Three
theories
of child
development

Harper Series in Social Work,
Werner W. Boehm, *Series Editor*

Three Theories of child development

Third Edition

Henry W. Maier
University of Washington

HARPER & ROW, Publishers
NEW YORK   HAGERSTOWN   SAN FRANCISCO   LONDON

To Jeanne

Photo Credits:
page 71—Jon Erikson, page 133—Stanford University

Sponsoring Editor: Dale Tharp

Project Editor: Pamela Landau

Designer: Michel Craig

Production Supervisor: Stefania J. Taflinska

Compositor: Bi-Comp, Incorporated

Printer and Binder: The Maple Press Company

Art Studio: J & R Technical Services, Inc.

Three Theories of Child Development, Third Edition

Library of Congress Cataloging in Publication Data

Maier, Henry William.
  Three theories of child development.

  (Harper series in social work)
  Bibliography: p.
  Includes index.
  1. Child psychology.   2. Erickson, Erik Homburger,
1902–   3. Piaget, Jean, 1896–   4. Sears, Robert Richardson, 1908–   I. Title.
BF721.M196   1978   155.41′092′2   77-11085
ISBN 0-06-044176-3

Contents

Editor's Foreword   vii

Preface   ix

PART ONE
Three Dimensions of Child Development   **1**

Introduction to Part One   2

    1. *The Cognitive Theory of Jean Piaget*   12
    2. *The Affective Theory of Erik H. Erikson*   71
    3. *The Behavioral Theory of Robert R. Sears*   133
    4. *The Three Theories Viewed as Parallel and An Integration
       of Affect-Behavioral-Cognitive Development*   165

PART TWO
Applying One's Knowledge of Child Development   **193**

    5. *The Helping Process*   195
    6. *The Three Dimensions of Child Development
       Applied*   223

Bibliography of Text References   257

Appendix: *Complete Bibliographies of Original and
         Collaborative Works of the Three Theories*   276

Index   289

Editor's Foreword

Much has happened since the first edition of this book was introduced to readers in 1965. Not only have social work programs for undergraduates considerably enlarged the student audience for a work on child development theories, but ideas regarding child care have undergone change. While methods of child care beyond custodial tasks have reflected educational concerns for some time, as a result of the struggle for equal opportunity and the legislation of the sixties, we are now convinced that tasks that seek to enhance the developmental potential of children are essential. The third edition of Professor Maier's book felicitously reflects this new trend.

Certain professions have been traditionally interested in material on child development. But now, in social work, we have broadened our concept of child welfare to include child care and education and psychology, child care personnel seem to be more interested in the theoretical underpinnings of their practice and the implications of theories for practice. Nurses too have enhanced their practice skills on the basis of increased knowledge of child development.

While serving various fields even better than before, this book seeks to do justice to recent developments, current theories, and societal changes. Professor Maier's third edition is more than just an update of earlier material; it is itself a development and in many ways a new book. A few years ago, when Harper & Row established a textbook series in social welfare to stimulate the production of books for the burgeoning undergraduate population, graduate social-work students, and students in related professions, our best judgment about the path to follow was to reflect both what is and what will be. Staying close to tradition certain times and venturing toward new views at others, Professor Maier's book includes appropriate current developments as well as what is emerging on the horizon.

Werner W. Boehm

Preface

What can a book about three different formulations of child development tell us? This study builds upon the belief that a human being is a manifold being who acts, feels, and thinks. No one account about human development, whether behavioral, psychodynamic, or cognitive, can fully explain human development. To assist us in comprehending and relating to children and youth, and to people in general, these dimensions of human development have to be considered together.

This book is written with the conviction that study, research, and actual work with children or youth should build upon that which is already known. The attempt to present the works of Jean Piaget, Erik H. Erikson, and Robert R. Sears under one cover was undertaken in the hope that such an effort would generate new ideas, enhance our commitments, and guide our actions in our own lives and in our work with children and youth.

Why a broadly revised edition? Times are changing. Contemporary perspectives focus less on the word of experts and more on the importance of widening one's own knowledge base. The original publication was written as a presentation of the research and thinking of three scholars of three distinct spheres of scientific effort. It was intended to be a resource book based on the knowledge of three wise men. The revised edition is primarily conceived as a sharing of knowledge about three central dimensions of human development, which happened to be researched by these three experts. The focus of the current edition is on what can be learned about human development rather than on who developed the knowledge about that subject.

Times are changing. Change is reflected not only in the perspectives of the authority of knowledge *(193; 194a)*, but also in the meaning of previous knowledge within the context of contemporary interests and events. The works of Piaget, Erikson, and Sears deserve a second (and maybe a third) look if we are to comprehend their findings in the light of present-day happenings. For example, predominant contemporary concerns with behavior acquisitions and accountability necessitate a reminder of parallel and congruent aspects of human functioning. Moreover, in the intervening years, time and experience have brought a recognition of sexual equality and a multicultural outlook, which has altered all perspectives, including the material in the earlier publications of this book.

Times are changing. Not only have the readers and the author altered their perspectives; the original investigators of the three dimensions of human development have updated and altered their own research and perceptions, especially Erikson and Piaget. Thus, this rewriting is more in order than a mere revision.

How did this work proceed? The presentation of a study of cognitive, affective, and behavioral development is based, essentially, on research in the primary literature of the three theorists. In the case of Piaget, English translations have been utilized almost throughout. This practice, hopefully, does not do injustice to Piaget's material. He himself states, "I feel that my original somewhat difficult text has become more understandable in English, thanks to the efforts of my translators" *(267, v)*. Each chapter on these three dimensions presents a synthesis of all the work done in the particular area. The most recent research is presented whenever the newer material has superseded earlier findings. Technical terms employed by each of the theorists are retained. Since chronological age levels are used by each of the three as points of reference rather than as data, age references are cited merely for the sake of orientation. A basic notion of the original book remains: human development and interpersonal helping deals with developmental rather than chronological age norms.

A concentration upon psychological and behavioral development seems to deny maturational (that is, physical, physiological, and neurological) development. Hopefully, readers will supplement this void with their own study in these areas. Furthermore, Dr. Edmund A. Smith, as he reviewed the original manuscript, reminded me that these formulations have been developed primarily by *men*. In addition, the synthesis and interpretation of these theories have been accomplished by a male author who depended upon other men to critique this manuscript to a large extent. Concerning this shortcoming, it is only hoped that I managed, as author of this book, to remove the sex biases which were unwittingly communicated in earlier editions.

The book could not have been written without the creative contributions of Jean Piaget, Erik H. Erikson, and Robert R. Sears, who also generously provided their photographs. They and their numerous publishers kindly granted permission to use the selected excerpts from their publications that appear throughout. The publishers are enumerated in the bibliography. I am particularly indebted to Professors Erikson and Sears for the use of their unpublished manuscripts which are also cited in the bibliography.

Although responsibility for this book's ultimate accuracy rests completely with the author, it could not have been written without the interest and the critical and helpful suggestions of many students, research assistants, colleagues, and astute reviewers. In addition, many painstaking typists struggled with corrections on top of corrections and pages upon pages of manuscripts. I would like to name all of these true coauthors, but there are too many. My warm thanks—affectively, cognitively, and (hopefully) also behaviorally—are given to each and every one of them. One editor and reviewer must be specifically mentioned—Faith N. Smith. Ms. Smith labored with me from the first to this third edition, providing a viable critique as editor of the manuscript. To her, I give my special thanks in appreciation.

Finally, the original publication gives special recognition to my sons, Mark, Peter, and Scott, for their patience, and above all, for their physical participation in helping with the sorting of the manuscript pages. Later, as their participation included probing questions, they brought vividly before me the many facets of human development. Today, each one writes and publishes his own works. They make this book alive for me because they illustrate the development of human participation—first by physical activities, then through empathetic inquisitiveness, and finally by means of identification. Earlier, I thanked them for their assistance; now I thank them for being so fully on their own while we are also together.

Through the years of gestation and the several "lives" of this book, I had one partner who lived with them all. She shared in my ups and downs, in my ponderings over ideas and searchings for words, and in the questions and satisfactions when each task was done. To Jeanne, my life partner, this book is dedicated.

Henry W. Maier

University of Washington
Seattle, Washington

PART ONE
THREE DIMENSIONS OF CHILD DEVELOPMENT

Introduction to Part I

Time and experience . . . alter all perspectives . . . HENRY ADAMS

TIME, EXPERIENCE, AND HUMAN DEVELOPMENT

"Time and experience alter all perspectives" is the theme of this book.[1] From the first to the last breath, human beings develop and change by minute but continuously different experiences in behaving, thinking, and feeling. It is the minute reaction, reflection of attitude, and exchange of thought which turn a casual encounter into a personal contact. Early in life, the ability of infants to hold on to a rattle or stick evolves out of their recurrent purely reflexive reactions of grasping. The infant learns to hold on by the experience of doing the grasping repeatedly. With this earliest conquest, infants are on the way to learning controlled adaptation of their behavior in relation to the impinging environment as they encounter it in time, space, and social context. Just try to take away an object an infant is holding and you will encounter such holding on.

In turn, experiences of holding onto an object by grasping, sucking, looking, and listening also alter all perspectives. As chance encounters become controlled behavior, infants simultaneously experience a predictable world in which they can begin to anticipate experiences. Rudimentary thinking is in process. This means the beginning of differentiating, ordering, classifying, and integrating events for a rational existence in a definable world. When we place a familiar object within the infant's visual, grasp-

---

[1] Throughout this book an attempt has been made to avoid use of the terms *he, him, she,* or *her* per se as generic terms.

ing, sucking, or auditory sphere, we can almost see the infant's power of thinking—recognition, which demonstrates a knowing of knowing.

Over time, an infant's experience of being able to grasp and hold with certainty simultaneously influences the development of cognition and emotional development. This emotional (affective) experience of certainty and comfort feels good, and, in association with physiological experiences of tranquility or excitement, serves as a stepping stone for venturing trustingly into new experiences. Infants, in essence, learn to experience and manage their emotions. When they lose an object they feel temporarily attached to, the loss is experienced as a very personal deprivation, as if their whole security had been undermined.

Reflexive movements are the rudimentary experiences for the development of *doing, thinking,* and *feeling,* which continue throughout life. To illustrate, newborns develop their hand reflex reactions into holding actions. Fifteen years later, as full teenagers, they are preoccupied with social control, exploring ways to manage themselves in order to obtain the supportive responses of others. By then, behavioral choice involves rational decisions between many alternatives which teenagers come to understand for their consequences. In other words, getting hold of the situation at hand becomes an interweaving of the behavioral repetoire,[2] the comprehension of the circumstances associated with the situation, and the personal feelings about the actions and people involved. Each minute experience of doing, thinking, and feeling builds upon what has been learned by participation and continuous opportunities are unfolded for experiencing events anew and differently. Time and experience do alter all perspectives.

Development, the theme of this book, is best described by the continuous interaction of constancy and change. In this context, deviant or just momentarily puzzling behavior in the events of daily living in human beings of any age becomes understandable, and helpful intervention is possible in terms of the developmental issues involved. The designations *normal* and *abnormal* give way to a clarification of the developmental issues involved in this type of study of people's management of their daily life. The puzzling and the deviant (or pathological) can be understood in specific cases as a particular child's ongoing functioning within a progression of potential achievement rather than as a problem in behavior per se.

---

[2] Such an awareness brings into question the applicability of findings from animal experiments with single behavioral dimensions to an explanation of the functioning of human beings beyond rudimentary learning.

For example, when seven-year-olds cling to a parent while visiting a new setting, the meaning can be explained as the uncertainty they experience in predicting their new social environment. Knowing what to do about such babylike clinging behavior requires relating this behavior to developmental knowledge. To handle clinging behavior (referred to above as holding on), look for the experiences that will make it possible for infants and very young children to learn to manage, to strike out on their own. Discover what actions in that moment will provide them with a sense of power or control over themselves, even within the new setting.

In contrast to such maturational indices as bone age, physical growth, or chronological age, there are no established norms for specifying developmental capabilities, progress, or phases. Individuals can be appraised only in terms of their status *within* a general continuum and within the context of their own unique evolvement vis-a-vis a specific life situation.

THREE DIMENSIONS OF HUMAN FUNCTIONING

The assumption underlying the three dimensions of development as postulated by Piaget, Erikson, and Sears is that the action of development progresses as a unity-in-continuity. Development (1) evolves within an orderly and continuous progression and (2) unfolds through well-established successive phases (or stages). What emerges in behavior, affect, or thought at one phase becomes transformed into something akin to, but also different from, what existed earlier. The processes unfold as an oscillating movement which is both *differentiating* and *integrating*. Such a developmental movement implies increasingly complex levels of organization.

The main features of this developmental model can be summed up as follows: (1) The stages of development are known a priori; they are always in the same order. (2) Development proceeds from an identified first phase and unfolds in the same order with no phase left out. Later development can be traced back to an earlier antecedent and, ultimately, to a first phase, although a retrospective analysis cannot fully explain the current development. (3) Each phase is more complex and differentiated than the one preceding it. Each phase has its central core of differentiation and integration of developmental acquisitions, involving a transformation of previous development into a new and more functional level. (4) Each phase builds upon the previous one and becomes the launching phase for the next one. Thus, each new phase, with time and added experience, alters all perspectives.

The oscillations between development and change and change and development are a major theme of this book. In describing that theme the discussion will alternate between cognitive, affective (emotional),[3] and behavioral processes.[4] Each dimension—cognition, affect, and behavior—has its own distinct developmental processes within a separate developmental continuum, and each is intertwined with and dependent upon the processes of the other two. These dimensions of development always operate together and constitute the state of a person's social functioning. Theoretically, each dimension of human functioning can be perceived, studied, and conceptualized as a separate entity. In the reality of everyday life, however, human beings function as a whole, with all three dimensions in operation. (190, 60–71)[5] People are known for what they are—that is, for what they *do, know,* and *stand for* (feel). When we meet people, we want to know what they do, what they actually know about it, and how they feel about it.

The concept of the wholeness of the human being creates a paradox. While people are whole to each other, in their actual responses to one another they relate to parts of each other. In everyday life, four-year-olds may be ready to manage by themselves. In fact, they are apt to play by themselves for hours on end. Yet, if left alone for some time, their play as organized activity may give way to disorganized behavior because they feel deserted. They can manage behaviorally but not emotionally. In contrast, many four-year-olds will dare to go far beyond their actual margin of safety, because they feel secure beyond their behavioral capabilities. We know from experience that many preschoolers move from joyful play to tears because they have trouble comprehending the notion of taking turns due to the behavioral changes required in the ongoing activity. The caring elder is apt to deal with the whole child rather than zeroing in on the part of the child which is the problem. In the last example, it is the cognitive dimension which is significant. Youngsters cannot appreciate that taking turns does not mean being left out. With help, they can discover that they remain a part and are included even while others have their turn.

The preceding illustrations show that child development is not merely a matter of individual growth. Child development is very

[3] The terms *affect* and *emotion* are used interchangeably throughout this book as they are in books by other writers. (8, 69–70)

[4] The emphasis is upon psychosocial development. Although physiological, neurological, and bodily development are also perceived as extremely relevant to human development, they are not covered here.

[5] Numbers in parentheses refer to numbered works in the bibliography at the end of the book. Page numbers within the work are also sometimes given, they are in roman script.

much a social affair. Development proceeds in a world of people, and the people include themselves in the processes of development. This factor is clearly brought out in a few lines by M. Schwebel. "It is during infancy," Schwebel writes, "that the initial feelings about the self and others develop. Is the world a safe, responsive and exciting place? Or is it full of prohibitions and unfulfilled needs? Are people helpful and encouraging or do they only limit and coerce? The young child may not question these factors. Nevertheless, this may be the most important area of learning." (324, 129) Taken separately or together, childrens' emotional relationships, behavioral interactions, and conceptions of events define their developing value of self. This is true over their lives in general and in small instances as well.

Helping persons in the course of their everyday life or in their professional capacity have to decide at various points whether to deal with the affective, cognitive, or behavioral aspect of an individual's development. This requires a full understanding that a change in the *affective* process can help a person understand life experiences more clearly and behave more competently; that a change in *cognitive* functioning can help a person feel differently and behave differently; and that acquisition of more competent *behavior* will foster changes in cognitive and affective experiences. *(190)*

THREE THEORIES OF CHILD DEVELOPMENT

The focus throughout the following chapters will be upon cognitive, affective, and behavioral development. Each dimension of development is considered for its own distinct processes within its continuum *and* for the implications of such knowledge for growing up and living and working with children, youth, and people in general. This book brings together the theories of Jean Piaget, Erik H. Erikson, and Robert R. Sears as three parallel and congruent theories of child development. Each theory explains one of the three dimensions of development.

Jean Piaget's work encompasses the study of cognitive development and functioning. In the past quarter of a century his research has been recognized in the United States and most of the Western world. Recently there has been increased interest in his work, with translations into English of almost all of his voluminous writings. In the following chapter Piaget's research findings and theoretical formulations are synthesized into a unified theory of *cognitive* development.

Erik H. Erikson's work on emotional development parallels

Piaget's contributions. While Piaget is today's pioneer in charting the content and course of cognitive development, Erikson is the contemporary architect of theories of affective development. As a body of work, Erikson's writings bring about an integration of psychoanalytic insight and wisdom from such fields as cultural anthropology, social psychology, the study of man in history, the arts, and above all, child development. Chapter 2 contains Erikson's contributions toward the formulation of a single theory of *affective* development.

Robert R. Sears' research and essays on learning theories, which attempt to explain the acquisition and alteration of learned behaviors, exemplifies the beginning of a theory on social behavior. He explores some aspects of child rearing and describes the impact of environmental forces on the development of the child in contemporary American middle-class families with two parents. Most importantly, Sears ventures where other learning theorists have not dared to tread. He draws inferences from empirical studies on child development for the benefit of the practitioner (parent or professional caring person).

In the chapter on behavioral development (Chapter 3), the research of Sears and his associates is integrated into a single framework. This is a rudimentary attempt to set up a theory of behavioral development as a *guide*. Why are these three theories selected among the many possible choices in personality theories? This book deals with personality development as a continuous and sequential process comprised of discrete multidimensional subprocesses universal to all human beings. The developing child is to be seen, understood, and experienced for his thinking, feeling, and doing. While children's physical development, especially physiological and sociocultural development are equally important dimensions of personality development, these dimensions have been omitted.[6]

Surprisingly, although there are a number of personality theories available, only a small number include a developmental perspective. Most personality theories are concerned with human beings as virtually completed entities. For example, the greats of yesterday, Carl Jung, Kurt Lewin, and the leading psychologists of today, Albert Bandura, Carl Rogers, B. F. Skinner, have contributed to an understanding of a person's relationships to others *(148)*, but they add little information for understanding the continuum of human development. Although the teachings of Sigmund Freud, Clark L. Hull, Lewin, Rogers, and Skinner have been

---

[6] Special attention should be called to Lawrence Kohlberg's research on moral development, a rich integrative developmental continuum of cognition and acculturation *(170)*.

applied to explain the development of children, none of these theorists actually studied and worked with children. Only Erikson, Freud, very minimally, Piaget, Sears, and Robert W. White deal with human beings over time as organisms with many seasons.

The selection of a theorist of cognitive development was easy. Piaget's work on cognitive development is unequaled, even though his research and conceptual contributions are seldom used by professional helpers and the lay public.

For an understanding of emotional development, Erikson's formulations were chosen in preference to those of Freud and his associates (Alfred Adler, Carl Jung, Otto Rank) or more recent students of the analytic schools (Anna Freud, Melanie Klein, and White, among others). In Chapter 3 it is argued that only Erikson's and White's work *(386)* are sufficiently different to warrant recognition as a separable formulation from the Freudian psychoanalytic one. *(27)* In many ways White's formulations represent another thrust forward in ego psychology beyond the thinking of Erikson. *(384)* White's work reflects the contemporary concern with competence rather than adaptive development. *(194a; 386)* It is Erikson's theory, given its scope and depth in clinical and empirical investigations, public appeal, and scholarly logic which remains the theory of the day on the subject of affect. *(27)*

For an exploration of behavioral development, Sears' approach to learning theory was chosen in preference to the work of his former colleague O. H. Mowrer. Sears has been less eclectic and has apparently found a wider audience than Mowrer, who attempted to integrate learning theory and psychoanalytic concepts. Among contemporary learning theorists, research, and publications concerned with operant conditioning (behavior modification), neither Alfred Bandura's *(10)* nor Sidney Bijou's *(20; 21)* extensive work and writings on children yield much data on the developmental continuum. Sears' work remains the best contribution concerning development within a learning theory perspective.

Although the scholarly interests and research methodology of the three theorists are diverse, the compatible aspects of their theories are more significant. As will become apparent within subsequent chapters, Piaget's cognitive theory is compatible with and supplementary to psychoanalytic theory, and vice versa. Charles Odier has observed:

> . . . the strongest aspect of the Freudian psychoanalytic doctrine is the weakest of Piaget's doctrine, and vice versa. . . . Comparing the evaluation of the individual to a river, I should say that Freud [with his psychoanalytic approach] and Piaget both ascended it to its source but each from

his own bank. By definition, this parallelism condemned them never to meet. (213, 32)

Peter H. Wolff adds, in a monograph published in 1960:

Despite their methodological differences and divergent goals, the two methods [Piagetian analysis and Freudian psychoanalysis] may complement each other in providing a comprehensive picture of the developmental process, each supplying that data in those areas where the other is deficient. (394, 11–12)

In one of his recent discourses, Erikson links his work with Piaget's findings as if each of them were weaving with different strands the same cloth of development. *(128; 304)* Sears' own conscious effort to unite basic concepts of psychoanalytic theory with those of learning theory *(347; 349)* lends further support to an effort to interrelate these three theories. A recent observation by T. Newcomb underscores such a perspective; he reflects on the fact that attitudes (a component of affect) shape behavior as surely as behavior shapes attitudes. "An attitude is a label for residuals of previous learning—affective, cognitive, behavioral—with regard to a specific object. Such learning influences subsequent behavior, and of course it is an outcome of previous behavior. . . . When circumstances force one to change behavior, attitudes may follow suit. Attitudes and behavior have a cyclical relationship." *(211, 78)*

AN ASSOCIATED FRAME OF REFERENCE ON CHILD DEVELOPMENT

Theoretical concepts define, explain, and serve to make sense out of apparent interrelated data and events. However, theoretical concepts neither verify as fact that which has been hypothesized nor fully predict that which is to come. Theoretical formulations serve as heuristic guidelines in the absence of a full constellation of empirical data. In one way, theoretical formulations serve as the precursors for empirical research in order that what has been predicted can be verified or refuted for its empirical validity. In another way, theoretical formulations serve as the lattices which link and anchor empirical findings, in order to give them substance and relevance. In the subsequent accounts of theoretical propositions, we learn of conceptual formulations based upon tested and verified empirical research as well as of those yet to be tested. Together, they can provide heuristic guidelines for further research and, above all, for comprehending in human development that which is known and that which is yet to be fully known.

The theories of Piaget, Erikson, and Sears deal with distinctly separate but complementary approaches to personality development. Each contributes one part to an understanding of the individual as an indivisible whole. Each interlocks, cogwheel fashion, with the others, while each sequential phase of development remains undisturbed within its own conceptual framework. Considered longitudinally, each theory might be said to possess its own internal consistency in portraying a continuum of development, while supplementing and upholding the integrity of the other two theories. Considered laterally, each theory may deal at any given point with a more or less distinct episode which may be defined in terms of one theory without absolving or refuting principles embodied in the others.

In everyday life or professional practice the applicability of each theory is determined by the nature of the activity. For example, if the reason for intervention involves a question of social behavior, Sears' particular findings stand out as most pertinent. If the need for help has to do with the child's comprehension of a situation, Piaget's detailed account of intellectual development will be instructive and reliable. And if the child's problem is one of emotional uneasiness, Erikson's concepts will assist in helping the child find greater personal comfort. It is necessary to consider all three dimensions of human functioning when assisting a child with his development or assessing and treating a developmental question.

Each person, more likely than not, relies upon an array of favored concepts of child development, garnished by flashes of wisdom derived from his or her own experiences. Yet, a wider understanding of human development, whether by studying, rearing, treating, or guaranteeing children their developmental rights (1; 144), is a prerequisite for working with children and youth more knowledgeably and more competently. Such an effort represents a challenge and a conquest and a belief in human beings as persons with a future.

AN OVERVIEW OF THE BOOK

In this book three dimensions of human functioning, thinking, feeling, and doing, are brought together in the form of three parallel and congruent theories of child development. This frame of reference lends perspective to the contributions of time and experience in human development, from birth to adulthood and from child care to world citizenship.

Part I is a study of the cognitive, affective, and behavioral development of children and adolescents, with a special focus on one basic theory in each of these dimensions. Part II is a study of purposeful intervention, with an emphasis on full application of developmental knowledge.

Since the book places the dimensions of affect, behavior, and cognition parallel to each other, no hierarchy is acknowledged or implied. In the actual presentation of the three dimensions an order has to be established. Cognitive development is presented first because Piaget's scheme appears to be the fullest and most comprehensive theory of the three. The theories of Erikson and Sears follow in order of the aforementioned criterion of degree of extensiveness.

In the presentation of each dimension of functioning, a brief biographical sketch introduces the particular theorist for his work and as a person of his time. Each theorist's basic assumptions and scientific stance on development introduces each developmental progression, which is then presented by its developmental phases. A cursory comparison of the three formulations with the focus upon forming an associated frame of reference rounds off Part I.

In the second part, the reader is introduced to the author's perception of the intervention process—the helping effort of the caring person in everyday life and in socially engineered helping situations. This is normally defined as the *professional* helping scene. A chapter on the helping process serves as backdrop for the concluding chapter which contains a systematic discussion of the *application* of the content of this book.

It is the contention of the author that *knowledge exists to be used*. The reader is hopefully challenged to learn to apply knowledge as well as to learn the essence of child development. In short, the book brings reader and writer together to learn.

CHAPTER 1
The cognitive theory of Jean Piaget

PIAGET'S LIFE AND WORK

For the student of child development, Jean Piaget's writings are a treasure chest of knowledge about cognitive development. Piaget, like Freud, became a pioneering psychologist, inventing the means for his investigation while exploring unknown territory. A student of Piaget's teachings is apt never to see children in the same way again. (5, 10)

Jean Piaget was born in the Swiss university town of Neuchâtel in 1896. He describes his own development in childhood as having been influenced by an intelligent, energetic, somewhat neurotic mother and a scholarly father who had little time for his son's abortive scientific studies. Piaget writes:

> I started to forego playing for serious work very early. Indeed, I have always detested any departure from reality, an attitude which I relate to . . . my mother's poor mental health. It was this disturbing factor which at the beginning of my studies in psychology made me intensely interested in questions of psychoanalysis and pathological psychology. Though this interest helped me to achieve independence and to widen my cultural background, I have never since felt any desire to involve myself deeper in that direction, always much preferring the study of normalcy and of the workings of the intellect to that of the tricks of the unconscious. (219, 238)

At the age of ten Piaget published his first article, a study of a rare albino sparrow, in the *Journal of Natural History of Neuchâtel*. This article brought him an invitation to consider the position of curator of the Geneva Museum of Natural History, until the director of the museum discovered that the author of this article was still a pupil in knee pants in secondary school. Later, as a *gymnasium* student, his research on mollusks introduced him to the biological sciences. He continued his biological studies at the University of Neuchâtel (1915–1918), and his doctoral dissertation was *The Mollusks of Vallais*. His scientific studies, in general, had already won recognition beyond Switzerland's borders.

During his university years, Piaget discovered philosophy and psychology. The writings of Bergson awoke in him a feverish interest in the idea of identifying God with life. This notion, as he describes it,

> . . . *stirred me almost to ecstasy because it enabled me to see in biology the explanation of all things and of mind itself. . . . [However] instead of finding science's last word therein . . . I got the impression of an ingenious construction without an experimental basis: Between biology and the analysis of knowledge I needed something other than philosophy. I believe it was at that moment that I discovered a need that could be satisfied only by psychology.* (219, 240)

Young Piaget must have found himself in a constant turmoil in his search for a scientific explanation of the psychological existence of human beings. He refers to this period as the time when he read everything which came into his hand—Kant, Spencer, Comte, and Durkheim among the philosophers, and in psychology, William James, Janet, Jung and Freud. (*219*, 241) This intense period of reading was followed by a writing spree in "forty days" of isolation. In a novel never to be published, he formulated his rudimentary concepts of intellectual development which forecast the kind of research he would do for the next thirty years. Piaget's life task was to fill the void left by the biologists *and* the philosophers, namely, to find out how we "know." His invention was to be a general theory of cognitive adaptation.

As a young postdoctoral researcher at Alfred Binet's experimental laboratory in Paris (1919–1921), Piaget was introduced to Binet's epochal work on intelligence testing. Interestingly, he became fascinated by the wrong answers of children. He noted that the apparently incorrect answers of children in fact represented a different and earlier conception of things. Thus, with age, children become not only brighter, but also *qualitatively* different. Piaget had now located his research material: the changing patterns of thoughts in a child's development. Moreover, in his work with Binet he noted that a child's response and spontaneous questions, rather than the questions posed by the examiner, were the source for data. This discovery became basic for his research methodology and for the over fifty new—and, at times, most ingenious—research techniques to be developed by him and his associates.

Piaget's tireless research, now spanning more than half a century of work, and his innumerable publications in Swiss, French, German, and American professional periodicals and in books can be divided into four distinct periods. In the first period of research, 1921–1932, he based the study of children in their language behavior. This was a limitation he corrected in subsequent studies. Five major publications (225; 227; 256; 257; 261) from this period introduced his research to the university centers of Europe and the United States. In fact, these publications found a wider audience in this country than any of his later writings did. Much of the present-day criticism of Piaget's research in this country is still leveled at these early works. Piaget himself was the first to acknowledge and to correct the limitations of his starkly verbal-oriented work. (219, 247) Piaget likes to call himself the number one Piagetian revisionist. (157)

Personal and professional experiences paved the way to a second period of distinct research (1933–1939). The birth of his three children in 1925, 1927, and 1931 brought him into continuous and intimate contact with developing individuals, an experience unparalleled by the most ideal laboratory arrangements. He designed and detailed observations of the *manipulative* behavior of children, recognizing perceptual and conceptual processes as interrelated rather than synonymous operations. The publications of this period present the basic framework of his cognitive theory, including a revised and most detailed account of experiences concerning the interaction between nature and nurture and between biological and environmental experience in the very early years of life. (232; 265; 267; 276)

A third, and in part overlapping, period (1937–1955) covers his and his collaborators' research on children's acquisition of specific phenomena of knowledge permanency, causality, space, and time. (230; 251; 258; 289; 293; 301; etc.) Albert Einstein's personal delight over Piaget's detailed research on thinking processes heightened Piaget's research on the concept of time. Einstein wondered with Piaget whether it was the notion of speed or of time that was learned first. (275, 82) Piaget's research probed the question which had plagued philosophers through the ages: How do we know what we know?

Partly, Piagetian research in this third period focused upon cognitive development, when conceptual thought is being developed in the school-age child and young adolescent. In another way, his research paved the way for his fourth and current period of inquiry, starting in 1959, in which he is essentially a genetic epistemologist—a student of the developmental growth of knowledge. Piaget refers to the interlinkage of these endeavors.

"The problem of epistemology is to explain how real human thought is capable of producing scientific knowledge. In order to do that we must establish a certain coordination between logic [ordering of concepts] and psychology [development of concepts]." (249, 12) "The nature of knowledge is related to how knowledge is acquired. Thus, [for instance,] the history of physics and the genesis of physical concepts in the child are part of one and the same enterprise." (203, 131) Piaget now sees himself prepared to attend to the task he set himself when he selected psychology as his discipline. (221; 244; 249; 271; 275; 282)

Piaget the researcher is also Piaget the teacher-citizen. His writings, lectures, and public responsibilities take him as much away from his research at the J. J. Rousseau Institute in Geneva, Switzerland, as his numerous ingenious research projects keep him in continuous contact with children and *their* way of thinking. Piaget has been a professor, teaching the history of scientific thought at the University of Geneva, a director of the J. J. Rousseau Institute, a director of the Bureau of the International Office of Education, and a chairperson for a number of UNESCO projects.

Aside from numerous honorary degrees in at least four different countries[1] he was honored with the first professor's chair to be occupied by a non-Frenchman since Erasmus in 1530 at the Sorbonne, Paris. Piaget is a strong advocate of research scholars being independent rather than disciples of his own endeavors. His research center serves as a form of think tank for critical reflection on research but never as a research production center. In essence, Piaget is more interested in the true search, the methodology of knowing how to know, than in the search for truth per se. He is, therefore, constantly in contact with the scholars of his time, through reading and personal discourse. In 1956 he created for the latter purpose, the Center for Genetic Epistemology and for the former he inaugurated the monograph series Studies in Genetic Epistemology.

By 1965, his prolific writings, translated into many languages, were estimated at 18,000 pages (284, 164).[2] By 1976, he was credited with over forty books, and at eighty years of age, he is still writing. (262)

Interestingly, while Piaget's experiments are clear and quickly comprehensible, his writings tend to be complex and laborious,

---

[1] Harvard University (1936), Sorbonne (1946), University of Brussels, (1949), University of Rio de Janeiro (1949), The University of Chicago (1953), and University of Pennsylvania (1965).

[2] Also see the *Appendix* for a bibliography of over seventy Piagetian publications in English.

akin to the waves of a flood tide.[3] Like waves, each publication covers previous ground and a bit more, and with each one a new gem is apt to emerge to captivate and awaken the serious reader.

While the questions Jean Piaget poses are those of a philosopher, his answers are those of a scientific psychologist.[4] His creative mind opened up new frontiers of knowledge and research methodology, and his cognitive theory not only logically consistent but also built upon empirical investigations, is repeatedly validated, based on cross-cultural research. It is both astonishing and reassuring that the data of thousands of observations match—data from the dry bushland of Australia and the Eskimo villages at the windy North Slope of Alaska *(132)*; from American children, of middle- or lower-class homes (5, 83); from American natives such as Hopi, Papago, and Navajo *(51,* 116; *5,* 83; *132)*; from children of Uganda in Africa; and from Arabic, Hindu, Japanese and Somali homes. (5, 33; *141,* 129–139) It is also astonishing and reassuring that these and additional cross-cultural studies bear out the basic information gathered on the children of Geneva, and, initially, on only Piaget's own three children.

It is not only Piaget's research and writings that achieved international acclaim, but Piaget himself. His magnetic personality serves as an "international glue" *(317)* for linking conversant ideas and contemporary psychologists throughout many lands. To learn from Piaget, it is important to understand, in addition to his research and writings, the inquiring attitude of mind that characterizes his work. *(4,* 177) Possibly, the contributions of such a giant as Piaget were best summed up by Albert Einstein, another giant, who appraised Piaget's work as "The idea of a genius, such simplicity." *(138,* 6)

PIAGET'S THEORY IN
RELATION TO OTHER PREVAILING THEORIES

Piaget, an avid reader, borrows liberally from the thinkers around him, "transposing and amplifying all that he borrows while generously acknowledging the sources." (7, 34) In his writings he links or differentiates, accepts or disputes the findings of others as he searches for new insights in relation to his own material.

Both Piagetian theory and psychoanalytic theory attempt to explain human behavior in terms of variations in the qualitative data about development at the expense of the quantitative data. In ear-

---

[3] His abstruse language has been dubbed "piagenetic." (*61,* p. 121)
[4] Observation made by my editor Faith N. Smith.

lier writings, Piaget saw affect as another dimension of development and beyond his concern. *(219)* More recently, he places the issue of affect more within the realm of physiological development and considers it to be an area of knowledge yet to be explored. *(221)*

Although in earlier publications Piaget gave little attention to learning theory, *(135, 3–4)* in more recent writings he contrasts his work with behavioral approaches. (e.g., *221*) "Even learning," he says, "depends upon [the] laws of development." *(268, 281)* Piaget conceives of learning as a modification of development, while learning theory considers development to be a product of learning. For Piaget, "In the Beginning was the *Response!*"[5] Stimulus → Response, S → R, is replaced by the interactional symbols S ⇄ R or S → (A) → R, where A equals cognitive adaptation. *(221, 8)*

Piaget's cognitive theory takes a third route to the essentially nature-prone, preprogrammed concepts of affect theory. Affect theory has a strong association with internal, maturational (physiological) regulations. Piaget's theory also takes a third route to the nurture-prone, programming concepts of behavioral theory and their complete association with environmental events. *(288, 192–194; 139)* Piaget's position is not a compromise between these two stances. It is a viable alternative to analytic and behavioral traditions which, in effect, allows for integration of the other two traditions.

In fact, Piaget, a very human being, has neither interest in a person's life story nor in an individual's cognitive development. His full interest centers upon the development of cognition per se. His students are left to apply his findings to the study of individuals, to child care, child rearing, teaching, therapeutic intervention, and above all to the everyday encounters with children.

ASSUMPTIONS BASIC TO PIAGET'S COGNITIVE THEORY

Prior to studying Piaget's cognitive theory, it is advisable to examine the basic assumptions which underlie the theory. They involve the following elements:

1. Approach to theory formation
2. Order of human life
3. Basic human values
4. Etiology of human behavior
5. Definition of Piaget's key developmental terms

[5] Italics added by author.

6. Core of human functioning
7. The newborn
8. The physical, social, cultural, and ideational environment.

Approach to Theory Formation

Basic to the formation of any theory is its author's scientific stance, in this case, Piaget the biologist complemented by Piaget the philosopher. Piaget the philosopher deals with questions such as what is reality (permanency)? what is thought (knowledge)? what is causality, what are space, time, and movement? As philosopher, Piaget is basically occupied with finding the most decisive questions, for only the most logical question can lead to the most telling response. We might note that Piaget the philosopher precedes Piaget the answer-testing scientist. The complications of his dual approach rest less with his thinking than with the fact that he integrates two disciplines which are conceived of and operate far apart from each other in the academic settings of today.

Piaget the scientist proceeds with the assumption that a detailed investigation of any small sample of a species can yield the same basic information inherent in all members of that species. For example, the children of Geneva, his own particularly, are representative for him of children everywhere. Since the forties, Piaget's research has shown a consistent increase in the number of subjects used for the testing of each new hypothesis.

Not until much of his work on cognitive development had been formulated did he pay attention to the variable of sex in his samples. For example, he observed in a roundtable discussion in 1955 that he had become aware that boys consistently approached problems related to questions of space in a different manner from girls. (237, 114) Yet, a child's chronological age continued to remain the most notable variable for him. Furthermore, the reliability of any of his findings is directly related to the completeness of the data furnished by the informant. He measures validity by the degree to which his findings are consistent with his theoretical propositions. In other words, Piaget sees empirical research as a tool to substantiate or refute facts previously established by logic.[6] His focus is upon qualitative analysis. He intentionally by-passes statistical analysis, since he is concerned with the tendency toward patterning and the order of a sequence of events rather than with statistical measures of central tendencies.

Two of Piaget's basic methods of research are also utilized in the nuclear sciences: (272)

---

[6] John H. Flavell challenges the validity of some of Piaget's work in his observation that at times Piaget forces the findings of his empirical research in order to validate his theoretical hypothesis. (135)

1. Step-by-step analysis based upon an investigation of causes and effect forms a network characterized by hierarchical relationships and connections. Empirical investigation and inductive reasoning are the major tools, which entails an application of the clinical method of investigation to the study of thinking (cognition).
2. The analysis of implications by considering both the field as a whole and the coordination of its parts. This is comparable to the group in mathematics and to propositional hypothesis in logic. Hypothetical and deductive reasoning are inherent in this second approach. Nothing can be viewed in isolation, because everything gains its meaning from the larger context of which it is a part.

Logic, Piaget stresses, can be applied as a research tool as scientifically as the more commonly used statistical techniques. It is of interest to note that the point at which Piaget stops in his projection of development is when individual achievement is at the same level of thinking employed in his own research endeavors.[7]

The Order of Human Life

Piaget believes in universal order and suggests a single unity of all things biological, social, psychological, and ideational in living as well as nonliving systems. For him, as a biological scientist, "all living forms grow and develop in coherent, logical patterns." (371, 34) All science is interrelated, and a theorem established in one branch of science is directly relevant to the laws and principles of other branches. Altogether, Piaget insists upon cosmic unity, which provides one explanation for his notion that his samples are representative. He assumes that any deviation, whether cultural or hereditary, is an *inconsequential* variation to the regular process of development. Four spontaneous actions are always present as inherent parts of life anywhere:

1. The action of the whole on itself (producing the law of preservation and survival)—a thrust toward homeostasis.
2. The action of all the parts (producing the law of alteration and preservation)—a thrust toward heterostasis.
3. The action of the parts on themselves (producing the law of preservation and survival)—a thrust towards homeostasis.
4. The action of the parts on the whole (producing the law of alteration and preservation)—a thrust towards heterostasis.[8]

Spontaneous action and inherent, constant dynamic change sustain each organism's evolutionary development, with move-

[7] E. A. Smith, professor emeritus, University of Washington, shared this observation with the author while studying an earlier edition of this book.

[8] Under this formulation fall both developmental (evolutionary) and accidental (mutational) change. Piaget had a vivid interest in mutation; for instance, his doctoral studies dealt with the mutation of mollusks. He ascribed order in disorder to the phenomenon of mutation.

ments in the direction of greater mobility, complexity, versatility, and increased unity for all actions of the parts involved. Though Piaget implies the interaction of opposing (polar) pulls in the counterbalancing of assimilative and accommodative processes, the process can be better comprehended if it is conceived not as one of polarity but rather as a process of oscillation. Constant motion and change are the essence of human life. "Nothing remains identical during normal mental evolution, not even identity, in spite of its very function." (294, 25) The greatest unity for all life experience can be achieved when a person approaches cognitive (intellectual) maturity.

Basic Human Values

Piaget, philosopher and scientist, strikes us foremost as a very *human* being. He refers only rarely to himself, but we do get to know him as a warm person with wit and high integrity. His work and his way of working convey an unshakeable belief in people and their capacity to succeed. Human beings learn, teach, know, and are known for their actions. With Piaget, although verbal and written communication are his media (personal conferences, seminars, lectures, and of course, his numerous writings), *action* is his message. In almost every research undertaking, the child's actions convey what the child is really all about. For Piaget, it is his work, his inquiry, and his personal involvement that stand for what he believes in. His commitments to UNESCO and other institutions and educational organizations which can make use of his rich fund of knowledge about children's development operationalize his belief that real knowing means participation and doing.

As a scientist, Piaget is objective, first clarifying specifically what needs to be observed, then making the observable yield verifiable data, and finally checking out the data with the subjects from whom they have been obtained. We learn that the researcher, his subjects, and the data are continuously and intimately interwoven, part and parcel of the same undertaking. This kind of working process is a prototype of a democratic form of human interaction. In fact, Piaget believes that democratic interaction and equity for all is the "mature" state of interaction; in his conception of development, these qualities present the ultimate and natural mode of a mature person.

Piaget's belief in the universality of people is reflected in his international collegial work and his dedication to the United Nations. While reading any of his research protocols, one is immediately struck by his belief in children and, above all, by his belief that each child knows best what he or she is all about and is always ready and capable of learning more. Piaget truly believes in children and in an orderly world; for him, both can only be good.

Etiology of Human Behavior

Piaget sees himself as a researcher of cognitive development; questions of affect or behavioral changes are beyond his field of study. His formulation builds upon two basic assumptions. First, biological growth indicates that all mental processes are continuations of inborn motor processes. Second, the processes of experience serve as the origin of all acquired acquisitions. Individuals learn from experiencing their experiences. In other words, experience rather than maturation defines the essence of cognitive development. In experiencing one's own native reflexes, the individual is led to use and apply them, resulting in the acquisition of new developmental processes. Consequently, human development (human learning) is neither purely social nor purely maturational; rather development evolves from individuals' experience of themselves and the patterns of living.

The evolution of cognitive organization in an individual is explained by two alternate assumptions, which Piaget usually pursues simultaneously in his inquiries:

1. It is presumed, a priori, that in the organization of objects, causality, space, time, and their interrelationships, definite patterns of intellectual development already exist.
2. The intellect organizes its own structure by virtue of its experience with objects, causality, space, time, and the interrelationship of these environmental realities.

All attributes of personality depend primarily upon the evolving intellectual capacity of the individual to organize his experience. Concomitantly, the totality of experience shapes the interests of an individual and the specific experiences he tends to pursue. Most importantly, as we learn from Piaget, it is not the knowledge of certain facts which enables us to act. Knowledge does not provide us with a blueprint of the realities of life. (221, 6) Rather, our use of and reaction to knowledge allow us to master what we know. When we try to understand the latest data about the surface of Mars, we have to react to them first with personal interest, scientific pride, or naive wonderment, and then translate them into some visible and comparable experience at hand in order to comprehend them. We are apt to know an object or an event when we know how it came about, when we try to know through reconstructing the information, skill, or event ourselves.

In short, we acquire knowledge to the extent to which we ourselves can discover or make the thing to be learned. John Dewey wrote: "We know an object when we know how it is made, and we know how it is made in the degree in which we ourselves make it." (306, 78)

Cognitive human behavior can always be traced to a *combination* of four factors:

1. Maturation of bodily processes (i.e., differentiation of the nervous system)
2. Experience (i.e., bodily interaction with the physical world)
3. Social transmission (i.e., humans taking care of and educating individuals and affecting the nature of the individual's experience)
4. Equilibration (i.e., self-regulation), "the overriding principle of mental development in which mental growth progresses toward ever more complex and stable levels of organization." (284, 1)

What is basic to all these assumptions, what constitutes the creed for all developmental and learning theories, is that once an individual has the ability, the individual uses it. Once people know, they incorporate the knowing.

Definition of Piaget's Key Developmental Terms

To comprehend Piaget's theory of cognitive development, it is necessary to become familiar with the meaning of his key terms. These terms are not a mere vocabulary for specific human mental processes. They incorporate Piaget's conception of the essence of human development.

Adaptation

Piaget postulates that adaptation is the cognitive striving of organisms—thinking persons—to balance their personal experience within the context of the environment as it impacts upon them. The qualifiers are (1) the individual's adaptation of his personal (internal) experience, which involves the Piagetian process of assimilation, and (2) the individual's adaptation to the environmental (external) experience, which involves the Piagetian concept of accommodation. It could be argued, as Piaget himself observed, that "all knowledge is always an assimilation of factors external to the person's overall life experience." (252, 8) Adaptation is, therefore, the intellectual aspect in any change of behavior which occurs in the interaction with changes in the environment; it is both the action and the conception of such action.

Assimilation and Accommodation-Adaptation

Assimilation is the mental process of experiencing an event in terms of past (internal) experience. People conceive of an event in terms of their existing way of thinking. An experience is then incorporated, without a break of continuity, into a person's ongoing way of thinking, the way the present understanding permits.

In short, assimilation is understanding the new by what is already known.

Accommodation, conversely to assimilation, involves the impact of the environment upon the individual. To accommodate is to adjust, to change an earlier conception in order to fit it more correctly into the demands of the actual event. Most importantly, to accommodate constitutes an attempt to incorporate the environmental (external) factors as far as they can be understood and managed. Therefore, it is not an accommodation to reality, but rather to reality as it is understood and manageable at that time. In short, accommodation is understanding a new experience so that it can alter the previous understanding.

Thus, assimilative and accommodative processes always act together. Piaget stresses that events can never exist unto themselves, they always involve assimilation and accommodation on the part of the experiencer. (265) Every interaction requires an individual to think, to feel, and to act as previous experience dictates, and such interaction is always challenged by environmental experience to think, to feel, and to act according to the impact of the new situation. Piaget builds upon these biological models of evolutionary homeostasis. His model implies (1) that old structures are fitted (assimilated) to new functions and (2) that new structures serve (accommodate) old functions under new demands. (289)

Equilibration

A basic Piagetian concept, equilibration constitutes feedback and forecasting, (53, 42) a series of active adaptations which are retroactive and also anticipatory of the outcome of more complex (more adaptive) ways of comprehending and managing environmental factors. Each phase of development has its pseudoequilibration, the achievement of a level of more realistic thinking, until towards the end of the final phase a near perfect equilibration is achievable.

To explain more fully, individuals first attempt to understand a new experience by using what they know. When such comprehension does not suffice to explain the new experience fully, people are apt to change their previous conception so that eventually the new happening is in better harmony with their personal conception of events. Repeated experiences with these new forms of thinking lead to new ways of thinking. (See "operations," below.) Each phase's equilibration constitutes the most advanced form of thinking that individuals are capable at that point of their life experiences. (252, 202) Whenever an individual is nudged further to more advanced thinking, the process of equilibration is going on. (247)

Operations

Operations refer to mental processes which deal with the comprehension of actions symbolically rather than purely experientially. Operations specify mental actions such as ordering, classifying, creating seriation, enumerating, and grouping. Operations are reversible thought processes (they can be done and undone) and are always part of a larger thought system. Operations interconnect mental structures in such a way that they form operational systems. (53, 36)

Schema

A Piagetian term with a number of varied definitions, a schema is understood in this account as "an instrument of generalization." (294, 362) For Piaget, "whatever is repeatable and generalizable in an action [thought and behavior sequence] is a scheme." (248b, xlviii) Descriptively, a schema can be explained as a tool of thinking which, in the thinking process, places the subject matter into similar classes or obtains a law of reasoning as the outcome of thinking.[9,10]

In concluding these definitions, it may be important to remind ourselves that Piaget parts with both the maturational and behavioral camps. Piaget contends that mental development does not depend on completing the human mechanisms for a greater and more accurate intake, such as improving with age, growth, and maturity. Nor is development a function of more precise learning, that is, more effective and complex input-programming. Mental development fundamentally evolves out of the *experience with experience*. Knowledge acquisition, in essence, is not "a copy of the environment but a system of real interactions reflecting the autoregulatory organization of life just as much as the things themselves do." (221, 27) Knowledge extends the physiological reach of the body as well as the initial adaptive and organizing functions of the nervous system. (221, 216–219) "Cognitive functions are an extension of organic regulations and constitute a differentiated organ for regulating exchanges and the external world." (221, 369)

Core of Human Functioning

The core of human functioning rests upon continuous experience, which may involve either operations (previously defined) or primary processes. These primary processes, as defined by Piaget,

---

[9] J. H. Flavell defines a schema as "a cognitive structure which has reference to a class of similar action sequences, these sequences of necessity being strong, bounded totalities in which the constituent behavioral elements are tightly interrelated." (135, 52–53)

[10] Additional "native" Piagetian terms are defined in footnotes.

refer to two original expressions of the individual. First, primary processes specify all original activities of the organism and all immediate forms of human interactions (bodily and perceptive) which unfold from them. Second, the term equally applies to all undifferentiated mental processes roughly up to the age of seven, at which time a child starts to apply operations, a logical mode of reasoning, in his thinking.

There is no doubt that, for Piaget, the story of intellectual development is also the story of personality formation. He suggests that the faculty of knowing serves as the coordinator, and is parallel to affective (emotional) development.

The human processes conceived of as major features of human functioning can be accounted for within Piaget's formulation as follows: *Identification*, as a cognitive process, is closely related to the mental capacity of conceiving of another model in relation to the self. *Imitation*, similarly is accepted as an intellectual function of repeating as exactly as possible environmental actions without much concern for the model, the source for the imitative actions.

Memory, customarily portrayed as a system of coding and decoding, is also subject to development; namely, the development of the code, basic to recall, is the central issue here. Memory is not simply reproduction of previous input; it is what a person conceives and reconstructs. Whereas imitation constitutes mere replay of experience as observed and understood, memory involves intelligent (selective and applicative) reconstruction of past experience. (294) Piaget's separation of the processes of recall, memory, and retention from the core processes of cognition has been validated by recent neurological findings on the learning and "retention" spheres of the brain. (306)

Play, an essential part of the evolution of intelligence, is adaptation dominated by assimilation; that is, personal satisfactions rather than environment influence an individual's thinking. *Language* is a product of mental activities. In spite of its pivotal position later in life, language, like play, emerges as part of the continuum of intellectual development. Language is a creator of thought, since the symbolic representation of thinking induces added thinking, and is also the object of thought, because only with thought do words and syntax make language.

Perception, by contrast, is a subordinate process of cognition. Perceptual experiences are activated from stimulus to stimulus, biological events (responses to stimuli) which are mastered as well by the lower animals. Just as the lungs furnish oxygen to the body, so perceptual inputs furnish impressions to the intellect. Impressions must be understood for their impact and adapted in terms of the individual's ongoing organization of comprehension to become operational at all. Therefore, perceptive input has to be neither completely novel nor without novelty to become perceptual at all. For Piaget, perception is merely a vehicle for thinking, perception provides the backdrop for making understandable what can be understood (151, 17) Piaget reiterated one of his fundamental ideas in a recent review of his fifty years of research: "First of all, knowledge comes from action and not simply from perception." (262) After all, a very young child does not perceive a difference between one animal and another till he *conceives* such a difference.

Piaget assumes that human affect (emotion) evolves from the same primary processes as its intellectual counterpart. He vacillates in his assumptions of whether affect assumes an equal rank or a subordinate position to intellectual organization. More recently, he has equated affective expressions with physiological processes. His overall position, however, is that intellect and affect are like two sides of a coin. "Both are always together as one. Both serve the adaptation to the environment." (274, 275) Affect and cognition are distinguishable but inseparable. (284, 33–34) "Reason and feelings are not independent faculties, they are always united in the facts." (2, 3) "We do not love without seeking to understand, and we do not even hate without a subtle use of judgment." (267, 207)

Piaget maintains that achieving a near equilibrium in a constantly changing situation is the goal of all human functions— biological, affective, and above all mental. He defines equilibrium as a state in which "all the virtual transformations compatible with the relationships of the system compensate each other." (258, 41) There is a state of permanent striving towards an equilibrium, a balancing effort with a state of disbalance as its constant outcome, similar to the activities in constructing an ever-expanding inverse pyramid. Life is a progressive series of attempts to balance forms; each attempt rests upon previous acquisitions, and each, with increasing complexity, creates new forms which furnish in turn the foundations for later balances.

The Newborn

The infant is born as a biological organism with a series of native reflexes. These reflexes, purely biological, are immediately modified on the basis of environmental events. In fact, these reflexive environmental encounters most likely started long before birth. These encounters, primarily assimilative in nature, constitute the initial adaptive experience, while cognitive processes are in the making. Thus, to quote Flavell, "birth reflexes are truly the building blocks of the [very early phases of cognition]; intelligence begins with them and is constituted as a function of their adaptation to the environment." (135, 89)

The Physical, Social, Cultural, and Ideational Environment

Piaget assumes that all social realities are created by humans. Curiously, the made-by-humans experience becomes as much a part of an individual's environment as the physical objects in a person's life space. The nature of these life experiences—their degree of availability and variation—can bolster, accelerate, retard and vary the rate of a person's development, including whether development can progress to any extent at all. (293, 337)

Thus, cognitive development is very much within the purview of socialization of the child. Society is in many ways what was once ascribed to instinct—a direction giver. Since the process of thinking always contains an interaction between the individual's ongoing mode of thinking and that which each individual encounters in the environment, individual and environmental can only be viewed as a syncretic whole.

PIAGET'S CONCEPTION OF DEVELOPMENT

Piaget's view of development as a distinct progression of phases maintains essentially an evolutionary perspective. A relatively homogeneous patterning of thinking, within the many facets in an individual's life, lasts for the duration of the particular phase. Piaget explains this phenomenon with an analogy: Development constitutes an "ensemble of elements" not unlike an orchestra which, as an organized and coordinated whole, produces the music of many pieces. (245)

Piaget locates five such major developmental phases, each of which has one or several substages. *Phase,* throughout this chapter, refers to any one of these five major developmental progressions, while *stage* designates a subphase within a phase. The fifth and final phase (formal operations) is assumed to bring about full equilibration.[11] This final form of equilibration occurs after a quasi-equilibration has taken place within each phase, that is, the individual functions at optimum to become more and more accurate (more knowledgeable) in a phase yet to come.

Piaget's and other descriptive accounts of the phases of cognition, tend to create the erroneous impression of a step-by-step phasal development, as if an individual were to ascend to the next developmental phase within one quick stride whenever the time was ripe. More correctly, each individual is always as much in transition as within a phase.

Piaget's associates, Inhelder, Sinclair, and Bovet, have more

[11] Most recently, Piaget and Piagetian scholars hint that there might be a successive cognitive phase to formal operation, a sixth (adult) phase of cognitive adaptation. (221; 250; 316b; 361b; 371)

recently analyzed four *transitional* occurrences between phases in which the following progressive developments can be identified: Phasal operation (pseudoequilibration) occurs when a feature of a situation is conceived within the particular phase's distinct conceptual scheme. No contradictions are apparent because each subsequent experience with a similar situation is understood and explained in the same manner. A new conception is in the making when differences are sensed but old conceptions and explanations are employed not so much as a matter of fact but as a matter of justification. Old ways of thinking dominate and perservere in spite of uncertainty and questionable impressions. As this uncertainty increases and gives way to new questions, conflicts, rather than protestations, arise between several alternative ways of thinking. The situation results in confusion and hesitation, and attempts are made to reconcile two or more contradictory conceptions. Finally, different conceptions are resolved via differentiation and generalization. A new scheme for a new structure of thinking emerges. These progressions of thinking can occur with specific learnings regarding new or newly conceived information, including values as well as the conceptual perspective (logic) of thinking. (163)

Although Piaget's developmental phases are frequently cited as if they were entities, they are actually no more than points of reference for understanding the sequence of development. They serve primarily to denote the course of development; they do not present development itself. Altogether, they serve as convenient "handles" for the study of cognitive development. Individuals are never aware of being in one phase or another; they merely interact as if they knew their phases—and as if they functioned accordingly.

Each phase reflects a range of organizational patterns of thinking. The phases occur in a definite sequence at approximate age spans in the continuum of chronological development. The completion of one phase provides a passing equilibrium, as well as the beginning imbalance leading to a new phase. Most important is the order of succession of these phases. The order remains always the same. According to Piaget's observations, then, developmental phases are age bound, since they depend on the completion of the previous phase, but they are also age free, since the age does not determine their occurrence. A wide spectrum of research on these phasal progressions in children on all five continents of the globe has thus far revealed that while the chronological ages cited by Piaget vary from place to place at times, the Piagetian sequential order of stages and phases never vary. (5; 47; 132; 141, 124–139) It is most important in Piaget's theory that his phases and stages are not merely descriptive and conceptual handles; they are verifiable and predictive! (50, 12–14)

Cognitive development can be summarized as follows:

1. Development is continuous and always within the same sequential progression, though the rate of development and at what chronological point it occurs in a child's development are apt to vary.
2. Development proceeds through a continuous process which includes structuring, bringing into hierarchical order, consolidation, and equilibration. (60) The latter involves the transformation of previous understanding into new comprehension.
3. Each progression of development depends on the progression of previous learning. Each developmental phase and substage has roots in a previous phase and contains precursors for the following one. Thus, cognitive development entails an evolutionary process of continuous development.
4. Each phasal development entails a period of formation and a period of attainment. New patterns of thinking, constituting a new provisional equilibration, replace previous levels of cognition. These changes are cumulative and irreversible. Thus, cognitive development is discontinuous as well as continuous as stated in number 3 above.
5. The sequence of development (the progression of developmental phases and the relevant substages) creates a hierarchy of cognitive experience. Each novel pattern entails a more complex and effective form of cognition. Once such a new form of thinking is achieved, the capacity to do so leads necessarily to new and advanced perspectives of cognition. Moreover, each aspect of knowledge—object permanency, cause and effect, space, time, moral judgment, etc.— that is, each mental perspective and abstraction, has to proceed through its own developmental-prone progression. Each developmental period is defined by new questions, and, concomitantly, each cognitive acquisition poses new questions.
6. Each individual is apt to achieve a different level of cognitive development though by native structure (brain) each individual has the possibility for all these developments but they are not necessarily realized by each one.

THE FIVE PHASES OF
PIAGET'S DEVELOPMENTAL THEORY

Cognitive development falls fundamentally, according to Piaget's general formulation, into three major phases:

1. Sensorimotor development (roughly, from birth to two years of age)
2. Concrete operations (roughly, from ages two to eleven or twelve)
3. Formal operations (roughly, over the age of eleven or twelve)

However, for the purpose of a more detailed comprehension of cognitive development and to establish a better linkage with affective and behavioral development (see Chapters 2 and 3) the five phases of Piaget's more inclusive developmental theory are employed in this discussion. This fivefold division represents not only Piagetian thinking in greater detail, it also reflects a practice employed by such Piagetian scholars as David Elkind *(56)* among others.

1. Sensorimotor
2. Preconceptual
3. Intuitive thought
4. Concrete Operations
5. Formal Operations

The meaning of the names for these five phases will become apparent in the presentations that follow.

The Sensorimotor Phase

Sensorimotor fittingly describes the initial period of cognitive development, a period of life in which predominantly sensory and motor experiences are molded into sequential and focus activities. This period takes up roughly a child's first twenty-four months. During this first phase of life, the infant will become an active partner in these scattered immediate experiences and will render the scatter into patterns but separate events. A whole developmental phase is achieved before the actual advent of language. Or, conversely, knowing and thinking emerge out of action. Sensorimotor knowledge develops before language and is the foundation for all subsequent understanding, including the knowledge of language.[12] *(221; 249)*

This first period of human development receives more detailed analysis than any subsequent period. *(232; 265; 274; 276)* Six distinct stages of sensorimotor development can be described and explained within the overall developmental phases, which are successive and always in the same order. The six stages are characterized as follows:

1. Exercise of reflexes
2. Primary circular reactions
3. Secondary circular reactions
4. Coordination of secondary schemata and application to new situations
5. Tertiary circular reactions
6. Invention of new means through mental combinations

---

[12] Interestingly, in R. Brown's account of early language development, the first stage of language development coincides with the sensorimotor phase. *(31,* 166–201).

Exercise of Reflexes

This first stage of the sensorimotor phases is characterized by reflexive activities, which are a continuation of the prenatal mode of living and fill much of an infant's first month of wakeful life. An infant's individuality is expressed by crying, sucking, and variations in the rhythm of breathing and resting. These early life experiences, though all reflexive, are the beginnings of personality development. The very nature of reflexes and their spontaneous repetition provide what is necessary for actively experiencing early activities. Repetitive experience establishes an activity for its rhythm, which denotes certain qualities. Rhythmicity is important in the early care of the child and also for pleasure in later life. Repetition and rhythmicity ("guaranteed repetition") furnish the foundation for regularity (affective dependability) and cognitive predictability.

Also furnished are the first traces of sequential use of events and the beginning of a notion of order. For instance, the sucking reflex depends upon practice for proper functioning. The location of the nipple and the immediate experience of having something to suck provide an experience cycle fundamental to all later development. It should be noted that this encounter reflects vividly the dynamic as well as the environmental aspects of Piaget's formulation. Change or development comes about by experiencing, that is, by living. Individuals cannot incorporate an experience on the preoperational (preconceptual) level until they have acted upon it. Moreover, the organism never *is* something, but is always *becoming* something, since the environment, simply because we exist in it, makes constant demands upon us.

Repetitive use of reflexes, enriched by neurological and physical maturation, tends to form the beginning of learned behavior, including habits. In this stage, such behavior is still months away; but it is clearly in the making in this very first month, if not before.

As stated earlier, cognitive functioning rests primarily upon the process of adaptation, which comprises the interplay of the processes of assimilation and accommodation. Growth of understanding is a dual process. Exploration leads the infant to note and order the world of external things, and at the same time the inner world of an infant's mind is taking shape. Adaptation, as a central cognitive process, has its start in these very early variations of reflexive actions and in the ever-increasing variation in activities. The dictum holds that there is no perception without novelty. First, perception involves a generalized assimilation, with the infant incorporating more and more of his own momentary reactions to environmental or internal stimulation. For instance, an infant will accelerate his response to a sudden change in light. This incorporative process is nonselective and includes those stimulations to which his sensory equipment is capable of responding. Repetition and sequential experience prepare the way for rudimentary generalization and recognitory assimilation. The generalization of practical experiences into such abstract categories as palpable, tactile, and visual experiences implies ordering. Although at this point ordering is solely on the experiential level, there is yet a hint of cognition. Separating visual from tactile, comfort from discomfort, etc., also initiates a process of differentiation in an active environment previously undifferentiated.

One-month-old infants are in a purely autistic phase. They adapt (assimilate) their environment entirely according to their organic demands. They experience all events either to their own satisfaction or dissatisfaction. Yet, each of their activities involve one or several of the five basic reflexes which are rudimentary to much of life to come: (1) vision (looking), (2) hearing (listening), (3) prehension (grasping), (4) ingesting (sucking), (5) vocalization (crying), and, of course, general limb movements. (*395, 229*)

Primary Circular Reactions

These mark the beginning of the second stage within this first phase (sensorimotor development). Within this stage reflexive behavior is slowly replaced by voluntary movements. Maturational neurological readiness is requisite to this development. An infant's psychic life starts when maturation "no longer alters assimilated objects in a physio-chemical manner but simply incorporates them in its own form of activity." (*276*, 8) In about the second month, the infant can consciously repeat an action, and activities primarily involve repeating voluntarily what was previously merely automatic behavior. This repetition of behavior is now a deliberate response to what becomes more and more recognized as the stimulation of a previous experience. We note that accidentally acquired responses (such as manual reaching or pushing) become new sensorimotor experiences. They open new and ever-multiplying "environments" (a plural term which stresses that the infant knows many environments and is as yet incapable of coordinating the parts of an experience into one or several integrated wholes.) Each event is a whole and, we should note, each behavior is moving on its own course and rhythm.

Primary circular reactions, however simple, provide an organizational pattern, a schema by which two or three factors are organized into a relationship pattern and superimposed upon the previous patterns of merely reproductive, repetitious, sequential actions. Most likely, in the second to fourth month of life,[13] reac-

[13] Please note that stages and phases within Chapters 1, 2 and 3 are made more explicit by references to children's *possible* corresponding chronological ages. These references are for illustrative not necessarily normative purposes.

tions become closely linked with stimuli, and the infant's experience is closely tied to the environmental event which stimulates the reaction. Repetition of actions—especially sequential repetition—leads to the infant's realization that a repeatedly experienced stimulus has a signal value. It is no coincidence that the effects of an infant's interaction with movements, sounds, and lights are almost always repeated. In fact, rhythmic repeat movements or sounds are the hallmarks of "babystuff" (e.g.; rattles and twirling tops). (194b)

In such circular experience is also the start of a new behavior sequence. This new cognitive behavioral pattern (or schema) is characterized by the assimilation of a previous experience and the recognition of the stimulus which triggers the reaction. It involves the emergence of the accommodative process. The child incorporates and accommodates reactions to an environmental impact. The synthesis of assimilation and accommodation which occurs is, in essence, adaptation.

New sensorimotor functions emerge. Vision, for example, becomes a continuous experience. Sucking, prehension, and hearing provide experiential episodes with newly evolving patterns of circular reactions.

Objects as stimuli become closely related to the ongoing experience. Each object is distinct and separate from it's context and the sequence of events; each experience with an object remains an isolated experience and a momentary life event. For example, grasping the nursing person's finger outside the field of vision and sucking the nipple (breast or bottle) provide two centers of experience, while smelling the nipple, touching it with the mouth, and seeing the person's face become part of one sequence of experiences in the baby's world. Most importantly, eye-hand coordination begins to emerge as an essential developmental achievement. (163)

Two new areas of organization have their roots in this second stage. First, a notion of causality, which can be traced to this early recognition of the sequence of events. Food, for example, as an extension of sucking or grasping, is related to these early intuitive experiences. "A child's first sense of causal relation, then, is simply a diffuse connection between an action on the one hand and a result on the other, without comprehension of spatial relations or intermediary objects." (222, 50) Second, a notion of temporal space finds its genetic roots in the seriation of experienced events. For years, however, the child senses all seriation as the extended present. Sequentiality also leads to increased incorporation of a relationship between action and the stimulation of action. This suggests that laws of stimulus-response (S-R) processes gain importance with development but seem to be nonoperative during the very early developmental periods.

The major theme of this period is the capacity of children to incorporate the new results of their behavior as part of their continuing behavior. New or past experiences have no meaning unless they become part of a primary circular reaction pattern. Infants have to experience any new event (or object) through their accustomed repertoire of sensory activities—sucking, touching, etc. Children learn from the process of interaction with the object rather than from the object itself. For example, babies will coo happily if a new baby-sitter handles them in much the same way as before. Infants thus beginning their own behavior patterns clearly start to interact differently with different objects.

Secondary Circular Reactions

The third stage of development involves a continuation of the primary circular reactions patterns and the incorporation of a more lasting behavior. In this period, which tends to be between an infant's fourth and eighth month, the sensorimotor apparatus tunes in and becomes more and more aware of accustomed events. Behavior is directed toward retention—toward making events last. Grasping and holding a finger and repeatedly banging an object for noise production are typical infant activities in this period. These activities constitute rich learning events and result in further awareness of and accommodation to environmental experiences. Environmental forces become more and more recognizable and concrete, and consequently, impinge more and more upon the infant's experiences.

Specifically, primary circular reactions are repeated and prolonged by these new secondary reactions. The grasping reflex, a sequence of grasping and holding, evolves into unified activities such as shaking, pulling, and tugging. Increasingly the infant widens the scope of activities by relating two or more sensorimotor activities (e.g., vision and touch) into one experiential sequence, that is, into a schema. Visible fractions of an object can serve to trigger an action sequence. To illustrate: the sight of the end of a familiar string can be sufficient to induce a child to pull it, perhaps to shake an object overhead. The string, the shaking, and the motion of the object are one universe, although infants are not yet aware that they themselves belong to this same universe. *(232)* These actions sequences contain the potential for future cognitive understanding which takes root in this early sensorimotor phase as follows:

1. Children, in interaction with objects, consider ends and means as one; yet, in their responses, they start to note a beginning and a subsequent action. Cognition of cause and effect is on its way.

2. Qualitative and quantitative judgments find their roots in these simple experiences. The notion of more and less come vaguely into the thought repertoire.
3. The child begins to note a number of different response patterns, they can comprise single unified action sequences. Behavior starts to be developed; it no longer just happens.
4. This coordination of separate experiences into one schema leads to an awakening awareness that the self plays a part in the action, that is, to a conception of self.
5. The notion of time finds a cursory introduction with the dim beginning awareness of the concepts of *before* and *after* in the various action sequences.
6. The recognition of a particular stimulus as a part of an action sequence introduces the use of symbols and opens the way to effective communication.
7. Variety in available patterns of action, the dawning recognition of symbols, a rudimentary projection of time, as well as increased accommodation all tend to stress the volitional aspects of the child's prospective behavior.

Each of these seven beginnings has significance for the development of imitation, play, and affect in human behavior.

Imitation depends upon the capacity to differentiate among several events and to react selectively. It all starts with the process of repetition, which is nothing else but self-imitation, with no alternative behavior; the repeating of already acquired actions involving no new model. Nothing, equally in later life, can be imitated until the individual has mastered the doing of it in the same way that children imitate that which they have done already. At this point of development (around the fifth to sixth month of life), systematic imitation becomes possible when the infant can integrate schemas of seeing, hearing, grasping, and specific body movements.

Play is hard to describe in its beginning, but once it has made an appearance, its development can be retroactively traced to repetition and cyclical activities. The skill of shaking, for instance, can become play at the moment the skill is mastered. Accommodation is essentially completed, and pure assimilative activity—doing as one pleases—occurs. There is no doubt that an activity is play if an individual repeats it as the happy display of comprehended behavior. *(267)* However, the exact boundary between ordinary behavior and behavior during play is hard to establish.

Affect (emotion), originally indivisible from bodily experiences, emerges as a distinguishable, separate, but related function in this phase. The increase in environmental contact, particularly in those actions which are beyond mere organic expressions, introduces a variation in potential actions. Affective processes emerge in relation to these differences in experience, which also eventually establish a person's interests and become a direction-giving force for the choice of human behavior.

For roughly the first half-year of life, affect has situational significance. The infant has no sense of permanency. For infants, an object lasts only as long as they perceive it. Once beyond perceptive range, the object, whether mother or rattle, is nonexistent. Thus, early attachment is momentary and without context; it is attachment without history.

Secondary Schemata

The fourth sensorimotor stage tends to culminate around an infant's first birthday (from eight to twelve months). During this stage, previous behavioral achievements serve as the staging grounds for the now rapidly expanding repertoire of behaviors.

Familiar modes of sensorimotor activities are applied to new situations. Increased experimentation is facilitated by the child's greater mobility. The child encounters and experiments with countless new objects. Life is full of new discoveries and experimentations with new events. For example, the child begins to discover that hiding an object occurs prior to finding it. The moment children are aware of the continued existence of an object once it is beyond their immediate perception, they are capable of reasoning to the degree that the object can be returned to their immediate sensory experience again. Ends and means are further differentiated by experimentation with and discovery of means which are quite apart of the usual outcome. The child is involved in continued and repeated experimentation, despite the fact that to the casual observer the emergence of new skills and awareness often appear to have been learned spontaneously.

Toward the end of the first year, children have refined their capacity to differentiate and generalize that experiential episodes can be generalized into classes of experience. Each experiential episode is distinguished from the others by recognized signs, and each evokes different sets of action sequences. When children can read these signs, anticipate action, and perceive their universe beyond the boundaries of their sensorimotor sphere of action, the capacity for intelligent reasoning has begun to emerge. Trial-and-error behavior continues to lead to the employment of previous behavioral patterns in new ways, and to select those results most useful to the achievement of desired goals. Adaptive behavior leads to random experimentation. In adaptation, the child fits new activities and objects of experience to previously acquired ways of conceiving (reactive patterns).

The infant now can distinguish objects for the related activity, can perceive them as objects, and can begin to distinguish end products from their means. An infant will recover a ball, for instance, return it to a thrower, be all set to have the ball rolled to a desired location, and await it there. This action and thought sequence calls to our attention how complex thinking can become even at the very beginning of cognitive development! The full ability to recognize signs and the capacity to anticipate appropriate responses to them create in the child a sense of independence from the action in progress. For example, the child seeing the ball roll and then scampering after it is able to remain apart from the action sequence, to experience action by observation. The child lets the thing happen and observes the results. When children observe in order to understand that which is beyond their immediate active involvement, intellectual activities are clearly present.

Tertiary Circular Reactions

These reactions involve the discovery of new means through active experimentation and occur in the fifth stage—generally the first half of the second year of life. Active experimentation continues to take up a large share of the day's activities. It almost seems as if children were saying to themselves, "Let's try it this time in a new way!" Understanding of what occurs coincides with experiencing the event. Children incorporate into their knowledge the actions of this new experimentation and its results. Rational judgment and, ultimately, intellectual reasoning are at hand.

Reasoning must be given credit for this cyclical repetition. The child tries to grasp the ongoing situation as it is and begins to observe its components. The child can now enter into an action sequence which the child had experienced before at any point in order to start the total sequence.

With an awareness that objects are independent from their action sequence, the child gains an intensified interest in his environment. Piaget suggests that sensory cues, perception, and continuous perceptive awareness entail three distinctly separate acquisitions. Sensory cues neither necessarily indicate perception nor guarantee awareness of perception if it occurs. Not until the current developmental level is achieved is the child capable of forming a beginning concept of a thing—a beginning awareness of an object as an entity with its own distinct properties. Prior to this period, the sensory cue has been only a necessary part of the whole action sequence. A very important development is the child's ability to observe that the discovery of new objects and new methods of behavior and the utilization of this discovery present two distinct steps. The first precedes the second, but the second does not necessarily follow immediately or, for that matter, at all. Throughout life, the awareness of the availability of an activity does not imply its utilization. From this point on, as an illustration of this pertinent cognitive acquisition, children no longer have to eat what is discovered as edible. They can now wait knowingly and delay an activity, not merely obediently but with the knowledge that the activity will still be there even after the delay.

An infant can retain previous behavior patterns so long as they have become part of a behavior sequence. Now, with the capacity to separate objects from the ongoing action, the child, no longer an infant, can continue to envisage an object beyond the immediate experience as long as there is an immediate relationship to what remains after the action sequence. In other words, the awareness of an object's relationship to other objects (including its use) is essential to the remembrance of the object. The failure to remember, therefore, is due to a failure to understand relationships. Of course, during this early period of the child's development, only immediate relationships are understood and reflected in actions.

The discovery of objects as objects introduces the awareness of their spatial relationships. For example, the filling and emptying of hollow objects with smaller objects and the fitting of differently shaped blocks into corresponding openings are typical experiments of children of this age. And these discoveries have a developmental progression. Full forms (circles and squares) are recognized for their shape before triangles and more complex shapes are.[14] (260, 198–205) The recognition of spatial relationships between objects and of rotations and reversals of objects in space leads to an awareness of one's own movements and the movements of other people.

At this point, causal relations begin to assume a new dimension. Children recognize the existence of causes which are completely independent of their activity. Other people become autonomous centers of action. Practically, this means children turn to adults not for actions but for help. Moreover, children distinguish themselves as actors, as the power behind the movement of inanimate objects, and simultaneously differentiate themselves from other people's ability to cause action. This new outlook is essential for the evolving capacity to relate to different people and for the enhancement of affect, competition, and rivalry. In everyday life, the child's growing desire expressed as "Me do" is anchored in this cognitive progress.

With more effective accommodative capacities, habit training becomes easier. Simultaneously, these gains also constantly threaten the maintenance of previous patterns as alternatives become more recognizable. In Piaget's words

[14] These findings are concomitant with data on neurological maturation. (155; 221; 260, and especially 306)

> *. . . the external environment imposes a constant enlarging of the subject's reactions and that new experience always causes the old framework to crack. That is why acquired habits are sooner or later superimposed on reflex schemata and on the former are superimposed the schemata of intelligence. And, of course, it can also be said that the subject accepts this necessity with pleasure since the "circular action" at all levels is precisely an attempt to conserve novelties and establish them by reproductive assimilation. (265, 265–266)*

The capacity to imitate depends upon systematic accommodation, upon the ability to discern differences between objects. Now, in the second year of life, the child can imitate the action phase of his model. He can *do* but not necessarily *be* what the model stands for; the latter requires retention of a model as a mental symbol in itself.

Play increasingly becomes an expressive function of developing children, primarily involving the repetition of their learned behavior as a self-satisfying occupation. In play, a child repeats that action phase which is not meant to represent any particular concept. For instance, a child playing at "going to sleep" imitates the action of going to sleep, not the concept of bedtime or night time. Play is an activity calculated to amuse and to excite the playing individual. Play becomes progressively less involved in the context of the existing environment, and it begins to have meaning only within the context of the child's own personal (assimilative) world.[15] Here is possibly a hint at the therapeutic feature of play: play "legalizes" the predominance of assimilation—of doing with life as only the playing one conceives it.

Invention of New Means Through Mental Combinations
This final stage of the sensorimotor phase is generally entered sometime during the second half of a child's second year of life (from eighteen to twenty-four months). There is a gradual shift in focus from the actual sensorimotor experiences to an increased reflection about these experiences. That this is done through mental combinations suggests a greater emphasis upon intellectual behavior. Obviously, this developmental stage represents a climax of previous acquisitions and constitutes a bridge to the next developmental phase.

In this final stage of sensorimotor development, the child becomes clearly aware of objects as independent, autonomous centers with their own properties beyond one's own intent and ac-

---

[15] Piaget is challenged by B. Sutton-Smith who believes that play fundamentally deals with novel but investigative behavior: "Play is basically a form of mind-making activity: It is a primitive process of presentation sometimes artistic, sometimes social, through which the child attempts to comprehend this world." (370, 31)

tion. Above all, the child utilizes objects for their own innate qualities and can use them beyond a personal immediate experience with them. First, individuals discern themselves as one object among many. Then they discover that objects can endure in the passage of time. It is then possible for newly acquired mental images of objects to be retained beyond immediate sensory experiences with them. Closely linked with the remembered image of an object are its properties: use, form, size, and color. For the comprehension of each property of the object, a separate level of cognitive maturity is required. For example, a child may readily pack a *big red* ball in the trunk of a car to take on a trip. Later, the child can readily and assuredly state that the ball is in the trunk. But if someone should inquire whether the *big* ball is in the trunk, the child would most likely clarify by saying, "No, the red one."

Notice must be taken of children's new relationship to their environment. They not only experience themselves as one among many, they also understand themselves as a single entity. In simple situations, they can think of themselves in relation to situations in the past and immediate future as well as to those in the present. They can also conceive of an object without having a detailed personal experience with it. Their previously acquired capacity to perceive cause is extended to a point where they can envisage themselves as the potential cause or initiator of action.

Sensorimotor patterns are slowly replaced by semimental functioning. Children then have a beginning ability to recall without having to repeat an activity with their sensorimotor system. They perceive simple causality by perception alone and can initiate detours or alternatives to most simple forms of action without actually performing them. A new era is dawning. They begin to predict. They can infer causes from observing effect, and they predict effects from observing causes.

Imitation now proceeds with the attempt to copy either the action itself or the representative symbol of the action. For example, children might imitate a parent's work or imitate a particular action in order to convey the idea that they are going to work just as their parents do. In either case, the imitative process, in essence, is an effort to accommodate an environmental model. This mode of behavior is of importance in incorporating the message of symbols, especially in language development.

In play, the beginning capacity to imitate actions and connotations of actions opens the possibility of playing at life's events for the richness of the possibilities. Play becomes life and life is, most likely, almost all play for the two-year-old.

Egocentricity, the state of confusion of self and the external world, is the undifferentiating state of awareness upon which all infant and early childhood behavior rests. The lack of differentiation is between the self and the environment. It is a lack of social perspective rather than a failure in social sensitivity. Egocentricity, in fact, is a stepping-stone to cognition of the self.

Identification as a cognitive process becomes evident toward the end of the child's second year. Identification evolves from imitation. First, individuals becomes cognizant of the worth (to them) of the person to be imitated, then of the model's imitable characteristics. In other words identification requires (1) a person the child considers worthwhile (a desire for attachment which is an affect issue) and (2) the ability to conceive the person's relevance to the behavior to be imitated.

All these powerful experiences present giant steps in thinking. As we observe very young children we can see more minute steps of learning, which also tend to proceed very gradually and in two phases. First, whether new noises, new tastes, new personal encounters, or strange objects or activities are involved, children will experiment to discover the nature and quality of new experiences. Then, frequently to the puzzlement of the adults, children tend to leave new experiences alone for awhile before returning to them with a clearer notion in mind of how the experience can start to fit into an emerging understanding (schema). Development is always in progress.

The Preconceptual Phase

The life of the child in the period from two to four years old appears to be one of continuous investigation of the environment and the possibilities of activity within it.[16] Children discover new symbols every day to use in communication with themselves and others. Primarily, these symbols have a personal reference for the child. Thus, even though children and adults employ much the same language and experience similar daily events, they do not necessarily mean or understand the same thing, even when they use identical language.

The child's thinking is largely preconceptual in content. For Piaget, this and the subsequent period is frequently placed within the concrete operational phase as one overall piece, preparatory for conceptual thinking (formal operation). This phase of preoperational representations (262) would then cover the developmental span from two to about eleven or twelve years of age. In this chapter, Piaget's alternate conception, which concerns the existence of a distinct but clearly preconceptual phase of thinking, is

---

[16] Jean Piaget's material concerning the period from two to four years old is elusive. These years involve a transition sandwiched between the life patterns of purely self-satisfying behavior and those of rudimentary socialized behavior.

presented. Noteworthy for this stance which is also collaborated by Piaget: (1) It takes a great deal of time to interiorize actions, as opposed to executing actions, and (2) a broad decentering process must take place in this phase in which children must situate themselves in relation to all events and people around them. (283, 31)

The basically egocentric approach of this phase reflects a decisive advance over the autistic behavior of the previous phase: "The interplay of practical relationships in the world of reality teaches the child to shift centers of space and its objects from his action to himself, and thus locate himself at the middle point of this world which is being born." (270, 38) Children know the world only as they see it; they know no alternatives. Moreover, they also take it for granted that everyone thinks as they do and understands them. Necessarily, during this phase, assimilation continues as the paramount process of thinking.

Play, as a major assimilative process, occupies most of the child's waking hours. With its emphases on how and why, play becomes the primary tool for adaptation. For instance, children will behave as if they had mastered the routine of dressing as soon as they can put their clothing on in one way or another. Thus, getting dressed becomes play even if their method of dressing varies considerably from the standards of their elders. Through play, the child is actually accomplishing real-life tasks. Play that is imaginary or symbolic has a rich egocentric character. Although to the uninitiated bystander play, with its *as if* quality, appears to be sheer fantasy, to a child it has all the elements of reality. For example, one wooden block might represent a rabbit eating, while another might represent a carrot. Children in this phase may be said to play their way through life.

Language, as play, also serves as a vehicle of development. With the recent acquisition of language, two- or three-year-olds employ language in order to convey their experience. Language slowly replaces sensorimotor experiences, symbolically expressing desires and experiences, and labeling. Speech becomes the conveyor of thought and actions. Language becomes possible the moment children relinquish some of their autistic world of self-imitation and are able to employ systematically representative symbols, such as a knowing smile or a verbal utterance, for that which they want done.

The imitation of others and symbolic imitation are mostly spontaneous processes in children of these ages. Children who sit crouched with a pen in one hand meaning to imitate the entire action sequence of their father writing a note are engaged in symbolic imitation. Similarly, merely wearing a police badge can make children think they are being police officers. Children imitate as they perceive. They try to incorporate, often in one gesture, their own perception of the entire action sequence demonstrated by their model. Imitation furnishes them with a wealth of new symbols for objects and also enriches their repertoire of available behavior. The process of shifting their attention from themselves to others and then back again further helps them refine their imitations and approximate more closely the action sequences of others.

Above all, during this phase, there is an awareness and an ever-increasing interest in and stimulation by objects and actions in the environment. The very assimilative experiences with which young children primarily started bring them continuously into situations which demand accommodation. Children are constantly challenged to evaluate and reevaluate their conception of the environment. For instance, in their repeated and much enjoyed play with water, they experience not only fun but also the properties of water as it runs over, runs out of tub, splashes over, etc.

The absence or severe retardation of play, language, or imitative behavior leaves a child more in his autistic world and less subject to the impact of his environment. Play involving language and imitation leads to communication with an outside world and a gradual process of socialization. Rapaport refers to this period of development:

> The mere fact, then, of telling one's thought, or telling it to others, or of keeping silence and telling it only to oneself must be of enormous importance to the structure and functioning of thought in general, and of child logic in particular. Now between autism and intelligence there are many degrees, varying with their capacity of being communicated. These intermediate varieties must therefore be subject to a special logic, intermediate too between the logic of autism and that of intelligence. The chief of those intermediate forms . . . we propose to call egocentric thought. (308b, 158)

Thought and reason for the child over two years old are based predominantly upon self-reference. Each event is seen as an independent event, *as if* life is a set of slides not even a series yet. Connections between events are noted; but whatever things happen together or after one another thereby belongs to each other. A child begins to reason that *proximity* makes causal relationship. Technically speaking, cause and effect are juxtapositional. For example, if a toy rolls off a table by chance and at the same moment an adult says something to the child who is busy with the toy, the child is likely to think the adult's comment made the toy fall.

Children order their concept of space and spatial relationships by their subjective experiences; life to them is logical within their own frames of reference. This same level of behavior is continued in adult life when a point of view or action can only be explained and justified by self-reference in terms of the person's own history.

Cognitive development during the period of preconceptual thought is characterized by the following forms (schemas) of thinking. First, experiences are judged by their outward appearance, regardless of their objective logic. The process "is simply a reflective level of internalization and of symbolization, permitting reasoning, but originating at the sensorimotor level, before the development of language and inner thought." (236, 61) It is based entirely upon subjective judgments. For example, children will select a glass filled to the brim in preference to three quarters of a glass twice the size, basing the selection upon their own idea of fullness. Though they may have witnessed a greater amount of milk being poured into the latter glass, they judge as they see things; that is, comparisons are purely visual. (301) Second, children tend to experience either the qualitative or quantitative aspect of an event. They do not perceive both at once or any connective relationship between the notions of quantity and quality. The child has not reached the point where he is able to merge concepts of objects, space, and causality into temporal interrelationships with a concept of time.

Close to the preconcept of causality by juxtaposition is the fact that a child is apt to bestow power upon an object, and its activity or events happening within its juxtaposition are conceived as causally associated with one-and-another. Animism, the attribution of life and consciousness to inanimate objects, is a natural way of explaining happenings. When children stumble over the leg of a chair they think the chair tripped them. In one way, it is primitive thinking; in another way it is one step removed from the individual. No longer do all actions emanate from the child. The child "thereby invests another person (or physical objects) with an exaggerated power over the universe, a sort of artificialization due to projection of personal activity into those new centers of forces constituted by the other 'selves'." (232, 308) Basically, children's thinking reflects a confusion between their own actions and those of the object. Goals and means are one.

Investing a model with unusual desirability and/or power leads to identification. Piaget explains the emergence of identification as follows:

> He [the child] feels close to those who satisfy his immediate needs and interests. He selects them as his model. These spontaneously selected models become the measuring stick for value judgments for years. In spite of unavoidable conflicts, particularly during the period of negativism around the age of three, the spontaneously selected model, usually the caring adult, remains the object of identification and obedience. Under ordinary conditions the young child maintains a sense of respect and awe for the superior powers of his caretaker[s]. He places them in an omnipotent position. The

child's sense of obedience and awe . . . is derived from a combination of love and fear and provides the foundation for his conscience. Obedience to the demand only becomes a moral obligation when the person requesting obedience is held in awe. Respect for the caretaker requires obedience to the values established by him. (Translated from 274, 308)

Identification on this level emerges from a combination of imitation and a sense of awe for the model. These experiences of identification become guideposts for judgment. With an increased capacity for refined differentiation of affect, children build up their system of values, their conscience. Identification is also strengthened by the child's accommodation to the pressure of the environment. Adult restraints and demands for obedience are as real to a child's experience as are episodes of self-satisfaction.

Long before children have a conception of obedience, they comprehend the activity of "doing as they are told." They equate this with pleasing the persons who care for them and conceive a causal relationship between the two. After all, it occurs in juxtaposition. A "good child" is the one who fulfills a caring adult's commands.

Requests are taken literally, as if words were the same as actions. Children frequently find themselves in a dilemma since they are unable to carry out orders as they perceive them. For instance, the command "be good" may leave a child at sea. The child does not know what to do in the absence of a specific behavioral request. A generalized concept of goodness does not yet exist in the child's form of thinking.

Just as obedience to adults is in the order of things, so are the rules of games conceived as sacred and unalterable. With three- and four-year-olds, the children's own activities continue to remain the center of their play. Consequently, "to win" means to carry out their activities successfully. Unless their winning necessitates elimination of the other children, they see no inconsistency in several simultaneous winners. All that matters is the successful completion of their play.

The Phase of Intuitive Thought

Most important for children from four to seven years old are their widening social contacts in the world around them, which necessarily reduce egocentricity and increase social participation. It involves a gradual shift in self-identity from thinking "it's me" to thinking "I see what is happening." (294, 19) This period is fundamentally an extension of the previous one. Both periods, as has already been pointed out, entail preoperational thought. They form a bridge between a child's passive acceptance of the environment as it is experienced and the child's ability to react to it realistically.

In this second transitional period (the phase of intuitive thought) children begin to use words as part of their thinking process. At first, thinking and reasoning are still acted out. Just as they had to coordinate sensorimotor experience on an earlier level, so on this level of intuitive thought children have to coordinate perspectives of different conceptual impressions. They must coordinate their subjective and egocentric versions of the world with the real world around him. They depend heavily upon perceptual experiences; applicable thought structures are just about in the making. Yet, more and more, they tend to behave similarly to their elders, as if they knew intuitively what life was all about; they exhibit real beginnings in conceptual thinking.

When children are old enough to begin school, a large part of their thinking involves verbalization of their mental activities. Just as they once employed their motor apparatus to act out their thinking, they now employ speech to form their thinking. Thinking remains largely egocentric, with a continuous shift to incorporate the thinking of key adults as their own. Though this gradual shift in centering spells progress, it also has an inherent danger if a belief in self is merely replaced with a belief in authority. (283, 179)

The child still struggles to find a better equilibrium between assimilation and accommodation. "Those parts of reality which are again encountered are fraught with a multitude of new shades and elements which can at first be ignored in assimilating occurrences to the habitual schema, but which in the long run must be taken into account." (267, 83) Accommodative processes are extended to verify, to stabilize, and to generalize the various models in order that individuals can assimilate more universal precepts.

With the aid of language and other symbols children gain in experience and in capacity to generalize their mental experiences. For example, children having two large red marbles and three small blue marbles envisage them as a collection of five marbles. The symbols "two plus three," can be manipulated mentally and altered into the representative symbol "five." Also, to wear a sheriff's badge, which in the preconceptual period meant "I *am* sheriff," means for children in this phase that they are playing the part of what, in their opinion, a sheriff represents (i.e., law and order). In other words, assimilative processes build upon early images that are frequently beyond the conscious awareness of the child involved. It must be stressed, however, that children must first understand the preconcept of being a sheriff before they can realize that the concept stands for justice, law, and order.

It is still difficult in this period for children to entertain two ideas simultaneously; they can only think of one idea at a time. This whole developmental struggle can be best explained by Piaget's concept of conservation. Conservation involves the knowledge (schema) that attributes of an object (number, weight, mass, etc.) remain invariant (unaltered) in the face of perceptual transformation. (248b, xlviii) Children are moving toward conservation when the difference between how things look and how they really are forces them to apply added understanding. In dealing with the problem of conservation, children will still ask for the candy bar that *appears* larger, even though they know they are all of the same sort (e.g., all in the same box).

In this period, children are preoccupied with parts. Their reasoning is pseudoempirical. Each part is envisaged as a separate whole. If they attempted to think of the whole as unifier of the parts, they would lose sight of the parts and their relationships to each other, which they are just beginning to grasp. This loss (childish amnesia) frequently occurs when the environment is altered or when events the child cannot comprehend intervene in a situation. One of Piaget's experiments serves to illustrate this problem. When the same number of matching buttons were placed in two parallel lines, children recognized the matching quantities as long as each additional button was placed in close proximity to the others in a given group. However, if the children saw the buttons rearranged into two groups of different dimensions, they indicated the group that *appeared* larger as having more buttons (because it was spread out more), even though each pile actually contained the same number of buttons. Thus, the concept of an unaltered whole requires an inspection of the parts. As long as the groups of buttons looked equal and were in juxtaposition, the children would explain that no buttons had been taken from or added to either group, and they would deny a difference in the quantity contained in each group. (163, chapter 2; 251) The alteration of the perceptual field, the change from two matched lines of buttons to uneven groups, even though still of the same number, created an environmental intervention and a new situation beyond the intellectual grasp of the children, obliterating their previous ideas.

In this phase, experiences are judged by outside appearances; there are no intrinsic indicators. Outside clues define each new situation. It is not surprising that children will count their pieces of candy again after they are placed in a paper bag; they have been regrouped after an initial count.

The child thinks in terms of the ongoing event. Activities are judged by their end stage or product—that is, their outcome. Gifts, speed, amount of work, and other accumulative events are evaluated by their appearance at the time of completion. For instance, any work the child might complete first is pronounced as the "easiest." A toy car which arrives first in a race is the "fastest," regardless of the shorter distance it may have covered in comparison with that covered by the others. The child judges by a single clue, usually spatial, and, above all, he reasons on the basis of a personal experience, not logic. His reasoning proceeds from the personal premise to the conclusion in a single jump. The outcome justifies the logic applied. A certain event *had* to happen. The child attempts logical reasoning, though spuriously, and such reasoning is a step forward.

Although children are continuing an earlier pattern, an important variation in thinking has occurred: they now select an objective point of reference. This new form (schema) of thinking does make a difference, and it provides new ways of understanding and a springboard for immense new comprehensions—actual cognition. In one sense, their reasoning is transductive; that is, it relates particular to particular. In another sense, it is syncretic in its depiction of things as a whole. The child is unaware of this contradiction. As long as children reason primarily from their own vantage point, they are not capable of assigning fixed laws to causality, nor do they see a need for it. Visual representation and personal experience, however, permit them to perceive simple relationships and to establish their precepts.

Children of this age explain dreams in the same way as they explain their objective world. Dreams are assumed to exist outside the dreamer, and persons and creatures that caused events in the dream are said to be real. Later, a dream is explained as it was visualized during the time of dreaming.

Naturally, increased accommodation during these years calls for children's added attention to, and extended understanding of their objective world. They begin to note in objects multiple properties such as form, color, and utility. Each attribute of an object or a person, however, is seen as an absolute. It is common for a child of this age to see the night as always black and the hero of a story as always brave. The child has no notion of valuation, rank, or relativity. Experiences are graded in absolutes and dichotomous opposites, such as in TV westerns or crime thrillers, where there is only "goodest" or "worst," where thinking and action are reduced to two choices, and where answers are either yes or no. A child's thinking then, in the absence of a hierarchy of values, remains essentially egocentric. Piaget characterizes it as "immediate, illegitimate generalization." (256)

The new awareness of such multiple properties as form, speed, utility, and moral value does not necessarily suggest a comprehension of the basic concepts related to these properties, although the child is acquiring the prerequisites for such understanding. Children slowly become aware that one property, such as height, does not exclude the simultaneous presence of a second one, such as width. Once aware of this much, children will detect further patterns of relationships and eventually note that total quantity or quality can be maintained even when one attribute is reduced or another increased. It should be stressed that children can evaluate only those relationships which pertain to one object or precept. Relationships between two or more objects or ideas are still beyond their comprehension, because they cannot conceive of several points or ideas beyond those of a single object as being part of a still larger whole. Children will easily comprehend that they will visit a person in a city different from their own, but the notion that both cities are in the same state is as yet incomprehensible. The latter notion is complicated because the *same state* involves a larger whole as well as an abstraction, not a readily visible unit of classification.

Although it may seem self-evident, it is important to state that children of preschool age may know how to count even though they have no concept of numbers. A year or so later, they usually acquire a concept of numbers, regardless of their capability in counting. Piaget maintains that children must master the principles of conservation of quantity, such as permanency and continuity, before they can develop a concept of numbers. The former is a logical notion and involves the schema of the next phase of cognitive development.

During the phase of intuitive thought, children retain their preconceptual notion that anything active is alive. A child's notion of animism was illustrated earlier by the case of a child who was tripped by a "bad" chair. Towards the latter part of this phase, however, life is attributed only to objects capable of motion or the production of energy. Furthermore, in the absence of a better understanding of causality and natural laws, children will reason along their own personal perspectives, explaining for instance, that clouds are alive and traverse the sky on their own. The physical and psychological worlds are still intertwined from the child's vantage point; thoughts, things, and persons are experienced as if on one plane. This may explain the observation that children's respect for a toy is equal to their respect for people.

Much of the foregoing discussion serves to present a number of important Piagetian formulations. People first behave as if they knew what it was all about. Moreover, while understanding may occur at different times in a person's life, the sequence of comprehension is always the same. Objects are first conceived as alike, then dichotomized (e.g., small and large), then grouped into sizes (e.g., small, medium, large), then ordered empirically, and eventually ordered methodologically. Similarly, while familiar objects in immediate proximity are fully perceived for what they are in the preconceptual phase, distant objects of more casual familiarity are fully comprehended only later in life. For example, children are apt to speak of a "new" sun appearing every day although they grant permanent existence to a ball even when it is missing; they will not grant such permanency to the remoter sun. Though the ball is recognized as an object which must depend upon an outside force for its motion, the sun continues to be vested with animism. For children, the sun "wakes up" on its own every morning. After all, the sun, by their conception, shines for them. Each change in field requires a new appraisal; a new visual arrangement alters the conditions of the parts. *(293)*

Intuitive thought introduces a rudimentary awareness of relationships, which, in turn, introduces a beginning notion of hierarchies; but usually such early understandings are related to concrete events. For children in this phase, the family consists of all living things in their immediate physical proximity, often including family pets. The family is not yet separated in time and space. It is almost impossible for children to understand fully that they belong to a particular family, a particular town, and a particular country all at the same time. These observations have important implications of understanding a child's sense of not being able to belong to more than one person at the same time. Most likely, the reader has had experience with children who protest that they cannot belong to an aunt because they belong to their mother.

Language at this level serves a threefold purpose. First, as an important tool of intuitive thought, it is employed to reflect upon an event and to project it into the future. Self-conversation is a common occurrence at this age and is popularly described as "thinking aloud." Second, speech remains primarily a vehicle of egocentric communication, with assimilation as its most potent adaptive process. Children assume that everyone thinks as they do. Arguments are simply conflicts of contrary affirmations, with much confusion over the concern of other people for "working out" such differences. Verbal arguments become vehement because words are readily accepted as thoughts and deeds. For example, two children may argue about their preference for a Ford or a Chevrolet. Having heard their fathers engage in a similar discussion, neither child has any real knowledge of the merits of his or her championed car, although both children affirm what they accept as correct. Both press the argument, thinking that the affirmation, the power of words, makes it valid. Similarly, children might cry for having been called "dumb" because they feel being called dumb actually makes them dumb. Finally, speech is a means of social communication in the accommodative sense. It serves as a means for understanding the external environment and adapting to it. Conversation is an extension of thinking aloud, and it projects individual thoughts into the social plane and encourages collective expressions. In the earlier years of this phase, speech involves a "collective monologue" analogous to parallel play. Speech serves as a mutual excitation to action rather than as a means of exchanging messages and ideas. (284, 20–21)

The child increasingly employs appropriate language without fully comprehending its implications. For example, children in the early years of this phase may use the words *right* and *left,* but they have no notion of the concepts of right and left. In this phase, children speak and act *as if* they knew. Their cognition, as this phase headlines it, is essentially intuitive.

Play reflects much of the evolutionary intellectual development of these early childhood years. On the surface, play becomes noticeably social, while its underlying thinking processes still maintain their egocentric quality. In play, a child now uses a more extended symbolic imagination. For example, as stated above, the understanding of "being a sheriff" progresses from merely wearing the sheriff's badge in the previous phase, to playing as if one were a sheriff in this phase, to playing the role of the sheriff as a guardian of justice, law, and order in the next phase. Games which depend upon finding or replacing missing objects, such as hide-and-seek and guessing games, become central in the child's play repertoire, and make-believe play is engaged in with much gusto. Children have achieved a new level of thinking and can now project themselves into other roles and begin to think in terms of other people.

Most important, however, is the fact that the child's play becomes more social. In social thinking, there is a reliance upon commonly understood (collective) rules, which one by one replace individually established rules. Traditional games such as tag, which are typical for this phase, replace private play. In fact, most play is now social, and to play means to be with others. Cognitive development from this phase on occurs in inverse ratio to symbolic play. The more accommodation to reality there is, the more opportunity there will be to adapt without recourse to assimilative play. Play, work, fantasy, and creative thought ultimately become interchangeable without clear boundaries for each other.

In an earlier phase, imitation was an end in itself and was employed by children without full awareness of their model's intrinsic values; activity and objective were confused. With a budding awareness of some of the relationship patterns of their social world, children in this phase tend to imitate other people in order to capture the values of these people or the status which such values or status represent. This effort at imitation does not necessarily involve identification or lead to it. Imitation serves only the immediate objective to copy a specific behavior without any plans for the use of such behavior in the future.

Moral values for the young child, it must be remembered, are generalized as they are learned. The child, so far, tends to view moral laws as absolute values in real things. Rules, moral obligations, and their phenomenalistic sources are seen as one. Just as its name and its attributes are part of an object, so moral values and rules exist as an indivisible part of the object. For example, the command "do not touch the scissors" becomes a property of the scissors. Also, mother and obedience to mother are perceived as one.

Increased social contacts combined with more accurate imitation gradually lead to new understandings of moral values. Adult rules are observed to be elastic and are no longer as absolutes. This puts children in a situation of conflict because they have no new ways of dealing with this new problem, nor can they find a solution until they combine a higher level of thinking with an understanding of the relativity of social obligations. As before, the first change will occur in behavior that is related to daily practice and well-mastered habits. Values that are less related to daily life are not challenged until later. Altogether, obedience to adults remains the prevailing moral code for children from four to seven years old. Obedience to adults still means "being good," and disobedience means "being bad." A child in this phase still expects all adult actions to be fair.

In play and fantasy, children enact the rules and values of their elders. They may behave as if they had adopted their elders' social conventions as their own. A sense of mutual cooperation and social responsibility may be reflected in the play and speech of children, but it does not exist in their pattern of thinking. Consequently, to hold the group responsible for the behavior of a few makes little sense to a child of this age. Mutual responsibility and group solidarity are still beyond comprehension.

The young child judges a lie by the degree of disobedience involved; motives or underlying circumstances are not considered. The child judges a lie for its size, rather than for its intended purpose. "The obligation not to lie, imposed upon him by adult constraint, appears from the first in its most external form: lie is what does not agree with the truth independently of the subject's intentions." (261, 143–144) Disobedience in this phase is an interruption of adult authority rather than a violation of moral obligation. For instance, so called naughty words are linguistic taboos.

Using them is considered bad because the taboos they break are imposed by adults. The sense of propriety involved in avoiding unpleasant terms cannot occur until children see themselves as part of a larger social grouping and until they understand the need for mutual cooperation to replace restrictive, unilateral respect for adults.

Piaget never traces the development of guilt and its underlying dynamics. Although he questions the psychoanalytic assumption of guilt prior to memory, he seems to accept the hypothesis that guilt is a product and expression of the conscience in later ages. The child sees noncompliance as an insult to adult authority even if such noncompliance is unavoidable, as in situations of involuntary awkwardness. If children feel responsible for an incident, they feel little relief in escaping an adult censor. "The sense of guilt is proportional not to the incidental negligence . . . but to physical acts themselves." (261, 177) Reproof is expected by the young child as a natural consequence of a perceived misdeed. Children perceive punishment as a necessary sequence following any transgression against adult standards. They see a necessity for atonement and punishment in due proportion to the gravity of the misdeed, regardless of the underlying circumstances. The expectation of punishment during these early years is related to the child's belief in automatic punishment and immanent justice. Immanent justice occurs when individuals confer a verdict of guilty on themselves and subsequently inflict punishment upon themselves whenever they commit a wrong. This process relating to a conception of the justice of life remains with the child until the end of this phase.

As we have suggested, unilateral respect for adults slowly evolves to an awareness of many adult authorities whose rules vary, and to the inconsistencies even within one adult's rules. Simultaneously, children slowly turn from their single authority, usually a parent, and tend to cooperate with other authorities, even without full awareness of the meaning of social cooperation. A six-year-old might be very apt to participate with others in a minor exploit which is contrary to adult wishes. But the six-year-old is merely going along with the group's actions, and in thought he or she fully accepts adult authority, even though the incident may appear to adults to be a deliberate affront to their authority.

The material Piaget presents for this phase highlights particularly vividly an observation of his about development which is operative throughout the length and breadth of human life:

Thought always lags behind action and cooperation has to be practiced for a long time before its consequences can be brought fully to light by reflective thought.

The idea of autonomy appears in the child about a year later than cooperative behavior and the practical consciousness of autonomy. . . . We may therefore advance the hypothesis that the verbal and theoretical judgment of the child corresponds, broadly speaking, with the concrete and practical judgment which the child may have made on the occasion of his own actions during the years preceding the interrogatory [gathering of data]. (261, 114–115)

The Phase of Concrete Operation

We learned that toward the end of the previous developmental progression, children have (1) an emerging perspective in which they see themselves as actors among other people (2) and a capacity to conceive of variables that occur together in environmental events. Spatially expressed, thinking becomes mobile. Children can now fully employ thought structures rather than relying primarily upon perceptual or body-motor cues as they did previously. Piaget terms this *concrete operational* thought. His research locates this form of cognition around the middle childhood years, usually within a range of seven to eleven years of age.

Concrete operational cognition involves conceptual thinking in combination with a concrete image or performance of the thought processes while reasoning out, explaining to others, or trying to comprehend by oneself the problem before one. Concrete operational thinking is likely to occur when any one of us is asked to explain a complex phenomenon such as *spiral behavior*. Most likely, we could only explain and comprehend spiral behavior by supplementing our conceptual formulation with a descriptive and explanatory finger movement.

Concrete operation, the first level of conceptual (logical) thought, involves foremost the mental capacity to order and relate experience within an organized whole. In this phase, children can state, and even eventually sum up, what they intend to tell. Previously, for example, children who were asked about what they were trying to tell you could only respond, likely with utter frustration, "I am telling you." (The story and the title of the story were one.) Two essential structures of thinking are capable of being applied within this phase: reversibility and conservation.[17]

Children have practiced reversibility in their daily actions and contacts for years, long before they could apply reversibility in their thinking and reasoning. But now, with the capacity to move beyond one-dimensional thinking and the ability to apply a manifold perspective, or at least a two-dimensional one, they become more and more aware of reversibility.

---

[17] Structure, as Piaget uses the term, refers to a system of thinking which has laws of its own. It is both an autonomous system and part of a larger one. (259, 7)

Reversibility constitutes a level of thinking by which the individual is capable of relating any one event or thought to a total system of interrelated parts in order to conceive of the event or thought from beginning to end and vice versa. In short, reversibility is "the permanent possibility of returning to the starting point of the operation in question." (293, 272) In daily life, it means that individuals can be questioned about any one point in the account they are relating to someone. They can be interrupted; they can interrupt themselves; they can go back to an earlier point of their story. They can do any of these mental movements without losing their thread of thought, their point, or the story as a whole. Reversibility entails the capacity to shift parts of one's thinking, as in an equation; to reverse or to review an idea from any one point, in any sequence, while still dealing with the subject at hand. Children's readiness to let others join in and their ability to deal with many beginnings at variant points in their play reflect evidence that they are employing the structure of reversibility in their thinking.

Conservation, mentioned earlier, is an acknowledgement of "variability *within* things." (61, 172) It is a mode of thinking which includes the capacity for mobile thought (reversibility). During conservation, an individual's conception of events is not distorted by deceptive perceptual or symbolic input; nor does this conception have to be verified, necessarily, through repeated experience. By means of conservation, human beings come to terms with their physical world. In our daily lives, conservation means that the scoop of ice cream is no different whether in a dish or in a cone; that every package weighing sixteen ounces weighs a pound, regardless of its size, attractiveness, shabbiness, or variations in labels or manufacturers. There is no need to check out each instance—unless there is a substantive change, in which case a developmental progression has to be reexperienced, but most likely rather rapidly.

As suggested, children's cognitive development centers in their facility to think, to employ mental processes for discovering their ever-expanding world for what it is and how it is made up and actually functions. They have moved from conceiving things and relationships for what they do and their use, to encountering things and events in order to classify, order, group, and eventually subsitute and replace them with other alternatives. An ice cream cone is no longer just "yummy" and "mine"; it is also chocolate, perhaps too soft, possibly cost thirty-five cents when the twenty-five-cent one down the street was just as big, and may represent money too quickly gone which could have been better used for popcorn at the movie later on.

Concrete thought, as stated, involves a different perspective of thinking. Assimilative and accommodative processes become less opposing pulls; rather they interact jointly as pulls towards a "mobile equilibrium." (258) Movements toward equilibration move into the foreground. Until this point of development, assimilation and accommodation tended to compete for dominance in the absence of a child's capacities to conceive and to integrate several points of reference simultaneously. With the mental facility to think about and explore several possible solutions without immediately adopting any one, the child can mentally return to any solution, including the original one. The previously one-dimensional, and consequently decisively rigid and basically intuitive way of thinking, becomes elasticized.

The developmental progression apparently occurs in two steps for all major cognition components, whether time, space, or number concepts are involved. In most recent Piagetian research, these steps are on two levels: the first is roughly during the ages from four to six, and the second is in the subsequent two years, ages nine to eleven. (249) Thinking in this phase has the freedom to develop along two levels of cognitive thought. Both cognitive expansions deal with a fitting together of the whole and the part, as well as with a sorting out of which parts belong to what whole. Children enter the age of reason and deal with premise and conclusion, sometimes in one jump, but they do deal with it and also engage in conceptual reasoning. They essentially deal with two rational issues: (1) which means can accomplish which ends and, conversely, which ends require what means; (2) establishing systems of classification.

In dealing with means and ends, children are out to discover the consequences one part has for the other. They ponder the internal relationships of any one event as if setting up an equation. To illustrate, as children watch the driver of a car, they learn to drive by exploring what happens when the driver does a certain thing and what has to happen in order to lead to a specific outcome. They relate themselves to both sides of the equation—action and outcome.

Along with these cognitive explorations, children are equally preoccupied with establishing for themselves systems of classification. Without children's knowledge of it, this process began long ago in all their everyday interactions with their physical and social environment. For instance, the concepts of weight and variation of weight have been encountered and dealt with effectively since early experiences with objects in the crib. At this point of cognitive development, however, children begin to abstract and conceptualize from their experience in order to create a sense of order in their conception of things. Note, the focus shifts from experience with things to conceptions of things. The acquisition of the concept of weight began with the experience of being able to lift or not being able to lift various items. Eventually, children experienced and noted the distinctions between heavy and light and, subsequently, between heavier and lighter. At this point they become preoccupied with how they can classify objects or actions in order to conceive of them together within a larger system. They search for systems of hierarchical relationships. These theoretical concerns find their application and become observable in children's play, for example, in collecting baseball cards, in making up stories of family intrigues, and in accounts of mystery stories which they view on television.

Nesting is classifying an internal relationship between smaller parts and their all-inclusive whole, as with nesting blocks, a set of boxes which fit into each other. Nesting specifies that all classes are additive. Each larger whole sums up all previous parts, so that many pieces of understanding and previously unconnected knowledge make sense. The new comprehension opens up various kinds of understanding. To illustrate, the discovery that all mammals bear live young ones frees a person from puzzling about the mode of procreation for each animal of this type. Simultaneously, as always, each new understanding poses new questions. For example, what is the relationship of the various animal groups to each other, and what is their order of classification?

Lattices refer to a form of classification in which the focus is upon the connective link and the parts which are linked together. Ordering conceptually by means of a hierarchy of lattices places stress upon creating subclasses of related objects. Related classes are conceptually linked together in order to create a coordinated whole. The link between pieces of knowledge is established by their logical relationship to each other rather than by mere proximity in experience. When children begin to envisage an object in relation to one or several wholes which, in turn, become part of a still larger unity or system, their life can proceed in an ordered world where they can organize their experiences, either separately or as part of such a unity.

The ability to order experiences and to be aware of their realistic relationship to each other helps children in ranking more lasting choices. Yet, within their cognitive modes of thinking, ordering is still done one experience at a time with the aid of a concrete model. Children cannot choose unless they can weigh each choice and perceive the relationships between them; making choices between alternatives and weighing the prospect of alternatives may still involve either touching or enacting each alternative.

First, a child masters the seriation of small aggregates with small quantitative units of familiar classes. Ordering by seriation involves the active manipulation of symbols or objects into new hierarchies. To review, objects are first separated by colors, later sorted by shapes, much later grouped by shape and color.[18] Initially, this sorting is by trial and error; only in middle childhood does classification by kind, form, and utility occur. Classification leads to seriation, first by constant comparisons, later by deduction. (249, 27–32)

In summary, classification proceeds on the basis of similarities and differences, subsequently by differential groupings which eventually merge into seriation—arrangements by increasing or decreasing first quantities and later also qualities. Such groupings again occur and are understood within a developmental progression from clustering by identical or equivalent quality, to grouping by logical systems of classes (nesting) or relationship variables (lattices). The child's earlier puzzlement at simultaneously belonging to a family, city, state and country can be resolved by organizing his or her thinking. Knowledge, in the last analysis, deals with transforming thought systems to comprehensible thought. "To know," says Piaget, "is to transform." (262, 6)

Regardless of what conceptualization the particular developmental progression involves—that of permanency in objects, that of heights, numbers or, below that, of space, time and speed— each progression starts with a general undifferentiated notion of absolute necessity ("give me candy") followed by continuously more specific requests ("I want some licorice"). Intermediate notions establish rudimentary features—usually relationships between parts, such as spatial comparisons or special cognition of specific but not necessarily critical features—and thus far without a cognition of the whole. (Buy me licorice, little round ones.) Finally, several features are interrelated with the hint of making up a whole, a classification. (Please, buy me some licorice, the tidbits kind in the red and yellow box.) Added experience in conceptualization, provides cognition of classification, categories, and a grouping of these classifications into an apparent orderly world. (Could you please stop at the candy counter and buy me a box of tidbits or any other package of black licorice?) This latter request involves conceptual thinking with a clear mastery of conservation.[19]

[18] Full forms (circles and squares) are discerned as distinct shapes before the recognition of triangles and more irregular shapes. These progressions are concomitant with our knowledge of neurological maturation. (155; 260)

[19] Conservation skills are necessarily universal for cognitive experience with time, numbers, quantity, and space; they are "reflecting just one part of a person's coming to terms with his physical world." Different explanations for conservation problems are apt to vary with class and cultural differences. The experiential sequence, however, of placing in order → combining → repeating → separating → dividing → ordering and then → substituting are continuous and universal. (359, 510)

Within concrete operational thought, with the conquest of conservation, a child is aware that the amount of milk poured into a smaller container can be the same as it was in the original container. The concept of reversibility, regardless of phenomenalistic appearance, opens the way to new vistas of understanding. Equilibration is within sight. It might be important to remind ourselves that learning is spotty and always proceeds differently in various areas. Children might comprehend that the amount of milk is constant in different sizes of containers, but in spite of the comprehension, they might still break up their candy bar to have more.

At this point a person shifts gradually from an inductive to a deductive mode of thinking. Noteworthy are Piaget's findings that deductive reasoning hardly ever occurs before children are well on their way in concrete operational thoughts. (Likely, they have to be eight years or older.)[20] In all of their mental operations, their reasoning takes cognition of a larger whole and the logical relationship to it. Awareness of repetition and rhythmic regularity have pointed toward an ordering of experiences. Generalization and differentiation of such experiences introduce classes which hold potential for hierarchical relationships. These experiential steps are essential precursors for conceptualization. Children learn to generalize and to deduce from simple experiences. Each new understanding occurs at the expense of their personal (egocentric) beliefs. In an explanation of natural phenomenon, for instance, the sun no longer would "just come out of the clouds." The sun now traverses the sky and the clouds drift independently in their speed. The child's world shifts from one of mythology to one of science (284, 42) and logic. (258) In other words, on this long path where sensorimotor and perceptual experiences have been the stepping stones for cognition, conceptual rather than behavioral experience increasingly provides the major road for thought.

Properties of space are also mastered in a definite sequence. A child first appraises size in terms of length, then after a year or more, in terms of weight; size as an expression of volume is usually not comprehended until near the end of this phase.[21] Concepts related to space precede the learning of concepts related to time and speed. For instance, the comprehension that a flower maintains its identical size and shape under the magnifying glass does not necessarily imply that the child will comprehend that fifteen

[20] P. Bryant questions Piaget's contentions. He suggests that children's inability to think deductively under eight years of age is a question of memory rather than a shift in the nature of reasoning. (33)

[21] Children can draw shapes, see differences between open and closed spaces and create forms similar to models of circular and triangular shapes within the preconceptual phase. (249, 32) Children have an early awareness of many correct things without being aware of the judgment involved. (163, 37)

minutes of watching TV actually involves the same time span as fifteen minutes of chores. Commonly, children will confuse different perspectives in one event in their reasoning. Mental operations "develop separately field by field, and result in a progressive structuralization of these fields, without complete generality being attained." (258, 15–16) Each field of understanding forms an island of knowledge without necessarily forming a unified approach to life.

As children become more accustomed to operational thinking, they can conceive of two hypotheses and can understand their relationship without being able to explain or apply it. Again, knowing precedes a capacity to verbalize and apply this knowledge.

Cognition of time requires a manipulation of several points of reference (object-space-causality) within one concept. (226, 86) The notion of time evolves out of the experience of rhythmicity of sequential actions with a *before* and an *after*. Early differences in time are measured by spatial distances. External events, as envisaged by spatial differentiation, are eventually placed in temporal order (early or past, now or present, later or future). This interlinkage of space and time is not too surprising because space can be conceived as a *slot* of time, while time is space in motion. (226) Time becomes independent of perceptual data. Subsequently, children can conceive and deal with such concepts as equal distance, duration, and speed. Naturally, in its beginning, conceptualization necessitates the use of symbols within the perceptive awareness. We can understand these theoretical observations more clearly by reminding ourselves that in a child's life, clocks, watches, and calendars at this point, and historical time and dates a bit later, have real importance and become features of everyday life. The concept of time becomes fully understood with the coordination of the concepts of equal distance and speed. Eventually, after repeated experiences, young adolescents can explain their understanding that an hour of work has equal duration regardless of the content of the work assignment.[22] Conservation is in full bloom.

In the acquisition of language, the child adopts words without full awareness of all they convey, employing symbolic speech

---

[22] It might be of interest to recall that Jean Piaget's research on the conceptualization of time was prompted by Albert Einstein's interest in Piaget's detailed studies of conservation. Einstein wondered which was learned first, the intuition of speed or of time. (275, 110) Though an intuition of speed emerges first, full comprehension of speed follows full comprehension of time, whereas the concepts of simultaneity and duration are subordinates of movement, which is speed. (275, 15) Cross-cultural studies validated Piaget's findings. Hopi children and children from Geneva, Switzerland, progress similarly in their comprehension of time concepts. (51, 116)

without a full understanding of its meaning. On the concrete operation level of cognition, language continues to be a tool of communication with the added utility—a tool for thinking. Language also follows a developmental continuum from verbal expression to verbal exchange. This involves internalization of words, thoughts, and mental findings, and, slowly, an internalization of actions along with mental experimentation. (284, 17–18). Furthermore, the structure of language assumes significance and also becomes a tool of thinking and communication. Whereas in the previous developmental phase, children will only have been able to hear and perceive words for the moment, in the operative phase, they are capable of taking cognition of the structure of the sentence. For instance, the statement "some of you" not only communicates a message, but also defines thinking, ordering and classifying; conceptualization by nesting is in order. Both communication and conceptual judgments are preceded by a year or more of clearly manifested relevant behavior without full awareness of its significance or the necessary symbols for explaining this new understanding. Third graders might readily announce that "everybody should be on time" although they would be at a loss in explaining what being on time means. Again, thoughts and words follow the potential action and the action phase.

The child's contacts with his physical world become more productive. First, increase in accommodation stimulates a real desire for verification of the accommodative process, which is accelerated by a decrease in egocentricity. Second, more accurate perception and an awareness of the process of perception extend children's understanding of their experience with the environment. Above all, children knowingly apply their interpretation of their perceptions of the environment. When they have points of reference and can anchor their experiences in a rational and communicable system, they have moved out of the center in their study of their world. They will then be apt to employ tools for measuring, rather than relying upon self-references such as their own body. Measurement allows for the possibility of establishing a chain of systematic comparisons and, gradually, for a discovery of the laws of ordering and grouping. We note that the notion of measurements can not be comprehended until the child acquires a notion of space.

Systematic comparison and independent measurements of events and things bring into the foreground a more realistic appraisal of the physical world. These new forms of thinking concomitantly also create a new level of self-identity. Identity of objects is the key to identifying the body in relation to other bodies, and correspondingly, in identifying the self in relation to other selves. In other words, identity is one element in the process of change rather than the source of change. (263, 27–37)

Notions of animism continue in this phase. In fact, underlying most objective interpretations is an animistic formula. The child still conceives of natural phenomena as being made by man for man, and more complicated events still receive a circular explanation. In other words, children's immediate explanation for their environment does not coincide with their own reasoning and ultimate convictions. Events beyond their reach are still centered in a socialized egocentrism. For instance, they may think that the sun rises because we need light.

Intellectual advances also find expression in a child's explanations of involuntary behavior. Dreams, a child is apt to explain, are perceived only by the dreamer; they are in the head, and become visible while one is asleep. The latter explanation hints at the remaining confusion of things and symbols.

A widening awareness of physical factors always precedes an awareness of social factors. Children first have to experience their new perspective of physical phenomena before they can extend this pattern, or schema, to their social sphere. Emancipation from parental dominance and greater participation in the social world bring about a shift in the child's models of imitation. Observation, comparison, and comprehension of others assume an important part in the life of children. They are eager to avoid self-contradiction, a common phenomenon in previous phases, and they attempt to understand variations in behavioral expectations. Play and language are no longer merely the means of self-expression; they become media for understanding the physical and social worlds.

Eventually, an important new level of social behavior is attained by understanding others in terms of their social position. The notion of mutuality, from the previous level, evolves into a concept of mutual respect toward the end of this phase. Mutual respect requires a widened social perspective. "It is indispensable that there should be established between them [the children] and oneself [the adult] those simultaneous relationships of differentiation and reciprocity which characterize the coordination of view points." (276, 162) Recognition of the seriation and hierarchy of nesting give children a new perspective for understanding their family. The family is now seen to be comprised of those people immediately related to one another, which means that pets lose their status as immediate family members.

Imitation proceeds along two different lines. Refinement in the accommodative process is achieved within the first years of this phase. Accuracy in imitation assures the mastery of mechanical details. Simultaneously, an awareness of a model's symbolic aspects detracts from copying details; the model's message becomes the medium for purposes of imitation.

Similarly in play, rules earlier were adhered to both for obedience to the order of the adult world and pleasure in regularity. Social obligations, mutality, and rules of the group become variables later. Situational (collective) rules replace universal ones. Above all, progressively complicated rules replace simpler ones; the playing with rules becomes the play. This tendency is also reflected in the fact that curiosity no longer finds much expression in active play, but reaches more and more into intellectual experimentation.

Commitments to the values of conscience find their anchoring points in newly acquired centers of mutual respect and of awareness of the necessity for collective obedience. In this new level, cognitive thought manages to internalize moral values. The new concept of time tends to free moral standards from temporary and specific situations. Children bring together into several systems the standards they have acquired and practiced in the past. They also incorporate their elders' comments, standards, and expectations. Basically, they relate fragmentary practices, hearsay, and knowledge into one practical system, although the theoretical implications of the system will not be comprehended until later.

Children from the ages of nine to eleven generally become most interested in the rules which regulate their lives. They examine rules for all their details. They inquire into the meaning of the parts in order to establish verifiable relationships and guarantee themselves a sense of permanency.

The children's awareness of social reciprocity and equality carries over into concepts of fairness and justice. Justice requires fair punishment. Equality in punishment, exact compensation for the damage done, and doing to another exactly what was done to oneself are conceived as fair judgment. The child strives towards complete objectivity in the enforcement of rules and disciplinary actions. A boy or girl of preadolescent age insists upon a shift in emphasis from mere adult authority to respect for established standards. Violation of reciprocity seems to be the worst crime. Furthermore, lies are defined objectively. The more a lie attempts to deceive and to deny mutual respect, the worse it is. Such an attitude represents a reversal of the views held by the younger child. At the same time, it becomes permissible, in the teenagers' eyes, to lie "a little" to adults. Expiatory judgment continues in more remote relationships, such as in stories, religion, and the political order.

The Phase of Formal Operations

The last phase of cognitive development, as conceived by Piaget, occurs from the ages of eleven to fifteen.[23] The nature of thought undergoes new changes. Unlike the child, the youth becomes "an individual who thinks beyond the present and forms theories about everything, delighting especially in considerations of that which is not." (276, 148) In popular terms, the child's life is as if in a continuous "rap" session. The young acquire the capacity to think and to reason beyond their own experiences and their own belief systems. They think about thinking. They enter into the world of ideas; the road has gone from a world of objects (physical world), through a world of social relations (social world), to a world of many perspectives (ideational world).

Thinking, reasoning, and remembering proceed primarily with the aid of symbolic, that is, conceptual thought. Cognition begins to build more upon the use of propositions. Propositions, hypothetical reasoning, serve as an alternative to experimental (empirical) thinking. Assimilative and accommodative processes find a near equilibrium in the acquisition of a complex and comprehensive mental structure which allows for dealing logically and effectively with the complex demands of everyday living. Within this phase's developmental progression, three substages can be located: (1) thinking stereotypically, (2) thinking in terms of an egocentrically conceived universal order, and (3) eventually thinking in terms of a universal, utilitarian order.

Not until the present level does the youth begin to comprehend geometric relationships and questions dealing with proportional relationships. Piaget establishes through his research the following progression of cognition relating to geometric questions:

1. Recognition of objects as objects: pregeometrical considerations (Piaget's phase 1 and 2)
2. Qualitative understanding of objects and events (Piaget's phase 3)
   a. Distance and length
   b. Area and interior volume
   c. Comparisons of objects and events
3. Comprehension of metrical activities (Piaget's phase 4)
   a. Measurement of length in one, two, or three dimensions
   b. Coordination of planes, angles and areas
4. Mental operations with symbols (Piaget's phase 5)
   a. Calculation of relationships

[23] Formal operation as a cognitive progression has been verified by Lawson's and Renner's research (172), but its onset occurred at a much later age than predicted by Piaget. This variation might be an artifact in the research or, as conjectured, possibly due to factors associated with the American's educational system. (172) Piaget speculates that differences in developmental rate might be a variable of what is stressed and tested in cognitive acquisition. (254, 10–12)

b. Relating different systems to one another (*301*, 389)
c. Logico-mathematical knowledge acquired independently of experience.

About Logico-mathematical knowledge Piaget says: "It springs not from the object as such but from the general coordinations of the actions exerted by the subject on the objects around it." (*221*, 266–267)

These advances in cognition have implications beyond the mastery of geometric problems; they affect problems of social relationships. The concept of probability now becomes part of the person's schema of thinking. No wonder that for the youth a pair of dice is no longer a toy to determine actions but a symbol of the alternatives of life. This new schema of thought heralds a comprehension of relativity, of balance between issues, and of equality in concepts, actions, and reactions. The objective cognition of propositions opens the way to understanding relativity in ordinary life situations.

A concept of relativity is anchored in two other processes basic for formal operation: first, reasoning by hypothesis, that is, the application of propositional statements; and second, the use of implication. Systematic ordering and reasoning by hypothesis is an endeavor, writes Piaget,

> . . . *to formulate all possible hypotheses concerning the operative factors [of the phenomenon under consideration], and then arrange [these] experiments as a function of these factors.*
> *The consequences of this new attitude are as follows. In the first place thought no longer proceeds from the actual to the theoretical, but starts from theory so as to establish or verify actual relationships between things. Instead of just coordinating facts about the actual world, hypothetico-deductive reasoning draws out the implications of possible statements and thus gives rise to a unique synthesis of the possible and necessary.* (258, 19)

Hypothetical thinking requires a reliance upon reasoning by propositions (conceptual tools), rather than by symbols (perceptual tools), and uses the forms of if . . . or, . . . , then and either. This ability furnishes the youth with a new tool for understanding his or her physical world and the social relationships within that world: the use of logical deduction by implication. (*253*, 23–24) Children have already managed the deduction of relationships on the basis of juxtaposition, proximity, transduction, and other irreversible relationship patterns. Now, reasoning by implication permits the youth to introduce simple, logical assumptions by taking a third position without resorting to verification by means other than logic. The youth undertakes a search for general hypotheses which can account for the observed and possible events which have occurred to him or her. Each partial link is grouped in relation to the whole, which is a set structured from all subsets with an integration of all parts into this whole. Reasoning acts continually as a function of a structured whole, with all deductions anchored in the possible and not merely in observed empirical facts. Reality becomes secondary to possibility. (293) For instance, a youth might mull over the factors involved when seeing someone walk up a downward moving escalator.

Adolescence is known as an age which thinks beyond the present. Adolescents form notions, ideas, and, eventually, concepts. about everything from the past through the present into the future. Interests center around broad issues and around most minute details. Around the ages of fourteen to fifteen, young people reflect maturity in cognitive thought when they can depend upon conceptual thinking. When they can think about thinking, they form concepts of concepts.

It is noteworthy that adolescents are no longer satisfied with empirical events. They regard their observations of life's events merely as points of departure, as proofs of the larger domain of the possible. With the aid of new mental capacities to formulate hypotheses, they structure a wide variety of possible combinations of events as they might occur. Simultaneously, they attempt to prove empirically which possibilities could materialize. Once they have established a range of hypotheses, they view these temporary findings or new insights as starting points for new combinations of possible approaches to life's problems.

Interestingly, in a much earlier work, Piaget locates a similar development in the child's explanation of the meaning of dreams. (267) At this final level of cognition the youth justifies dreams as instruments of thought; dreams are internal thoughts, thoughts with oneself.

Prior to formal operation, Piaget reminds us, language is largely "marginal to real thinking which, even though verbalized, remains until about eleven to twelve years of age centered upon actions." (269, xii) Language seems to develop more fully, and furthers cognitive thought and behavior: "Language conveys to each an already prepared system of ideas, classification, relationships, an inexhaustible stock of concepts which are reconstructed in each individual after the age-old patterns which previously molded earlier generations." (276, 159)

The youth's physical environment appears in many new shadings. Objects become relative in terms of their appropriate use. Distant objects, such as the sun and the moon, find explanation in a rational system. Youths find their place along with other living organisms in an ever-evocative world. Topological structures are conquered last, long after mathematical and algebraic ones. (249, 24–25) And since position in the family has already been established, the young see themselves, their family, and family members in relation to other families in society.[24] It is a period when the youth struggles with a life plan and life objectives.[25]

Adolescents find pleasure in this new power of manipulating ideas without seriously committing themselves to anyone. The tenuous character of their manipulation of ideas and social practices can be compared with their former practice of imitating the behavior of others with no real intention of adopting any of it permanently. Just as adolescents find pleasure in anticipating all possible outcomes and codifying them into complicated rules, so do they toy with new concepts, common and extreme, to anticipate all possible eventualities. Their major interest, however, centers in weighing, classifying, and reevaluating different social points of view. Their manipulation of social issues, of political social, ethical, and religious ideational expressions, and of scientific intangibles follows a progression similar to that of comprehension of physical properties. At this point, an individual can be in love with love as well as in love with a person.

The young can, so to say, dream up the probability of their position. Deduction by hypothesis and judgment by implication furnish them with opportunities to reason beyond cause and effect. For example, if two youngsters fight over taking turns, cause-and-effect judgment bases the decision on the question "who was first?" Judgment by implication necessitates a total evaluation of each person's situation in relation to a larger context. From this a new logic of moral values emerges, a sense for equity. Piaget's very early empirical research on lying points toward this new level of cognition. (261) Around eleven or twelve years, youths start to define lying quite differently from the way they did in childhood. Anything intentionally false is a lie because of its intentional aspect, its implicative meaning. This new concept also reflects a new awareness of relativity. The previous sense of equality evolves into a sense of equity. This sense of equity applies the principal of "never defining equality without taking account of the

---

[24] Yet, when young adolescents are asked to account for other children's thinking, especially those within different cultures, their conception is initially most stereotypic with stark perseverance of egocentricity. Contradictory as it may sound, an adolescent is apt to have an egocentric world view. Piaget argues that egocentricity sharply diminishes on one plane and reemerges on another broader plane as each new life conflict arises. (233)

[25] We learned earlier that Piaget, as was customary for European youth of his time, wrote his "life plan" at that age. In this country, students in high school are asked to submit plans for the future when applying for entrance into college. ("What can college education do for you?")

way in which each individual is situated. In the domain of distributive justice, equity consists of taking account of age, of previous services rendered, etc., in short, in establishing shades of equality." *(261,* 284)

The principal orientation in the latter part of the phase of formal operations is toward confirmation of the actually established social rules and also toward an adherence to self-chosen ethical principles which involve an appeal to logical comprehensiveness, universality, and consistency. *(316b)*

Adolescence is known for its acquisition of more complex thinking and its adherence to contradictory values which eventually will come into near balance with adulthood. Equilibration occurs on the basis of four developmental accomplishments:

1. An individual can take another person's point of view and engage in true communication on the basis of subject matter. (Knowledge can be truly exchanged.)
2. Individuals can compare what they hear, see, and say with what they know and deduct from these things. (Validity can be established.)
3. An individual can link the general with related parts and the parts to the relevant context. (Rules and order can be known.)
4. An individual can utilize that which has been conceived. (Thought creates thought and becomes practical).

Piaget sees the individual finding equilibrium around the ages of fourteen and fifteen, because the youth can envisage potential operations which will compensate each other. Basically, propositional operations are tied together into structured patterns of relationships and systems, which eventually are structured into a single unity. "The structured 'whole,' " Piaget maintains, is "the form of equilibrium of the subject's operational behavior." *(258,* 45) Although Piaget does not commit himself, he does imply that at this point the individual has reached intellectual maturity.[26]

SUMMARY

It must be repeated that the charted course in this chapter describes *potential* cognitive development. The actual rate and degree of completion of each phase varies with each individual. Also, developmental phenomena may easily continue beyond their

---

[26] "It would seem that the formal operational stage needs not be the final stage," C. Svoboda reminds us; but it will "as long as reality is viewed rigidly by means of the same model of reality. When a new conceptual model is adopted, new aspects of reality will be attended to; the cognitive balance should be upset; and man's integrative forces set in motion anew." *(371,* 38)

TABLE 1.1 THE CONTINUUM OF COGNITIVE DEVELOPMENT

Piaget's Basic Modalities of Intelligence	Phases as in this Chapter	Stages	Approximate Chronological Age
I. Sensorimotor intelligence	Sensorimotor phase	1. Use of reflexes	0 to 1 month
		2. First habits and "primary" circular reactions	1 to 4½ months
		3. Coordination of vision and prehension, "secondary" circular reactions	4½ to 9 months
		4. Coordination of secondary schemata and their application to new situations	9 to 12 months
		5. Differentiation of action schemata through "tertiary" circular reactions, discovery of new means	12 to 18 months
		6. First internalization of schemata and solution of some problems by deduction	18 to 24 months
II. Representative intelligence by means of concrete operations	Preconceptual phase	1. Appearance of symbolic function and the beginning of internalized actions accompanied by representation	2 to 4 years
	Intuitive thought phase	2. Representational organizations based on either static configurations or on assimilation to one's own action	4 to 5½ years
		3. Articulated representational regulations	5½ to 7 years
	Concrete operational phase	1. Simple operations (classifications, seriations, term-by-term correspondences, etc.)	7 to 9 years
		2. Whole systems (Euclidian coordinates, projective concepts, simultaneity)	9 to 11 years
III. Representative intelligence by means of formal operations	Formal operational phase	1. Hypothetico-deductive logic and combinatorial operations	11 to 14 years
		2. Structure of "lattice" and the group of 4 transformations	14 years—on

SOURCE: Adapted from Piaget's paper "Les Stades du Developpement intellectuel de l'Enfant et de l'Adolescent" (1956, pp. 37 ff.). Adapted for this book from Table 1, "Intelligence Is an Ultimate Goal," in T. G. Décarie, *Intelligence and Affectivity in Early Childhood*, New York, International Universities Press, Inc., 1965, p. 15. (50) (Used with kind permission of original publishers, Delachaux & Niestlé s.a., Neuchâtel, Switzerland.)

usual approximate age levels. Very likely an individual will achieve completion (maturity) in one area while still struggling with other aspects of development. Cognitive development can be schematized on the basis of the Piagetian continuum shown in Table 1.1.

Altogether, Piaget's theory furnishes us with a frame of reference on cognitive development. The actual developmental profile on each individual resembles a barogram showing peaks in some areas and depressions in others. Basically, however, cognitive development proceeds within an orderly, predictive progression which is universal in sequence but which varies in rate and chronological reference points from child to child, and between sociocultural groupings. Such a frame of reference on intellectual development allows us to predict an individual's mode and range of cognition all along the person's course of development.

CHAPTER 2

The affective theory of Erik H. Erikson

A BIOGRAPHICAL SKETCH

ERIK H. ERIKSON clinician, educator, and theorist—one of the foremost psychoanalytic scholars of the second half of our century—was born of Danish parents in Frankfurt, Germany, in 1902. An identity crisis was to be his fate and destiny. His father abandoned his mother prior to his birth. Theodor Homburger became Erik's adoptive father when his mother married his pediatrician during his early childhood. When Erikson faced a "rebirth" as an American citizen in 1939, he chose to be known by his original father's name and used Homburger from then on as a middle name.[1] Erikson observed that the question of origin looms large in persons who are driven to be original. (*63*, 742)

Erikson's childhood years were spent in Karlsruhe, Germany, in a household enlivened by his mother's friends from the arts and distinguished by his adoptive father's role as a physician. Yet, neither formal education nor his father's wish for him to become a pediatrician provided the adolescent Erik with sufficient anchoring points. His yearning for the arts and his wish to search out life on his own caused him to drop out of high school. He left home to begin his *wanderjahre* as a "young man with some talent but nowhere to go." (*83b*, 40) He painted and worked on large woodcuts for several years. Erikson's friend Peter Bloss noticed the

---

[1] For this reason, his publications before 1939 appear under the name of Erik Homburger.

young artist's interest in children and their play. In 1927 Peter Bloss invited the drifting Erikson, now twenty-five years old, to teach art in a small American experimental school in Vienna. This school, funded by Dorothy Burlingham, served American children whose parents had come to Vienna to join the Freudian circle for psychoanalytic training and analysis.

Intimate involvement with his work and stimulation from the Freudian circle helped Erikson focus his work on children and their requirements. His teaching at the school brought him in touch with Anna Freud and her emerging interest in psychoanalytic work with children. She became the teacher of the children's teacher by accepting Erikson for psychoanalytic training and analysis. Erikson found a new home away from home and a life task very close to his home's calling. In his words, "Here a circle . . . admitted me to the kind of training that came as close to the role of a children's doctor as one could possibly come without going to medical school." (63, 744) He became a healer of children, using artistic components to augment scientific ones.

From 1927 to 1933, while in Vienna, Erikson completed his professional training in child psychoanalysis. He obtained his only formal academic certificate as a Montessori teacher and is probably one of the few men with such a certificate. During this period he met his wife-to-be, a young American artist, Joan Mowat Serson.[2] While in analysis with Anna Freud, he came into the Freudian household and made the personal acquaintance of Sigmund Freud. Erikson himself started to practice, teach, and write, and his first publications merged his dual training. His subject was the application of psychoanalytic inquiry to educational issues. (106; 110)

The clouds of fascism in Europe and an invitation from Boston brought the Eriksons and their two sons to the United States, where a daughter was born later. From 1933 to 1936 Erikson served as the first analyst of children in Boston and as a research fellow in psychology in the Department of Neuropsychiatry of the Harvard Medical School. An appointment to Yale's Department of Psychiatry and Institute of Human Relations came after that for three more years. In those years Erikson worked on issues of human development that had caused much unrest in his own developmental progression. Erikson, the wanderer, immigrant, and artist whose own childhood and youth lacked apparent continuity, studied children at play in their own microsphere, (72, 113, 116, 143) conducted anthropological inquiries into the meaning of child rearing and other life practices among the original Indian inhabitants in

---

[2] Joan Serson Erikson became a professional in her own rights as an artistic occupational therapist and a gifted writer; she also collaborated closely with Erikson as his personal literary critic.

his newly chosen country, *(96, 97)* and began work on the continuum of ego development, the major work of his life. *(105)* Erikson, once a restless explorer, settled down to live in the intimacy of family life and to research the minutia of daily life experiences.

From 1939 to 1951, Erikson lived on the West Coast where he continued his anthropological inquiries into the development of native American children. *(97)* His research on sex differences in children's play configurations, which was part of the longitudinal child development study at the University of California, brought him both acclaim and scorn. This study was questioned recently by segments of the women's liberation movement; *(201; 312; 362; 367)* it has also been upheld in replication studies *(112; 158)* as recently as 1974. *(380)* Erikson himself is devoting some of his "retirement" years to further investigation of sexual and cultural differences in children's play. *(115a; 212)* His alleged sexism is more fully reviewed below in the section on Erikson and the current scene.

In the post–World War II years, Erikson was in his mid-forties and fully productive, teaching at the San Francisco Psychoanalytic Institute and the University of California and, periodically, at the Menninger Foundation in Topeka, Kansas. He gave the coveted Goethe lecture in Frankfurt, Germany, his own birthplace, in honor of Sigmund Freud's one-hundreth birthday. *(80b)* He presented his theoretical framework in his first book, *Childhood and Society,* *(65)* the title of which sums up his major proposition: human development is a synthesis of developmental and social tasks. He converted the Freudian notion of the psychosexual development of libidinal phases to one of psychosocial stages of ego development. The publication of *Childhood and Society (65)* established Erikson as one of the leading proponents of ego psychology in this country, a position his former teacher, Anna Freud, had achieved for herself in Great Britain. Erikson's subsequent writings on healthy personality development *(99; 109b; 114)* clearly brought forth a new theory of child development, *(65; 85; 87; 99; 114)* which is the foundation for this chapter. Erikson considers the development of affect the basis of human development. He set forth eight ages of man, during which, in Shakespearean fashion, all the world's a stage.[3]

In 1951, Erikson moved East and joined the staff of the Austen Riggs Center at Stockbridge, Massachusetts, while teaching at the University of Pittsburgh and the Massachusetts Institute of

---

[3] William Shakespeare refers to such a stage and to "seven ages of man" in *As You Like It,* act 2, scene 7. Shakespeare's ages are: infancy, school days, adulthood-courtship, the period of service, the time of establishment, declining years, and second childhood.

Technology. Ten years later, nearing sixty years of age, he dropped his commitments to become a scholar-in-residence at the Center for Advanced Study in the Behavioral Sciences at Palo Alto, California, and, simultaneously, professor of human development (since 1970, professor emeritus) at Harvard University—an unusual accomplishment and academic distinction for a high school dropout with no formal academic career and only a Montessori teacher's certificate. After retiring from Harvard, Erikson returned to California to write, guest lecture, and, since 1972, serve as clinician and senior consultant in psychiatry for the Mount Zion Hospital in San Francisco.

Erikson's writings become progressively more concerned with societal events rather than with the intrapsychic struggle, except as the intrapsychic person and the person's contemporary society are an interacting whole. He increasingly embraced dialectic thinking (discussed later in the section on Erikson and the current scene). Freudian concepts which were polarities in opposition became, for Erikson, dualities with which an individual struggles concurrently at all points of life. He had moved, as he acknowledged himself, from the explanatory analysis of historical sketches of personality formation, to an existential comprehension of how the present becomes what it is. (126, 108–110) "Does it make sense or not?" is a question he and Huey P. Newton ask as they consider the dilemmas they face. (126, 113)

In recent years, Erikson has reflected more on his own life history. His struggles and his searching inquiries are one; his theory is his life story. He recognizes himself as an immigrant (73, 12) who is at one with his community and its history; and the identity of the new world is a central theme in the formation of his own identity and in his personal legacy. (73, 27–28) For him, "personality is destiny." (212, 87)

"Gifted with a poetic literary style, the observing eye of a trained artist, and the probing mind of an analyst," (58, 26) Erikson portrayed the personal and historic developments in the lives of Martin Luther, (120) Mahatma Gandhi, (82) and Thomas Jefferson. (73) He was awarded the Pulitzer Prize and the National Book Award in philosophy and religion for his biography of Gandhi. (82) The book was an analysis of the origins of militant nonviolence, written and published when this nation was in agony over its own violent militancy and militant nonviolence in connection with its war in Southeast Asia.

Erikson was criticized for using words instead of marching and for explaining events rather than protesting them. Did he really remain outside the stream of events? When California's "loyalty oath" threatened to shackle his individual and academic freedom in

the midst of the McCarthy era, Erikson resigned and publicly de-
nounced the demand to compromise freedom. (64) Twenty years
later he wrote to a psychology student saying that at moments of
severe crisis "two things [are] more important than writing—one
is action and the other is silence." (212, 86) Erikson pursued both
courses. He signed protest statements (64; 212; 376) and remained
a silent although involved man of his times. He wrote continually
of the young and their struggle, (87; 90; 93; 95; 121; 122) of
minorities and their indignities, (70; 82; 94; 126) and of the perspectives of men and women in their struggle with modern life.
(71, 89; 119)

   In his professional career, the observing analyst became an analytical observer, a clinician, like his teachers, Sigmund and Anna
Freud. However, where Sigmund Freud had relied upon clinical
cases, the couch, and Greek mythological drama, Erikson researched individuals and families in the spheres of their everyday
lives and at a given moment in the history of their culture.[4] And
where Anna Freud had studied children's fantasies in play; Erikson delved into a study of children's play to understand children's
life struggles. His formulations were to be different than those of
his teachers'—the Freuds.

   Erikson's writings are those of an artist; he paints backdrops
with broad strokes and fills in intimate and minute details in the
immediate foreground. His theoretical formulations are those of an
analyst turned philosopher.

ERIKSON'S THEORY AND
FREUDIAN PSYCHOANALYTIC THEORY

   Erikson builds solidly upon Freudian analytic theory. He terms
Freud's work as the "rock" upon which all advancement of personality theory is based. (153, 8) He believed that even today Freud
would consider his theory to be essentially biological. (128, 85)
Recently, Erikson acknowledged his own contributions and his
departures from Freudian psychology. The contrast between these
two psychoanalytical thinkers is clear. While Freud was challenged
by technological advances and the constriction of moral and sexual
codes, Erikson related himself to the challenges and dilemmas of
changing social conditions and movements in an era of social and
moral diversity. (71; 87; 92; 95; 98; 109a; 118)

   Erikson's theory diverges from the Freudian model in three
major areas. First, rather than the id, it is the ego which is the life

---

[4] In his work as therapist, Erikson visited the client's home and had dinner with
the family; quite a departure in practice for an analyst of his generation. (58, 26)

force for human development. Erikson's emphasis upon the continuity of interpersonal experience involves functions of the ego beyond those of Freud's sexual (libidinal) developmental progression. Erikson reformulates the Freudian organ phases so that they lose many of their biosexual implications; yet, he breaks neither with the Freudian perspective of *man*kind nor with topological terminology. For Erikson, unconscious motivation is an accepted fact. Nevertheless, his major preoccupations are with the processes of socialization, the relations of the ego to society.[5] Essentially he broadens psychoanalytical inquiries without sacrificing Freud's particular approach to psychic life. For him, it is the *ego*, the affective aspects of life, and the innate inner self, which relate *to* society.

Second, Erikson introduces a new social matrix; individuals in their relationship to their caretakers within the context of their particular family and its historical-cultural heritage in direct relationship to the social and political demands of the items. This complex social configuration replaces the classical Freudian matrix: the child-mother-father triad. Such a shift comes about when an analyst takes a look at "ordinary" people (who are not patients) or "different people who live in other segments of the world." (45, 58) For Erikson it is not so much a preoccupation with the mystical drama of Oedipus as the power struggle within the sociocultural reality of the family. As he comments in 1968: "We cannot separate personal growth and communal change, nor can we separate . . . identity crises in individual life and contemporary crisis in historic development, because the two help to define each other and are truly relative to each other." (87, 23)

Erikson questioned the essence of the Oedipus formulation when he observed that if a father trusts and enacts his trust that he can bring up a little boy, then neither has to fear the other. Then, unlike the father of Oedipus, this father does not have to order the slaying of his son to prevent him from becoming a patricide. In Erikson's words, "trust would not make a myth but it would make history." (126, 117) And with such insightful words, Erikson drastically alters analytical thinking. The family as a product of society and culture lends shape and content to the developing ego. In human terms, ego is society.

There is a third way in which Erikson's theory diverges from Freud. Whereas Freud's mission was to prove the existence and operation of the unconscious, Erikson was challenged to chart the opportunities and developmental progression afforded each indi-

---

[5] David Rapaport aptly calls Erikson's formulation a "theory of reality relationships." (85, 14)

vidual. Freud's concern for social doom if people were left to their innate strivings is answered in Erikson's optimistic premise that every personal and social crisis furnishes components that are conducive to growth. Freud made his inquiry within the confines of pathological development; Erikson addressed the potentials of successful resolution of developmental crises.

If we look at Erikson's work from today's perspective, we can perceive him as a theoretical bridge between psychoanalytic and existential thinkers. "Although Erikson starts from and remains loyal to Freud's developmental stages, the actual polarities which he posits are existential crises." Erikson provides "a developmental timetable for the resolution of existential crises and relates it smoothly to Freudian psycho-sexual stages,"[6] which are now completely "reconditioned and as good as new" in Erikson's eight stages of men. (85)

Erikson, like Freud, grounded his initial inquiries in clinical work, but eventually turned his career almost solely to teaching and writing. They each stand out in the center of their half of this century for formulations concerning affective development. For Freud affective development involved the inner strength and knowledge people are capable of mastering for harnessing or being harnessed by their own inner strivings; affective development meant finding a manageable balance within a conceivable reality. For Erikson, affective development revolves around people's ongoing struggle to achieve a power through which they can partake of rather than be left out by the sweep of events going on in their particular space and time in history; (44, 22) affective development denotes an affirmation of a person's individuality within his or her social reality. Reality, for Erikson, is not a conceptual phenomenon; reality, like life, is lived continuously within events of the moment.[7] An American concept of reality demands active participation of the parties involved so that reality and actuality are one. (73, 36; 126, 106)

ASSUMPTIONS BASIC TO ERIKSON'S THEORY

A statement on Erikson's basic theoretic assumptions must necessarily include Freudian formulations which Erikson takes for granted. In the following paragraphs Freudian assumptions are

[6] Special recognition is due to W. Larry Ventis of Williamsburg, Virginia, for helping me highlight these observations through our correspondence from February 1973 to July 1974.

[7] In other words, Freud's reality dealt with the "oughts" and what is assumed to be over time. Erikson's reality is phenomenological and time bound.

labeled as such. Assumptions which are not so labeled may be credited to Erikson. The assumptions are summarized under seven subheadings:

1. Approach to theory formation
2. Order of human life
3. Basic human values
4. Etiology of human behavior
5. Core of human functioning
6. The newborn
7. Environments (physical, social, cultural, ideational)

Approach to Theory Formation

Erikson relies upon psychoanalytic methods and techniques for obtaining and processing his data. What counts is the *meaning* of a behavior or constellation of events *to the individual* in the context of the person's past history and surrounding circumstances. While Piaget's questions concern a person's process of thinking, and while Sears studies the impact of behavior on learning, Erikson searches. for the affective forces which make individuals act. Psychoanalytic investigation, according to Erikson, depends on understanding individuals' most personal perspectives, good or bad, concerning their everyday life experiences. While Freud's couch was his lab, Erikson's lab is the space, time, and cultural scene of each person's daily life sphere. Freud had people come to his territory; Erikson meets people within theirs.

For Erikson, psychoanalysis is something between science and art. (*128*, 62) No scientific investigation can be undertaken without an underlying theory. Any one aspect of development must be evaluated within an understanding of the total context of development. Each case study must test and add to the fabric of his total theory. He writes: "We are more interested here in the overall *configuration* and *integration* of [a child's] developing approaches to the world than in the *first appearance of specific abilities* which are so well described in the child development literature." (*114*, 104) Altogether, Erikson exhibits a bold confidence in his own intuitive sense of timing, selection of samples, and choice of techniques. His interest is in qualitative data more than in quantitative measurements. His theory formation is essentially deductive based upon his own insight into personally selected and defined problems. His model is a fusion of his own psychoanalytic efforts and the application of knowledge from allied fields—Freudian psychology, child development, cultural anthropology, and history.

Order of Human Life

Psychological phenomena, Erikson postulates, have undergone an evolutionary history similar to biological structures. For him, biological and psychological phenomena are closely interrelated. In the life of a human being there is a simultaneous development of physiological structure and of psychological endowment. For instance, the primary structure of the most primitive living organisms consists almost entirely of an oral cavity, and their primary mode of life is to ingest, that is, to incorporate. More complex organisms possess additional functional structures and more complex psychological modes. For Erikson, ontogeny recapitulates phylogeny in psychological development. The infant's incorporative strivings in the first developmental phase is not very different from the jelly fish's basic nature. Each developmental phase finds a counterpart in the phylogenic evolution of man; personality development follows biological principles.

However, biological evolvement at birth is replaced by psycho-social development. "The maturing organism continues to unfold, not by developing new organs, but by a prescribed sequence of locomotive, sensory, and social capacities." (114, 97) "The same acts which help the baby to survive help the culture to survive in him. (66, 325)

In fact, cultural programming by developmental phases tend to be in tune with the progression of developmental readiness of the maturing individual. An individual's culture socializes the individual into distinct periods of development. These periods or phases specify clearly what people are to be, to do, to think, to feel, and to be recognized for within the ranges of their socialization capabilities. In other words, Erikson's reliance upon developmental phases builds upon the basic assumption that they are distinct entities.

Conversely, Erikson gives credence to the expectations of the society and the subculture for development. (154) The societal tasks jibe with human nature. He assumes that phase developmental laws operate wherever human growth takes place: "Growing is a differentiation in preplanned parts during a given sequence of critical periods. In personality growth, it is the task of the ego (in the psychoanalytic sense) and of the social process together to maintain that continuity which bridges the inescapable discontinuity between each of these stages." (78, 7)

The individual unites biological, psychological, and social forces. To quote Erikson, "A human being, thus, is at all times an organism, an ego, and a member of society and is involved in all three processes of organization." (65, 32) In fact, it is his outlook on life which makes Erikson as much a humanistic philosopher as a developmental psychologist. Erikson's stress upon the interlinkage of biological, psychological, and social development gives equal weight to each dimension and also accents their shared participation in the development of an individual. Life histories and mutual events unite individuals with each other, unite generations with generations, and unite humanity with its universe.

Basic Human Values

Erikson wants to know individuals for their own creative and adaptive powers. He believes that individuals have unique capacities to create their own way of life, to bring to bear their own faith and indignations. He calls this "what the best in you lives by, the loss of which would make you less human." (126, 128) He sees human behavior as neither good nor bad, but rather capable of producing good and bad. He reminds us of one of Freud's more hope-inspiring axioms: "Men are not only worse, but also better than they think they are." (65, 288) Erikson's own faith in human creativity is revealed in his observation that "there is little that cannot be remedied later, there is much that can be prevented from happening at all." (114, 104)

Yet, no person being an island, the sanctity of the individual is endowed by each individual's culture and society. In turn, these social institutions require for their perpetuation a corresponding respect and recognition from the individuals who depend upon them. These circular interactive forces are highlighted by Erikson: "In order to make the world safer for democracy, we must make democracy safe for the healthy child." (114, 145) In a conversation with Huey P. Newton, Erikson accented again his fundamental belief that what happens to the individual defines the destiny of each group. "We must stand ready to expect and to respond to human love in any of our fellow men so long as they do not set out to kill that human dignity in us without which we could not really love anybody. For only people with equal dignity can love each other." (126, 79)

Etiology of Human Behavior

Erikson accepts the Freudian notion of a psychosexual energy-filled organism. This energy is inherent, generates all psychological processes, and is a basic motivating force.[8]

---

[8] In his earlier writings, Erikson employed the Freudian term *libido*; in more recent publications, such Freudian terminology is almost extinct. *Libido* must be defined as an innate, undifferentiated energy which in part is sexual (incorporating Freud's interpretation); but it is largely an unspecified aspect of the human system

Erikson got himself into hot water and was branded as a sexist *(119; 201; 312; 362)* by interlinking biological and psychological factors as if biological factors create psychological facts and psychological experiences endow a person with biological existence. For Erikson, biological and psychological realities are inseparable. He believes "we live a somatic, social, and a personal order . . . the perpetual conflict of these three which make human destiny." *(212, 87)* He hopes women will "add maternal concerns to the cares of world governing" *(212, 87)* because women are more likely than men to add nurturing concerns to international affairs. For Erikson, it is hard to attribute to nature that which is biological and hard to nurture that which is sociocultural. The human body and the culture, he stresses, are intertwined. Women's liberation material proceeds with dichotomous thinking while Erikson thinks dialetically. (See later section on the current scene for elaborations on this issue.)

Erikson's multidimensional perception creates difficulties for him in his encounters with social activists *(119; 126)* and with those whose stance is oriented toward the development of social changes. For Erikson, development occurs within the context of the present and is rooted in the past. He recognizes that the social order has "recklessly enslaved the personal and the somatic order (in both sexes) in the service of the oldest establishment—male dominance." *(212, 87)* Yet, for Erikson, change is not knocking loudly at the door. He believes in maturation; that is, change will come as individuals create it, separately and together, over time and within a historical perspective.

The human psychological system gains its human strivings from dynamically opposed drives (forces) which create polarity. The drives to live, to gratify oneself, and to reach out beyond oneself exist simultaneously with the counterpull, an urge to return to the condition prior to birth or, at least, to an earlier phase of lesser complexity. This desire to return or to regress implies a desire for self-destruction.[9] These two opposing forces are ever present and create a polarity which energizes behavior through all the developmental phases of life. This assumption of the inherent motion of coexisting and continuously activating counterpulls underpins Erikson's theory concerning the problem of dealing with life's ever-present crises. The individual struggle has its

---

which impels its realization. In essence libidinal energy is a term for the as yet unknown force which directs the human system's epigenetic development. In this text the terms *drive, desire, urge,* or *energy* are used in place of *libido.*

[9] These concepts are akin to the Freudian notions of a will to live, to expand, to be gratified and the "death instinct" with its desire to undo all connections with life.

societal counterpart in the strife between progressive and reactionary forces.

The psychological components of masculinity and femininity represent another basic polarity within the individual; bisexuality is inherent in all beings. With all behavior originating from the interplay of polarities, Erikson hints that the etiology of conflict and the recurrence of crises are essential and ever-present components of life. His formulation have a dialectical quality, and his psychoanalytic contentions are clearly of the second half of the twentieth century.

Erikson, like Freud, recognizes conscious, preconscious, and unconscious levels of awareness and assumes that the id comprises the sum of unexpended, unreconstructed, and unconscious attached energy. He ascribes to the id phylogenetical depositions of the unfulfilled strivings of the organism's evolutionary history. These strivings "which would make us mere creatures [are] the sum of the desire which must be overcome to be quite human." (65, 167) The ego, in contrast, is assumed to be a psychological configuration which controls the conscious actions—the synthesis and integration of past experiences with the tasks confronting individuals in their present. Yet, Erikson, with his shift from an id to an ego theory, discards the notion of the "dynasty" of unconscious forces and stresses highly flexible, transferable, and, above all, adaptable and unlimited styles of life. (128, 87)[10] Erikson reminds us that psychoanalytic theorists since Freud continue to contribute to the understanding of irrational thinking. His bridge to that focus is the study of the actual human management of life. (89b; 92; 128)

For Erikson, the ego provides the individual with specific direction and "makes it possible for man to bind together the two great evolutionary developments, his *inner life* and his *social planning*." (111, 149) Ego is no longer the Freudian product of id and superego pressures; rather it forges each individual's developmental history in terms of the social expectations of culture and society, a description that would never fit into a pure Freudian perspective. The direction of individual behavior is determined by the individual's capacity to develop and utilize his ego processes. Freud's defense mechanisms lose their importance for the management of id processes. In Eriksonian analytic thought, the ego processes of behavior, play, work, speech, thought, and actions contain the "mechanisms for activation" (128, 92) of the influence of inner and outer

---

[10] This shift has become more and more marked over the years; interestingly, only as recently as 1967 Erikson acknowledged that he is a man of the twentieth century who swings toward the elements. Freud, in the Darwinian period, had his sights upon man's affinity with the animal kingdom. (128)

forces. Effective and wholesome *activation,* therefore, becomes not only a way, but also a triumph of human life.

Core of Human Functioning

Erikson follows Freud in his assumption that the emotional aspects of life permeate all human functions. Yet he differs with Freud by assuming that the nature of emotional content, or the quality of interpersonal relationships, determines the core of a person's makeup.

In the very beginning of life, the *quality* of interaction between infant and caring adult determines the impact such interaction has upon them both. Erikson recognizes the possibility of constitutional differences in initial sensitivity to various caring experiences. Basically, however, he holds to the notion that the first two years of life constitute the formative years. He stresses that the same factors which determine healthy interpersonal relations also contribute to difficult relationships. Disturbance in interpersonal relationships represent, in essence, an imbalance in the total "emotional household." Emotional difficulties or deviations involve neither a product nor an irreversible condition; a deviant interpersonal interaction possesses a different configuration of the same ongoing processes that are found in ordinary (expected) encounters.

A stress upon the quality of interpersonal relations also implies that neither the child nor the adult is the sole initiator of events. It is not one alone but both together who are responsible for the flow of events. Erikson's notion of *mutual regulation* is central to his whole theoretical position. Such a perception of mutality places the accent not only on the biological development and bodily orientation of individuals but on the partnership in the mutuality of participation. In such a partnership, we find "the development of an individual [anchored in] living through his life history and a series of mutualities which unite men with each other, generations with generation, and man with cosmos." (28, 204) To paraphrase Erikson, maturity requires individual happiness combined with responsible citizenship.

In human development, particularly in early childhood, Erikson considers play to be one of the major ego functions. Play deals with life experiences which children attempt to repeat, master, or negate in order to organize their inner world in relation to their outer world. Further, play involves self-teaching and self-healing: "The child uses play to make up for defeats, sufferings, and frustrations, especially those resulting from a technically and culturally limited use of language." (113, 561) "Playing it out" is a common expression for this form of behavior. Play usually involves three major dimensions: (1) the content and configuration of its parts, which create the underlying theme, (2) verbal and nonverbal communicative components, and (3) modes of renewal and termination (or play disruption). Play activity becomes the means of reasoning and permits children to free themselves from the ego boundaries of time, space, and reality while maintaining a reality orientation, because they and others know it is "just play." Play assures the individual of "free movement within presented limits. . . . It connotes both carefree oscillation and a quality of being engaged, committed." (103, 133) In other words, play is the ego's acceptable tool for self-expression just as dreams afford expression for the id. For Erikson, the playing child advances toward new mastery and new developmental stages. Erikson quotes William Blake: "The child's toys and the old man's reasons are the fruit of the two seasons." (65, 195)

The Newborn
The newborn baby is not much different from his prenatal counterpart. Psychologically, babies are already endowed with *personal* qualities; they have their individual inheritance as well as all the innate potentials for unique personality development.

A newborn can be described as a generalist who becomes more and more specialized during childhood. (101, 606) Erikson assumes that sex differences denote different developmental experiences and that environment is a heavy influence at birth and possibly even before birth. As children mature, they influence the family as much as they are influenced by it. Society needs the newborn for its continuation, and the newborn needs society for its own nurturing. Yet, individuals are the central movers and eventually forge their own destiny.

Environmental Forces
Physical, social, and ideational environmental influences are intertwined as coparticipants along with innate biological and psychological processes in shaping an individual's personality development. An individual's life course is already decisively influenced by the era, area, and arrangements into which he or she is born. Much subsequent development depends upon events, be they chance or destiny, and upon where, when, how, and how much other persons respond to the ever-developing individual.

Environmental forces both limit and free the individual. The typical environment provides ample freedom for individual choice. Individuals want direction from their society concerning what choices to make as much as society wishes to direct the individual toward making the appropriate choices. Since advanced civilization provides a division of labor, present-day children find themselves in the hands of various training, teaching, and helping adults who assume responsibility for a proper balance of the child's behavior, learning, and well-being. As can be expected, these adults tend to direct a child's development according to the patterns of their own particular life style. Religion and ideation serve as guidelines for molding present values and for explaining a future beyond life's certainties, the limits of reason.

Culture adds the humanistic aspect of living. People live by biological (instinctual) forces, and culture insists upon the proper and appropriate use of these life forces. It is the cultural environment, as interpreted by the individual, which selects the range of each individual's experience. Children and their parents are never alone. Through the consciences of caring persons, generations are looking upon the actions of children, helping them integrate their relationships by giving approval, or dividing these relationships into countless disturbing details by disapproval. (105)

Infants first experience society through their body. Significant physical contacts are children's first social events, and these begin to form psychological patterns for their later social experiences. Early bodily experiences tie individuals forever to their original milieu, because of the way their culture, class, and ethnic group organizes the experiences which become their natural and preferred way of life. Not only does child rearing keep the small dependent individual alive and well, it also automatically preserves for each ethnic group and society the unique qualities needed for survival. Child-rearing practices have absorbed the understanding of "by what measures and in what situations [the child] will feel activated to use his best potential and to activate others likewise." (128, 192) "The growing child must, at every step, derive a vitalizing sense of reality from the awareness that his individual way of mastering experience (his ego synthesis) is a successful variant of a group identity and is in accord with its space-time and life plan." (65, 208)[11]

Erikson assumes that prolonged adolescence, which is found in most of the western world, creates a considerable gulf between biological and psychosocial maturation, and impacts upon human development as much as the years of early childhood do: "It is human to have a long childhood; it is civilized to have an even

---

[11] The importance of ethnic variation and differential emphasis in phasal development is brought out by Huey P. Newton when he states that "80 percent of all black suicides occur . . . [due to] lack or loss of love in general." Whites commit suicide "because they suffer the loss of prestige or position or economic security." These later themes are anchored in other than this early developmental phase. (34; 126, 138)

longer childhood. Long childhood makes a technical and mental virtuoso out of man, but it also leaves a lifelong residue of emotional immaturity in him." (65, 12)

Recently, Erikson stressed that we are seeing a divorce between traditional culture and the tasks of our present-day society. The accent upon "here and now" is transmitted in contemporary child-rearing practices. As children perceive in their parents a peer consciousness and a preoccupation with contemporary cultural variables, a new society is in the making. (87; 193; 194a)

One current cultural ideational force is the advent of female liberation. The liberated perception of the biological female body and the increased activity of women in more and more spheres of everyday life highlight Erikson's contention that "body and culture impinge upon each other." (119, 323) The contemporary roles of women and men provide leeways "within the limits of what bodily constitution can sustain, social structure [can] make workable and personality formation [can] integrate." (119, 320) Erikson seems to respond to his feminist challengers of the seventies (201; 362, 367) when he writes: "At the end, only a renewal of social creativity can liberate both men and women from reciprocal roles which, in fact, have exploited both." (119, 331)

Erikson maintains that the social environment needs the individual as much as the individual requires it. "There can be such a waste of human resources," to quote Erikson in a conversation with Huey P. Newton, "when the simplest emotions are misunderstood." (126, 139) When in an earlier writing Erikson said: "The developing child needs society and society needs him;" (65) today, Erikson would more likely say that the developing child needs society, and changing society needs both the female and male child.

ERIKSON'S CONCEPT OF DEVELOPMENT

Development is an evolutional process based upon a universally experienced sequence of biological, psychological, and social events, including autotherapeutic "healing" of developmental complications encountered in the course of growing up.

In one way, Erikson's first five psychosocial stages are essentially a reformulation and expansion of Freud's psychosexual ones. In another way, Erikson presents an entirely new and different framework. For Erikson, there is constant motion. An individual has neither a personality nor a character structure; a person is always a personality in the making, developing and redeveloping. The Freudian conception of biological development as a homeostatic steplike progression has been mutated to Erikson's evolutionary perspective of heterostasic development—a zigzag course from phase to phase and within each phase, a constant state of imbalance, a striving to incorporate irreconcilable opposites.

Freud in the context of his time, introduced an electromagnetic image of human development, where polar forces propelled or repressed development. Erikson, as a person of his time, proceeds with a dialectic conception. The human being is an evolving system; in each moment of life development, the individual, in one sense, chooses between opposites and, in another sense, incorporates such opposites in order to create a new and unique life situation.[12] In addition, this very solution generates different dilemmas with new opposing pulls and with promises for and threats of synthesis.

Erikson's concept of development is pictured by Anderson and Carter as a set of teeterboards being balanced upon each other. Each new balance in one stratum depends upon the balance achieved in the preceding phases and demands subsequent adaptation to this new state; and such an adjustment will affect all previous balances. (6, 120) Most importantly, Erikson's developmental scheme has to be understood for its dialectic premise: the solution of the dilemma of each phase generates the struggle for the next developmental conquest.[13]

Although development proceeds along a zigzag course from phase to phase, it is actually first acknowledged for its regularity. Development follows a predictive sequence which lends parents and kin "an almost somatic conviction that there is meaning to what they are doing." (114, 107) Erikson in this connection quotes Benjamin Spock: "To be a good parent you have to believe in the species—somehow." (114, 107)

It is the progression from a central problem or dilemma of one phase to that of the next which Erikson sees as universal, although the particular context for the dilemma is culturally defined. For example, in many western cultures, weaning is treated as a developmental crisis. Actually, it is a crisis in learning to trust and accept change as part of the regularity and predictability of major life

[12] This particular Eriksonian perspective has become more evident in recent publications (73; 92; 118).

[13] Originally, Erikson employed in his earlier writings (65; 85; 109b) the term *versus*, as if he were dealing with merely opposing forces like in the reporting of a ballgame score. This designation has remained with all descriptions of his phases into the present. The author holds that the use of *versus* or *vs.* to designate opposing poles does not fit with the present perspective in Erikson's current writings. Thus the author has substituted a verb for Erikson's use of *versus* in order to describe more specifically the process which is assumed to take place, and to avoid an erroneous implication that the counterdirectional pulls could serve to neutralize each other.

events. As each dilemma is fully dealt with, the individual moves into the next phase. The individual has to deal with the dominant theses of each phase; there is no mention that anyone has to solve these dilemmas; hardly any person does. Each successive phase provides the possibility of new solutions for previous struggles. At the same time, any earlier theme can remain dominant in a person's destiny. (103, 131)

The developmental phases serve the individual (or the ego) as timetable and mirror for discerning the structure of the relevant social institutions. Individuals develop and move into subsequent phases as soon as they are biologically, psychologically, and socially ready, and such individual readiness is matched by societal readiness. Individuals not only develop, they are socialized. Development requires a variety of subenvironments, depending on the phase the child has reached and on the environments experienced during preceeding stages. Erikson's psychosocial development phases are the products of interactional experiences between each child and his or her world.

Graphically, development for Erikson is tridimensional. First, there is the progression from one phase to another, which includes the pull back and forward between the previous and future developmental phases. The progression in anyone's life chart is linear, though rather wavy, and is always in the same order. Second, development involves sets of mutualities, first between infant and one child-caring person, later on between child and child-caring persons, still later, between child and peers, then between adolescents and the world of their peers. Mutuality in early adulthood is between intimate friends, work associates, and other types of partners, and later on between adults and their generation. In the late years of adulthood, mutuality is between elders and their world of successors, that is, between generations. Third, development is relative. Old developmental issues are taken up anew and differently in each subsequent phase. For instance, issues of trust and autonomy, once major themes, emerge as much in facing the *new* world of peers in the early teens. These issues are dealt with differently but are still vital, being carried over from previous life encounters.

It should be stated again that temporary regression in any of the major areas of development is a natural side effect of the process. To cite Erikson's faith in the elasticity of human development: "Children 'fall apart repeatedly, and unlike Humpty Dumpty, grow together again." (114, 83) Children, adolescents, and adults grow and develop, first, on the basis of innate laws of development which, like biological processes, are irreversible. Second, they develop on the basis of sociocultural influences which specify the desirable rate of development and favor selected aspects of biological development at the expense of others. Third, their development is based on the idiosyncratic way they manage their development, on their native endowment, and on the way society responds to them.

Erikson describes eight developmental phases, attributing five phases to childhood and three to adulthood. (The latter three phases represent another major alteration of Freud's five ages of man.)[14] In the following list of Erikson's five phases of childhood, the word *sense* underscores the affective states being dealt with in the progression of development: (1) a sense of basic trust while overcoming a sense of basic mistrust, (2) a sense of autonomy while combating a sense of doubt and shame, (3) a sense of initiative while overcoming a sense of guilt, (4) a sense of industry while fending off a sense of inferiority, and (5) a sense of identity while overcoming a sense of identity diffusion. The struggle over a sense of basic trust and basic mistrust and the dilemma over a sense of identity and identity diffusion received more painstaking attention than the other six phases combined, perhaps because of Erikson's personal preoccupation with these periods, perhaps due to their importance in contemporary child-rearing efforts.

Although this chapter on Erikson limits itself to a study of child development, an understanding of the eight phases, which cover the total span of development, is essential, particularly since helping adults are dealing with their own development as well as the child's.

Phase I: Acquiring a Sense of Basic Trust
While Overcoming a Sense of Basic Mistrust
—a Realization of Hope

Affective development, that is, emotional development, is anchored in the very early experience of this first phase. After a life of rhythmic regularity, warmth, and protection in the uterus, infants experience the reality of life in their first contacts with the outer world. Although children are born naked, meek, and vulnerable, each one

> is endowed with an appearance and with responses which appeal to the tending adults' tenderness and make them wish to attend his needs. . . . [The] vulnerability of being newly born and the meekness of innocent needfulness have a power all of their own. Defenseless as babies are there are mothers at their command, families to protect the mothers,

---

[14] In fact, while Plato and other philosophers of the past have specified stages of development beyond adolescence, modern theorists have treated human development as if there were no continuous development through adulthood.

> *societies to support the structure of families and traditions to give a cultural continuity to systems of tending and training.* (111, 150–151)

Infants develop a sense of expectancy through a mixture of trust and mistrust. Their sense of basic trust—as opposed to mistrust—becomes the critical theme in their first developmental phase. In these very early experiences the infant begins to learn to what degree hope is realizable.

For the newborn, a sense of trust requires a feeling of physical comfort and a minimum amount of uncertainty and discomfort. If these are assured, individuals will extend their trust to new experiences. In contrast, a sense of mistrust arises from unsatisfactory physical experiences and the association of frustration with them. Frustration leads to fearful apprehension, a lack of hope for finding desired change in trying anew.

A sense of basic trust helps an individual to grow psychologically and to face new experiences willingly. Each successful outcome of his trust tends to produce favorable expectations of new experiences; yet, experiences will always offer occasions for mistrust. One can learn to trust even one's own mistrust—a believe the world is good. For example, trusting the experience of mouthing new objects also includes a mistrust of the unknown. Only the trustworthy atmosphere of the immediate environment maintains the infant's overall confidence, balance, and emotional well-being. During infancy, the faith and conviction of parents assure the child's basic trust in, and genuine dependence upon, a world that is predictable and knowable but also unknown and unpredictable. Parents themselves can find assurance in spite of their own uncertainties and mistrust through their religious or philosophical outlook on life.

The first and fundamental task of establishing a sense of basic trust coincides with the rapid maturational period of early life, when body growth can be overwhelming and can invite much mistrust unless new modes of bodily behavior provide adequate compensation. Maintaining the bodily functions of respiration, ingestion, digestion, and motor movements are the only concerns of young organisms, and these functions comprise their immediate purpose for interacting with their environment. Thus, bodily experiences provide the basis for a psychological state of trust; bodily sensations become the first social experience and are generalized for future reference. Whether infants become trusting and easily satisfied people or mistrusting and demanding people who are essentially preoccupied with bodily requirements is determined in large measure by the nature of their experiences during these early life encounters.

To understand the intertwining physical and psychological conditions, it is necessary to trace the origin of all psychological forces. Psychological energy is present with birth and impels the organism to survive and to ward off destruction. This energy evolves from psychosocial experiences, bodily sensations. Surplus or unused energy, unassociated to any life experience thus far, are potential id forces, ready to find expression whenever and wherever appropriate. The infant's crying, sucking, visional reflexes, and motor movements become invested with psychic energy. As they become more and more cortically controlled, they become distinct ego processes.[15] Infants' dependence upon external care and control becomes supplemented and more and more impacted by their own competence in affecting their environmental input.

Body Experience-Early Life Experience
Psychic energy becomes closely intertwined with the body zones around which the most crucial life experiences revolve; consequently, these zones become significant erotic centers for affective processes. During the first three to four months, much of the infant's routine centers around the intake of food, light, sound, and around general bodily tactile stimulations. Of these, food intake involves the most regular and significant contact between infants and their social environment. Their mouths and sucking activity establish primary contact with the outside world. Oral contact and suction alleviate a generalized sense of discomfort, while simultaneously providing a source of satisfaction in themselves. Essentially, infants meet their society orally. They receive and give love with their mouths. The length of oral contact and the quality of sucking are not as important as the nature of the interpersonal contact in the organization of the infant's feelings about these life experiences.

The mother or a caring person brings the social world to the infant. The environment expresses itself through the mother's breast or the bottle. Love and the pleasure of dependency, which is so important in this phase, are conveyed to the child by the caring person's embrace, by his or her comforting warmth, smile, and way of talking to the child, and also through the quality of the care.

Much of this phase involves the incorporation of sensory experiences. The sense of trust or mistrust is closely related to these first social encounters in which the infant accepts the environment as it is given. Very early experiences are somatic and not yet connected by the infant's perception of the outside world. The young or-

---

[15] Erikson recognized neurological maturation as an important component of ego development.

ganism learns to regulate its system in accordance with the way in which the caring environment organizes its methods of child care. How infants associate receiving with trusting depends on the way their mother or any other central caring person combines giving with trustworthiness in her care of them.

As infants mature, receiving includes reaching for, appropriating, and testing orally everything within their grasp. The degree of an individual's desire to cope may be lessened if these early efforts are experienced as severely thwarted. The acts of receiving and reaching lead to the next social modality, which is grasping. Grasping and gripping are connected with objects such as the nipple and also with other tactile experiences, visual perception, and the localization of sounds. In situations where the initial sense of trust through receiving has been unsatisfactorily developed, infants tend to reach out at random in an effort to obtain what they feel they are lacking in the satisfaction of their needs. Dissatisfaction emanates from a lack of adequate integration. A sense of distrust of living results from a meager experience of receiving.

While learning creates new experiences of trust and a sense that one can rely on the environment, it also calls forth anxiety and uncertainty. Babies are involved in the coordination of perceptions and internal states, so that wishing for an item they see, judging its closeness, and being able to grasp it produce a situation which can result in trust and fulfillment although it is also a moment of anxiety.

Early Social Outreach
As the baby grows, new pleasure is found through more aggressive interaction with his environment. Erikson designates this as the second oral stage. The incorporative mode becomes particularly prominent at the time the first teeth develop. Grasping is now under full voluntary control, and visual perception extends to a larger field. In this second incorporative stage, the social mode of gripping is analogous to the process of clamping down (biting) with the new teeth. Psychologically, children tend to incorporate completely to keep as their own what they acquire or are given. Experience has taught them by now that they can maintain their environment through their own efforts. As Erikson explains it, this desire to hold is a reaction to the somatic experiences of teething, colic, and other early discomforts. Yet, to hold on through biting frequently causes the withdrawal of the mother's breast or bottle's nipple, and an even more vehement urge to hold on is thus stimulated in the child. Biting as the response to a sense of frustration is a secondary expression, similar to the previously described random reaching for what was felt to be inadequately given.

Thus, during oral development, an experience of regularity and continuity in the relationship between the child and the caring person begins. Through oral development, children experience their earliest appropriate and consistent satisfaction of basic needs. Thus, they establish unique patterns and limits of behavior for their developing ego. More and more the infant's inner state of well-being becomes associated with consistent behavior, on the part of the caring person. Adverse experiences may retard children's ego development, but if trust has dominated their early experiences, they will readily face new situations and overcome any initial mistrust. The early interactions between mother and child Erikson says, builds a "cradle of faith [and] permits a mother to respond to the needs and demands of the baby's body and mind in such a way that he learns once and for all to trust her, to trust himself and to trust the world." (123, 101)

Play

Although Erikson sees young infants as participants within a social matrix, he recognizes that they appear to be totally egocentric, behaving as if they were all that existed and counted. In very early forms of play, they rely entirely upon themselves. Their activity begins and centers upon their own body, with repeated of sensory perceptions, kinesthetic sensations, and vocalizations. In play, the developmental theme of incorporating and holding is reflected. Experiences during play, such as the visual integration of cognition of a well-known human face, are intimately associated with the development of relationships later on and the outreach for and trust upon others. Gradually, play activities begin to include whatever is within the baby's reach in his or her objective world. In these very early forms of play, the ability of humans to experiment and plan is developing. Infants practice by playing, by creating model situations for simple life tasks. For example, much of play revolves around making "things do"—e.g., a rattle rattle, two blocks fit on each other, etc. Play can have a cathartic value when the outside world is not providing stability for the young infant.

Roots for Identification

The person caring for the child and the feeling toward him or her that that person produces in the child constitute outer predictability and inner reality. A caring person's healthy identification with her nurturing role further increases the incentive to become the significant person in the child's life. During child caring, each moment presents an opportunity for regeneration in the life and world of the caring person. Young children assimilate this person's qualities while projecting onto the person some of their own feelings. Children's tendency to identify and project also includes aspects of the immediate environment which affect them strongly in any way. This growing sense of belonging to a central person becomes evident around the sixth month of life in instances of separation. Consequently, during this acute formative stage, separation, however temporary, can be highly influential in an adverse way.

Erikson includes joint experience and mutual regulation of frustration as essential components of identification in establishing a basic sense of trust. The very experience of establishing mutual regulation results in moments of frustration for both child and caring person. Frustration only leads to feelings of uncertainty and a basic sense of mistrust when it is not eventually resolved into trust. Children tend to sense the unconscious insecurities and intentions as well as the conscious thoughts and overt behavior of their parents, even though they do not understand their parents conscious or unconscious intentions. In fact, Erikson does not ascribe much importance to individual habits or acts of skill in the care of the child. Instead he points to the underlying emotional and attitudinal themes which motivate the parent in the handling, care, and training of his or her child. He suggests that early training efforts fail when they primarily revolve around training parents rather than the care of children. (65, 270)

Mother substitutes for nurturing purposes can have considerable influence and even be a deterrent to nurture. The quality of care also depends on the support that the central caring person receives from a husband and/or other adults in the household, on the family into which the child is born, on the society's recognition of the family as one of its basic institutions, and on the culture's guarantee for the continuation of fundamental societal mores and values. In other words, the society and the cultural heritage into which each child is born or adopted also determine what the limits and possibilities will be and what each boy or girl can hope for in his or her dreams and aspirations. The nurturing experience defines the mode and degree of mistrust and trust, and determines to what extent to mistrust will be trusted as a basic affective mode later in life.

Phase II: Acquiring a Sense of Autonomy
While Combating a Sense of Doubt
and Shame—a Realization of Will

As infants gain trust in their caring person, environment, and way of life, they discover that they can determine their own behavior and with it acquire a sense of autonomy; they realize their will.

Simultaneously, however, their continued dependency creates a sense of doubt concerning their capacity and freedom to assert their autonomy and exist as an independent unit. This doubt becomes compounded by a certain shame for their instinctive revolt against their previously much enjoyed dependency, and by a fear of perhaps exceeding their own or their environmental limits. According to Erikson, the conflict of these opposing pulls to simultaneously assert oneself and deny oneself the right and capacity to make this assertion provide the major theme of the second phase.

In this struggle to be a *self* without insulating this self too drastically from others, the urge to assert one's will and prove one's muscular mobility is accompanied by a reluctance to experiment with one's potential capacities because of the danger of being on one's own. Children need sympathetic guidance and support at this time, lest they find themselves at a loss, as if out on a limb, feeling shame and doubt for their helplessness. During this period, roughly between the ages of eighteen months and three years, the child "must learn to *will* what *can* be, and to convince himself that he *willed* what *had* to be." (*111*, 155)

Body Control–Self-control

Physically, the young child is undergoing an acceleration of maturation. Movements and mobility become well coordinated and mastered to the extent that reaching, walking, climbing, holding, and releasing are no longer activities in themselves, but rather the means for new encounters. Youngsters find it increasingly difficult and undesirable to stay within their designated activity space; they want to explore their world on their own and accomplish new feats. Newly improved and refined muscle control helps children regulate their eliminative functions; they become capable of controlling their urethral and anal sphincter muscles. The eliminatory zones become centers for denoting the degree to which the child masters or refuses to master physical, social, and psychological functions.

Physical maturation is paralleled by an increase in energy and the channeling of such energy into more and more life experiences. Children in this period are analogous to toys tightly wound up. At times, the impulses are stronger than the child's capacity to cope with them. They also tax the capacity of parents or other caring persons to deal with them. Generally, however, increased energy coincides with further ego growth. Greater mobility, more refined perception, improved memory, and greater neurological and social integration all point toward added ego strength. This constantly fluctuating balance between energy which can be expended and energy which can be channeled is further influenced by the emergence of conscience (superego processes). However rudimentary, conscience increases as children gain and utilize their autonomy. As children become autonomous in certain areas of their life, they integrate the guidance which previously, in their utter dependency, provided them with direction and control.

Erikson focuses upon the ego in this psychogenic development. When individuals see that they can be what they will and when they perceive the boundaries between themselves and their parents (or surrogates), they expand their sense of trust within their expanding selves. Although this trust, under ordinary circumstances, can no longer be so easily destroyed by strivings for independence or the demands of the controlling environment, the fear of failing in situations beyond one's capacity to cope still creates some self doubt.

Many of the psychosocial contacts of this period center around the newly gained capability of holding on and letting go. The child is preoccupied with activities of retaining and releasing perceptions, ideas, interpersonal relationships, verbal messages and communication of wants, and manipulative objects. The capacity to alternate between retaining and releasing becomes a power issue. Deciding *what* to will and *when* to will it requires an integration of the individual will and the social will, and also creates an authority issue concerning *whose will* is involved. For young children this is a struggle between themselves and the interference (actual or remembered) of their caring persons. To hold and to let go with the hands, mouth, eyes, sphincters, become incidents of real ambiguity and ambivalence; for such actions operate under the inner conflict between the desire to continue with or return to old dependency situations and the desire to try on one's own initiative.

As long as sphincter control and toilet training carry considerable cultural importance, they become associated with the concurrent struggle for autonomy. The whole concern that the child eliminate at a designated place and time is closely associated with the caring person's approval of and trust in the child, his or her own self-esteem regarding how well the job is being done, and the child's feelings of discomfort, tension, and release of tension as the elimination routine becomes established. Such experiences provide a theme and a test for the child's general notion of self-regulation versus regulation by others. Toilet training leads to both greater autonomy and subordination to adult direction, and in an area where behavior has heretofore been completely uninhibited.

In a social culture where effective bowel training is not an essential concern during this particular developmental age, other behavioral areas may be treated similarly or analogously by the parent. Naturally, if the area of concern becomes heavily charged with feeling, children will transfer the meaning of this struggle into other areas of their life. They will tend to treat other related activities as if they were also retainable and accessible to touch and disarrangement, or as if they needed to be expelled, avoided, or cleansed. Many such activities center around collecting, hoarding, and piling up rather than discarding things and putting them in their proper places.

It has already been implied that much of the child's initial self-esteem and the release of his infantile sense of omnipotence depend upon his capacity to maintain the reassurance of trust in himself until he finds his ultimate balance of power. Any frustration of this real or potential power of self-expression is of ever-increasing significance. The child must incorporate the experience of frustration as a reality of his life and view it as a natural part of life events rather than as a total threat to his life. Thus, it is important that the child sees, in this period, that an insult to his autonomy (such as frustration) in any one area does not render him impotent in all others.

Play

Play assumes special importance during this phase and provides the child with a safe island where he can develop his autonomy within his own set of boundaries or laws. Doubt and shame are conquered when play proceeds according to these laws. Erikson says that "the small world of manageable toys is a harbor which the child establishes, to return to when he needs to overhaul his ego." (65, 194)

The child's play and his quick changes of mood from joyful certainty to utter helplessness and despair provide visible proof that opposites are very close together, including the proximal qualities of love and hate. This stage is decisive in establishing a ratio between love and hate, cooperation and willfulness, and the freedom of self-expression and its suppression. From a sense of *self-control without loss of self-esteem* comes a lasting sense of autonomy and pride, from a sense of muscular lack of control or loss of self-control, and out of parental overcontrol, comes a lasting sense of doubt and shame. (114, 112)

Relationship Formation

In these early childhood years, the relationship between child and caring person shifts. They devoted much effort during the first phase of their joint history to establishing mutual trust and a willingness to face new situations together. In the second phase, young children violate this mutual trust and try to establish their autonomy in distinct areas. Vigorously, they try to do all on their own; to feed, walk, and dress themselves and to open and shut things. At this stage, to live means to expand aggressively, to act on one's own terms, to insist on one's own boundaries.[16] It is a common experience at this point in development for parents to dress their children and then find them undressed and proudly trying to do it all by themselves. "Me do!" is a vital request at this point in life. The theme of child-parent relations is the establishment of mutual regulations.

The sense of autonomy and the effort to combat a sense of self-doubt are fostered "by a handling of the small individual which expresses a sense of dignity and independence on the part of the parents and a confident expectation that the kind of autonomy fostered earlier will not be frustrated later." (*114,* 120) In this give-and-take between child and caring person, much depends upon the caring person's capacity to grant to the child gradual independence, at least within areas which are relatively safe. The caring person's comfortable enjoyment of granting freedom in some areas while maintaining firmness in others will be reflected in the child's sense of tolerance and self-assurance. A parent's firmness, Erikson warns, "must protect [the child] against the potential anarchy of his yet untrained sense of discrimination, his inability to hold on and to let go with circumspection." (*114,* 112)

Most importantly, the responsibility for establishing wise limits rests with the parent. Children are still pliable; if they know and fully understand the range of their limits and what they are supposed to do, their growth will be largely healthy. Conversely, they become almost unapproachable when they find themselves involved in activities which they feel they understand and should be allowed to do but which are not permissible. It is at this point that the adult's tolerant firmness spells the difference between childrens' establishment of their own capacity for self-management and self-control and their establishment of a gradually increasing sense of doubt and shame in themselves. In the latter case, self-doubt becomes an intolerable burden, because either children feel inadequate at proving themselves or they sense their unharnessed urges to control, which become overwhelming to them; in either situation, they doubt their capacity to become an independent being.

A parent is readily apt to sense the child's precarious position, especially when the newly developing conscience is still very

---

[16] These normal developmental attitudes of the young 2- to 4-year old remind one of the spirit and proud nationalism usually associated with the life of a young nation.

fragile. This is a period when children learn to "blackmail" their parent with the threat of regression. (69) At the same time, however, this form of demanding, compared with the one based upon the complete dependency of the previous phase, fosters mutual regulation. Children learn to get somebody to do for them what they want done, while they learn to give, since all receiving involves an aspect of giving.

Identification Formation

Father, elder siblings, or any adults other than the mother in the child's immediate environment assume an ever-increasing significance in the awareness of children and in their efforts to find the boundaries of the self. Constantly in contact with different adults and different degrees of freedom in different areas of behavior, children quickly learn to utilize these differences and tend to make distinctions as they do relate to each adult. Trust and mistrust in their relations with each person in the household depend on the degree to which children have safely established an autonomy with the particular person. Similarly, for the first time, other children assume meaning, but only to the extent that they serve as play objects or as additional caterers to the need for attention. When the newborn sibling is experienced as a rival for the mother's attention and met with jealousy, the detraction from the child of the attention he or she has always had is compounded in its effect by the strong desire for dependency which still vies with the desire for autonomy.

The social setting of children has direct bearing on their ultimate realization of their sense of autonomy, or on their doubts of it. For children to release thoughts and feelings through their behavior is intrinsically neither good nor bad for them; these values depend on the cultural definition ascribed to the natural urges to assert oneself and they will determine the kind of child-training devices used to regulate the child's behavior. All child-rearing patterns, Erikson points out, lead to some sense of doubt and shame. It is merely the particular behavior to which a positive or negative value is attached which varies from culture to culture, or from family to family. The degree and type of behavior permitted the child and the way in which the control of his behavior is handled will have direct bearing upon the individual's attitude toward social organizations and ideals later in life. It is basic to Erikson's concept that the pattern of child training determines the eventual form of political authority the child finds most satisfactory as an adult. In turn, the political ideology of the time has an influence on the boundaries and nature of acceptable child-rearing patterns.

Phase III: Acquiring a Sense of Initiative
and Overcoming a Sense of Guilt
—a Realization of Purpose

Having learned some measure of conscious control over themselves and their environment, children can rapidly move forward to new conquests in ever-widening social and spacial spheres. A sense of initiative permeates most of their life at a time when their social environment challenges them to be active and purposeful by mastering specific tasks. They are asked to assume responsibility for themselves and for the things in their world—their bodies, toys, pets, and, occasionally, younger siblings. They and their society realize that each child *is* counted as a person, and that life has a purpose for each of them. Such a realization starts a flood of new questions—obscure variations of "but what am I here for?" As children search for and create fantasies about the active person they want to become, they consciously and unconsciously tests their powers, skills, and potential capacities. They initiate behavior, the implications of which go beyond themselves. They intrude into others' spheres and get others involved with them and their behavior.

Whatever autonomy they have achieved is frustrated to some degree when the separate autonomous behavior of others is not in accord with their own. This behavior to some extent negates the previous trust they formed in their caring adults and their dependency. Consequently, they experience and have to overcome a sense of guilt and a corresponding desire to curtail their initiative whenever conflict arises. The struggle over whether to move beyond such boundaries or remain as they are causes further affective stirrings because the developing individuals are denying their own desires and the opportunities offered them by their environment. This polarity of initiative versus either passivity or guilt for having gone too far—that is, living too strongly or too weakly compared to their inner strivings—provides the major theme of this period, usually encompassing the preschool and kindergarten years.

Erikson stresses that psychological mastery of the ambulatory field encourages and reflects children's maturational accomplishments. They have mastered the skills of reaching, taking, and holding and are now combining these capabilities with walking, running, skipping, etc. They can move about with more freedom, knowledge, and energy in an ever-expanding environment. They discover that in their greater mobility, they are not unlike the adults of their environment. Their use of language has been improved; they now ask questions through which they begin to understand many old and new mysteries. Permissiveness towards such trying out, daring, and investigating is an essential feature of development—as is the establishment of certain boundaries to circumscribe just what *is* permissible. What is at stake, then, is the authenticity of the caring person's permissiveness and strictness. (92, 218)

Reaching out with language and locomotion permits children to expand their fields of activity and imagination. Inevitably, some of the possibilities will frighten them. They can easily feel and fear the thought "I am what I can imagine I will be." (114, 127) On the whole, the child is faced with the universal crisis of turning from an "attachment to his parents to the slow process of becoming a parent, a carrier of tradition." (65, 225) The first step in becoming one's own parent is to supervise oneself, a role requiring parentlike behavior. This process begins during this phase. Children's consciences increasingly assume the supporting and controlling functions of the significant adults in their environment. As the conscience (superego) is built, external "voices heard firmly enough" are being more and more absorbed by it as the inner voices of the child.

In one sense, the conscience is built from the model of the caring persons'; in a truer sense, it is built of the caring persons' superegos and the culture's values—the sociocultural heritage. (104) The superegos of parents or caring persons and, to a considerable degree, of the developing child include the tastes, class standards, characteristics, and traditions of their society's culture. (77) Thus, children will incorporate into their conscience what the parent or caring person really is as a person, and not merely what he or she tries to teach the child.

In spite of the emerging conscience (superego), the ego continues to determine major developmental accomplishments. Children invest much in refining muscular activities, accuracy in perception, assessment of others, and skills in communication. Speech represents more than mere communication; it involves assuming a particular position on a given situation and a verbal acknowledgement of the awareness of variances in situations. The child's behavioral capacities are directed toward a purposeful existence and a manifestation of a self-identity which replaces the previous sense of egocentricity. However, this self-identity also includes mistrust, doubts, and fears—residues of the polar conflicts with which the child still wrestles in his or her conscious and unconscious efforts to cope with the everyday questions of life.

Identity Formation

Psychological development in this phase centers in two major tasks. First, the individual becomes a social unit, an integrated personality in his or her own right. From now on, as development proceeds, the child is a being in relationship to other beings—parents, peers, and other social entities in the child's expanding universe. Second, young individuals begin to notice sex and other role differences among those in their environment which affect both their own self-definition and the course they must pursue according to the social demands of their society.

The child now faces a period of energetic learning. Much of the time, children associate with others of their own age. They enter actively into the lives of others and, thus, into a multitude of new experiences. Above all, in their learning and associations, they experience being a boy or a girl. As members of a social grouping, their sex identity is more fully sensed through others in their midst.

At the same time, the child cannot escape the fact that his or her learning, social contacts, and experience all introduce new thoughts, feelings, and imagined or accomplished deeds which will provide a new area for a sense of guilt. Children frequently fear they have gone beyond their rights, which in fact they frequently do. They continuously question their sex role to determine whether their behavior is in line with what is expected of their sex and whether it is all right that they are not of the other sex. Thus, this phase provides moments of feeling a sense of real accomplishment, and moments when a fear of danger and a sense of guilt are engendered.

In psychoanalytic psychology this developmental phase is noted for its Oedipal complications. In his earlier writings, Erikson accepted the Freudian theme of a central developmental crisis for children, their parents (especially the parent of the opposite sex), and the family as a representative of societal mores. In more recent publications, Erikson questions the generalization and oversimplification which, he suggests, grew out of others' interpretation of Freud's concept of an Oedipus complex. Erikson does not doubt the attachment to the opposite sex, but he notes that this most important person of the opposite sex has thus far been the true and only representative of that sex. (128, 24) Recently, Erikson suggested another drastically different perspective of the *Oedipus* phenomenon. He sees in the myth, and in life, as much a father's fear of son as a son's fear of father and asks, why not prove the oracle wrong rather than acknowledge a self-fulfilling prophecy? As noted earlier, Erikson remarked in 1973 that if a father trusts his ability, and a mother hers, to bring up the little boy or girl, "such trust would not make a myth but it might make history." (126, 113)

Strivings for the opposite sex occur when children discover they are *counted upon* within the context of a family group and when they can express *purposeful affection*. The child's affectionate outreach is not incestuous in terms of our western mores; but rather it involves the fact that love always reaches to those who have most proven themselves and are really available. A boy tends to reach out for his mother, his most available love object, because she is the one who has given him constant comfort. The mother is apt to accept and to encourage her son's attachment because she senses the maleness in her son who is becoming a man. At the same time, society challenges the boy to shift his *identification* to his father. The boy usually finds it easy to admire his father, because the father stands for those symbols of maleness (ego behavior and superego values) which his culture (particularly the specific culture of his home) values as desirable and admirable. A girl, tends to attach her desire to the most trusted and available man, usually her father, while he sees and encourages her feminity and, most likely, enjoys it. Again, this involves a question of propinquity rather than of incest. A girl's Oedipal relationship is one step removed from a boy's because her desires are not usually attached to the same person upon whom she relied in her infantile dependency. Her Oedipal relationship to father is romantic, while her identification continues with the mother, who stands for all that is embodied in her own strivings for femaleness.[17]

As the boy or girl finds a romantic attachment in the parent of the opposite sex, he or she tends to express mistrust of all those who will interfere with this new relationship. Essentially, the so-called Oedipal struggle is not so much a fight of boy against father nor girl against mother, but rather a fight against the controlling person. (126, 116) It is a power struggle rather than a sexual struggle, a conflict of wills; the parents are confronting the budding will of the new generation. Again, old feelings of mistrust are aroused as the child senses the tenuous character of this new relationship. The child finds the desired parent emotionally unattainable and, naturally, develops a sense of rivalry with the parent of the same sex. This leads to two interdependent sequences. One involves the gradual replacement of the desired parent by other more accessible love objects, that is, persons who can safely become the recipients of the child's emotional investment. The other sequence is linked with the child's more appropriate reality perception. While the parent is successfully replaced as the immediate love object, his or her position becomes enhanced as the ego ideal for the opposite sex. The parent of the same sex becomes the model for the child's superego and the major person with whom the child identifies. For

---

[17] "Romantic" implies an unreal make-believe situation with ample opportunity for practicing flirtation and other skills ascribed in the romantic literature to the art of conquering one's love.

children of both sexes the modality of expression has an actively aggressive undertone, with a thrust toward searching out and expanding the territory under their control as urgent goals.

Human Modalities

Boys, during this phase, tend to be intrusive, thrusting forward into space, time, new areas of knowledge, and people's lives. Erikson developed these propositions from his research on play configurations in the late thirties. *(65; 68; 72; 113; 116)* These tentative findings were retested in later studies *(103; 112; 115a)* and also in studies by others. *(158; 380)*[18] Boys' play is marked by intense motor activities penetrating through space with few holds barred. They urgently explore unknown spheres with searching curiosity, attacking problems head on. Such ordinary life events are getting dressed, meeting people, as well as talking and questioning have an intrusive quality. Boys more and more shift from an emphasis on experience with people to a preoccupation with the world of actions and things.

The modality of expression for girls seems to have an inceptive quality with an urge to include others and to be included into others' lives.[19] Erikson perceives much of a potential maternal role being formed at this point. Overall cultural values are "willed" to girls and boys at these periods of their development. Sex roles are also assigned and are to be practiced. The young girl who gets a boy to do a task for her (or vice versa) is no longer controlling the other person but rather *winning* the other sex over to the management of daily routines. The form and content of such management are also in question from now on.

In recent writings, Erikson acknowledges the strong cultural components in human modalities. Essentially, however, he maintains the basically biological position that differential inclinations are an adaptation to the body's language and a cultural acknowledgment of nature's sexual differentiation. Erikson does question, at the same time, the politics of sex—the attribution of greater power, authority, or choice in life opportunities to one or the other sex. *(89a; 92; 118; 119)* For further exploration of Erikson's perception of sex differentiation and sexism see later in this chapter.

Play

Erikson refers to these developmental years as the "play age." Play is the way of life for a child and serves as a most indispensable

---

[18] Wambach's study *(380)* is particularly noteworthy. He started out in 1970 to question Erikson's findings of thirty years before and found, through careful research, that essentially the same sexual differentiations occurred in play configurations, even with children of "modern" families, as the ones Erikson had found before World War II among children born in the late twenties.

[19] See footnote 18 for recent research on these propositions.

and natural autotherapeutic agent. Play takes two essential forms in this phase. First, children need time to themselves to indulge in solitary activities and undisturbed daydreaming, during which they can play out or dream out phasal conflicts and resolutions. Secondly, the company of other children is required in order to play out individual and mutual life crises. Sometimes play objects are employed to portray the forces of conflict experienced by the child in his life (113); at the other times, play relationships with real people serve as opportunities for solving previous difficulties or in anticipating new problems. "The imaginative anticipation of future roles is played out with toys and costumes, in tales and games." (92, 213)

A child's greater sense of reality sometimes becomes a liability in play, because he or she frequently attaches a forbidden (though necessary) meaning to play fantasies, and this leads to a further sense of guilt. In these cases, the child is tensely ready to interrupt "forbidden" play for fear of being discovered, and he or she often does so at the very moment when the play has reached the autotherapeutic point. Children at this age can be seen to interrupt suddenly a very active encounter, such as making toys cars crash together, to ask for a noncombatant activity, such as watching TV or getting a drink of water.

Relationship Formation

The developmental phase places the child-parent relationship in a triangular situation in which the child becomes an independent and active, if not competitive, partner. As we have suggested, only the child who has successfully experienced autonomy can relinquish his or her romantic possession of the parent. Children who have been less successful need to cling to such support to be certain of themselves as individuals; otherwise they become entangled again in the question "what is me?" instead of "what is not me but the other?"

Children and parents work together on problems related to the child's development but beyond his or her immediate capacities and comprehension. As he or she works and plays with the child, the own parent, most likely, conveys a common cause with people, ideas, and values beyond their family unit. At this stage, the child needs other people besides family members in order to experiment with various alternative types of behavior and goals beyond the family's life sphere. Children begin to realize differences between their own family standards and those of others. Moreover, they begin to note that a parent seems to be allowed to do things they are not allowed to do. Rivalry shifts from competition for dependency satisfaction to competition for full partnership.

Children enter with all their inquisitiveness and adventurousness into their ever-widening social circle. They want to find out about their world, and are increasingly encouraged to conform to the teachings of the society in their unfolding world. Nursery schools, kindergartens, and primary grades, and churches are the major social institutions which, along with the home, indicate to children the range of initiative appropriate for them at this particular time of life. Gradation of inquisitiveness and permissible aggression by age, sex, and social roles are cultural devices which, ideally, direct individuals to develop to their best advantage within the context of their culture.

Erikson draws a relationship between the degree of individual initiative, fostered or permitted, and the community's economic system. He implies that the individual's potential capacity to work and achieve economic success within the framework of society's economic order depends upon his or her mastery of this developmental phase. It is a period of realizing a sense of purpose.

Children seem to grow integratively into a physical and psychological unit. They test forward-surging independence in relation to the many facets of the immediate and expanding environment. They gradually gain glimpses of their society's institutions and of the opportunities and roles which will permit and demand their responsible participation when they become adults. For the present, however, children find it a pleasurable accomplishment to manipulate meaningful toys, wield tools, or take responsibility for themselves and younger children. Their great energy permits them to overcome disappointments, failures, unfulfilled goals, and above all, to try again with new more channeled purpose. They find that they are moving in the right direction; they are on their way. Failures are compensated by new accomplishments. "The future is emphasized as against the past. The future absolves the past." (77, 385)

Phase IV: Acquiring a Sense of Industry and Fending Off a Sense of Inferiority —a Realization of Competence

Children's forward searching brought them into contact and involved them with a wealth of new experiences in which they found others of their own age. The major theme of this phase reflects their determination to master the tasks before them. They direct their abundant energies toward working as an equal with age mates and toward those social problems of their world that they can successfully master.

The polarity of this phase is, as Erikson phrases it, a sense of industry versus a sense of inferiority. There is abundant energy for invention and for all possible effort in producing. Opposing this is the ever-present pull toward the comfort of staying as one is, toward being satisfied with lesser production. The strength of the latter is supported by the very fact that the child is still an incomplete person, which tends to give him or her feelings that just trying is good enough. After all, what else can be done by a "mere child"? Roughly between the ages of seven and eleven, the child delves diligently into all opportunities to learn by doing, by experimenting with the rudimentary skills required of his or her culture. Children try to prove their competence, lest they perceive themselves as inferior. As they learn to wield the tools and symbols of their culture, children seem to understand that this sort of learning will help them become competent and more competent than they were before.

Physical maturation slows as if to consolidate what has already been acquired. Psychological development reflects a similar pattern. Boys and girls have found, for awhile, their respective psychological and social boundaries. Each of them can work on filling in the vast gaps in their capabilities within the present limits of his or her capacities. The Freudian notion of latency has to be rephrased: There is nothing latent in the middle years except the strivings toward intimate involvement with a partner of the opposite sex. During the "latent" period, children continue to invest as much of themselves and their apparently unceasing energy as they did before. They work incessantly on their physical and perceptive skills, as well as on their growing knowledge of the world, which becomes increasingly important to them. Above all, they concentrate on their capacity to communicate with, to relate to, and to team up with those individuals who are most significant to them—their peers. A sense of accomplishment for having done well in the midst of peers, being the strongest, best, wittiest, or fastest are the successes which count.

Their society hints that their very handling of the ongoing situation will determine their future. They sense that if they prove their skills within the areas of their greatest competence, their successful future will be assured. Thus, failures have to be warded off at almost any price. We have all seen children working feverishly to be able "to do it"—at least once—so they know they can. In trying to excel in anything and everything they try, children are not attempting any psychological or real elimination of others. On the contrary, children want and need the continued association and cooperation of others; but they need their contemporaries primarily for measuring their own skills and worth. They become particularly interested in the operations of the material world, which they try to translate in terms of their own social life. An example of the relationship between strength, skills, and social

power is the fact that children who excel in outdoor play or otherwise prove their dexterity in peer interactions are more likely to be
afforded prestige.

Play

In play, children rely upon their growing sense of the social
perspective. They incorporate real-life situations into play. The
two sexes tend to have separate play habits, although, upon occasion, they enter each other's worlds and participate in play which
is generally thought of and culturally assigned as particularly appropriate for the other sex. Nevertheless, the basic modalities related to psychosocial sex roles ultimately determine the major form
and content of an individual's play. As has been alluded to on
preceding pages, boys' and girls' play themes, especially their use
of the spatial fields, correspond to the male and female principles
in body construction. For instance, while boys tend to build ex-
terior scenes, girls tend to build interior ones. *(89a, 591; 380)* Beginning with puberty and the onset of adolescent values, what
once had been an industrious involvement in play slowly merges
into semiplayful activity and, eventually, an involvement in work.
Adolescents, as we shall see, tend to steer a middle course between
play and work; between childhood and adulthood.

Identification Formation

Child-parent relationships maintain a level of dependency in
areas where dependency is still necessary or desirable, while in
other areas, children tend to relate to their parents and other adults
on a more equal basis. Children begin to recognize that they must
eventually break with their accustomed family life. By this age,
they have overcome, temporarily at least, the power (Oedipal)
struggle. Since children see their caring persons as representatives
of the society in which they must operate, they now begin to
measure them against other representatives. Friends of their parents and parents of their friends assume a new importance.
Neighborhood and school become significant social determiners,
and strangers become intriguing and important discoveries. Other
adults also become sources of identification. Boys and girls will
identify with those aspects of people which are most meaningful
without necessarily considering the total personality or situation of
the person.

The world of peers assumes a position equally as important as
that of adults. Peers are needed for self-esteem and to provide
criteria for the measurement of one's own success or failure.
Among peers, the child finds another source of extrafamilial identification. Interestingly, siblings are no longer significant com-

petitors unless they happen to be members of the pe
"Nobody to play with" is a common complaint of chil\
developmental age group even though they might be s\
by brothers and sisters. After all they are just "sibs."

As children develop, society seems to become more ar\
concerned with admitting them on an equal basis; s\
churches, and youth organizations encourage them toward \ .e
advanced participation. The focus has shifted, then, from dependence upon the parent as the child's major influence, to dependence upon social institutions. As in each previous and subsequent phase, the child becomes a very different person. To quote
Erikson, the child becomes "a person with increased cognitive
capacities and a much greater ability to interact with a much wider
range of people in whom he is interested, whom he understands,
and who react to him." (128, 26)

Erikson stresses that many of the individual's later attitudes
toward work and work habits can be traced to the degree of success with which a sense of industry has been fostered during this
phase. For young people, the basic technology for doing their job
arises from native abilities that allow the development of those
skills prized by their culture. For example, a stress upon the virtue
of skilled craftsmanship lays the roots for later scientific or other
painstaking pursuits.

In acquiring a sense of industry and in fending off a sense of
inferiority children must find their sense of competence while accepting, though with misgivings, their limitations. During this
time, young people are frequently described as being "too big for
their boots." They devote their abundant energies to improving
their *capacity* to deal effectively with people and things. Their
drive to succeed includes an awareness of both the threat of failure
and the management of failure. Above all, young people experience an urge to work harder to succeed, because any halfway
measure, any mediocrity, will lead them too close to a sense of
inferiority, a feeling they must both combat and accept as a fact of
life in order to move on with self-assurance toward their
adulthood.

Phase V: Acquiring a Sense of Identity
While Overcoming a Sense of Identity
Diffusion—a Realization of Fidelity

"A sense of identity means a sense of being at one with oneself
as one grows and develops; and it means a sense of affinity with a
community's sense of being at one with its future as well as its
history—or mythology." (73, 21–22) This Eriksonian definition
more likely specifies identity for the adolescent as perceived and

by the adult world. For the adolescent, a sense of identity carries with it a sense of mastery of childhood issues. It also implies a genuine readiness to face the challenges of the adult community as a potential equal. Identity development is closely linked with the mastery of skills. Competence without conviction is, to be sure, no more than a form of slavery to facts;conviction without competence is also less than liberation. (73, 105) Competence with conviction concerning one's place and purpose allows for a self-chosen form of being.

Just as the quality of trust qualifies how infants branch out into new childhood experiences, so an individual's identity formation is instrumental in creating the quality of the decisions and commitments the individual will make as an adult. This includes the degree of investment in the choice of work and in the work itself, personal alliances, and the degree of mutuality and involvement in one's community for the community's sake. It follows then that one's perception of oneself is reflected not only in a clinical context but also in a life context, in what one thinks, feels, and does about the minute as well as the major life choices.

It is timely that Erikson focuses more on identity evolvement than on other developmental factors; in fact, his writings made identity a household word. He is astutely aware of what a crucial concern identity formation was for him as an adopted child, an immigrant, and a professor who, although distinguished, was not academically established. Moreover, he reminds us that in Freud's day we saw how psychosexual energies were misspent. Presently, there are questions all over the world related to identy, on a personal level as well as on vocational, racial, and national levels. We cannot separate personal growth and communal change," to quote Erikson, "nor can we separate . . . the identity crisis in historical development because the two help define each other and are truly relative to each other." (87, 23, 28, 29) Identity formation is not only a developmental issue, it has also become a social issue for countries at times of change.

It is not surprising, as G. V. Coehlo and associates state, that "Erikson is widely read by adolescents themselves and, in part, has become a blueprint for them as well as parents, teachers, mental health professionals." His descriptions are apt to become prescriptions. (43, 104) "Identity consciousness then is a new edition of the original *doubt*, which concerned the trustworthiness of the training adults and the trustworthiness of the child himself. In adolescence, such self-conscious doubt concerns the reliability and reconcilability of the whole span of childhood which is now to be left behind." (104, 99) "Psychosocial identity is not feasible before and is indispensable after the end of adolescence." (109b, 61)

The young do not question who they are but rather what and in what context they can be and become. For identity one needs to be counted upon, as an accountable part of a larger whole. Identity is an individual *and* a communal issue. This has special relevance for young persons, especially for minorities whose share in and contribution to community life are primarily perceived as negative or absent. At this point of development the adolescent requires a personal and cultural identity.

Achieving a sense of identity as well as overcoming a sense of identity diffusion represents the polarity of this developmental phase. At one end, there is a striving toward an integration of inner and outer directions; at the opposite end, there is diffusion, leading to a sense of instability in the midst of many confusing inner and outer demands. This polarity must be solved within the span of adolescence if adulthood is not to be further complicated by a continuation of old struggles. Erikson, it must be noted, recognizes the wide variation between early and late adolescence. Yet, his formulation denotes no essential differentiation between such subphases. A certainty of one's place in the present and future assures individuals of their immediate confidence and their advance beyond the previous levels of development. Erikson quotes an aphorism posted at a western bar: "I ain't what I ought to be, I ain't what I'm going to be, but I ain't what I was." (*114*, 139)

A struggle over one's identity, or an identity crisis, is neither a fatal event nor a pathological condition, it is rather "an inescapable turning point for better or for worse." *Better* means a confluence of energies of the individual and his particular society (a state of "social actualness"); *worse* means a prolonged period of identity confusion for the young individual and divergent efforts invested by communal bodies. (*70*, 160) Identity confusion, in many ways, is a phenomenon of the second half of this century, just as "neurotic manifestations" were akin to personal dilemmas in life during the first half of this century. (*92*, 22)

As children physically mature into adulthood, they experience rapid body growth with important physiological and anatomical changes. Previous trust in their body and their mastery of its functions is suddenly shaken and must be regained by reevaluating themselves. They seek assurance from their peers who are also in a stage of change and seeking approval. Puberty rites and religious confirmation frequently serve as cultural seals of the individual's new status within the continuity of his developmental self, and specifically in the acknowledgment of the fact of maturation as a welcome event. Internal and external events validate bodily integrity and social order. The individual is assured of being at one with his or her world (*92*, 45) because a feeling of wholeness and self-consistency has to be coordinated with the ever-increasing perception of self as separate from others, despite, or on the basis of, ties with them. *(103)*

Major maturational changes invariably upset previous balances. The new physio-psychological forces, the Freudian id energies, have to be integrated. Earlier dormant strivings demand the fuller attention of the adolescent. Desire for sexual fulfillment can no longer be diverted as inappropriate or ridiculous. It is the adolescent and the communal mores which must contain these strivings and balance them within a different social matrix than in childhood. No longer confined to his or her dependent position within the family, the adolescent now has a dual arena: a family and a social world, as the arena for life's practices.

Acquisition of Social Status

Young adolescents experience a close attachment to their parents while they search for new and more satisfactory contacts in associations outside of the family. The relationship of parents and children is transitory, anchored solely in their joint past and their mutual anticipation of the youth's life based on their social and psychological history and their common belief in his future. Parents are eventually on a par with other significant adults in the adolescent's life.

Identity acquisition, and with it the inherent identity crisis, needs to be perceived and dealt with for its dual component. As already stated, it involves both an individual and a communal factor. Developmentally, as we saw earlier, young children see themselves, the caring person, and the world as one. At that point children live in a true community. At their very beginning, everything depends upon the way they are handled, the way they are cared for, all of which already expresses the community's style of life. In this arrangement, children are never alone; they are from the very beginning members of a community. *(126, 134)* Later, they learn to interact with more and more people at given times and they learn in which way they should relate to them. In this process they become individuals in and members of their community.

This progression from inherently belonging to the primary or familial community to becoming members in their own right is in many ways the story of early adolescent development; specifically, it is the theme of the struggle in the adolescent (or second) Oedipal phase. As explained previously, it is essentially a power struggle rather than a sexual one. Father and son, mother and daughter fight for control. Who is to control whom? *(126, 116)* Eventually, the struggle over membership rights and power status *within* the family gives way to a reaching out to control others beyond the family's spheres. In essence, the drama of the Oedipal triangle can be reinterpreted as a struggle of the haves and the have-not-yets.

In adolescence, the individual gradually establishes a synthesis of his past, present, and future. It can be denoted as a period of self-standardization in the search for identity as an adolescent and as a member of a sexual group, an age group, and a community.

Role Selection and Role Diffusion

The youth's search for a sense of self implies a commitment to specific roles selected from many alternatives, because identification with a special person (ego ideal) no longer serves its full usefulness. At this period of life, young people integrate all previous identifications. Their gradual but full integration comprises an ego identity. They then realize their fidelity to their new position as persons in their ultimate psychosocial ethnic and communal spheres. Only in adolescence, as we saw with Piaget's cognitive formulations, can individuals reverse a sequence of events in their minds, so that it becomes clear why what *did* happen *had* to happen, and feel out their choices among a permutation of choices. (86, 63) They find promise for an expanded future with the aid of a more universal identity.

Adolescents, as part of their development, are faced with continued identity diffusion concerning their own potentialities and their prospective place within their society. The question of this phase, "Who am I to be?" continues to be ever present. The adolescent continuously faces a hierarchy of positive and negative elements. Previously, these were really not alternatives, because in order not to be "bad" he had to be "good." Now, he comprehends, masters, and can feel that he can be somewhat bad and still be good. As a child he had been "warned not to become what he has no intention of becoming so that he can learn to anticipate what he must avoid." (70, 155) As an adolescent he has to verify the consequences in order to test the proposition. The alternatives and choices for the adolescents are vast, and every combination has a road ahead. It is no wonder that adolescents, in their sense of diffusion, periodically beg others to tell them what to do and then protest that it wasn't the proper suggestion. How can they choose or be told what the proper behavior or action is when there are so many?

Many an adolescent is apt to solve this dilemma by becoming deviant, choosing the identity opposite to the one society suggests, in preference to remaining a nonentity. Negative identity reflects "a desperate attempt to regain some mastery in a situation in which available positive identity elements cancel each other out." (104, 88) In many ways, negative identity is not only an individual solution; it is also an effective step in breaking up the status quo of communal standards. Many characteristics of the hippie of 1967 can also be found in the conventional youth of 1976. Contrary to their society's expectations, their happenings became their society's happenings.

The foregoing observations on negative identity crises are particularly relevant for our contemporary societal dilemmas. In this country's recent history, themes such as assertiveness, black, native, and other ethnic power, stay-ins, female equality, and "We Shall Overcome," a moving song of the sixties, have spoken to the inaudibility, invisibility, namelessness, and facelessness of the young in their communities. (87, 25–27) In order to bring about change, the Black Power movement created a separate, or negative, identity. This allowed individuals, the community, and eventually the society to identify with it and be admitted.[20] The formation of such a negative identity can be part of the process of individual or communal adaptation, but it can also accentuate alienation. When such alienation separates the young, not only from society, but also from the self, it is particularly acute.

The Concept of a Moratorium

Adolescence extends childhood by a legitimate delay of adulthood status. Social institutions grant a period of grace, a moratorium for selected individuals who need to delay or momentarily slow down their development into adults, by providing extended formal education, apprenticeship, military conscription, internship, etc. The concept of a moratorium is "at worst, a no-man's-land between childhood and maturity, and at best, a normal time of sports and horseplay, of gangs and cliques and parties." (65, 298) The moratorium sanctions identity diffusion as a temporary pivotal component of adolescent development. Erikson writes:

> A moratorium is a period of delay [of entry into adulthood]. Here I mean delay of adult commitments, and yet not only a delay. I mean a period that is characterized by a selective permissiveness on the part of society and of provocative playfulness on the part of youth; and yet also a period of deep (if often transitory) commitment on the part of youth and ceremonial acceptance of commitment on the part of society. Such moratoria show highly individual variations, which are especially pronounced in the very gifted (gifted for better or for worse); and there are, of course, institutional variations linked with the ways of life of cultures and subcultures. (78, 5)

[20] Credit to Mark Shifflette for these observations in his discussions with me on the relationship of Erikson's formulations to developments in countercultural groups.

Thus, individuals require time to find themselves and their integration into consistently acting, thinking, and feeling persons as part of their adolescent development, and society grants them this time. The young experiment with patterns of identity before they have to come to a more complete decision. A true moratorium provides leeway for timeless values and removes the pressure of time, but it must end eventually. (108, 157) Each of the following seven areas represents a partial polarization of developmental crises on the developmental continuum during a moratorium. (78; 85; 91)

1. *Time Perspective vs. Time Diffusion.* A concept of time is essential to identity. If the time perspective of young people is a problem, they may either demand immediate action or immobilize themselves completely, in the desperate hope that time will stand still and that feared disappointment will then never materialize. (392) Intermittently, adolescents utilize opportunities to delay planning or to recall the past. Only when they can see their life in a definite perspective does their sense of time lead to a sense of full identity.
2. *Self-certainty vs. Apathy.* Self-certainty involves a struggle between identity consciousness and an escape into apathy. Adolescents, may convey an air either of stark vanity regarding their appearance, as if it were all that mattered, or else callousness, as if it were of no consequence. Only when their awareness of self and the impressions they convey to others are congruent do they gain certainty of self and a sense of their own identity. Meanwhile self-consciousness, with its attendant feelings of doubt and confusion about oneself and one's autonomy, recedes.
3. *Role Experimentations vs. Negative Identity.* While the developing child finds many opportunities to experiment with various roles, adolescents find experimentation critical, and qualified by dangers and commitments. Interests in extremes and experiments with opposites, especially those frowned upon by elders, become the center of their role experimentations with their self-images. Eventually, positive or negative identity will depend upon successful experimentation with a wide range of roles.
4. *Anticipation of Achievement vs. Work Paralysis.* Adolescents bring their sense of industry to bear in a persistent pattern, in preference to unrelated situational opportunities. A struggle to complete a task, or sometimes even to start one at all, becomes a crucial issue as youths ponder their sense of the adequacy of their own equipment. "It does not usually betoken lack of ability; in fact [at times], some of the most gifted suffer from it most extremely." (78, 3) Persistency and integration of work capabilities are essential for forging a work readiness and for making plans.
5. *Sexual Identity vs. Bisexual Diffusion.* Adolescents move toward resolving bisexual conflicts and, eventually, toward feeling identification with their own sex role. They need to experience comfort in their range of contacts with members of the same as well as the opposite sex. They need to see themselves first as wholly male or female. Adolescence furnishes situations and attitudes for con-

tinued experimentations and for resolutions which are needed if a
sexual identity is to contribute toward a fuller identity and toward
behavior prescribed by the relevant culture as appropriate adult
sexual activity.

6. *Leadership Polarization vs. Authority Diffusion.* Adolescents' capacity
   to lead and follow coincides with the authority index of their society. A realistically clear appraisal of authority and a readiness to be
   in authority if called upon are closely linked with the successful
   mastery of previous developmental phases and with the eventual
   acceptance of a positive identity.

7. *Ideological Polarization vs. Diffusion of Ideals.* Adolescents are on their
   way to selecting a basic philosophy, ideology, or religion, which
   will provide an anchoring trust in life and society. Adolescence
   affords many choices. However, "adolescents tend to be uncom-
   promising in their prejudices and belligerently loyal to their own
   group's ideas and values. This being against something is one of
   their greatest needs, for through contrasting themselves and their
   ideas with an opposite group's, they firm up their sense of themselves." (78, 4)

Adolescents have the opportunity to utilize the additional time
during a moratorium to work on these seven areas. The "extremes
of *subjective experience,* alternatives of *ideological choice,* and potentialities of *realistic commitment* can become the subject of social
play and of joint mastery." (104, 119) In the light of rapidly changing standards in contemporary society, a moratorium allows and
also enhances social change, as the youth doesn't have to reify the
conditions of the adult's world. Added time allows a greater likelihood for breaking with rather than being engulfed by one's developmental continuum.

A moratorium sometimes fails when individuals have defined
themselves too early and are committed to adult society before
they are ready or when they have strong feelings of inadequacy
from being left to the uncertainty of their developmental period
and their time for an eventual progression in development. They
will find themselves fully at a loss as to who they actually are, who
they want to be, and who they are in the eyes of others.

Speech

In an adolescent's life, speech often merely reflects thinking
aloud. (184) The adolescent habit of talking things over endlessly
with a special friend within the age group is one means of searching for a comfortable position for one's identity. Once an identity
commitment is made, speech goes beyond communication; it also
serves as a commitment to social values in tune with one's identity. This is not too different from our everyday life experience.
When we meet a new acquaintance, we want to hear what the
person does, how he does what he does, and what it really means
to the person.

Play

Play loses importance as a major developmental function. The youth no longer has to play at being important. He or she is now more apt to find himself playing at being younger as an outlet for dealing with earlier life issues because society frowns on childish play behavior at his or her age. A teenager will play with enthusiasm with younger children for the joy of interactions as well as for a chance to play. Erikson sees role playing excursions into fantasy in adolescence as an appropriate handling of identity diffusion. The "I dare you" and "I dare myself" variety of play is a form of social play and a legitimate successor to childhood play. *(75)* "In the healthy adolescent, a great capacity for phantasy is matched by ego mechanisms that permit him to go far into dangerous regions of phantasy or social experiment and to catch himself at the last moment and divert himself in company, in activity, in literature or music." *(78, 13)* This play is a social experimentation with attitudes and roles of adult significance— occupational behavior, preparation for communal life, the selection of intimate associates, etc.

Play moves more and more into those areas of life where it counts such as babysitting, sport, or time out for play. Moreover, close friendship, gangs, cliques, and crowd behavior, with its insistence upon rituals and loyalty for the members of the group, involve a basic aspect of role playing and an urge for in-group (minisocietal) norms.

Relationship Selection

Youths will select significant adults who have come to mean most to them through past influence or ongoing pivotal relationships. Adults from the past might include parents, teachers, neighbors, and other familiar persons. The ongoing pivotal relationships are selected for their meaning in the adolescent's temporary role diffusion rather than for their societal functions. Teachers, social workers, bosses, psychologists, priests, judges, recruiting officers, play managers, dance instructors, or any individuals to whom the youth might turn in his or her search for close adult relationships can become influential persons in adolescent development, if they are acceptable to the youth.

The role of parents as the essential supports and value givers is now shared with peers, who are age mates and partners. Compatible partnership with and among age mates began in previous phases and is an essential component in this one. Peers stand as intermediaries in the society, where the adolescent must eventually find his or her inner identity and the continuity of this identity and become a cooperating partner, a person with a place, a social career, and some kind of a perception of a future.

A Normative Crisis

The crisis of this phase involves making a choice compatible with oneself and with the opportunities of one's society. For society, the crisis involves extending sufficient time, space, and social freedom to adolescents without denying its ultimate range of control and guidance over them. Actually, in spite of the apparent discrepancies between the standards and aims of the young and those of their society, there is little danger of them deviating too far from communal social norms. Much of their efforts are directed toward the clarification of their role as a member of their society. Adolescence constitutes not an affirmative but a normative crisis. "In youth, then, the [individual's] life history intersects with history; here individuals are confirmed in their identities, societies regenerated in their life style." (122, 23) Youth crises intersect, aggravate, as well as heal the tensions of the time. (108, 154)

The normative crisis of our times takes on a new dimension. In one way adolescents are transitory in their existence, and existentialists by nature. They can become intensely involved in acute contemporary conflicts, which they isolate both from all historical antecedents and commitments for the future. (128, 39) Love-ins, be-ins, crash-ins, happenings all require the ingredient of immediate intense involvement without commitment to the consequences. Conversely, social alienation and the isolation of drugs or pot represent an avoidance or, at best, a delay of intimacy. Society's struggling experience with youth complicates but is also an ingredient of the development of youth. The unique developmental experience of contemporary youth undoubtedly affects their subsequent development. In Erikson's words, "we are witnessing a situation where youths sport identity confusion very openly and almost mockingly, for they prefer to find their own way to new ethical commitments." (128, 38)

Societal and Cultural Anchorage

The individual slowly moves into society as a unit and as a member of a unit in his or her own right. Individuals create and continue to establish their communal membership. They abandoned a stark dependency on family two phases ago; they now require full status alongside their peers in the society. The youth's gradual growth and transformation make sense to others, and others begin to make sense to the youth. Youths find increasingly new and more inclusive identifications, whether they are with peers, neighborhood, school, work, play group, or a kindred mind. (122) Their new identity is anchored, first, in their new sense of reality and new way of experiencing unified events; second, through the factuality of fully observable actual data and processes; third, via their new way of relating; and fourth on the basis of chance—the grace of intertwining time, place, and social context with each individual involved. That is, reality + factuality + actuality + chance = identity. (73, 33)

Adolescents both mock and long for the cultural image of adulthood. Their previous trust and anchorage in their culture's environment and their understanding of themselves as creative units in it set the tone for their ultimate level of participation in the adult realm. Young people find themselves as they find their commonality. Whenever these foundations have not solidified, there is the danger that their elders will assign them an identity which was only a part of them in their identity diffusion. In such instances, society may stamp them as deviant, poor worker, clown, delinquent, misfit, superathlete, brain, Mr. or Ms. Clean, etc., even though the individual might have only temporarily maintained such a special identity. Erikson quotes a character from a Faulkner novel: "It ain't none of us pure crazy and ain't none of us pure sane until the balance of us talks him that-a-way." (124, 43) At no other phase of the life cycle, then, are the promise of finding oneself and the threat of losing oneself in society so closely allied. (122)

The young also look to their culture's heritage, ideology, and religion as a confirmed source of trust. Religion and social heritage provide perspective and counteract the surge for an autonomous and individual identity. The young search for something and somebody to be true. They represents a "bewildering combination of shifting devotion and sudden perversity, sometimes more devotedly perverse, sometimes more perversely devoted." (122, 6) Above all, the oscillating experiences assure genetic continuity of one's identity and self-esteem as a member of one's society and culture—the integration of the two-way pull: to be and not to be a part of one's society. (75) A sense of identity assures individuals a definite place within their own corner of society. The young find their fidelity.[21] He finds "progressive continuity between that which he has come to be during the long years of childhood and that which he promises to become in the anticipated future; between that which he conceives himself to be and that which he perceives others to see in him and to expect of him." (117, 165)

Identity formation "is a continuous process with a special crisis in youth." It is a developmental and a "dialectical process." (126, 109) Toward the end of adolescence the youth is forming "a sense of identity" firm and informed enough to permit him to act. This requires "enough experience to acknowledge the power of facts

---

[21] *Fidelity* is a word Erikson adroitly applies since 1961 in his accounts of identity development.

and the facts of power; enough practical idealism to attach infantile ideals to live persons and issues; and enough rebellious commitment to the future to leave behind some of the internalized debt of infantile guilt." (73, 72–73) Identity development is psychological and social. Identity development moves from the reality of being to the reality of becoming—a very contemporary preoccupation. This perspective, in contrast to the earlier childhood wish, constitutes a desire to become in order to be. (92, 18–19)

Phase VI: Acquiring a Sense of Intimacy and Solidarity and Avoiding a Sense of Isolation —a Realization of Love

As young adults, individuals become full members in our western society. They are asked to settle down seriously to the task of full participation in the community. This period is a time to enjoy life with adult liberty and responsibility. For Erikson, psychological adulthood entails continued development. Developmental energies are invested in the search and pursuit of career, work, and love. Career extends from intimate relationships between individuals, to investment through study and labor, to social participation as a citizen.

The major developmental theme now involves psychological readiness and a commitment to mutual intimacy in the partnership of marriage or its alternatives. Readiness includes the ability and willingness to share mutual trust, to regulate cycles of work, procreation, and recreation for each partner's fullest and most self-satisfying participation in society. In this phase a foundation is prepared for the couple's own life and the lives of others. To find a sense of solidarity in choosing a partner, usually of the opposite sex, is a difficult undertaking. The young adult has to overcome inclinations for safe social distances, for repudiation of others, and for destroying those who may become potentially close. (87, 136)[22] Fears of closeness are exchanged with feelings of social emptiness and of being an isolated unit within a world of intimate friendships and family units. Young men and women need to experience an intimate oneness with their society lest they experience isolation. The essential developmental task for this phase is to maintain and further "individual identity in joint intimacy." (111, 159)

In the worlds of work and of love career efforts are directed toward improving and interpreting patterns of cooperation, with varying allowances for competition and for each person's individuation. While graduation from adolescence requires a sense of identity, graduation from the first phase of adulthood requires

---

[22] In a 1968 publication, Erikson states that early adulthood denotes a crisis of intimacy versus "distantiation." (87, 136)

finding a sense of *shared* identity. The solidarity of the marriage or partnership is an evolutionary and individual achievement of the selectivity of sexual love for "mutual verification through an experience of finding oneself, as one loses oneself, in another." (*111*, *158*) Intimacy involves a balance between giving to others and maintaining oneself. (*357*, *31*) Young adults' energies are directed toward success in the assigned tasks of their work—avocations and hobbies included.

Erikson suggests that men and women are alike in their capacity for a career in work, partnership, and citizenry. Yet, woman's modalities in relating themselves to these aspects of life are different from men's. Technical advances have made a difference in political and social norms, so that women have been brought into life spheres beyond the former boundaries of homemaker, husband-keeper, and mother. Women are entering fields previously perceived as "for men only"—political sciences, engineering, truck driving, and executive functions, for example—and thus integrating females and males into these pheres of the work world. (*389*)[23]

Phase VII: Acquiring a Sense of Generativity and Avoiding a Sense of Self-absorption —a Realization of Care

Establishing a new unit based upon mutual trust and intimacy includes the preparation of a new cycle of development within a new generational unit. A secure adulthood serves as the foundation for assuring care for the new generation—the theme of the second developmental phase of adulthood. It should be noted that *generativity* does not refer to the procreating individuals, but to the care they provide as a unit in society at large to the next generation so that it can also find hope, virtue, and wisdom. It is the period in life when individuals are productive in work or leisure to satisfy themselves and, at times, people beyond their own family bounds.[24]

A sense of generativity includes parental or communal responsibility for society's efforts and interests in supporting child care, education, the arts, the sciences, and the traditions which are to nurture the newly developing individual's life span. Each individual's life involves care for his or her generation and for the next.

[23] Lois E. Whitman made this author aware in her research paper on Erikson's adult developmental tasks that Erikson speaks much more to and about women than this author had noted. (*389*) A woman undoubtedly would have written quite a different book from the one written by this author.

[24] The individuals whose lives Erikson chose to study for their generativity were all in their generative phase when they broke forth: Ghandi *(82)*, Luther *(120)*, and Jefferson *(73)*. Erikson himself was forty-eight when his first and major book *Childhood and Society (65)* was originally published.

Full adults are able to take care of what they care to be and who they care to be with. (*126*, 125) The personal ideational life and the community life become one, unless self-absorption drains the person's energy and estranges the individual and his or her efforts from the community. Each adult accepts or rejects the challenge of responsibility for the next generation and for assuring this new generation the trust it requires for its development.

Phase VIII: Acquiring a Sense of Integrity
and Avoiding a Sense of Despair
—a Realization of Wisdom

Finally, as adults witness the development of a new generation, they gain a fuller perspective of their own cycle. They develop a sense of integrity by an assured reliance on others' integrity. Thus, the first developmental theme evolves into the final one, while the final theme clearly has its roots in the first one.

Integrity rests upon an acceptance of the collective and individual life cycles of human beings as "something that has to be and that, by necessity, permitted no substitutions: It thus means a new, different love of one's parents. It is a comradeship with the ordering ways of distant times and different pursuits." (*65*, 232) If in old age one prefers not to be what one was not meant to be, one has found a sense of integrity. A sense of integrity includes overcoming a sense of despair, a sense of disgust at certain life styles, and a fear of death as the end of a never complete life.

In this final phase, one often finds wisdom and a philosophy of life which extends beyond one's own life cycle to future developmental cycles. Erikson best describes this phase when he accounts for Ghandi in his later years as manifesting a sense of integrity:

> Ghandi . . . *straight, and yet not stiff; shy, and yet not withdrawn; fearful, and yet determined; intelligent, and yet not bookish; willful, and yet not stubborn; sensual, and yet not soft; all of which adds up to an integrity that is, in essence, unexplainable, and without which no evaluation holds.*
> (81, 633)

With a faith and trust in generations, Erikson says, "healthy children will not fear life, if their parents have integrity enough not to fear death." (*65*, 233)

CONTEMPORARY AMERICAN ISSUES AND THEIR INFLUENCES ON DEVELOPMENT

Erikson addresses himself to a number of distinctly culture-bound developmental issues that are of particular importance to the child and family in contemporary America.

1. Identity

Rapid changes in societal norms and conditions *(193; 194a)* are linked with Erikson's preoccupation with social trends and their historical moments. Our moving times shift the accreditation of membership, be it social, ethnic, national, or even familial, to one earned not so much by one's birth rights (ascription) as by one's own contributions (acquisition). Erikson, considering his own history, observes: "One can become an American to some extent in one's own lifetime even if one started elsewhere. And once an American, one has to continue becoming an American even if he was one at the beginning." *(99, 136)*

The concept of identity becomes especially important in a country and in a time of change. *(128, 29)* Identity lends anchorage and direction to a person when guiding images and ego ideals cease to be historic facts. At a time of rapid change, the authority which counts is the one who can prove his or her competence at the moment, rather than the one who has been tested through the ages. *(194a)* This means that personal development finds its direction less from old heroes and time-proven practices than from contemporaries and timely happenings. For child-rearing it means that children will be more conscious of what parents *do* than what they did when they were the child's age. The reality of the present rather than the ego ideal, the encounter of parent as quasi-peer rather than as Oedipal elder (discussed earlier in this chapter) makes the struggle not of ages but of the age. It is the age of a new reality, based on the actuality of the present and on the factuality of one's personal strength, resources, and capability to perform and find receptiveness for one's performance. The latter emphasizes the mutual constructive interchange between the individual and his or her environment.

The contemporary concern for the environment and the maintenance of nature's balance is, then, as much a developmental as a social issue. Identity formation is as much rooted in the conditions of the time as ongoing conditions are shaped by the generation of the time. Eriksonian identity reflects and determines the making of history. *(73, 16)* These factors are well exemplified by the changes in the historic Uncle Sam recruiting posters. Uncle Sam no longer *tells young men* that they ought to join him; rather he *asks men and women* for an opportunity to join them.

2. Affect Development

Affect development is life betwixt alternatives, a course between polarities. In fact, Erikson presents us with a dialectical formulation concerning the coexistence of opposites in human strivings which is, essentially, very much akin to the American culture of opposites *(65)* and contradictions. *(126)* Americans in the

United States live with two sets of truths: It is a child-centered nation which, nevertheless, has a tolerance for child abuse and neglect. (165) Two other contradictory American values are "respect a person's point of view" and "give them hell—tell them what you really think—it's a free country!"

Erikson's strong appeal to the youth of the late sixties can be attributed, in part, to his dialectical thinking. In affective development, especially for youth, opposing desires coexist. Erikson perceives affective development (1) as parallel and congruent with the dual expectations of our society and its cultures; (2) as essentially meeting contradictory demands (phasal alternatives); and (3) as simultaneously responding to the push and pull requirements of both progressive development and maintenance (phasal change). Just as American culture insists that a multicultural approach to child-rearing should be the national standard, so the individual also has many alternatives for his or her personality development. To be a "real American" is to be different from others, but true to oneself.

As stated, opposing poles have a seductive quality; both pulls can be met, usually if one is in the service of the other. A reliance upon secure dependence, call it Eriksonian trust, always incorporates leeway for independence, that is, for doubting and secure mistrust. Conversely, extended mistrust always implies submitting oneself mistrustingly to dependent trust situations. This incorporation of opposing stances is not only inherent in our interpersonal relations, it is also characteristic of our social norms. We see in this decade a stress upon accountability, but we also see a questioning of norm-setting systems. The incorporation of countercultures as essential components of our culture is another illustration from our conflicted contemporary American scene. Everyone, and society as a whole, has a set of self-images which serve a person as models to strive for and another set of images as models to avoid. The individual and society always need both; human development, especially identity formation, always involves an interplay of these factors. (126, 110) The reason society tolerates some individuals who commit undesirable acts, and some who toy in various degrees with the idea of committing them, is so that each individual can effectively deal with the avoidance of such behavior, feelings, or thoughts.

Dialectically, each phase in a way opposes and in a way incorporates, and always reaches beyond, that which was before. The solution to any one struggle, situational or developmental, generates a stage for the next dilemma and struggle. Each individual is simultaneously and persistently faced with the satisfaction of doing and the frustration of not doing the task at hand.

3. Child Rearing

Child-rearing in the northern segment of the Americas is a major enterprise. Nowhere do individual infants receive so much recognition and so much opportunity to experiment with all the facets of life. They can be active and wait; laugh and scream; love and reject; endear and separate; remember and experience over again; and, above all, integrate all of that experience as genuine and essential for a full life later on.

The very fact that early childhood development receives so much attention makes the American infant also into a "model of all oppression and enslavement." As in all colonization, the child in its dependency accepts the master's world, while the masters believe that without them the child cannot live and without their sacrificial help the child would become prey to all the fears the adult world fears for itself. (126, 52) "We see," to quote Erikson, "the suppression of badness in children related to the repression of what is unacceptable in ourselves and the oppression of people deemed inferior." (212, 85). At the same time, the investment in child development brings forth an immense treasure of knowledge and a sense of inquiry about child development which renders child development into human development.

4. Adolescence

Erikson's special preoccupation with adolescent development, particularly his concepts on identity formation and the moratorium from early adult commitments, are very contemporary phenomena on the American scene. American life tends to be open for experimentation with new roles and values. In fact, its tendency to continuously delay national commitments while attempting to solve all the world's crises is adolescent in character.

Identity formation "is a continuous process with a special crisis in youth" (126, 100) and one which has unique meaning within our contemporary arena where each individual, adolescent, youth, and adult evaluates and reevaluates what he or she cares to do and cares to be. (73)

Adolescence and the adolescent moratorium are nowhere as universally accepted as within the American cultures. Fluctuating attitudes toward authority are not only adolescent ones, they are also strictly American attitudes. Moreover, the American adolescent tends to have a composite father and mother image, made up of many figures. In fact, parents and children identify jointly with some of the same idols. Furthermore, mood swings are apt to focus more on peers than on the family, because at this point of development, it is largely in the peer group where questions pertaining to the family are tackled.

> *Likewise at times . . . when rapid social and technological change breaks down many traditional values, it may be difficult for young people to find continuity between what they learned and experienced as children and what they learn and experience as adolescents. At such times young people often seek "causes" that give their lives meaning and direction. The activism of the [immediate past] generation of young people may well stem, in part at least, from this search.* (58, 92)[25]

Adolescent, youth, and adult are presently working together on new guidelines for their expectations of each other. Individuals alone and with others review those qualities which they care to have, both in work situations and in private life.

5. Young Adulthood

Erikson recognizes the most recent special situation of young adults, or older adolescents, in specific articles devoted to their dilemma. (63; 73; 87; 90; 92; 93; 94; 95; 108; 118; 122) Yet, his scheme, like the actual life situation of these youth, has no real place for them. He locates them as society sees them, either on both sides or on neither side of the aisle. Youths vote as adult citizens yet in certain states they are concurrently denied access to such adult institutions as taverns, bars, clubs, elected offices, and important positions.

Even if Erikson has not altered his eight-phase developmental ladder, his writings imply that the young are beyond the adolescence struggle for identity of phase 5 but not yet in phase 6 where the young adult finds solidarity with the generations of the adult world. They are struggling with acquiring a sense of individuation while avoiding a sense of standardization and working on the validation of the self. Most likely another interim phase, a youth phase, is emerging.

6. The Family in the U.S.A.

Point 4 below alluded to a shift in authority alignments within the family. Concomitant with this shift, the process of decision-making has changed from one of a hierarchical down-the-line chain of command to a more parliamentary process of temporary coalitions of family members for their particular interests. With a lessening of reliance upon the tradition of the elders of the family, which was once the major cultural regulator, the family tends to depend more and more upon *mutual* regulation. (194a) Family members tend to see to it that no one pressure group is eliminated by any combination of others. Family members are tolerant of different interests because "nobody can be sure he is right, but everybody must compromise for the sake of his future." (65, 277).

In the American culture, the family group has lost its importance as a regulator of family standards. It lacks control from within because each family member seeks autonomy and substitutes authority from outside the family. In the contemporary family unit, the child is seen as the adult's quasi partner. In the American family unit, especially the white middle-class one, the rights of each individual member, adult and child alike, are guarded against domination by any other member or group of members (parents, children, older children, grandparents, males, females, etc.) Put another way, mutual regulation is aimed toward self-preservation rather than family preservation.

These recent changes in the family structure and family roles, intertwined with the altering perceptions of sex roles (more fully discussed below), have created decisive changes in the psychological positions of father, mother, husband, and wife in the family. Father along with mother has not only become a child-caring parent to *all* the children (rather than merely to first born son(s) as in earlier American families); he has also entered the family as a co-homemaker and a spouse to the wife. These recent changes place mothers and fathers in a new position for which they have neither a prototype nor an image of their own. Rapid change suggests to the parent that he does not want to be like his own parent. He cannot turn to his parents for advice and support on questions of child rearing and family matters. So he turns to fellow parents, the journals, and family therapists.

7. Sexuality

The activities of men and women have changed, both in the family and in other spheres of our daily lives. Since World War II, men have been more and more ready to admit their bisexual tendencies and to pursue interests such as child care, homemaking, culinary arts, and hobbies once thought of as for women only. More recently, women, with their accent on liberation, have learned to insist upon their rights and opportunities for equal access to roles, occupations, and strata of life that were once for men only.

At a time when sex roles and power alignments between the sexes are in a state of flux, any person who analyzes, explains, or publishes accounts of either sex is apt to be in hot water. Erikson, like most analysts and psychologists of his time and before him, studied mankind primarily as *male*kind. His perspective is all male and so are his clinical subjects (65, chapters I and III) and his historical subjects (Hitler, Gorky, Shaw, Luther, Gandhi, Newton,

Jefferson). The content of his research on human development, however, includes both sexual differentiation and human bisexuality. No doubt, his writings reflect the male bias and dominance of his and, in fact, this author's era. Regarding sexism, all of us who lived before the era of liberation can be critiqued for errors in our perception, scholarship, and attitude.

How did Erikson perceive the essence of maleness and femaleness? How did these perceptions change? Erikson, throughout his writings, tried to underscore as equal but different the life experience of males and females. (65; 66; 72; 85; 89; 89a; 103; 107; 112; 115a; 119) The author says "tried" because from the viewpoint of today, life was not equal; it was strictly oriented toward the male. Within his time, however, Erickson was considered scholarly and logical, and he was appraised as clinically sound and objective. Erikson accepted Freud's dictum that "anatomy is destiny," (212) but he came to grips with contemporary findings that anatomy's destiny is more defined by the culture's evaluations of the anatomy than the anatomy's designation of its destiny. In other words, it is not that the woman's menarcheal blood release renders her weak but rather that cultural perceptions of her as weakened result in her being treated as periodically weak and in need of protection. Erikson alters Freud's "anatomy is destiny" (which Freud adapted from Napoleon's "history is destiny") and postulates that "personality is destiny," since "we live in a "somatic," "social," and "personal" order. It is the perceptual conflict of these three which make human destiny." (212, 87) Social role and status are ideological and politically created. A role provides leeway within which the bodily constitution can sustain, social structure can make workable the tasks at hand and personality formation can integrate social expectations. (119, 330) "Equal opportunity for women, then, can only mean the right and the chance to give new meaning and new kind of competence to 'male' occupations." (119, 331)

Erikson's formulation establishes a person's experience of life as being basically influenced by his or her bodily experience. A person's life style is influenced by the experience of living life in an ambulatory or stationary fashion; the size, shape, and weight of the body; the reactive powers of the body; and the body's sexual makeup and functions. Spatial sense and disposition to procreation and life is influenced (in both sexes) by the experience of the growing body's build and function. "In women," to quote Erikson, "the sexual and procreative experience of an 'inner bodily space' is central both in personality development and social role." (212, 87) "The sexual and procreative orientation becomes and remains . . . a significant aspect of existence in space." (119, 327)

Anatomical and physiological differences do have an impact on life style and perspective. Female and male relate themselves differently and complementarily to the issues and tasks of life. Erikson asks that all tasks and positions be open to the different potential contributions of any sex. The two sexes counterpoint differences as they share sameness; (119, 331) However, each tries to imitate and compensate for the mode of the other. (119, 327)

> "Each sex overdeveloped what was given. . . . Each sex compensates for what it had to deny . . . ; thus each managed to get special approbation for a divided self-image—and to what oppressor and oppressed . . . colluded with each other in enslaving each other and themselves—these are the deals which men and women have to learn to study and to discuss." (119, 335)

Erikson acknowledges his severe critics. (201; 312; 362) First, he sympathizes with and applauds their thrust for equality but questions the accuracy of their study and of their comprehension regarding the ideas of his which are under attack; (92; 119) Secondly, Erikson states that his basic premise is and has been that there are male and female modalities above and beyond cultural imprinting, a contention he tries to verify in his current research on boys' and girls' play configurations. His earlier findings on sex differences in play behavior were also recently tested by Robert Wambach, whose findings—to his research sponsors' surprise—upheld Erikson's earlier data. (380) An awareness of these differences between the sexes, combined with equal opportunities for women and men, can provide a new meaning of competence in formerly "male" or "female" occupations. "At the end, only a renewal of social creativity can liberate both men and women from reciprocal roles which, in fact, have exploited both." (119, 331) Thirdly, in his more recent work, Erikson reformulates his analytical thinking so that, for culturally impacted affect development, culture constitutes destiny. Whether Erikson has changed or whether, because of the women's liberation movement and other contemporary events, he was challenged to make his position clear remains open for debate. He questions analysis which prejudicially suggests what a woman cannot be and cannot have instead of considering what she is, has been, and may yet become. (86, 64) In one of his rare critiques of his master's thinking, he points out that Freud's "judgment of the identity of women was probably the weakest part of his theory." (128, 43)

Most interestingly, his questions and challenges occurred before he came under major attack by the women's liberation press. His premise has consistently been that a person is as much a creator as a specimen of his time. No matter who or what furthered these changes, it is likely, in the words of Erikson that "modern life may come to permit a much freer inter-identification of the sexes in everyday life." (119, 333)

8. Minorities

The contemporary awareness of and struggle over the uneven position of minorities in this country and efforts to build a more equitable multicultural nation are closely linked with the form of child development that is allowed and that is willed upon reared and rearing persons. Erikson reminds us that minorities such as the American natives or the African blacks are a thousand years older than the prevailing culture.[26] It is not a minority's differentiation from the model culture but the contributions, of individuals which count, particularly in bringing their culture's historical heritage to the prevailing mode.

For minority groups, a parent's lot and impact in the larger community communicates as much to the child about the worth of the parent's care as the actual care the child receives in early childhood. For such a child the potential to care and be cared for can continue only to the extent that the caring person is cared about by the community. Thus, the equal employment of a minority person is an effective child development effort as well as being a sound economic enterprise and, above all, a moral necessity. (70) In the words of Erikson, "we must stand ready to expect and to respond to human love in any of our fellow men so long as they do not set out to kill that human dignity in us without which we could not really love anybody. For only people with equal dignity can love each other." (126, 79)

Most pertinent for minority issues in our contemporary scene is Erikson's contention that it is not the opportunity that individuals have but the *choice* of opportunities which is important. To provide equal schooling, employment, housing, and so on is a step forward; but real respect for and full acceptance of an individual and his development are measured by the opportunities individuals can avail themselves of as a matter of choice.

SUMMARY

In studying affective development, according to Erikson's teachings and writings, one must proceed from the individual's immediate affective experience to encompass the totality of his or her development. Erikson, as researcher, creative thinker, writer, and teacher, always approaches the individual in question in relation to the person's total situation. For an understanding of Erikson's formulation, an overview of his early worksheet of develop-

---

[26] In a speech at the Annual Meeting of Orthopsychiatry, April 1974, as related to the author by Peggy West, Seattle, Washington.

TABLE 2.1 ERIKSON'S WORKSHEET OF DEVELOPMENTAL PHASES

	Psychosocial Crises	Radius of Significant Relations	Related Elements of Social Order	Psychosocial Modalities	Psychosexual Stages
I	Trust vs. mistrust	Maternal person	Cosmic order	To get To give in return	Oral-respiratory, Sensory, kinesthetic (Incorporative Modes)
II	Autonomy vs. shame, doubt	Parental persons	"Law and order"	To hold (on) To let (go)	Anal-urethral, muscular (retentive-eliminative)
III	Initiative vs. guilt	Basic family	Ideal prototypes	To make (= going after) To "make like" (= playing)	Infantile-genital, Locomotor (intrusive, inclusive)
IV	Industry vs. inferiority	"Neighborhood," School	Technological elements	To make things (= completing) To make things together	"Latency"
V	Identity and repudiation vs. identity diffusion	Peer groups and outgroups; models of leadership	Ideological perspectives	To be oneself (or not to be) To share being oneself	Puberty
VI	Intimacy and solidarity vs. isolation	Partners in friendship, sex, competition, cooperation	Patterns of cooperation and competition	To lose and find oneself in another	Genitality
VII	Generativity vs. self-absorption	Divided labor and shared household	Currents of education and tradition	To make be To take care of	
VIII	Integrity vs. disgust, despair	"Mankind" "My kind"	Wisdom	To be, through having been To face not being	

SOURCE: Reprinted with permission from E. H. Erikson, "Identity and the Life Cycle: Selected Papers," p. 166, in *Psychological Issue*: (Monograph), New York, International Universities Press, 1959, vol. 1, p. 1. (85).

ment might be in order (see Table 2.1). We note in this worksheet"
Erikson's allegience to psychoanalytic thinking and terminology.
His glossary and many of the concepts have been adopted in contemporary language regarding developmental perceptions. This
chart presents affective development as a phasal sequence from
womb to tomb, with a succession of different key persons (variation of social matrices) and altering value systems in the making.
At each point of one's developmental progress, different modes of
behavior take on significance. Each of these factors assumes special
relevance in Erikson's scheme; yet, it is the *interrelationship* and
progression of development, always changing, always warding off
change, which makes his concepts into a dynamic and heuristic
theory.

Erikson's formulation deserves to be hailed as one of the major
breakthroughs in developmental theory since Freud. Affective
development as portrayed in the chart above is now understood
for the linkages of life experiences, the mutualities between
people—caring and cared for, peers with peers, partners with
partners, contemporaries with contemporaries, generation with
generation, and mankind with the cosmos. Growing older and
developing, from trusting infantile experiments in trust to con-
templation over the wisdom of life's experiment in old age, is an
experience of coparticipation, or growing *together,* throughout;
and what cannot be resolved at the moment can be resolved later.
Individuals are always a part of and a partner in their future. In
essence, "man experiences life and death, past and future—in
terms of the turnover of generations." (*98,* 725)

Erikson as a human developmentalist is departing from his
analytic forebears. Human development is a creative enterprise, in
which individuals utilize their developmental desires for meeting
environmental opportunities, while the immediate environment
wills them the way in which they can best utilize themselves. In
development, the process of maturation meets the process of education. The continuous life experiences of individuals, based on
the qualities they can make use of and on support by the environment, all subsequently define the essence of affective development.

In closing this account of Erik H. Erikson's affect theory, it
might be fitting to quote one of his more recent philosophical
observations. Reminding us, as a person of his time, that human
destiny is as much a developmental as a cultural (sociopolitical)
issue, he points to the need for "a world order which permits all
children chosen-to-be born anywhere on earth to develop to an
adulthood that learns to humanize its own inventions—
psychologically as well as technologically." (*119,* 339)

CHAPTER 3
The behavioral theory of Robert S. Sears

A BIOGRAPHICAL NOTE ON
THE LIFE AND PROFESSIONAL CAREER OF SEARS

ROBERT RICHARDSON SEARS the only American born of the three theorists presented in this book—provides a behavioral approach to the study of child development. Born in 1908 in Palo Alto, California, as the son of Jesse Brundage Sears and Stella Richardson Sears, Robert Richardson Sears grew up in the town of his birth while his father was professor of education at Stanford University. He was graduated from Stanford, and eventually his career as a psychology professor brought him back to Stanford as a distinguished scholar until his retirement as professor emeritus. In his twenty years at Stanford he earned distinction as department chairman, and, most important, as teacher and researcher of child development.

Sears had graduated at the age of twenty-one with majors in psychology and English. In his student years, his interest in psychology had been stimulated by Stanford's child psychologist, Lewis M. Terman, who encouraged young Sears to continue his psychological studies at Yale. After completing his doctoral research on the visual motor behavior of goldfish in 1932, Sears embarked upon an academic career and obtained a full professorship within ten years. His first academic appointments were to the University of Illinois and the Chicago Institute of Junveile Human Relations (1932–1936) and later to Yale University (1936–1942).

Sears moved in 1942 to the Iowa Child Welfare Research Station, where he was a teacher and researcher, and in 1949 to the Harvard Laboratory of Human Development. By 1953, Sears had returned to Stanford University, where he became head of the Department of Psychology and also served for several years as dean of Humanities and Sciences. In 1973, he became the David Starr Jordan Professor of Psychology, and served as chairman of Stanford's program on human biology until his retirement as professor emeritus (1974). Together with his research and teaching activities, Sears has held numerous administrative positions, the most distinguished of which was as president of the American Psychological Association (1950–1951 and 1960–1961). In 1974 he served as editor of the Monograph Series of the Society for Research in Child Development. Sears' interest in child development was also part of a family affair as in his marriage to Pauline Snedden (Sears) he married an accomplished researcher in child development. She herself became a professor of child development.

Sears' early psychological orientation was anchored in the teachings of his former Yale professor and later colleague, Clark L. Hull. Other impactive relationships were with his research collaborators, Dollard, Doob, Miller, and Mowrer, who were applying learning theory to immediate social problems *(52, 333)*. By the early forties, Sears had become preoccupied with the teaching of psychoanalytic theory. His investigation of research on psychoanalytic concepts convinced him of the significance of early parent-child relationships and the relevance of these dyadic relationships for learning theory research. Since then, his major research projects and formulations have concentrated on early childhood development and the essence of child-parent interactions.

In 1944, he described the challenge he saw before him:

> *It seems doubtful whether the sheer testing of psychoanalytic theory is an appropriate task for experimental psychology. Its general method is estimable but its available techniques are clumsy. Instead of trying to ride on the tail of a kite that was never meant to carry such a load, experimentalists would probably be wise to get all the hunches, intuitions, and experience possible from psychoanalysis and then for themselves, start the laborious task of constructing a systematic psychology of personality but a system based on behavioral rather than experiential data.* (332, 329)

The challenge Sears voiced for psychologists in general became his own major life task. He researched the early development of the child and its behavioral components within a dyadic, interpersonal context. In the early fifties, Sears was one of the behaviorists who stressed the interpersonal context; *(346; 348)* now, in the seventies, he is one of those who stresses the generational factor. *(351)*

Early in his career, Sears assumed the stance of philosopher-scientist—a role B. F. Skinner adopted much later in his professional life. *(361a)* In recent years Sears' research and writings reveal the influence of Skinnerian terminology, although not necessarily the thinking of Skinner. *(328; 337; 353)* His method of inquiry is pragmatic and empirical. His questions were formulated eclectically. Throughout his research, his attempts to reconcile psychoanalytic psychology with behavioral research reflect his desire to make use of the best of several worlds.

Sears formulated an array of behavioral questions and concepts which are parallel to those of theorists who attempt to deal with affective and cognitive development. His work is not as extensive and original as that of Piaget's or Erikson's.[1] They actually developed a theoretical system. Nevertheless, Sears' work, in over 70 research and theoretical papers or books, represents, the best developmental inquiries within a learning theory approach. Sears is a theorist who can teach us much about behavioral development as an interpersonal event of life.

SEARS' BEHAVIORAL THEORY

As a behaviorist, Sears' focuses his work on overt behavior, and he has documented the observable social interactions during personality development. Sears' emphasis upon reinforcement and secondary-drive behavior have their roots in Hullian learning theory. Thus, his preoccupation with resultant actions as the *learned* cause for future behavior and his emphasis upon reinforcement and secondary-drive behavior can be understood in that context.

Behavioral events, in general, can be studied from two quite different perspectives: (1) from a perspective where the emphasis is upon the sequence of cause and effect events within an action continuum; (2) by emphasizing the behavior which is learned so that the effect of the learning cycle itself is the factor which counts, and the *effect* becomes relevant as the *cause* for future behavioral expressions (actions). Sears is interested in this second perspective.

Behavioral expressions (actions) are the outcome of the innate force (drive) responding to an external cue or stimuli. Initially in a person's life, all behaviors are a product of and intimately associated with both the individual's expression of primary drives

---

[1] In fact, in a recent publication *(351)*, Sears cites Erikson's and Piaget's writings as major resources. He sees Erikson's and Piaget's contributions as fundamentally complementary to his own work.

(bodily experiences), such as hunger, fatigue, physical discomfort, etc., and the responses of others which have become associated with a drive's tension reduction. The degree of tension reduction, the resultant satisfaction or frustration, leads the individual to repeat the behavior involved or to be more available for an alternate behavior. Repeated satisfied experiences within an action cycle leads, in one way, to further acquisition of the behaviors involved as well as to the adoption of the associated experiences as basic, *as if* these secondary events were primary ones. For example: "The individual does not wait for the onset of the primary drive (stomach contraction or changes in chemistry of the blood) before engaging in the appropriate adaptive response (eating). Rather, he responds to the secondary-drive stimulation which may be linked to time, place, or verbal command." (199, 429) In other words, secondary-drive stimulations (cycles of secondary actions) such as the smell of food preparations replace primary ones such as the stomach contractions of hunger.

Basic in Sears' behavioral formulation is the stimulus-response (S-R) cycle. The stimuli which activate the individual's response also determine when, where, and how he or she will respond. The triggering of an action sequence directed toward a given goal concomitantly serves to reduce the intensity of the drive. Sears is particularly concerned with the quality (the reinforcement value) of each goal-directed response. It is the individual's experience which determines whether an action cycle will prove to be transitional, with little or no reinforcement value, or whether it will contribute substantially towards an individual's repertoire of behavior and thus have reinforcement value.

Behavioral differences in individuals can be traced to the reinforcement value derived from even minute variations of similar action cycles. Reinforcement of behavior occurs only if there is a variation in the reinforcement events. For example, a child accustomed to constant praise will cease to be affected by praise unless there is variation in the pattern in which priase is awarded.

In any S-R cycle, the response of one individual can serve as the stimulus for another. For instance, the wails let out by a child in response to a tumble can become the stimulus for a response of comforting the child. In fact, almost all human actions signify and become human *inter*actions. A person is always responding as well as socially corresponding.

Recognizing the social dimension of behavior as central in the human action cycle, Sears' perceives child development as always proceeding within a dyadic unit of behavior. (This latter approach was a decisive departure from the traditional single person units applied by the fellow psychologists at the time Sears began his work.) Adaptive behavior and its reinforcement in any one individual must therefore be studied in terms of the actual or anticipated response from another individual. Such dyadism demands complicated research designs because each S-R cycle (not sequence) had to be studied with respect to the interrelated behavior of two or more individuals; the stimulus and the response itself receive only secondary considerations.

Sears' research on dyadic behavior—with its stress upon (1) the action sequence and the action cycle as central factors, (2) the study of behavior which nurtures dependency (sucking, cooing, grasping, now called operant behavior), and (3) the caring person's response (now called operant response)—built a bridge between Hullian S-R learning theory and contemporary operant conditioning (Skinnerian) learning theory. (325, 2)

The role of bridge builder was not new for Sears. He tested a range of psychoanalytic concepts and incorporated an array of analytic concepts into his behavioral thinking. His research and writings deal with aggressive, projective, and sublimated behaviors and with such phasal action cycles as oralism, oedipalism, etc. Most important, Sears recognized human behavior as multidimensional, and departed from the traditional unidimensional behavioral stance. He stresses that "a given bit of behavior may serve to express more than one motive or be directed to securing more than one kind of reinforcement (i.e., negative attention seeking; aggression and winning others). . . . Behavior [can be] elicited (in part) by different internal instigational systems—[and] many different internal properties of the person [can] determine *meaning* to him." (325, 5)

Sears' writings demonstrate his intermittent commitment to deductive discourse, although he continuously tends to set himself "right" by returning to inductive thinking, thus remaining true to empiricism and the prevailing American approach to theory construction. His research is limited to native-born white primarily middle-class Americans. Dyadic parent-child relationships are, for the most part, those of the mother and child, as if such a dyad were the all-inclusive one.[2]

In addition to Sears' more inclusive approach to the construction of behavior theory, which is a notable deviation from B. F. Skinner's rigorously empirical stance, Sears' work differs from Skinner's in his perception of the all-encompassing power of behavioral control. While Skinner envisages that a proper utilization of learning can bring about utopian behavioral control, Sears, in

---

[2] He makes a notable exception to this mother-child matrix in his biographical study of Mark Twain, where he deals with matrices of both Mark Twain and his father and Mark Twain and his mother. (337)

contrast, questions whether parents can ever be in sufficient control of their children's environment to use learning theory for rearing children. Although it may be possible to manipulate specific behaviors, he doubts that it is possible to know in which way a single behavior unit such as outstretched arm can truly become a signifier of "pick me up and love me." Although Skinner implies that we shall know it all, Sears questions if we shall ever know enough.

Sears employs standard research techniques. He advocates that in the behavioral as well as in the physical sciences, theory must be based upon empirical research: "A theory stands or falls on its effectiveness in ordering empirical observations."[3] (349, 382) At the same time, Sears wanders beyond the scope of his research data and is apt to incorporate inferences from merely preliminary or statistically insignificant findings.

Essentially, however, the account of behavioral development that emerges out of Sears work can give us understanding, direction, and heuristic insight into human development because Sears' views the individual as a developing social being within an impactful environment. In an era where ecological thinking is in the foreground, a formulation which recognizes environmental forces as salient is an opportune one.

ASSUMPTIONS BASIC TO SEARS' BEHAVIORAL APPROACH

Universal Order and Fundamental Human Values

Sears, as scientist, believes in the discernibility of an orderly universe. However only occasionally, as in his collaborative efforts on the frustration-aggresion theorem (52, 96) and in his later inquiries into the processes of identification (334; 335; 353), does Sears venture to weigh his formulations as universal principles of human behavior.

Sears' research focuses on selected aspects of human behavior. To Sears each individual's destiny is determined by his or her interactions with others; each person is born with the same infinite capacity to learn; (334) and early experiences of eliciting care and being cared for determine an individual's development. Since the differences between individuals are in large part related to what information was available on child-rearing practices, access to the most advanced knowledge on child rearing becomes paramount.

---

[3] In more recent research, he readily applies this criterion to his own earlier work when later findings fail to support his previous data. (353)

Sears basically assumes that every parent could do better if he or she knew better.

Etiology of Behavior

Although Sears' work does not emphasize the source of human behavior, he seems to proceed on the basis of the following etiological assumptions. First, behavior is both the cause and the effect of subsequent behavior. Primary drives represent the instrumental energy for the beginning of behavior; but it is the social world which actually shapes behavior associated with the primary drives. For instance, from the very beginning of infant care, parents' reactions to sons tend to be different from their reactions to daughters. Consequently, each sex experiences different child-rearing practices and, thus, develops differently.

Second, behavior is self-motivated by its tension-reduction effect. Goal orientation is subordinate to the tension-reduction associated with the goal achievement. Third, when a certain behavior precedes the achievement of a goal the cycle receives a reinforcement potential, either because the behavior was repeated before the goal achievement, or because the behavior was subsequently repeated as a result of goal achievement. Fourth, all reinforced behaviors with drive-equivalent characteristics form secondary motivational systems. These secondary motivational systems, the stock of *learned* behavior, comprise an individual's culturally conforming behavior. Fifth, the action cycles which are known to have their own laws and patterns of development are aggression, frustration, dependency, and identification.

The action cycles of aggression and frustration are intertwined. Frustration is always the product of an anticipated or experienced interference with the goal achievement. *(333)* Frustration creates a drive for aggression which requires tension-release as if it were a basic-drive.[4] Identification, moreover, has its roots in the early experiences of spontaneous imitation of behavior; its reinforcement and personal satisfaction are a result of repeating the behavior of others in one's own action cycle; identification then becomes a drive force equivalent to the earlier primary ones. Behavior development and change, in essence, emerge out of a combination of physical maturation and socialization.

Core of Human Functioning

Sears views personality as a product of a "lifetime of *dyadic action* which has modified the individual's potentiality for further

---

[4] The original frustration-aggression hypothesis is now being questioned by Sears on the basis of his observation that frustration can also occur without any aggressive counterparts. (337, 92)

action." (*346,* 476) All human functionings are the outcome of the interactive effects of all the influences, constitutional and experiential, that have impinged on the individual. (*349*) A child's inherent desire to learn and a parent's desire to do right create a dyadic situation where the proper knowledge of actions produces the proper balance of human behavior. "If a mother knows the effect of a particular practice, she can decide whether to use it or not. She can base her judgments on a knowledge of the product she will get." (*349,* 17)

Emotions affect the quality of reinforcement which any action cycle might receive. Emotions are seen as qualitative-quantitative ingredients of anticipated or experienced actions. At no time are emotions viewed as entities. To illustrate, Sears stresses a parent's inherent warmth as paramount to the caring action. This warmth is conceived in the quality of the parent's action rather than in the parent's state (feelings) associated with the actions. As all social behavior is conceived as dyadic reinforced actions, child development becomes synonymous with child training.

Sears gives some consideration to play.[5] He designates play as learning by trial and error how things feel, taste, or perform and discovering rationally what things do and stand for, and what space and time they occupy. (*336*) On occasion, Sears ascribes an irrational component to play. Play, like fantasy, occurs "when some of the laws of the physical and social universes have been rescinded, and hence it is the product of the child's derives and habits when these have different constants in the behavior questions." (*331,* 498)

All human functions follow the same behavioral laws. Social behavior depends exclusively upon the impact of others, rather than upon any innate developmental laws. Human development is manageable for its unity in continuity.

The Newborn

The newborn infant has biological needs which result in primary drives. Some of them are hunger, thirst, sex tension; needs for activity, rest, waste elimination; and optimum temperature maintenance. These drives are the foundation for social learning: "The child is endowed, at birth, with a potentiality for securing many forms of gratification from his world. He can eat, he can eliminate when need be, he can be warmed or cooled, he can be fondled and loved. These experiences are not only gratifying; they are also the sources of learning." (*326,* 68) Therefore, infant care is

---

[5] Sears' position on play is cited because, for Piaget as well as for Erikson, play is basic for human development. Sears' position is open. He has concerned himself with play only in selected research projects.

the cradle of all learning and a study of infant care leads to the discovery of childhood development.

Physical and Social Environment

A behavioral approach is an environmental one. It is the environment (usually called society) which implants appropriate motives, interests, skills, and attitudes in children. They learn to act according to environmental expectations. Each society and culture sees to it that certain actions, at the expense of other actions, are reinforced. Those actions which are reinforced result in an incorporation of values which become a part of a person's social heritage. The role of the parents is crucial, for the parents are the most important reinforcing environmental agents. Sears does not recognize socioeconomic classes or other social clusters as independent variables for child-rearing practices. For him, the discriminating variable is what access the caring persons have to the most relevant understanding of the best child-rearing practices. Sears suggests that differences in child-rearing practices between socioeconomic groups will diminish with increased accessibility to the essential information and with the immediate dissemination of new learning to all socioeconomic layers of society. Therefore, what the environment can grant equally affects child-rearing practice.

SEARS' CONCEPTION OF DEVELOPMENT

Sears' writings imply two different stances on child development. His behavioral stance clearly suggests that he sees development as a continuous chain of events adding to and in part replacing previous acquisitions.

> Child-rearing is a continuous process. Every moment of a child's life that he spends in contact with his parents has some effect on both his present behavior and his potentialities for future actions.
> A child's development seems to be a fairly orderly process. He gives up modes of behavior that are no longer suitable, and acquires new actions appropriate for his age and his life conditions. (349; 314, 466)

At the same time, his research formulations and the presentation of his findings imply that he envisages developmental phases. In fact, we can readily infer from Sears' presentation of developmental progression that he conceptualizes development as a continuous, orderly sequence of conditions which creates actions, new motives for actions, and eventual patterns of behavior. As the thinking of everyday life proceeds with a notion of developmental phases as a reality, all social learning will tend to proceed in comparable patterns. To amplify, early training of the infant during weaning, feeding, toilet training, and object recognition, as well as the child's age-linked dependence, distinctly implies an expectancy of a level of readiness in the infant phase which is different from that of subsequent periods.

In essence, Sears proceeds with a mental image of developmental tasks, though he does not enunciate them as such. Socialization, in the final analysis amounts to the fulfillment of developmental tasks. Social expectancies imply developmental phases, regardless of whether they are fact or fiction. As long as they are responded to as if they exist, they do exist as reinforcing developmental variables. In fact, Sears speaks of an "infancy phase," lasting for the first 16 months of life. (329, 161) We will, therefore, present behavioral development in three developmental phases.[6]

> Phase I Rudimentary behavior based upon innate needs and initial behavioral learning in infancy
> Phase II Secondary motivational systems based upon family-centered learning
> Phase III Secondary motivational systems based upon learning beyond the family

The first phase involves the early months of life, when children's environmental experiences are intimately associated with their basic need requirements. The second phase covers the subsequent socialization within the family. And the third phase introduces developmental experiences largely beyond the hold of the family. This last phase, however, has only limited research by Sears and his associates and can consequently not be fully developed as a complete phase in itself; it merely contains material which extends beyond the first two phases.

These three phases are consistent with Sears' behavioral assumptions. They are like three expanding circles in a pool of water into which a stone has been dropped. The first, innermost circle represents the child's most intimate parental environment; the next circle stands for the child's emergence into a larger family environment; whereas the outermost circle symbolizes the child's gradual social penetration into his neighborhood. Each circle, as it expands, blends into the next larger circle, thereby losing its original boundaries.

Although Sears' work centers in early childhood development, he sees development as a continuous life-long process, in which

---

[6] The articulation of these three phases is entirely based upon this writer's interpretation of Sears' intent. The method of organization is hopefully consistent with Sears' thinking, even if this writer adds his own terminology.

each aspect of development depends upon every other: "Growth and change are dramatic in the first two decades of life, to be sure. But the next five or six decades are every bit as complex and important, not only to those adults who are passing through them but to their children, who must live with and understand parents and grandparents." (351, v) Thus, Sears view of development as interpersonal experience is expanded to include intergenerational family factors.

Phase I: Rudimentary Behavior:
Innate Needs and Initial Behavioral Learning

Within the first sixteen months, behavioral development primarily involves a progressive reduction of the inner tension that originates from inner drives. When basic human requirements are met, such experiences as food intake and rest become an integration of bodily (physiological) and social interpersonal behavior. An infant's bodily needs to secure food, to eliminate and to receive personal contact and stimulation along with physical comfort create the boundary conditions of the experience of social learning. The nurturing experiences are increasingly associated with the physiological stimulations until the social events become the prime instigator of behavior. It is this period of rudimentary learning which comprises the first phase.

In this early phase, innate needs produce the primary drives and cues for action. Hunger, fatigue, pain, etc., produce tensions which seek reduction through any gratifying response. Much of this initial gratification-seeking occurs by trial and error. Crying, struggling and holding one's breath, for instance, are actions based upon cues of pain, and are responses which merely happen. The child is in a purely autistic state unrelated to any social world. Slowly, the infant learns that the reduction of pain is related to some of his or her actions. Then he or she strives to imitate these previously successful actions. For instance, the cue of hunger becomes associated with the sequence of crying and receiving the breast (or bottle) with the hunger-reducing fluid. Infants' actions become more and more learned behavior; that is, their actions become part of a sequence with a learned, goal-directed response.

When the infant's behavior tends toward goal-directed behavior, each completed action which brings about a reduction in tension is the one which is most likely to be repeated again, whenever the tension arises. Repeatedly satisfied responses and the attendant events which lead to the satisfaction are viewed together as rewarding experiences. In the case of the infant, the caring person's promptness, dependability, regularity and personal warmth (close body contacts, fondling, etc.) provide the essential reinforcement. For instance, parents who devote appropriate attention to their child at the times he or she needs them are supportively reinforcing. Children in turn, are more apt to adapt their behavior to those forms which will assure him the parent's consistent attention. The child learns to ask for a parent's reciprocal behavior, and the range of behavior alternates available to the child is as much a function of child rearing as of age. (353, 38) Children consequently, are stimulated to select the responses their environment seems to expect from them. They tend to manipulate their environment in order to pursue gratifying responses, while their environment suggests to them the range of satisfactions it can supply. The key to socialization is embedded in this dyadic relationship. The infant learns both to control and to be controlled. As a quick learner, the child develops early "his techniques of cooperating with those who care for him, and of controlling them and insuring their nurturance." (349, 138)

Requirements For Socialization

From this time on, socialization takes place. "Every child always has a repertory of actions that needs replacing." (349, 464) Successful development is characterized by a decrease in autism and innate need-centered actions and by an increase in dyadic, socially centered behavior which assures dependence upon dependency. The failure to secure what is needed (and eventually what is *wanted*) results in a child's return to previously successful actions—be it crying, kicking or random actions. Thus, Sears' inquiry into early child development is guided by three essential questions:

1. Under what conditions is a child's behavioral repertoire learned?
2. In what circumstances does the social environment reinforce such learning?
3. What are the resultant behavior patterns in the child's learning?

Dependency Fulfillment

For Sears, a satisfactory experience in depending upon someone is basic to infant behavioral learning. (328; 337; 353) "Dependency is a type of operant behavior that has as its required environmental events affectionate and nurturant behavior performed by another person." (337, 15) A child learns to make supplications for such love; he or she is reinforced for such attention seeking and establishes patterns of actions which assure the attention and assistance of others as well as assuring others of his or her dependency. (337, 15) The experience of dependency becomes paramount to the specific series of satisfactory experiences which make up the total behavioral pattern of dyadic dependency. Rewarding reinforcement in all dyadic situations depends upon the child's having consistent contacts with one person.

Dyadic dependency has its beginning when in the earliest contacts between child and mother (or other caring person) the child shifts his or her processes of learning from those based upon trial and error to those based upon dyadic reinforcement. A dyadic relationship fosters dependency and thus reinforces it. Infants reveal dependent tendencies from birth. They tend to respond to people as recurring environmental phenomena during the first two months of life. They call upon them when hungry, cold, or otherwise in a state of biological need. The dependency requirements are nurtured through the dyadic relationship of feeding and other forms of being cared for during the child's fourth to twelfth months. (354)

Both child and caring person have a repertoire of significant actions that stimulate responses from the other person which are compatible with each one's expectations. For illustration, the parent or parent surrogate is an indispensable part of the activity of intake of all food. The caring person's image, smell, feel, voice, etc., are closely associated with hunger-stilling gratifications. The child "not only learns to expect her to come when [he is] hungry, he also learns that he needs her." (349, 66) The desire for food and the desire for a caring person (usually the parent) are linked with the caring person's wish to provide what is needed and to feel personally needed for these activities. The patterned behavioral cycles of dependency create a higher-level construct for the help-seeking and help-giving behaviors which are so essential to subsequent development during this phase.

Dependency, like other secondary behavioral systems, starts with the child being initially reinforced for specific behaviors which also bring about the experience of closeness and dyadic involvement with a person. Later on, it is not the specifically reinforced behavior but the maintenance of personal contact and dependency which is secured. Early an infant cries for a shift in position. Later he or she cries for *you*, because *your* reassuring presence is a welcome and needed "shift" for his or her life. In fact, this phenomenon continues throughout life. While we may want people's advice for the advice itself, later on we may find that it is not the advice but the person which adds to our life.

Dependency is determined by the need to regain control of the parental resources that provide the child with many forms of gratification, especially the expression of love. (328) The *learning* of active dependency, therefore, proceeds from a *state* of active dependency, in which both parties involved play a mutually sustaining dependency role. "Help given is appropriate to the help needed; what is asked for by the child is, in style and content, what will serve to evoke the needed help from the parent." (325, 11–12) It takes time for the caretaker's affection, loving and attention giving ". . . through smiling, talking, hugging and other means [to give] the child an understanding that he [she] is a desirable and sought-after object. Presumably such a concept of the self-as-worthy develops over many years" (343, 269) and only gradually finds expression in the child's life in general, including most likely a reciprocal effect of child on caring person which in some fashion leads a child's high self-concept to produce warmth in his/her being-cared-for experience.

The child's dependency becomes a powerful need which can be neither eliminated nor ignored. In fact, the more the child increases his or her efforts to satisfy frustrated dependency needs, the more insistent and all-absorbing become his or her demands for dependency. To illustrate, children around the age of one year who have formed little dependency (attachment) to any one set of selected elders, will attach themselves indiscriminately to almost any one *as if* any one will provide for them. Most noteworthy, a lack in dependency reinforcement will likely thwart future efforts and inclinations for seeking assistance. Children who have ample opportunities for attachment will have more discriminating and less demanding dependency requirements. Such children have behavioral assurance that they are loved objects and can be assured of their elder's readiness to do for them what they cannot (yet) handle themselves. In sum, permissiveness towards dependency tends to meet dependency needs. High dependency demands high preponderance of adult nurturing and care at this crucial period of development. (353)

It is notable that these beginning primary attachments and dependencies in the second half year of life, are not quite explainable in terms of ordinary and progression of learning. Attachment is in one way a behavioral event; yet, it is a very personal experience and only transferrable to other experiences over long periods of time. Dependencies, with the quality of attachment, require the presence or, at least, nearness of the depended-upon person but not necessarily the intervening actions of the person. (325)

The child's biological need for the reduction of his hunger drive, moreover, becomes quickly associated with two essentially interrelated components of his food-intake sequence: to suck and to be near the nursing person. Because of its constant repetition and powerful association with the goal-directed response, the instrumental act of sucking rapidly becomes an ingrained habit and an independent drive which gets stronger with age as long as it remains the primary means for getting pacifying attention. This latter factor suggests not only to the importance of the satisfaction recieved in a child's help-seeking efforts, but also to the relevance of a wider choice of operant responses as offered by the parents.

Attitude of Aggressiveness

According to Sears' early research, (52; 200; 333) aggression is an outgrowth of frustration. Yet aggression can readily become an early and vital aspect of learned behavior in its own right. Frustration occurs from the very moment the infant experiences discomfort or pain because of a delay in finding relief from the unpleasant inner experience. Aggression, which is usually manifested by a show of anger in the form of rage or a display of temper, can be conceived of as a response to the frustration. Infants or older individuals with an infantlike behavior reservoir express frustration in forms most basic to them: crying, screaming, or changes in the rhythm of breathing, in food intake, or in the entire body posture (a temper tantrum). Permissiveness as a response to frustration and permissiveness toward the expression of dependency have different meanings for the child. Parental permissiveness toward frustration results in a state of nonreinforcement of dependency and dependency denial and leaves the child with depersonalized and unchanneled aggression.

Considered specifically, if a parent uses permissiveness toward dependency and, in general, nonpermissiveness toward frustration, the result will be apt to overcome frustration and provide direct assistance with expressions of aggression. Meanwhile, the adult control and nurturance of dependency provides the beginning of the process of identification, because the attachment remains intact throughout.

Sex, Ordinal Position, and Social Status

Much of the social environment into which children are born has inherent implications for their eventual development. Sex, ordinal position in the family constellation, parents' basic happiness, families social position and educational status determine significant variables which direct the child's development in one way or another. Basically, the parent sees his or her child in the light of a general disposition toward bringing up children. Too, parents react to a child in terms of the feelings about his or her sex. From birth, a "child is allocated to one sex or the other, and society begins to implant in him motives, interests, skills and attitudes appropriate to such membership." (350, 221) The child's sex determines a social meaning that has decisive implications for training, especially as it relates to the nature of the child's allowed dependency. (329)

The ordinal position of the child becomes important because it defines the span of control from above. In large families the distance before one reaches the final control (the parent) is extended. The oldest child is exposed to the most direct parental training, while other siblings tend to have an additional intermediary with each older sibling. More important than ordinal position are the age spacing between children and the mother's freedom to deal directly with each child without having to "water down" such contacts with older children, who simultaneously compete for her attention. Furthermore, a parent tends to become less frustrated by daily chores with the second-born child. An only child tends to receive more attention from the parent of the same sex, while the youngest child of a large family seems to be left predominantly under the mother's discipline regardless of its sex. (349)

Much of a child's earliest development reflects the mother's personality: her capacity to be a caring mother and to regulate her permissiveness; her attitudes toward sex and toilet training; and the span of experience and education through which she finds the capacity to deal simultaneously, although differently, with children at various levels of their development. A mother's capacities are greatly associated with her own self-esteem, with her evaluation of the father, and with her feelings about her current life situation. A high rating in each of these three factors correlates with high enthusiasm and great warmth in child-caring.

The parent's social status, education, and cultural background predetermine many child-caring practices. The child has a greater probability for healthy development if the parent does not yearn for another station in life. This observation holds true for working parents as well as for foster parents as long as they consider their lot the most appropriate one for them. Parents' overall position on the socioeconomic scale seems to affect the child's development less than the extent of their education. It is the less educated parent (usually the lower-class parent) who uses inappropriate measures of permissiveness and control. Conversely, more education and access to contemporary understanding of child care prepares the parent for a more rational use of control and greater permissiveness toward dependency. Sears stresses that differences of socioeconomic class are primarily related to the degree of access to the major contemporary matrices of communication for obtaining current knowledge and methods for applying such knowledge.

This first phase interlinks the biological endowment of the newborn child with the endowment of his or her social environment. It ties the infant to his or her environment and provides the beginning of ever-increasing interactive experiences with the environment.

Phase II: Secondary Behavioral Systems:
Family-centered Learning

One by one, aspects of the rudimentary life of the infant become subject to social training. Rigorous socialization is carried out during this second phase, covering the early childhood years, the period between the second half of the child's second year and the age he or she enters school. Primary life requirements, combined with the previously cited secondary dependency, continue to motivate a child's actions. What is striking about this phase is the gradual incorporation of additional systems of secondary actions. These secondary behavioral cycles become the child's fundamental motives to action—unless his or her social environment fails to provide the necessary reinforcement. To illustrate, the child's hunger no longer depends entirely upon the contraction of his stomach, but becomes associated with the smell of food or such cues as the opening of the refrigerator.

Dependency Fulfillment

Parents continue to be the major reinforcing agents during the early stages of this phase. They perceive behavior which should be changed and reinforce more mature forms of action. First, they must reinforce the child's desire to become socialized. Once the attachment to parents is established through dependency, the child's learned dependence for nurturance includes advancement in more mature activities and responses. Children become aware that their personal happiness depends upon their readiness to do as they are expected; eventually, their happiness becomes more or less synonymous with doing right.

At this point, it is important to consider punishment as a variable of socialization. Thus far, only positive (rewarded) reinforcement has been cited as a socializing agent. Punishment is a response with a clear absence of reward. Sears himself gives little credence to punishment as an alternative to reward. Punishment, in general, neither tends to alter nor to extinguish behavior. Punishment, however, does elicit a reaction and create a response to the agent administering the punishment. For instance, children who have been punished by their parent experience the parent's punitive behavior as the expression of an angry person and a person to be avoided, rather than relating their parent's actions to their own actions. In other words, genuine social learning depends upon replacing previous learning with newer experiences based upon more appropriate satisfactions rather than upon fearing and avoiding unpleasant consequences. *(349; 353)*

As stated all along, early childhood development is anchored in the satisfaction gained from the learned dependency upon the caring person. The child now relies upon his dependency as if it were part of his nature. When dependency assumes drive equivalency, frustration or punishment of dependency results in the persistence of this secondary drive, because neither one stills this now "basic" need. Only gratification or gradual modification can produce a shift in the nature of dependency. Conversely, the more infrequently dependency is rewarded, the more persistent the child desires such reward. In the early years, sensory *attachment* seeking based on tactual, visual, auditory, and oral contacts becomes a generalized experience of having dependencies met. Within the developmental years of two to five, *proximity* seeking replaces attachment experiences. The child has become more person-centered and more oriented toward specific persons (less transferable). Conversely, interactions are less personal in form and more personal in content.

As the toddler grows older, a parent looks upon stark emotional dependency as behavior which should be altered. Frequently, this shift in emphasis will come when children's behavior permits them to manage their daily life requirements as if they were able to stand on their own two feet. *(325, 24)* The parent then is apt to alter the quality and nature of nurturing care for the child's sustenance. In Sears' words:

> It [*dependency*] has a little of the quality of something infantile, of something that must be put away in favor of more mature kinds of expressed affection. The child should love his mother, to be sure, but with a less embarrassing degree of openness. He should want her attention, but not hound her for it or insist on it as a complete gratuity. The ultimate aim of the socialization process, as it relates to dependency, is for the child to be fond of the mother rather than passionately attached to her, to be pleased by her attention and interest but not incessantly to demand it. (340, 140)

Some of the alteration in care, such as temporary withdrawal of doing for the child, occurs because children have learned to attend to their own needs. They spontaneously imitate action sequences previously carried out by the parent. This spontaneous imitation represents children's attempts to secure for themselves a satisfying response in relation to a goal. Imitation occurs and is reinforced both by the parent and by the child's self-activated responses concerning goal achievement. Slowly, children learn to gratify their dependency drives by performing actions that they previously anticipated and demanded from their parents. More and more children learn to imitate the parent and the model of the parent on the long road toward being a model parent themselves one day. *(345)*

Sex Typing

Dependency and weaning from dependency are viewed differently according to the sex of the child. Girls tend to be granted dependency longer than boys. *(349)* But then during their third and fourth years of life, mothers tend to require girls to relinquish their dependency in a greater variety of areas than boys. Yet, girls of preschool age tend to remain more persistent in their overall dependency behavior than do boys.[7]

Girls can continue using the mother model for dependency and imitation of behavior that is adultlike and sexually appropriate, while boys experience similar reinforcement from the nurturing parent (mother) without the benefit of the mother as a sexually appropriate model. It is a fact that girls experience less conflict with their models. *(353, 256)* For boys, consequently, dependency can no longer remain the major resource for sex identification; their development becomes diffused and slowed down and has to depend upon their conception of male roles. *(353, 261)*

Early Forms of Identification

Generally, however, dependency decreases with age, as children learn to rely on an increasing number of adults, and eventually on their peers. The dependent state of children gradually modifies into one of affection and esteem for those on whom they rely for care. This change leads to the fact that parents increasingly teach them to ask for signs of love, attention, and reassurance in a fashion which is less demanding, more subtle, and in accord with the propriety and dignity of adult behavior (i.e., nearness in place of direct full attention, verbal in place of touching contact). In one way dependency unfolds into a process of identification. In another way dependence upon a single person is spread out into dependence upon many, particularly the one which counts within each particular situation.

With less dependence upon a caring person, children become freer to compete with others. They learn that nothing is their sole monopoly and that they have to compete for their desired goals. The drive of competition is in the making. The eventual gratification of gaining the parents' goodwill fosters a sharing of dependency

---

[7] These data are related to a generation born and brought up in the fifties and sixties. Recent shifts in sex-role expectations and the tendency to achieve more unisex standards in child rearing will most likely bring about new child-rearing circumstances.

and encourages the child in the experience of competing for the attention of parents. He or she then behaves as if his or her goal is unshareable, while actually the experience of competing and the means of competitively sharing the goal become as relevant as the goal itself.

As long as dependence upon the nurturing person is still essential for the child, the threat or the actual withdrawal of activities that maintain dependency becomes a powerful weapon in the child-rearing effort. For the child, a sudden or untimely withdrawal of support of his dependency means "you don't care for me any longer." Children will instantly react to such a threat with behavior that will, in their estimation, secure for them the desired and needed range of dependency support. In other words, a withdrawal or threat of withdrawal of personal care, love, or support is the alternative to positive reinforcement. The thread of the loss of dependency support can then serve as a facet of punishment—as negative reinforcement (or extinction). Children will tend to change their behavior in order to assure themselves of continued support for as long as they find sufficient satisfaction in their dependency. If, on the other hand, dependency upon an adult is associated with nonsatisfying experiences, a threat or actual withdrawal of dependency will hardly motivate children to change because continued dependency has equally little promise for them. As an example, a visitor threatening a child that he will not come back if he or she keeps on misbehaving can only have a salutary influence if such a visitor has positive meaning for the child.

During the early childhood years, feeding and nurturing of dependency are intimately linked with each other. Changes in the feeding patterns not only interfere with the experiences of obtaining food, but also affect the mutually dependent relationship. The child's degree of sensitivity toward weaning, for instance, is related to the age when weaning has begun and to the preparation for the final steps of weaning. If weaning is started before the child is six to twelve months old, the completion of the weaning will take longer than if its is started later, but it will proceed with fewer setbacks than will occur during a subsequent period, when dependency development is in the forefront. On the other hand, at the point when dependency is securely established, roughly by the time the child is a year and a half, weaning is of less consequences to the child.

Furthermore, the parent's mode of behavior and the degree of decisiveness conveyed in the feeding techniques also influence the child's response. In essence, it is the parent who proposes, while the baby disposes. For the young child, weaning involves five learnings in one: (1) learning to acquire food by means other than sucking; (2) learning to like this new method of food intake; (3) learning to encounter solid food; (4) learning how to handle solid foods orally; and, (5) learning to eat in an upright position, probably with diminishing body contact with the caring (feeding) person. (349) Sears' findings suggest that girls seem to take longer to be weaned. This finding coincides with their extended dependency experience during this age period.

Toilet Training and Sexual Taboos

Toilet training, unlike weaning, requires socialized control over previously autonomous behavior. Usually, elimination control is demanded after weaning is completed and when the child-mother interdependent relationship has become more entrenched. In toilet training, the mother is not supporting or fulfilling an infant's requirement. The parent does nothing *for* the child, only *to* him. (354) In toilet training, consequently, the surrounding circumstances of reward and punishment become important, including the parent's greater attentiveness. The child is faced with the question of accepting a set of entirely new motivational systems which, at the time of their introduction, are irrelevant, as far as the child is concerned. Reward and punishment continue to be interpreted by the child as acceptance or rejection by his mother. Toilet training, consequently, must be related to the child's state of dependency and handled in concert with his dependency needs. Only gradually does the child himself learn to want bodily cleanliness and approved toilet habits. Toilet training incorporates additional behavioral learning and values: bodily regularity, modesty, and cleanliness.

Sexual modesty, like toilet training, is initially experienced as an inhibiting activity. Potential sexual experiences (i.e., activities of the masturbatory type) are curbed before the child has any notion that these social amenities have anything to do with sex. Getting dressed is the first step to "covering up" and denying the presence of sex organs. Sex organs are hardly ever specifically mentioned, in contrast to direct references to other organs. A child is apt to be admonished not to play with his nose, while the fingering of sex organs is met with the request "do not play with *yourself!*" Boys and girls must deal with undefined requests which have little direction for them but considerable meaning for their elders. Socialization regarding sex, in general, involves prohibitive instructions and proceeds differently from the way dependency, feeding, and toilet training proceed. Sex training rests upon implication and affect-laden terms. Avoidance of and attitudinal dispositions toward specific sexual behavior rather than acquisition of specific behavior become the essence of learning.

Sears suggests that conscience formation is a product of attitude modeling in which behavioral conduct becomes a dependent variable. This aspect is particularly relevant in modeling behavior in regard to sex or aggression. It is the attitudes of the parent toward control of sex or aggression that count.[8] High standards for circumscribed manners, toilet training, the inhibition of overt expression of aggression and sex interests, and a general tendency towards restrictiveness seem to contribute toward constricted behaviors for girls and boys. (329, 153; 353, 196) By placing high value on maintenance of the culture's social aggressiveness and freedom of expression, the tendency towards expressiveness encourages expansive attitudes in boys *and* girls. (329, 141; 353, 195) These personality development factors tend to create less complications for a girl's conscience formation because the shaping of her behavior and model most likely involve the same caring person.

Attitude of Aggressiveness

Aggressiveness as a part of socialization occurs as much by accident as by design. Aggression develops as a consequence of certain actions or a lack of them. First, aggression arises as a consequence of the inherent frustration of growing up. Aggression, from irritation to rage, can be viewed as a sequence to frustration, for it occurs as part of a strong but futile attempt to achieve a goal which individuals experience as inaccessible to them. When infants cry out "angrily" in frustration, they accidentally learn that this thrusting behavior becomes associated with responses to their wants. They learn that they can utilize their aggression to secure compliance with their wishes. By hurting the apparent frustrator, they can get what they (angrily) feel is withheld from them. Their aggression instigates responses. For example, when an adult retrieves a toy in response to a child's screams, the act becomes associated with the screams. Not unlike the way they treat dependency acts, children learn to initiate aggressive acts in order to have their wants met. Social learning slowly introduces a refinement and more goal-directed aggression. Simultaneously, children learn to estimate their parent's aggressiveness by the degree of counteraggression which the parent exercises against their own. Sears suggests that parents of the same sex as the child introduce the greater frustration by more demanding control and, consequently, are the instigators and recipients of greater aggression.[9]

The child's use of aggression as a means of controlling his envi-

---

[8] It is notable that Sears speaks of one parent's attitude. Parents, as a mother-father dyad, do not exist as far as Sears' formulations and research are concerned.

[9] This observation parallels the concept of the Oedipus complex.

ronment is a motivational system repeatedly confronting parents. The handling of aggression is intimately tied to the development of behavior within the standards and values of the child's culture. The child learns when, how much, and what modes of aggression will be tolerated in the various arenas of his life. These standards for aggression are well acquired by the time a child is three years old. *(349)* Social learning also introduces the possibility of expressing aggression indirectly and in fantasy, for example, in play. Through fantasy, children release their aggression uninhibitedly against a substitute for the real instigator of their frustration. *(354)* The punishment of aggression in everyday life increases imaginary aggressive activities in play and fantasy. *(331)*

Learning to inhibit or to redirect aggression appropriately depends upon a delicate balance of permissiveness and restraint during a child's early developmental years. Excessive permissiveness of aggression leads the child to place a positive value on aggressive behavior, and excessive restraint can lead to continued recourse to such behavior. When children are asked to endure their frustration and live with their anger, they experience an increase in these feelings. Permissiveness increases aggressiveness toward the parent but decreases it outside of the home; while *non*permissiveness decreases aggression at home but results in greater aggressiveness with nonparental contacts out of the home.

Since punishment of aggressive behavior occurs after the act has taken place and, thus, after the child has already found a reduction in tension and has undergone a reinforcement of his or her aggressive action, the result is that punishment competes with the satisfaction obtained by aggression. Punishment is apt to add new frustration and increase aggression without providing an outlet for it. For example, if a child is scolded for tearing off his or her coat while experiencing frustration over the difficulties in unbuttoning it, he or she will act relieved at getting out of the confining apparel but will also feel frustrated by and angered at the person who did not understand and thus interfered.

This double-bind situation becomes particularly acute in instances where children seek attention by negative behavior. They experience anxiety because they are caught in a futile situation where they must either forego the attention they deem necessary or continue to strive for it while experiencing punitive attention (censorship).

Sears' findings on aggression can be presented schematically by a curvilinear graph with minimal punishment or extreme permissiveness to aggression at one end and extreme punishment or minimal permissiveness for aggression at the other; either extreme fosters intensified aggressive feelings.

Identification

Around the third year of life, when much behavior tends to resemble that of the parent, the child has started to identify. The emergence of identification as a process can be traced to the quality of the mother-child relationship, that is, to the mother's previous provision of gratifying experiences for the infant and to the infant's successful experiencing of his or her need for mother.

> *By the time a child is a year old, he has become related to his mother in such a way that not only do many of his satisfying actions require her presence and cooperation, but her very orientation toward him—indeed, her simple existence near him—is a source of pleasure. He loves his mother; he is emotionally dependent on her. (349, 377)*

Thus, when the primary caring person is absent, children will seek to recover what they have lost by the person's absence. They do this by repeating certain action sequences *as if* the person were administering them. As far as possible, children try to maintain the satisfactions associated with the continually experienced but absent parent.[10] The pleasure they are able to reproduce through performing motherlike caring activities gratifies their needs, and their frustration over mother's temporary removal is reduced. Simultaneously, the successful imitation of mother's behavior reinforces the behavior sequence itself as well as the desire to behave like mother, whether she is present or not. The child discovers a new source of gratification from imitation of behavioral sequences which lead to acting like the other person. In short, children reward themselves for imitating dependent behavior without being directly dependent upon the caring person. Identification emerges and becomes a goal response.

Unlike the previously cited forms of trial and error and behavioral socialization reinforcements, identification evolves from children's own role playing practices and their success (reward) in securing for and from themselves what was initially secured from others. Learning to identify occurs without any specific teaching from the parents. Notably, neither nurturing of dependency nor withdrawal of care by themselves produce identifying behavior. Furthermore, identification does not necessarily produce behaviors desired by parents. Children are apt to adopt everything in an elder's behavior which they perceive as appropriate to the person's role. Identification depends upon a desirable person with whom to identify, and, similarly, such a person's qualities become the qual-

---

[10] Note the development of a sense of permanency regarding the object relationship in the child's simultaneous cognitive development and a sense of assured dependability in the child's affective development.

ity of a new generation: "The more identification there is in any one generation, the greater will be the absorption of those qualities that induce identification in the next." (349, 392)

Identification has thus far been conceived of as an outgrowth of imitative behavior leading behavior related to roles. Sears denoted this process as anaclitic, that is, identification based on dependency. (353, 27) He also denotes a secondary process of identification—defensive identification—in which "the already established anaclitic identification produces an internalization of punitive and restrictive qualities of a threatening parent." (353, 7) Defensive identification creates mediating processes in which children align their wishes with those of the parent of the same sex.[11] This identification is directly related to the degree of availability (more than accessibility) of the parent in order that children can copy his or her attitudes and receive reinforcement for their successful execution of valued behaviors.

Furthermore, defensive identification is inversely related to the degree of interference by other competing models. For example, a four-year-old girl will more likely model her behavior on the basis of the mother's attitude toward sex, aggression, etc., if she is not constantly confronted by father's different standards. A complete absence of father, however, negates an opportunity for reinforcement, and the girl is less likely to find reinforcement for her behavior from others of the opposite sex. In short, too much of father and no father have similar consequences. A corresponding hypothesis can also be established for a boy and his relationship to his mother. Clearly, this is the same formulation as the previously cited one on dependence, that is, that extreme dependency support and the absence of dependency support tend to have the same effect. (A parallel to the Oedipus myth is also inherent in Sears' formulation.)

Identification By Sex

Sears stresses that sexual typing—the reinforcement of "development of social behavior appropriate to the child's own sex" (349, 369)—is perhaps the most pervasive aspect of the identification process. Boys, for instance, are encouraged to switch their ongoing identification around the age of four, at which time the boy's identification with his father's sexual expectations becomes relevant. Girls continue their major identification with their mother, and they progress more rapidly to more mature forms of behavior than do boys because their identification is uninterruptedly fortified. Girls tend therefore to become more strongly identified at an ear-

[11] This formulation is akin to the folk wisdom "If you can't fight 'em, join 'em."

lier point in their life with adult roles, standards, and values. In this process, girls remain more sensitive to mother's approval and disapproval.

In contrast, boys' identification is complicated not only by the fact that they have to alter their identification with mother, but also because they depend upon father's capacity and availability to model behavior which also receives the esteem of mother—the person whose judgment counts at the outset of this developmental progression. *(345)* The same holds true for girls when father fortifies the girl's esteem by conveying respect and appreciation for mother through his own behavior towards her.

Play

Play provides an opportunity for children to explore the makeup of their immediate universe by trial and error. Play opens the door for exploring, relatively unhampered, physical properties, causality, and social relations. An early Searsian research project yielded the pertinent findings that toys (play blocks) with low realism elicited greater varieties of themes in children's play, while toys (blocks) with high realism were more frequently explored and used but involved more circumscribed play. Play occurs without promise of reinforcement by extrinsic rewards. Play provides children with a territory free from trespassing elders. They can incorporate parents' behavior at their leisure and can express joy, frustration, and anger through acceptable play activity. It is "just play," they will explain to the outside world, and the latter finds comfort in the thought that "the child is merely playing."

Dependency Behaviors

Sears calls our attention to five clusters of behavior related to dependency. Although statistical significance was established for only the first cluster, he attributes equal relevance to the other four categories. All five are presented, because Sears' formulation of behavioral patterns adds conceptual clarity to the organization of behavioral variables:

> 1. *Negative attention seeking:* Getting attention by joking, teasing, disruptive "aggressive activity with minimal provocation, defiance, or oppositional behavior (e.g., opposing and resisting direction, rules, routines and demands by ignoring, refusing or doing the opposite)." *(353, 33)*

The foregoing dependency patterns (also statistically verified) seem to be the direct consequence of such child-rearing patterns as "low demands and restrictions," that is, little dependency nurturing on the part of the mother and, in the case of girls, high participation of the father in the girl's child rearing. (353, 67) In essence, seeking negative attention is a fusion of aggressive anger and dependency.

> 2. *Reassurance seeking:* "Apologizing, asking unnecessary permission, or seeking protection, comfort, consolation, help or guidance;" (353, 33) also unusually strong reliance upon cuddly objects, toys and pets.

The above patterns of dependency behavior seem to be directly related to "high demands for achievement from both parents, plus possible sex anxiety produced by the father's sex permissiveness." (353, 67)

> 3. *Positive attention seeking:* "Seeking praise, seeking to join an in-group by inviting cooperative activity, or actually interrupting a group activity in progress." (353, 33)

The above behavioral patterns seem to be correlated with "low infant and current caretaking by the mother and a nonpermissiveness attitude toward aggression." (353, 68) The latter involves high aggression control by the mother and only quasi child-rearing participation by the father.

> 4. *Touching and holding:* "Nonaggressive touching, holding, and clasping onto others." (353, 33)
> 5. *Seeking to be near:* "Following or standing near a particular child or a group of children [or an adult]." (353, 33)

The dependency behavioral patterns for touching and holding and being near seem to be directly related to the child-rearing antecedent of "low demands and restrictions without the entrance of the father into the [child's] rearing." (353, 67)

Behavioral development in both attention-seeking and attention-awakening behaviors proceeds then in several dimensions simultaneously. There is the development in the direction of greater precision and greater complexity, that is, seeking and gaining attention goes from "gurgling" to "asking," from stirring to defining wants. (325, 11) There is also the development towards the preferred mode (quality) of behavior for seeking and awakening attention, which is much akin to the selection of one's preferred insurance policy; that is, the selection of forms of behavior most likely to insure dependency reinforcement when dependency is needed. "Help given [tends to be] appropriate to the help needed; what is asked for by the child is in style and content what will serve to evoke the needed help from the parent." To illustrate, seeking proximity can serve as an effort (and end) to gain personal assurance, which is obtained (self-reinforced) within the act of obtaining proximity; while seeking proximity can also be an effort (and means) toward securing attention, which in turn depends upon the other person's response for its validation or negation. Interestingly, the former effort has to be met within the situation, the latter is transferable. (325, 14)

A parent's ability to recognize more than one facet of behavior hints at the inherent difficulty in relying upon *consistency* in behavioral reinforcement. First, there is always the question of which facet of behavior the caring person should respond to. Secondly, any consistent response assures reinforcement of development and change. Consequently, effective consistency requires change in consistency because change is the venture (contingency) of consistency. (325, 11–12) The questions always remain: consistent for and in what?

For Sears, *labeling* is an essential prerequisite to reasoning. Reasoning involves the explanation and justification of a total behavioral system, while labeling specifies the intent and outcome of certain actions. In labeling, a mother will "explain to a child exactly what it is she does and does not want him to do. . . . Its main purpose is *directing* behavior rather than *sanctioning*." (349, 351) When reward or punishment is introduced within the process, labeling then tends to occur as a backward sequence; that is, after the labeled behavior has taken place, the parents' action is inserted and connected to what should have occurred prior to the labeled event.

At the beginning of this phase, around age two, the child progresses from parental control to partial self-control supported by parental guidance. Self-control is a process of adopting parental wishes and standards as one's own. Children tend to imitate those qualities in their parents which are most vital to parents and are apt to be reprimanded by withdrawal of parental love. A sense of conscience usually revolves around two aspects of each behavioral act: the task to be done and the idea of obeying whatever is demanded, that is, obedience for its own sake. In each aspect, children will be motivated by their expectancy of reciprocal affection for behaving according to the expectations of others. "Privation of opportunity for establishing a primary attachment [dependency upon the care-giver] in the first three years of life produces a character defect such that second and third major attachments [dependency upon additional care-givers and later mutual caring friendships] fail to develop." (325, 25)

Increase in identification and conscience lead children to behave more in keeping with their sex. At the same time, they must learn how the other sex behaves and what such behavior expects of them in return. As stated, the child has to deal simultaneously with acquiring adult-role and sex-appropriate behavior. Each parent's capacity to praise and withdraw affection appropriately is intimately correlated with the parent's own satisfaction and comfort in life as a social being. (349) Parents' sense of well-being is closely linked with their sense of oneness with their social setting and the larger community. Their sense of self-esteem depends upon their ready access to the latest available information including the current emphasis for child care. Parents must find their behavior in agreement with that expected by the larger environment, transcending existing class, ethnic, and educational differences.

During the second phase of development, children develop their own personality while being directed by their elders' child-rearing efforts. During this period, a child develops a full repertoire of responses based on dependency needs, for rewarded, punished, and *non*rewarded situations. Behaviors for nonreinforced (noncontingent) dependency requiring interactions become important learning requirements in a child's armature of behaviors. The success of each method of child rearing depends upon finding a middle ground; too much or too little dependency and too strong or too little identification and conscience will thwart the normal progress of development.

Phase III: Secondary Motivational Systems: Extrafamilial Learning

By the time children are chronologically and developmentally ready for school, they can absorb learning beyond the bounds of the family. Their behavioral acquisitions can guide them for limited periods in their thrusts into the public arena and the world of other families. This wider social environment now shares in socializing them.

Dependency and Independency Balance

At approximately age five, their dependency becomes reduced to specific spheres of family living. To illustrate, children depend upon eating within the family circle, although they are no longer fed by any one member of the family. Dependency has been widened from reliance upon one person to relying upon a family system. This enlargement of the base of dependency continues. Usually, the teacher becomes a new support for dependence. At first, children tend to relate personally to each new adult they meet, according to earlier childhood patterns; later the teacher is a representative of a social system. Most importantly, dependency continues to allow the child to seek and receive help and guidance regarding behavior, although, as has just been illustrated, it proceeds on a higher level.

As before, the manner and quality of dependency are influenced by previous experience. Development proceeds in terms of seeking and gaining admiration or approval from parents, peers, pets, and anyone who can lend personal assurance or status beyond the immediate interaction sequence. Behavior patterns for seeking positive attention, such as compliance with expectations, are perpetuated in cooperative efforts with peers. Negative behavior patterns for seeking attention also continue, for example, teasing, exhibitionism, and practical joking. If negative patterns are not checked, they can remain an integral part of one's personality in years to come. Sears illustrates this point in his analysis of Samuel Clemens (Mark Twain), whose dependent behavior was to hide and stay out all night. "Shame, terror and the loss of love were the prices he paid for the glories of attention sought and gained." (337, 28)

The desire of school age children for independence needs to be balanced by their acceptance of control and their awareness of their range of freedom. They will try to control other people in such a way that they can satisfy their wants. Their new skills in controlling others are met by an increase in the self-control demanded of them. More and more areas of life become known for their expected behaviors, while the range of permissiveness in undefined areas becomes narrower. Certain areas remain strictly controlled by parents, teachers, neighbors, and other everyday contacts. In other words, controls become more universally defined and more explicitly reinforced.

Attitude of Aggressiveness

With an emerging shift in environmental reinforcers, permissiveness and punishment slowly alter their significance for the school-age child. "Permissiveness [tends] to serve as both an instigator and a symbolic reinforcer, while punishment [has] its predominant effect as a further frustration and hence a goal to more aggression." (353, 22) Higher punishment for aggression reduces antisocial aggression but increases anxiety and socially acceptable aggression. In early adolescence, punishment produces an increase in the aggression that is projected into the activities of reading, viewing, and fantasizing. (342) Conversely, high permissiveness regarding aggression increases antisocial aggression, especially in the matrices involving immediate dependency. Interestingly, aggression anxiety correlates positively with behaviors in caring persons that are either high in aggressiveness or low in aggressiveness but highly influenced by conscience (self-imposed expectations) as deemed as expected by caring person.

While punishment for dependency behavior tends to foster self-aggression, strictness achieves only the desired results if it combines caring (dependency support) as well as controls. Punishment as an instrument of discipline becomes effective only if the punishing person is experienced by the child as affectionate (caring). Children who experience satisfying interactions with the agent of punishment, especially if this experience occurs in their initial dependency formation period *(342)*, show significantly greater resistance to deviation than youngsters who have either more impersonal or unsatisfactory contacts. In other words, non-permissiveness is more influential than punishment per se in the lives of school-age children. *(342)*

Identification

Identification continues with models which are desirable at least in terms of fulfilling the child's wants. If desirable models cannot be located among adults, highly appreciated peers serve as people with whom to identify. As the world of children expands beyond the home, they learn of and acquire social, religious, political, and economic values. These value absorptions tend to be an expansion of what they once learned from their parents. Most importantly, children continue to strive for their parents' acceptance of them in order to maintain and enhance the gratification of such acceptance. Dependency upon parental gratification now means the child is assured of being more and more gratifying to the parent.

SUMMARY OF SEARS' DEVELOPMENTAL THEORY

The foregoing effort to sum up and interpret the work of a contemporary learning theorist highlighted the changes in the degree of precision, efficiency, and speed with which the developing child can manipulate his or her own actions and communicate with others. More and more children become a product of their social environment, assuring for themselves the gratification they desire. These social gratifications invariably become incentives and goals for actions. Sears conceives and researches child development primarily as a mirror of child-rearing practices in relationship to a child's basic life requirements. The activities meeting these essential life demands become the secondary motivational drives. The secondary motivational drives supersede the earlier innate ones and ultimately determine an individual's behavioral patterns. Secondary motivational drives become the behavioral systems of feeding, toilet training, dependency, aggression, dyadic relationships, and identification. They become the critical variables of child-rearing practices and, consequently, of child development.

Sears' findings emphasize that child-rearing practices in these critical areas are neither linear nor accumulative; rather they follow curvilinear patterns. Child rearing depends upon finding a balance between providing too much and too little in any one area. In the case of dependency and aggression, proper development depends upon furnishing an appropriate permissiveness and an opportunity to depend and aggress, as well as upon appropriate limits in order to foster gradually more and more independent actions and control. In other words, curvilinear development implies that too much such permission and opportunity intensify the behavior in question and too many limiting or controlling actions inhibit behavior.

Altogether, the socially acquired motivational systems determine the development of internal desires for action and the control of it. Young infants start behaving in the direction toward which parental control steers them. Later on, they enact this parental control; they identify. Identification becomes another motivational system which "drives" them to behave as expected, as primary caretakers and larger social institutions want them to behave.

To conclude, behavioral development can be summed up in short: as children behave, they develop. Conversely, their behavior is the product of their immediate social experiences of being brought up. To put it another way, behavioral development is a consequence of learning. Yet, with Sears' stress upon human development as a consequence of learning, his conclusion on the ultimate utility of learning theory starkly deviates from his fellow learning theorist B. F. Skinner. *(361a)*

Sears more recently suggests: "There is little hope that average parents will become sufficiently skilled—or be in sufficient control of their child's environment—to use complex learning theory for rearing children." *(325, 5)* Sears muses that we know much about the sequence of learning, but it remains still a matter of wonderment how an outstretched arm can become a single communicative unit meaning "pick me up and love me" or later on "give me the car keys—and quick!" In other words, behavioral development is discernible, measurable, and informative for the study and comprehension of how humans develop.

CHAPTER 4

The three theories viewed as parallel and an integration of affect-behavior-cognitive development

Three theories of development have been presented. Each theory has been written up as a system of its own. Together, they are viewed as parallel and congruent. The aim of this book is to provide a conceptual reference system of human development for the professional, the parent, or anyone who works with children and youth.

We need to ask ourselves whether the points of view of these theories are similar or conflicting regarding the understanding, care, or treatment of children. We shall reflect in this chapter on the similarities and differences among these theories with the following subheadings in mind: terminology; basic assumptions of homeostatic or heterostatic existence; questions of structure; the developmental continuum; integration of affective behavioral and cognitive phasal development; and the three sets of phases viewed as parallel.

TERMINOLOGY

At first glance, differences in the terminology employed by each of the three theorists accentuate differences and raise problems beyond those of pure semantics. Each theorist's strict adherence to a set language usage creates obstacles for conceptualizing cross-theoretical integrations. By considering the contexts in which the terms are employed, the problem of integrating the theories becomes approachable. Whenever we deal with different terminologies, we can either limit ourselves to the particular context in which technical terms are used, and remain almost parochially wedded to that specific system, or we can apply the terms employed in the context for which they were thought of and search for the corresponding designators in the other formulations. In the former approach, we focus upon the comprehension of any one system; while in the latter we want to understand development in general. It is this second objective we endeavor here to achieve.

To illustrate, *reinforce* in learning theory implies the introduction of specific contingent variables which, at specific intervals for a particular selected behavior of a specified person, have predicted impact upon the very behavior under consideration. Within the affective or cognitive theories before us, *reinforce* more likely means to support (affectively) or to pursue further (cognitively) without the specificity which behavioral language implies.

Another problem is to reconcile unique terminology for similar ranges of observations and concepts. For example, Piaget labels the first phase of life the *sensorimotor phase*. Erikson calls it the *phase of basic trust*. Sears simply refers to the *infancy* period of learning. Each one is preoccupied with different facets of development, but each one also refers to the identical period of life. The important thing then is to recognize that each theory may account for the same individual at the same point in his life with a unique point of view.

Thus, it remains for us to go beyond the semantic variations among the theorists and to search out the essential ideas each theorist's terminology intends to convey. This perspective is particularly pertinent for this book, since its intent is to provide a bridge of understanding among the theories rather than to expound each theory for its own unique meaning.

BASIC ASSUMPTIONS

It is important to parallel and compare the basic premises of the three theories, reviewing the assumptions underlying the three theory constructions—etiology of human behavior, core facets of human behavior, and environmental issues. These are all fundamental considerations in determining the nature of human development.

Theory Construction

As scientists, Piaget, Erikson, and Sears aim for an increased understanding of human growth and interactions through specific investigations in their specialized areas. Piaget strives to establish a universal system of cognitive development that is consistent with the collective intellectual development of human beings anywhere. Individual differences and cultural variations are of less interest to him than the search for the universal in the human species.

Erikson, by contrast, endeavors to understand each individual for his or her uniquely complex situation in life, and in particular for his or her emotional development. From their respective preoccupations, Piaget and Erikson search for a different truth. Each theorist deals with a prescribed dimension of human functioning and development. (190) Piaget is after what is *common* in each person's development in order that each person can be known for his or her specific and particular state of development. Erikson pursues the uniqueness in each person in order to explain the individual for his or her variation and ultimate universality. It is no wonder that each one turns to different methods of investigation, analysis, and reporting of findings.

Sears has a third approach and proceeds differently; he is searching neither for what is true for all human beings nor for what is different for each human being. He is after the essence of the social aspects of key human interactions. He is there to study humans within their social learning matrix.

In their approaches to theory building, Piaget and Erikson operate deductively, Sears inductively. The first two agree that all research on human development has to proceed within the context of a unified theory. Their separate approaches might be compared to the explorer who insists upon mapping the complete course of a river, including its springs and its final delta, before he can satisfactorily locate and investigate the whirlpools and bends within the path of the river. Piaget first constructs his theoretical model, then proceeds to test each of its parts, and finally considers his research findings valid only if they are, first, theoretically consistent and, second, empirically substantiated. Erikson stays with his deductive material. Individual and clinical data serve either to illustrate or validate conceptual propositions but rarely to test them. Sears, in contrast, holds that the building of a theory is a laborious process which requires the systematic organization of empirically valid findings. Curiously, although Sears advocates empiricism— an inductive approach to theory formulation in the presentation of his findings, particularly in his later writings—(173; 328; 330; 349; 351; 353) he proceeds much as do the other two, with his generalizations venturing far beyond the data which would validate the theory empirically.

Although all three agree that the natural environment provides the most favorable laboratory conditions for studying human development, each differs with respect to methodology of investigation and that aspect of development which ought to be investigated. Piaget structures his research in order to isolate variables of thought (cognitive) processes, aiming to learn precisely how one individual thinks about any one problem. Having gathered all the information he can from one individual, he relates his findings to his theoretical structure. Sears relies upon quantitative data which reveal the typical behavioral (interactive) responses to certain stimuli under given (that is controlled) sets of circumstances. Erikson dispenses with controls. He attempts to analyze all variables operating in the individual's total affective (emotional) sphere—personal, familial, cultural, societal, cosmic, and historical. His focus is upon the affective components, in particular in association with the complexity of the interrelationships of the variables cited.

In essence, Sears tries to locate general tendencies—the most probable modes of interaction; Piaget searches for the most inclusive overall structures within which development proceeds; and Erikson hopes to define the most dominant characteristics in human development. Yet despite these markedly different perspectives and research procedures, the findings of each theorist are strikingly noncontradictory. When we note that the perspectives are actually complementary when superimposed upon one another.

Etiology of Human Behavior

All three theorists believe in a system of human development and the predictability of human behavior. Piaget goes so far as to hypothesize that there is a single universal order. He sees in the ultimate understanding of the nature of life processes a key to an understanding of universal laws, and conversely, in the discovery of universal laws, an ultimate explanation of everyday life events. Erikson, too, assumes a cosmic order, but considers it beyond his immediate reach and concern. Sears, with his reliance upon the laws of probability, assumes with Piaget the predictability of human behavior. In his work, however, he limits his studies to those fractions of the universe which can be controlled, observed, measured, and empirically validated. Thus, Piaget, Erikson, and Sears all assume that human life unfolds in an orderly process in an orderly world and each one takes on a "humanistic approach to system theory. [Each one] emphasizes the proactive, creative, stimulus-serving behavior of living organisms, especially man." (366, 104–5.)

All three build upon an evolutionary view of human development, but in dissimilar ways. Sears considers human behavior to be the product of stimulus-response learning—more advanced than but essentially like animal motivational conditioning. It can be assumed that Piaget perceives cognitive development as separate from and unequal to drives and, therefore, more likely a key determinant of behavioral shaping rather than its product. We could assume that Piaget would repeat to Sears his earlier wry reminder: "In the beginning there was the response (R)!" (See Chapter 1.) All three suggest that human behavior arises out of the interplay of opposing forces; Erikson ascribes this polarity entirely to the struggle between opposing internal pulls; Piaget allocates the polarity to an encounter between an individual's internal understanding and the reality conveyed to him or her by the outside world; and Sears considers that the interplay of stimulus-response functioning essentially goes on between two individuals.

Sears introduces a rapid shift from innate (or impulsive) to learned (or socialized) behavior. For Sears, outward behavior soon reflects the product of the social environment; infants eat when and what they have been taught, and not as their digestive tract urges. Sears' reliance upon external forces for impacting development actually does not negate the existence of internal mediating factors (359, 440). Piaget starts out with a pure biological formulation (reflexes as the root of thinking), but then proceeds with his concept of the intermediation of experiences. Erikson alternately sees nature or human beings' harnessing of nature as the main source of humanness.[1]

Yet, each theorist has his own accent. Piaget stresses that new comprehension prompts new behavior. Erikson emphasizes, on the other hand, that the satisfaction obtained in the interaction impacts new behavior. Sears is apt to differ with both; for him the gratification obtained (reinforced) as a consequence of specific interactions (stimuli) guarantees and expands the desired behaviors. Each formulation implies that change—whether toward more advanced comprehension, greater security, or more effective behavior—is for the betterment of the person, and there to stay. Each formulation builds upon the belief that what is developmentally acquired is permanently used.

The greatest difficulty lies in reconciling Eriksonian views concerning the origin of human interactions with those of Sears and Piaget. If the three were to join in a roundtable discussion, Piaget and Sears would have to take issue with Erikson's psychoanalytic assumption that human behavior evolves from internally nurtured motivation. Piaget would painstakingly explain that once reflexes have been metamorphically changed into behavioral expressions

---

[1] It is in their alteration between nature and nurture, to quote Erikson," that history *and* personality *and* anatomy are our joint destiny"—(119, 323) a perception which gets him into dispute with N. E. Millet (201).

within the early months of life, human interactions are the product and instigator of the very process of interaction between individuals and the environment they experience. Sears, if he were to pursue this argument, would stress the interactive aspect learned ("experienced" for Piaget) by an individual. As soon as either Piaget or Sears were to explain their premises, they would have to clarify their contradictory points of view. Piaget sees learning as a product of development, while Sears views development as a product of learning.

In a study of the origin of human behavior, their differences are starkly divergent. Piaget posits a ready-made sensorimotor human apparatus at birth, and has been supported by neurological anatomical prenatal studies; while Sears, like other behaviorists, proceeds with seeing the infant at birth as a *tabula rasa*. The major concern of these three theorists, however, is not in which way human development originates, but rather in which way it progresses. The three developmental theories do not necessarily explain the source of the river of development, but rather its course. Therefore, in spite of this divergence in locating the spring of development, they seem to study the same river.

Core Facets of Human Behavior

Each theory was selected for its different focus upon human behavior. They have to differ. Piaget's emphasis upon cognitive comprehension as the decisive factor in all human behavior is countered by Erikson's contention that affective (emotional) processes furnish the basic motivations for all human behavior. Sears suggests that a person's behavior is in itself of overriding importance and an instrumental aspect for subsequent behavior. Each theory alone provides only a partial understanding of personality development. The human being is more than purely rational, purely motivated, or purely behaving, *(190)* and has to be viewed as being subject to all three of these dimensions.[2]

Within the bounds of our understanding of human development, we need to recognize that the child or youth is an individual who *thinks, feels,* and *acts* uniquely. Human behavior cannot be simplified when it is complex, nor defined as fully explainable and controllable when there is still much to be learned.

Environmental Issues

It is worth noting that Piaget, Erikson, and Sears all unite in an unwavering belief in granting the individual the potential capacity

---

[2] Thérése G. Decarie points out her research has proven the existence of a close link between intellectual and emotional development. Both dimensions of human functioning have "a parallel genetic order." (50, 191) She also provides a charting of a young child's intellectual and affective development. (50, 192–211)

to hurdle environmental obstacles, although each one holds a different view of how and to what degree environmental factors affect the individual. Piaget considers only those physical, social, or ideational components of an individual's environment that are within the range of the person's comprehension. Sears includes all factors which impact behavior, regardless of whether or not they enter the person's cognitive threshold. Erikson would be likely to include all imaginable environmental factors—including those spheres which are outside of the individual's immediate life—maintaining that all have relevance to the emotional development of a person. Figuratively, for each theory, environmental factors generate separate dynamic currents and activate widely differing functions. It should be pointed out that Piaget and Erikson join in viewing environmental events as both stimulants and feedback factors, while Sears depicts environmental events as the essential stimulators for all actions.

Homeostatic or Heterostatic Existence?

It is puzzling to decide whether each theory can be classed as a homeostatic or heterostatic formulation. Both Piaget and Erikson employ homeostatic terminologies. Both trace the interactions of polar pulls. Yet, in either formulation it is not the polarity of counterpulls, but the helical oscillation, the constant fitting of acquired experience into new experience, which counts. (192) So for both, a successful solution, whether it is called equilibration (Piaget) or positive adaptation (Erikson), introduces new benefits, new ways to create interactions for life. Oscillation and dialectic contradictions within a heterostatic context rather than polarity within a homeostatic one are, for them, the essence of life. (377) New ways of doing take over all functions—not to solve them but to create new (changed) life requirements. In contrast, a homeostatic conception pictures human adaptation, cognitively and affectively, as an issue of survival—that is, of making it at all. Both, Piaget and Erikson, concern themselves with questions of living beyond "making it." Their concern in human development, is in finding new starts (imbalances) through discoveries of added opportunities rather than finding balance through successful solutions.

Sears in his research seems to stand on the sidelines in this discussion. Yet, a review of his work suggests that he leans toward Erikson's perspective in his stress upon momentary reduction of tension as a means of creating opportunity and receptivity for added stimulation. If no added stimulation occurs, the individual is at a loss rather than at peace.

In summary, each theory can be defined as a formulation with a heterostatic perspective and, consequently, as relevant for our contemporary, changing times. (194a, 127–129) Piaget's and Erikson's thinking, especially their more recent work, is akin to dialectic thought since both conceive of the interaction of opposing yet mutually satisfying and energizing forces as oscillating events. *(377)* Each event is different, with each event bringing the individual a step closer to balance, and each step creating new vistas of imbalance for our thinking.[3] The latter are not defeats but life's opportunities.

QUESTIONS OF STRUCTURE

In a review of structure, we may ask ourselves: What functional purpose does each structural framework serve? Actually, very little, as each of the formulations before us are pertinent for their inherent change processes. These formulations account for what occurs (process), but teach us little about what the nature (structure) is. To recapitulate, for Piaget, all cognitive processes are related to the scientific structure of assimilation and accommodation—an oscillation between the structural reference points of internal (egocentric perspective assimilation) and external reality adaptation (accommodation). In contrast, Erikson operates with the analytic trio of id-ego-superego, which is little mentioned but ever present in his writings. Sears specifies two interdependent structural determinants, the action-reinforcement sequence.

Piaget and Erikson overtly, and Sears implicitly, create a second but equally significant structural framework—namely, developmental phases. In one sense, developmental phases serve as criteria of developmental achievements. In another sense, developmental phases for Piaget and for Erikson serve as organizational (structural) matrices within which development takes place. Actually, these phases become basic to an understanding of each theory. They are the tools in the study, evaluation, and interpretation of human development. It is not surprising, therefore, that these developmental phases have become useful points of reference and psychological "bookkeeping" terms.

All three authors apply structure as theoretical rather than topological reference points. Erikson departs from this position when he conceives of human anatomy in regard to the sex variation as an important variable. In this respect he finds himself in conflict with Sears' and Piaget's form of thinking—and for that matter, with the tenor of our time.

---

[3] Balance is equilibration in Piagetian terms; mastery for Erikson (quite a difference from catharsis in Freudian thinking); and readiness for new reinforcement for Sears.

What is important, however, is the structural base each theorist locates for himself as his territory of study. For both Sears and Erikson alike, the central caring person (or persons) and the child in their joint social matrix are the targets of study. Both theorists deal with the support and limitation afforded by each party concerned. Both hold that it is the quality of interpersonal relationships—attitude and action—between parent and child which is more important than the child's behavior, per se. In other words, though only Sears utilizes the world, both concentrate on dyadic relations within a larger social context. Piaget, in contrast, never even considers child-parent relationships as variables pertinent to his research.

THE DEVELOPMENTAL CONTINUUM

All three theorists equate development with dynamic, continuous change, a process in which all new development finds its roots in previous acquisition. Development, additionally, provides opportunities for completing and correcting development which lags or is irregular. Piaget shares Erikson's optimism that development is essentially a growing and rectifying process. And, in Erikson's words, unlike Humpty Dumpty, human beings can grow together again (114, 83). Sears' scheme can more easily be described as an additive progression, in which each new acquisition significantly builds upon a previous one. This emphasis upon continuous change by all three implies a progressive outlook with a strand of conservatism by recognizing the impact of the continuation of previous acquisitions. No learning, no experience, is ever entirely new. Each experience becomes integrated within previously established modes of behavior in the history of personal traditions. Old experience acquires new perspectives, and as Sears and Piaget stress, old experience receives new labels.

The differences among the three theorists are to be found in their emphases concerning the impact of earlier developmental acquisitions upon later ones. Sears seems to find himself on both sides of the argument. He considers only the latest social experiences as the major behavioral determinants which either replace or reinforce previous behavior. Erikson believes that early childhood experiences have a lingering impact. Regardless of subsequent events, early experiences continue to mold the direction of future behavior. Piaget challenges this interpretation as "adultomorphic" thinking. He questions an infant's capacity to perceive and remember specific events within the cognitive realm at a time when the individual is incapable of cognitively ordering such events.

Piaget's emphasis rests upon the alteration of early experience, that is, the continuation of earlier learning in terms of new ways (schemes) of understanding.

Piaget and Sears implicitly come to similar conclusions in their recognition of the increasing relevance of ongoing encounters that provide new and dissonant experiences as the child matures. Piaget's research brings out pointedly that during early childhood, new events are perceived as they happen. As individuals mature, they see such events with increasingly new perspectives and conceive of different patterns of relationships. For Piaget, maturing means increased comprehension of patterns of relationship. For Sears, maturing means refinement in the selection of appropriate behavioral patterns.

Without denying an inherent conflict, all three are closer in agreement than it appears. In a roundtable discussion, Piaget and Erikson acknowledged the compatibility of their formulations concerning the impact and continuation of earlier developmental experiences in later life. (237, 154–160) Each approaches the question of change from a different angle. Piaget preoccupies himself with the etiology of cognitive acquisitions and change in behavioral life experience; while Erikson (and perhaps Sears also if he had been present at these roundtable discussions (235; 236; 237; 246)) is concerned with the causative factors leading a person to choose one life experience over another.

In reviewing the total stream of development, we note that only Erikson recognizes setbacks or reversals as essential ingredients of development which are explainable within his theory. This is not surprising, for Erikson is as much concerned with normal as with deviant development. His concepts on regression are not in conflict with either Sears' or Piaget's theory. He alone, however, recognizes regression as an acceptable deviation within the progression of development. The other two do not deal with regression, but acknowledge the occurrence of plateaus.

Individual differences are accounted for by Piaget as differences in the rate and environmental circumstances of development. Erikson and Sears also locate in external circumstances the decisive factors in determining the rate of development. Erikson gives added credence to cultural expectations, while Sears finds that the rate of development is basically influenced by the immediate social settings.

Piaget and Erikson are known for their inventions of their developmental phases. Sears' research and writings imply, but do not acknowledge specifically, the existence of such phases. Both Piaget and Erikson imply a dialectic crisis within each phase which has to be resolved. For Erikson, with his stress upon opposing poles within each phase, these opposites have to be integrated. For Piaget, merely a temporary equilibrium of opposing processes has to be achieved within each phase. Sears acknowledges the emerging foci within the process of learning but has apparently no desire to discern further the nature of such a process.

Charting the developmental phases of each developmental continuum next to each other affirms a high degree of accord between them as well as a number of differences. (See Table 4.1.) In a review of the differences, we note at once the extensiveness of Erikson's developmental continuum as compared to Sears' and Piaget's limited explorations. For Piaget and Sears, development ceases at the most advanced age level they happen to have investigated.

There is a wide gulf between Piaget's and Erikson's conception of what occurs in adolescence. Their two theories are congruent in regard to the adolescent's struggle to comprehend what Piaget calls the complexity of life and to find a sense of anchorage, that is identity, in a network of what Erikson terms manifold relationship patterns. Piaget, however, expects personality integration to be completed during these years, at least as far as intellectual development is concerned. (Freudian theory once terminated development at this point, a perspective which Erikson altered with his reformulation.) Erikson conceives a series of new dialectic crises which both challenges and integrates anew all previous conflicting pulls.

With the completion of the adolescent phase, Piaget sees the individual as a mature and complete personality who has made the transition from adolescence to adulthood in a single step. Erikson strongly challenges such a position. He views young adults as still forging their own place in their society. Genuine maturity (a sense of integrity) for Erikson is still three stages ahead. In other words, for Piaget (and also for Sears), growing people reach adulthood the moment they surrender their childish thinking and actions. For Erikson, adulthood means more than outgrowing one's childish ways. Psychological maturity—if it ever exists—depends upon continued development of one's self-awareness and understanding within a complex and perplexing world. Maturity in a complex society, unlike that in less complex cultures, is not automatically bestowed with the traditional "rites of passage" that take place at puberty. Full adulthood is recognized when the individual is accepted as an equal by other adults. It is interesting to note that it is Erikson, the clinician, who continues to see not only the adolescent, but also the adult as a developing individual. It is he who can go beyond the notion of equal citizenry. As a clinician, he can

TABLE 4.1 COMPARISON OF THE DEVELOPMENTAL PHASES OF THE THREE THEORIES

Age (Years)	Piaget (Cognition)	Erikson (Affect)	Sears (Behavior)	Integration
0	Phase I: sensorimotor thought	Phase I: sense of basic trust	Phase of rudimentary behavior	Phase I: establishing dependence upon dependence
1				
2	Phase II: preconceptual thought	. . . . . .	. . . . . .	. . . . . .
3		Phase II: sense of autonomy	Phase of secondary motivational systems: family-centered learning	Phase II: establishing dependence upon self-care
4	. . . . .	. . . . .		. . . . .
5	Phase III: intuitive thought	Phase III: sense of initiative		Phase III: establishing dependence upon primary relationships
6	. . . . .	. . . . .	. . . . . .	
7			Phase of secondary motivational systems: extrafamilial learning	Phase IV: establishing dependence upon personal competence and secondary relationship
8	Phase IV: concrete operations	Phase IV: sense of industry		
9	. . . . .	. . . . .	————	. . . . .
10				
11				
12				

TABLE 4.1 (Cont.)

Age (Years)	Piaget (Cognition)	Erikson (Affect)	Sears (Behavior)	Integration
11				
12				
13				
14	Phase V: formal operations	Phase V: sense of identity	Little research done by Sears	Phase V: establishing dependence upon primary relationship in a secondary world
15				
16				
17				
18				
19	Not investigated by Piaget	Phase VI: sense of intimacy"		Phase VI (youth phase): establishing dependence on a complex ideational world
20				
21				
etc.				Adulthood phases

" Two more progressive phases of adulthood follow: sense of generativity and sense of integrity.

NOTE: No steplike pattern is intended here; rather, development is continuous through phases which merge into each other.

consider from a position of authority differential maturity among social equals.[4]

INTEGRATION OF AFFECTIVE, BEHAVIORAL AND COGNITIVE PHASE DEVELOPMENT

By placing the developmental continua of the theories next to each other (as in Table 4.1), we note how starkly congruent and parallel they are. We note, as was stressed in the introductory chapter, that for each developmental continuum, time (maturation and chronological passage of time) and experience (environmental encounters and the experience of such experience) alter all perspectives. We note the parallelism and congruency of developmental phases. As is noted later in this chapter, the essential foci within each parallel phase are congruent with each other. On the basis of these observations, the following interpretation of phasal development could be established (see Table 4.1, fourth column).

It is remarkable that the three continua of human development contain almost identical phasal divisions. It becomes less of a coincidence when we remind ourselves that each phasal epoch involves a combination of maturational and societal contingencies. For instance, just to note some maturational factors, the first phase spans the period of most rapid postnatal physical growth, the second and third phases[5] overlap with a period of accelerated physical growth until the combined rates of growth (body weight and height) level off to a minimal growth period, which is the fourth phase for Piaget and Erikson. Finally, each theorist's fifth phase—development of a sense of identity or, in the case of Piaget, conceptualization by means of formal operations—coincides with a renewed period of accelerated maturation as illustrated by a highly steep combined rate of growth curve for this adolescent period.

Phases are not wired into the organism; they are products of interactional experience between a child and his or her social environment. These experiences inform the child's social world of his or her requirements and lead to the child's developmental progression. Societal conceptions and expectations are summed up by bestowing each period with a specific name. Each period has its set of expectations and social norms in which children are respectively socialized. Phase I is infancy; phase II is toddlerhood; phase

---

[4] This observation was made by Dr. E. A. Smith, a political-economic social scientist and professor emeritus of the University of Washington.

[5] These phases are least clearly defined and acknowledged in Piaget's and Erikson's writings. Curiously, they also have the least notable maturational counterperiods.

III is early childhood or the nursery school period; phase IV is childhood or the school-age period; phase V is adolescence. *(184)* In addition, a new youth phase is in the making; it is societal and, consequently, like a sixth developmental preadulthood phase. *(316b)* Each of these descriptive entities hint that the phasal concepts may also have biological realities.

In an integration of affective, behavioral, and cognitive phasal development, the author submits the following notion of progression. The first phase, establishing dependence upon dependence, deals essentially with eventual predictability that is rhythmic and regularity within a cognitive realm, while affectively, rhythmic repetition creates certainty (trust) with an ability to perform in the behavioral sphere. Altogether, be it in regard to feeling, knowing, or doing, depending upon dependence is at stake.

Once dependability is assured, a new phase is in the making—phase II, dependence upon self-care. Cognitively, labeling is important and also conveying thoughts with a beginning sense of order; affectively, we see the emergence of maintenance of self-care with a strong behavioral component in children to do it and control it themselves. Each of these developmental preoccupations imply a period in which young children find themselves as if they were the center of the universe and preoccupied with their own actions and the mastery of their actions.

A Copernican-like revolution occurs within the third phase. Dependence upon self-care frees the young child to become independent of this self-centered preoccupation while becoming more concerned with dependence upon primary relationships.[6] Agemates, family members, and others are discovered. Cognitively, the child moves beyond a one-dimensional world, and classification emerges in his mode of thinking. Affectively, differential primary relationships (family and immediate peers) become central; behaviorally, the child begins to master social controls. Altogether, dependence upon primary relationships is in order. After all, as contemporary social institutions will it, it is time for the child to learn how to be, to think, and to do with others. It is time for nursery school, head start, or play school.

With dependence upon primary relationships temporarily secured, greater independence from them provides for freedom to depend upon secondary contacts as well as for personal competence development. It is time for school and social organizations beyond the family, from playground to established organizations (scouts, clubs, leagues, 4-H clubs, etc.). Cognitively, conceptual

[6] For a fuller discussion of the notion of dependence-independence oscillation, see "A New Perspective on the Role of Dependence and Independence in Human Development." *(192)*

and multidimensional thinking, especially hierarchical ordering and the processes of reversibility and conservation, assist the child to deal realistically with his or her life experience. Competent mastery becomes the central issue, improving and exacting behavioral acquisition within space, time, and social contexts. Dependence upon personal competence and secondary relationships constitutes the child's life tasks within this phase.

Finally, on the basis of the developmental material presented in the preceding chapters, we see the young adolescent has acquired conceptual thinking and social capability. His dependence can shift (free of that particular dependence) to a new dependence in which conceptual conquest, comprehension of his or her multidimensional world and the relativism of every event moves into the center. Affectively, children have to find their own self in a complex system of relationship. In Eriksonian terms, they are now in the process of forging their sense of identity. Behaviorally, they have to locate, as Robin Hood did, the proper behaviors and social expectations—each according to the specific social context. Within this proposed integrated scheme, the adolescent is establishing dependence upon primary relationships within a secondary world.

In summary, the five phases just discussed are presented schematically parallel to the separate phasal progressions of cognition (Piaget), affect (Erikson), and behavior (Sears) in Table 4.1. The three developmental continua on affect, behavior and cognition are almost dovetailed with each other when viewed vertically, that is, developmentally. They do diverge from each other, as will be seen in the following section, when viewed horizontally. The latter is neither surprising nor necessarily inconsistent as each formulation relates itself to different dimensions of human functioning. (190)

THE THREE DEVELOPMENTAL DIMENSIONS VIEWED AS PARALLEL

Infancy and Toddlerhood Development

In scanning an individual's development simultaneously through the observational screens of Piaget, Erikson, and Sears, we find congruencies as well as contradictions. Piaget and Erikson concentrate upon the very early patterning of native responses. In the basic rhythms of living during the beginning weeks of life, they locate basic patterns of thinking, attitudes, and behaving. While Piaget and Erikson speak of early patterning, Sears speaks of conditioning. In essence, however, Sears' interpretation of this early conditioning remains true to Erikson's and Piaget's findings.

Actually, Sears deals as fully with whole complexes of behavior, which he denotes as clusters of behavioral sequences. Most strikingly, all three imply that an infant's experience of rhythmicity represents a cornerstone for later developments.

There are, nonetheless, noteworthy differences among the theorists' interpretations as they consider the meaning of early life experience in the context of the individual's current and subsequent experiences. Erikson hypothesizes a continuous thread of life events, beginning with experience associated with birth and weaving a pattern throughout an individual's life history. Piaget satisfies himself that early life experiences establish the essential although potentially alterable patterns for relating to events in later life. Sears sees earlier self-satisfying experiences impinging upon later ones only so long as their aggregate lends a directional impact upon later events. Moreover, Piaget and Erikson find different interpretations for a child's early self-centeredness; Piaget requires no explanation because for him the child knows no alternative.[7]

From Erikson's viewpoint, childhood egocentricity constitutes children's early efforts to establish their own sphere and to locate themselves as independent being among others. Sears tends to side with Erikson. He defines a child's self-centeredness as an expression of the central struggle between self-satisfaction and the acceptance of social controls. These theoretical differences bear directly upon everyday practice. They point to the necessity for differentiating distinctly between intellectual and emotional self-awareness. They imply the continuous separation between the states of feeling and the knowledge of one's independence and sense of self.

A similar problem arises in regard to sex differences. Erikson alone sees the infant child as sexually differentiated. Infants' sex defines their specific sexual, genetic, and sociocultural heritage. Sears recognizes sexual differences to the extent that these differences affect a child's immediate environment, since this environment will, in turn, impact the child. Piaget gives no cognizance to sexual differences in his study of intellectual development. In other words, the three theorists combined teach us that male and female employ *equal* intellectual processes but behaviorally and emotionally they differ; socially they are as equal as culture permits.

In another area of infancy development, Piaget questions the analytical contention that unconscious processes are as potent within the first phase of development as they are during sub-

---

[7] Piaget stresses that the egocentric aspect of speech starts to dissipate toward the middle of the second phase (around three years of age). He also reminds us that interpersonal feelings cannot take place until the child is able to perceive other as *others;* only then can he develop sympathies and antipathies (*284,* 17–18, 33–34).

sequent phases. According to Piaget, infants do not yet possess the intellectual capacity to conceive and to remember objects when they are in direct contact with them. Memory of experience and its conceptualization, at least on an intuitive level, are prerequisite to unconscious thought. Consequently, recall, conscious or unconscious, cannot occur until children have the capacity to symbolize, label, retain, and recall previous experiences—a capacity usually not achieved until the child is over one year old. Piaget repeatedly stresses that individuals cannot conceive others (another *self*) before they can perceive objects, at least vaguely, as being independent. In essence, it is narcissism without any alternative. Even then, memory of objects remains linked with the memory of the sequence of the total experience. Sears would not be apt to agree with this. Erikson maintains that unconscious processes such as emotional states can be reexperienced with little or no accurate intellectual ideation.

These differences are viewed for their impact upon the application of concepts once they are applied. In the actual application of theory, the practitioner does not deal directly with children's infantile image of their parents, real or implied, conscious or unconscious, except as it might apply to their overall feeling about other persons in their ongoing life experiences. The three theorists imply that the adult world deals with children as if they knew and remembered their previous experiences. Consequently, whether children can consciously or unconsciously remember their early life experiences, they react to adults' expectations as if they knew.

There is a conflict in the three theorists' interpretation of unconscious processes. For Erikson, unconscious processes are reality; for Piaget, beyond his questions about infantile unconscious retention, unconscious processes are a likelihood, but outside his sphere of interest and range of research. *(267)* Sears, like Erikson, but unlike other behaviorists, accepts them as an implied but unmeasurable reality. *(328; 337; 343; 348; 349)* He focuses upon the results of human motivations, conscious or otherwise. *(346)*

All three theorists view the process of perception differently without inherent conflict. For Piaget, perception is a neurological experience with little cognitive reference per se unless individuals mentally incorporate their perceptual experiences. In short, only as individuals cognize their perceptions do they perceive, however realistic or distorted their awareness may be. Erikson, on the other hand, acknowledges perception as part of a person's experience, but does not deal with this process as an area of specific interest to him. Sears describes perceptual processes only as response to stimulation. All three theorists agree that selective perception is as much impacted by developmental and maturational factors as by personality issues. We may assume then, that perception and comprehension are closely intertwined and can be viewed as one within the range of questions of this book.

Play, accepted seriously as a core process of human development by all three, is continuously reviewed as an accelerating factor of development. Sears' work is notable for his research on play and his perception of play as a practice arena for the integration of diversified behaviors. Erikson and Piaget also grant play equal time. The latter two conceive the function of play conversely. Erikson interprets play as an effort to adapt inner reality to outer experience, while Piaget, in contrast, signifies play as a process of adapting (assimilating) outer reality to inner perspectives. Each one, however, deals with different life functions. Erikson conceives play as a means for solving emotional conflicts, and only secondarily as instrumentally enjoyable. Piaget, again on the other side of the fence, accounts for play as a pleasurable activity for setting things right (cognitively) in terms of individuals' own pleasure—their very own perceptions of things.

Controversial views exist around imitative behavior. Imitative and habit-forming processes loom large in Sears' frame of reference. Piaget implies that habit formation occurs mainly during a child's first twelve months. For Piaget, habits constitute self-limitation; that is, persistence in behavioral patterns. The young child's ever-increasing capacity to perceive and to imitate outside models (to accommodate) simultaneously diminishes his or her inclination to live according to habits. More and more he or she adapts to the behavioral patterns of others rather than by habitual performances. Some of these adaptations will also involve the adaptation to common social practices, or generalized habits. Erikson pays little attention to the acquisition of behavioral patterns as such. Basically, all three are more concerned with the context in which habits occur than upon a study of habits per se.

Childhood Development

Piaget and Erikson recognize learning by trial and error as an essential factor in early childhood development, but in this they part ways with Sears by relegating this process of learning to a minor position in all later childhood development. Altogether, Erikson is the most willing to recognize a power within the infant which is knowingly exercised. Sears prefers to relegate the direction-giving power for most infant behavior to the stimuli outside the infant. Piaget, on the other hand, first counters Erikson's idea that early life experiences become generalized by the child for all subsequent experiences; but he then submits a similar observation—albeit with a different rationale—by stating that infants do build upon their own previous experiences because they know no alternative.

In all three dimensions of development, the process of identification is central. Trial and error and imitative learning are primarily precursors and supplementary processes to identification. For all three theorists, modeling is a vital part of the process of identification in which the selection of others as models, and living up to the behavior, ideas, or values assumed to be measured by the persons selected are constituent parts of the identification process.

Piaget conceives of identification as the process of choosing models according to existing patterns of the child's understanding. Sears conceptualizes a process of fitting available models to the satisfactions associated with them on the basis of similar and previously pleasing experiences. Particularly, Sears sees identification evolve from a delicate balance between the experience of support or frustration and love or denial of love. Interestingly, Sears' descriptive explanation of identification could readily be interpreted in terms of Erikson's schema. Thus, the degree of the caring person's love and his or her desire to guide the child without willfully pushing or letting the child flounder haphazardly, can be seen as efforts to deal with these wobbly balances. To Erikson, the selection of models is a natural need-fulfilling process and each phase demands the development of different qualities and a different range of models.

Altogether, the selection of the model is based upon each child's unique perspective as circumscribed by the range of available and appropriate models. Identification, as depicted by all three theorists, can be described in terms of Bronfenbrenner's three levels of identification: (30) (1) a behavioral activity, with emphasis on absorbing a model's overt action; (2) a motivational activity, with emphasis on the disposition to act like the selected models; and (3) a mental process, with the emphasis on mechanisms involved in emulating a person of special personal importance. Note that identification bestows symbolic significance upon the model apart from and beyond the previous ongoing relationship to the model and provides the child with additional significant persons within or beyond his or her immediate social matrix.

In his developmental scheme, each theorist maps a course for the transfer of personal attachment and behavior. Erikson stresses two factors. The first of these is the transfer and continuation of the symbolic significance of a previously important experience with one model to a contemporary model. Secondly, a fanning-out process takes place in which the identification with one person moves differentially to two and eventually several persons or even to groups of individuals. Piaget charts only the ongoing changes in the use of different models without defining specific patterns in the progress of relationships. In contrast, Sears cites the development of identification as an additive process. Each successful identification results in the potential for renewed and improved identification on a more complex and, presumably, more advanced level. All three, then, unite in viewing identification as a central process of development. Each formulation's emphasis supports and supplements the others' content.

Piaget, Erikson, and Sears share the conviction that whatever occurs during the early developmental years is impactful for a child's later adjustment. All three see early life experience as an initial period of socialization. Each recognizes that the social implications of new experiences are more important than the actual mastery of the tasks accomplished.

The actual processes of social learning, however, are accounted for quite differently by each. Piaget considers social learning to be a process of personal adaptation between what is understood and mastered previously and what is perceived as new and appropriate to be mastered. Erikson interprets learning that is "social" as an issue of "psychological digestibility." For him, social adaptation takes place concomitantly with psychological accessibility. Sears counts on the relationship between past experience and the rewards that socialization has in store. Piaget, then, sees social learning as an ongoing and balancing process between internal and external impressions. Erikson modifies this contention by maintaining that this balancing process is substantially influenced by children's individual efforts to make their social adaptation psychologically safe for them. Sears adds that the selection of the eventual balancing factors and the psychological mechanisms depend ultimately upon the satisfaction that the child tries to recapture in keeping with his or her past experiences.

When viewed together, the formulations are not too far apart but they emphasize different factors. For purposes of working with children, a choice is required concerning which shift of emphasis is appropriate at each given instance. Erikson's infants, who are testing their sense of basic trust, and Sears' infants, who are practicing their rudimentary behavioral skills and testing their environment, are probably very much the same as Piaget's infants, who are experimenting with objects around them, including their own body parts, to produce interesting effects.

The three theorists recognize the words and sentences of spoken language as the conveyor of symbolized meaning and implied messages. In addition, Piaget says that language has a second function as an auxiliary operation of the thinking process. In Sears' and Piaget's view, the child is a different person as he or she learns to use language. For Erikson, language is merely an additional, significant resource for transmitting as well as for camouflaging feelings, thinking, and actions. Moreover, he alone gives attention to verbal and nonverbal language and the inner consistency or divergence between these two forms of communication. (Naturally Erikson, as a student of deviant behavior, wants to know when an individual's communication systems are at one with each other and when they lack integration.) Language for Sears constitutes symbolized learned behavior.

For all three, the use of communicative language, combined with identification with a model, establishes the operation of a conscience. Erikson alone concerns himself with the progressive development of a conscience (superego) while Piaget attempts to trace the emergence of consciousness and self-awareness. Odier once suggested that Piagetian and analytical thinking come closer together in the sphere of superego (conscience) development than in any other aspects of their respective thinking. (213, 20) The three theorists agree that the parent's conscience serves as the child's conscience until children incorporate their caring adult's conscience as their own. Piaget also stresses the importance of the peer group as an alternate conscience. For Piaget, a child's conscience becomes operational at an earlier developmental level than that of the other two theorists, roughly a year ahead on the developmental continua.

To Piaget, conflicting feelings cannot be labeled as guilt until the child has atained the mental capacity to appraise adult prestige and authority. Thus, Piaget finds no place for a feeling of guilt or a desire for punishment on any level prior to the child's conscious awareness of the seat of authority. Erikson and Sears, on the other hand, define guilt as the product of conscious or unconscious experience from infancy on, even prior to the conscious awareness of taboos, since conscience is a learned phenomenon of social interaction. The child, for years, anticipates responses to his potential actions based on the responses to similar behaviors in the past. Sears, then, limits conscience to anticipatory behavior. Piaget and Erikson again present a dichotomy. Cognitive conscience does not exist until an individual *knows* of its existence. The affective conscience (superego) emerges years before an individual is consciously influenced by its effect.

The Oedipal conflict, a psychological phenomenon pertinent for psychoanalytic theories and still a reality in Erikson's new analytic construct, has no place in Piaget's or Sears' formulations. In the presentation of Erikson's affect theory, Erikson points to shifting as well as conflicting loyalties in varying attachments toward key elders of the opposite sex. These shifting and differential loyalties, in essence, are the "stuff" which led to the Oedipus formula. Piaget and Sears observe in their findings similar shifts and conflicting alignments in regard to imitative learning and the establishment of a single model as the source of primary identification.

Both observe an increase in the child's awareness of and interest in behaving like the parent model of the same sex, and a simultaneous endeavor to maintain and to ensure close ties with the model of the opposite sex. It is interesting to note that Piaget defines an intellectual conflict in a child's apparent sexual identification during the nursery-school years. For Piaget, much of a child's role confusion and conflict is parallel to the emotionally conflicting loyalties in the Oedipal situation. Sears stresses that during this particular developmental period the parent of the same sex as the child is apt to be the instigator as well as the recipient of greater aggression, while the opposite parent tends to be more lenient, and consequently more approachable (163). Erikson relates these observations to the Oedipal situation.

Erikson progressively changed his conception of the Oedipal phenomenon. He held earlier, in 1950, to a traditional analytic interpretation. (65) By 1967, he suggested that the Oedipal situation involves more diverse conflicting strivings than merely sexual attachments to the parent of the opposite sex. (128, 24) In a publication in 1973, he questioned the whole Oedipus mystique, (126, 113) interpreting it as a situation of perplexing and conflicting relationships rather than as an inherent developmental phenomenon.

Piaget's and Sears' findings imply that in the so-called Oedipal period the child attempts particularly painstaking behaviors in order to imitate the parent of the same, which, in turn, creates a more urgent attachment and added complications with the parent of the opposite sex. There is little fundamental conflict as long as the situation is viewed as a perplexing problem in the shifting of interpersonal attachments rather than a complexity of its own making.

Erikson sees the identity struggle at puberty (formerly designated as the second Oedipus conflict) as a developmental crisis, a struggle between gaining a sense of identity and being left with a sense of role diffusion. Piaget alludes to similar complications as adolescents attempt in their own mind to define their social relationships within a new and larger social matrix. Piaget conceives of a more advanced cognition of patterns of relationship as the solution to this period of stress. Erikson attributes the successful integration of this period to the mastery of conflicting affective processes. Both recognize this time of confusion and conflict as an essential ingredient of growth.

Erikson suggests that developmental processes differ according to sex. Piaget does not take sex differences into account, although he does note clear conflicts and dilemmas in adolescents' thinking, in which reality becomes secondary to possibility. Technically speaking, the identity crisis of this period is associated with formal operations. Piaget agrees with Erikson's emphasis on the need for the young during adolescence (identity crisis) to make their own choices from among many possibilities. Cognitively, Piaget discovered that only within adolescent development (formal operation) can an individual mentally reverse a sequence of events in such a way that it becomes clear why "what did happen . . . had to happen." (86, 63) Sears' work does not sufficiently extend into this developmental period to parallel his thinking on these questions.

School Age Development

In this section only Piaget's and Erikson's material will be compared for essential agreements and differences since Sears' work is mainly limited to the preschool child.

Piaget and Erikson assume distinctly different positions in regard to the fantasy life of children. For Piaget, fantasy remains a continuation of the egocentric phase of a child's life. He defines it as a compartmentalized continuation of a young child's one-dimensional life of which the child is the center. Erikson, in contrast, attributes to the child both an awareness of his fantasies and a conflict over such an awareness. Yet, both stress that the caring adult deals with the child as he or she perceives or wants to perceive the child's world. Erikson adds that the adult also relates unconsciously to the child's fantasies, which have been communicated by the child and sensed by the adult unconsciously. Adults tend to respond to these fantasies because they unconsciously relive their own childhood and strive to forestall the mobilization of feelings that were put aside a long time ago.

Piaget and Erikson see young school-age children as pushing forward incessantly, creating for themselves new horizons of skills, knowledge, and emotional maturity. Piaget and Erikson both recognize the children themselves to be the driving force. The adults in their environment, especially those who care for them, can substantially help or hinder their progress. At school age, the adults no longer simply "bend the twig," for children then have a life sphere of their own. In other words, Piaget and Erikson both acknowledge children's intense concentration to improve their understanding and techniques of living and the resulting gradual shift from dependency upon caring persons to dependency upon peers and new adult influences. Both recognize a change in the child's style of living without an alteration in the child's basic personality structure.

Adolescent Development

Piaget's approach to adolescent development as a finite process, the culmination of all previous development, is in conflict with Erikson's central theme that this period constitutes the second formative period of life—the years of youth and of becoming an adult. The differing positions center around two major points: (1) Piaget depicts adolescence as a period in which the youth finds unity with the world; a period in which the outside social world "falls into place" and can be fully comprehended for its division of roles, its interrelated laws, and its permeation with unity. Erikson, in contrast, defines adolescence as a period in which a relevant social position is sought with the full implication of this position yet to be established in the ensuing years of progressive maturing, which constitute an essential component of adulthood. (2) Piaget's approach to adolescence as a period of tying together loose ends, as a period of completion, is contradicted by Erikson's stress upon defining adolescence both as a period of delayed development and as a period of commencement.

These apparently conflicting positions can be reconciled in part by the fact that Piaget and Erikson deal with two different elements of personality—cognitive and affective. Yet both see adolescence as a developmental period in which the young find their societal place. For Piaget, it is a "life plan"; for Erikson, a "sense of identity." In addition, these differences might be further bridged by Piaget's findings that modes of action precede the corresponding mode of cognition, and, in particular, comprehension always precedes the capacity to explain that which is understood. Knowing and substantiating what is known are logically earlier than achieving the capacity to translate such comprehension into action.

Piaget and Erikson both suggest that their developmental progressions incorporate age norms only as points of reference. Their developmental charts stress that developmental sequences are based upon previous developmental acquisitions and that any advanced phase of development, such as adolescence, can occur at any time in life, even after individuals' chronological age has established them as adults and as accomplished citizens of their society. The apparent differences, therefore, are not necessarily contradictory; they merely apply to two different aspects of personality. Moreover, cognitive development likely has added phases beyond those thus far formulated by Piaget himself. Piaget recently implied this (221) as have several students of development. (316b; 371)

Beyond Adolescent Development

There is, however, a significant difference when one theory depicts total personality development as a life-long process and the other defines cognitive development as circumscribed and finite, similar to physiological maturation. These complications primarily effect the expectations set for the developing individual. While one theory implies that a person's range of mature comprehension should be near completion and at its highest level when the youth becomes a young adult, the other views development as far from completion. In this case, Piaget and Erikson live, expect, and create in different worlds.

SUMMARY OF MAJOR DIFFERENCES

In the foregoing discussion of similarities and differences of the three theories, we employed logical rather than empirical means for reconciling differences. Certain differences remain that are of particular importance.

1. The differences in terminology are most troublesome, but they can be partially overcome by absorbing technical terms for their message rather than for their technical definition. After all, technical language serves as a vehicle of communication rather than a tool to either isolate or substantiate.
2. Each theory is grounded in a different cluster of assumptions. Most striking, each theorist attempts to obtain his facts by starkly separate methodologies. Each has his own objective to pursue. Yet, the mutual compatibility of their findings remains more convincing than the different road each one chose for his research.
3. Each theorist explains the origins of human behavior differently, although they share major concerns, for example, to concentrate upon behavior as it unfolds.
4. A more complicated situation arises as each theory introduces different assumptions, data, and conclusions about the stabilizing factors in each child's development and especially in the child's efforts to locate added stimulation for advancing his or her development. Each theory introduces its own set of basic ingredients for its chosen core of development (affect, behavior, cognition). These ingredients are nontransferable and remain applicable only within the theory.
5. In a review of the developmental continua, the major difference rests with the question of when a mature person is "mature." Erikson alone recognizes a clearly open-ended continuum. Piaget grants the adolescent near-adult maturity during a period in which Erikson sees the emotional development of adolescents still very much below the threshold of psychological maturity. Because Piaget and Sears dealt far less with adulthood, we yield to Erikson by default; his work continues where the others' leaves off.

6. Only Erikson considers sexual differences as an essential variable. For Sears, it is the environmental reaction to maleness and femaleness which defines differences in the developmental paths of boys and girls. Cognitive development, for Piaget, remains asexual.

Thus, together, the three theories provide a three-dimensional approach. For the practitioner or student of human development, each theory adds understanding and lends direction to the understanding and helping of people. Jean Piaget's consideration of cognitive functions is certainly vital to one who tries to understand and work with children; but to consider only the intellectual functions would be highly inappropriate. Erik H. Erikson's concern for affective, interpersonal processes is needed to supplement Piaget's contribution. Robert R. Sears' stress upon the effects of immediate behavior becomes particularly applicable for parenting, day care, and other child-caring efforts, especially for impacting ongoing problem situations.

Each theory contains a partial and different answer concerning a child's development. But a child is not a disected being, and if children are to be helped toward successful development and social development, they must be viewed in light of their *total* development. Consequently, adherence to just one of these formulations is apt to result in an incomplete approach.

We should remind ourselves that Sears studied affective development in order to gain an added appraisal of human development. *(332; 347)* Erikson intermittently refers to Piaget's work, while Piaget frequently admonishes his readers that there is neither *pure* behavior nor pure affect nor pure cognition. All three dimensions are forever present. To quote Piaget:

> *There is no affective behavior and cognitive behavior. Behavior is always both. Thus, only an analysis, an abstraction for the study of their respective mechanisms separates these two aspects which in reality are always present* simultaneously. *Hence, if one acknowledges affectivity and cognition . . . as two aspects of behavior, it makes no sense to wonder which causes which or even which precedes which. One aspect does not cause another aspect or precede another aspect. They are complementary because neither process can function without the other.* (50, 199)

Altogether, the tendency of one formulation to supplement the other two presented in this book by far outweighs the existing and residual conflicts noted in this chapter.

PART TWO

APPLYING ONE'S KNOWLEDGE OF CHILD DEVELOPMENT

CHAPTER 5
The helping process

To understand fully how the three dimensions of human development presented in this book can be used in working with people, a review of the process of helping is in order. In any purposeful effort to help, certain activities are brought together, for example, assessment and intervention, observation and relationship, and empathy and rational judgment. It is only when an individual knows that the ordinary alternatives of daily life do not promise the desired changes that he or she will search out specialized professional help. The aim of a professional helping process is to alter the focus of some aspect of life which the individual and the helper mutually designate.

THE HELPING PROCESS DEFINED

Within the context of this discussion, the helping process is defined as follows:

A series of socially engineered intervention activities in which the practitioner (the helper) deliberately introduces specifically structured events into the experience of an individual or group of individuals, or into an organizational context, in order to facilitate ordinary developmental processes.

Whether intervention is supportive, rehabilitative, or preventive, the practitioner needs to regard the helping events as supplementary to the myriad experiences every individual encounters in his or her daily life which serve as ordinary enabling processes. For example, it is common for parents and teenagers to discuss and to disagree on appropriate curfew hours. Parent are, thereby, helping teenagers incorporate appropriate limits into their daily life. It is possible, however, for parent and adolescent to come to such an impasse that the curfew suggested by one brings about the wrath of the other. When such a conflict cannot be solved by parent, adolescent, family, or friend, a third, uninvolved, professionally equipped person can furnish the needed help.

In both these instances a helping process occurs, but the two differ significantly. In the first situation, the actual process is of parent helping adolescent and adolescent helping parent to work out a developmental task together. Together, parent and adolescent find and grant one another limits of independence and dependence acceptable within their shared social sphere. The second situation requires the special helping process of intervention by a third party. This supplementary helping includes the introduction of intervention activities which reduce the problem by promoting the developmental adjustment of adolescent and parent. Such an adjustment could include the introduction of societal conditions which will touch the parent's and adolescent's life experiences without necessarily requiring the personal adaptations of either one. For example, to arrange with the adolescent a special alternate educational experience for him or her which meets the adolescent's interests and parental expectations, while it also supports and expands the particular educational institution's purpose. Once parents and adolescents find *ways* of working on their differences, it is assumed that that experience will lead to more continuously successful interactive modes for solving future differences.

We note that several key notions are implied in the previous paragraphs: (1) As already stated, intervention occurs in order to enhance ordinary developmental processes. (2) Professional helping deals with the persons' capability to resolve the conflicting situation. Helping means assisting persons with their problem-solving capacity rather than removing problems or submitting solutions. (3) Helping requires that the helper relate to both parties involved for their interaction with each other rather than to just one of the parties. A relationship issue proceeds between people and does not belong to one person or the other.

Developmental Implications

In a professional context, the helping process involves a systematic procedure. Such a systematic procedure of intervention builds upon two basic assumptions which emerge out of our perspective of human development. First, ordinary human development is understandable and predictable; second, human development will take its course spontaneously if gross complications have been reduced or altered. Professional intervention, therefore, occurs with the knowledge that once the complicating circumstances have been corrected, regular development continues. The professional has to resolve an "if . . . then" proposition. That is, if specified intervention steps are introduced, then he can expect that specific developmental processes will assume their normal course. Figuratively, professional intervention initiates a play within a play in order that the play of life can go on.

CHOICE OF HELPER

Help is introduced in order to facilitate development. The person in distress may be a concerned family member or one of society's trouble spotters, such as a teacher, counselor, nurse, policeman, clergyman, physician, and personnel worker. The person who first notes or suspects the complication will define it within his or her own conceptual framework. This initial assessment of the problematic situation defines who the professional helper should be.

For example, consider a ten-year-old boy's inattentiveness combined with slow progress in school. The boy's mother might confer with his teacher about this concern. If parent and teacher think the complication has some physical connections, a medical examination by a health specialist would be in order. Parent or teacher might infer that the same complication was a problem in learning, in which case special educational testing and intervention would be considered appropriate, and the parent might explore the advisability of remedial work with an educational specialist. The same problem could be defined as emotional. Therapeutic help in this case might come from one of several helping professionals—social worker, psychiatrist, clinical counselor, or psychologist.

Within this specific definition there is a second more subtle question: Is this particular situation conceived as an emotional or behavioral complication? The answer can determine whether the helping agent ought to be psychodynamic or behaviorally oriented. The issue in this same situation might be considered as a psychosocial one. Then, parent or teacher might conclude that the best plan of action would be to foster the child's interpersonal associations with peers and/or adults. Then, one would seek the assistance of a social worker or a guidance worker specifically qualified to help children with their interactions with others. The selection of one of these helping professionals would depend upon the parents' estimate of the nature of the complications and upon their knowledge of the professionals most closely associated with treating such difficulties.

Hopefully, the issue in this situation would be seen as an educational challenge to alter the learning situation through a change in learning content, teaching method, or educational grouping. This would put the focus on the learning situation. Inattentiveness can be as much related to disinterest in either uninspiring or incomprehensible learning material as to personal issues beyond the immediate learning situation.

In each of the foregoing possibilities, the fact that the child's educational progress in school is in jeopardy remains constant, while the definition of the nature of the deviation and the corresponding effort to adjust it can vary. The point is that the selection of the helping agent and the associated helping efforts depend largely upon the *interpretation* of the problematic situation. To put it succinctly, different persons or different parties see different problems. *(372)* It is important to keep in mind, however, that the decision to ask for professional intervention remains a sociocultural one when complications are noted. In contemporary America, for example, learning difficulties in school are considered to be within the domain of the child's family. Any probing into the difficulties, from educational, psychological, or medical perspectives would occur only with parental sanction. In contrast, in other places (e.g., Great Britain) the educational institution would consider it *their* obligation to look into these difficulties as part of their responsibility and concern with *their* child.

THE HELPER'S PROFESSIONAL ROLE

Following a request for help, professionals review the situation once more for themselves to come to their own definition of the situation. Professionals want to decide for themselves whether their service or method of help is an appropriate form of intervention, should they choose to render the requested service. It is common practice, even in the referral from one professional to another, that the second person's agreement to enter into the situation hinges upon that person's own assessment of both the situation and his or her own ability to help.

Inherent in a successful helping process is the compatibility of help-seeker and help-giver. People seeking help are expected to commit themselves, however tentatively, to becoming a recipient of help as client, patient, counselee, trainee, charge, or consultee.

Professional practitioners, likewise, commit their energies toward helping the client by making the difference which makes change possible. Above all, the helper assumes the management of the client's experience of seeking and receiving help (215, 26) and becomes the agent of change—"the difference maker."

Together, helper and client create a system of interaction based upon mutual dependence, each contributing a share of help so that the helper is able to intervene and the client to profit from the intervention. The nature of the helping situation, however, destroys the very sense of parity which it attempts to induce. Individuals as clients are never fully on a par with their helpers because to be helped, the client must accept the social and psychological consequences of the promise of help, namely, the sense of dependence and the psychological relationship with the expert in the situation. It is important to keep in mind that in all other respects clients are on their own. Client and worker are equals as persons and citizens.

Nevertheless, parity in the social context is altered when individuals seek help, since society considers that they failed to be on their own in situations where they were expected to be able to manage. Altogether, entering into the client role and accepting dependence upon the help-giver is often very difficult; yet, as Werner Boehm states, "it is a necessary condition for the helping process, one goal of which is to eliminate or reduce the degree of dependence." (23a, 42)

ACTION SYSTEMS FOR HELPING

The foregoing points could lead to an exploration of professional territorialism, (9) role relationships, and the processes of the helping situation. (24) It is the latter to which the major content of this chapter is directed. From here on the focus will be on the dynamic process of interaction between client and helper.

In working with children and youth, the helping process can be structured within four different action systems. First, the individual child may be assisted through the interactive dyadic group of client and helping agent. This helping effort is the most traditional. It is known variously as the individual-interview system; the one-to-one therapeutic relationship; individual counseling, psychotherapy, or casework; interviewing; and advising. This term, the "difference maker", highlights the helper's responsibility and sense of accountability. We often hear the cliche that people can only help themselves; that a counselor cannot do it for the client. We must keep in mind that a client requires a counselor who will make the *difference* in order that the client *can* do it. Otherwise the counselor's involvement is superfluous and there is no justification for socially engineered intervention. (A fuller account is given on subsequent pages of one-to-one work, or individual counseling, as a dyadic group situation.)

Second, the child's family group can be selected or a special group can be formed as the most advisable system within which to apply the helping process. Third, parents, teachers, youth leaders, etc., can be selected as those with whom the professional will deal. This system, which depends upon cooperation between parents, child, and helper, provides auxiliary or consultative help. Fourth, the programs, structures, or policies directly related to the child's life can be brought to the foreground, and the helping process can assume the task of altering pertinent aspects of them to enable the child to develop more effectively. This would be an organizational action system.

Once the helping professional, client, and other parties involved agree to work with each other, the helping professional assumes responsibility for defining the system in which the helping effort is to be introduced. He or she needs to clarify the targets of the effort to bring about change; (6, 88) the action system that will best facilitate such a change; and the everyday experiences in the client's daily life which will be affected by the socially engineered helping system. After these are clarified, the helper can decide upon the appropriate helping systems to be utilized. Most importantly, helpers have to remain aware of the fact they and their clients operate within one system (305a) made up of two mutually interlocked interacting systems, as shown diagramatically in Figure 5.1.

Dyadic Group Systems in Individual Counseling

The joining together of an individual and a professional helper is the most common helping system. Client and worker form a group, or system, of two. This helping situation is purposely conceived of and labeled as a dyadic group system because the work of a group of two (a dyad) brings about a desirable conceptual shift which emphasizes the encounter as *interactive*. When the helping situation is seen as a one-to-one or a casework relationship, the helper is limited to relying solely on knowledge and skills about one-directional relationships in which one person has an impact on the behavior of another. However, if the helping situation is conceived of as consisting of a group of two, the worker is challenged to apply knowledge and intervention skills from communication theory, group dynamics, and system theory, in addition to using applicable skills from the various repertoires of individual

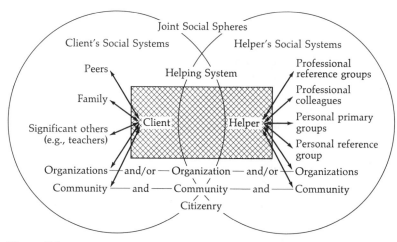

Figure 5.1

The Two Interacting Social Systems of the Action System

counseling and individual therapy. By such a conceptual shift, workers can see themselves more realistically as interacting parties within the process and can apply a more extensive range of knowledge and skills, simultaneously increasing the opportunity for effectiveness.

Conceiving of the intervention action system as a group gains further support when two additional factors are understood. First, from system theory we learn that each functional system exists, in part, in terms of other related systems. (6; 205) Thus, in perceiving the action system as a dyadic group, it is possible to go beyond relationship variables to see interaction for its constituent parts and to see the more inclusive systems of which interaction is a part. Secondly, when we reflect on the implication of Figure 5.1 or on our own observations, we are reminded that while we relate to individuals as individuals we are actually dealing with groups; namely, the invisible groups of others who are of pervasive significance in the life of a particular individual and in one's own spheres of commitments as well.

The child as client is conceived of as the one to be changed, the one to try out new forms of interactions, and the one to perpetuate change. Helping persons, in their role as interacting agents of change, introduce conditions to facilitate the processes of change. Although the child has temporarily gained a new key person, the helping professional, the child's everyday association with his or her immediate primary world continues. Regardless of the quality of the child's therapeutic relationship to the helping agent, he or she continues to depend fundamentally on contacts with parents, siblings, peers, and selected significant adults in most of his or her everyday experiences.

The dyadic group system can operate on two levels—the associate level and the primary level. The associate level, which occurs in social casework, clinical counseling, individual psychotherapy, and behavioral therapy, is intended to enable the individual client to function and develop more effectively in his or her ongoing primary (familial), social (peer), and extended (community) worlds.

Helping clients on a primary level takes place when a child is removed from his or her natural or established family environment and placed in a foster home or other residential situation. In these circumstances, the foster parent or child-care worker (teaching-parent, residential worker, life counselor, etc.) becomes both the key agent for change in the child's life and a parent surrogate as well. The nurturing and helping activities are aimed at fostering mutual dependence—that is, simulating as far as advisable the tenor of the parent-child relationship. *(186; 187; 191) Dependence* here means a sociopsychological condition of mutual trust; mutual reliance in areas in which activities, guidance, or support of a primary figure is needed. Caring depends upon the accepting of care when it is offered and the offering of care when it is needed.

Childhood always involves a state of dependence and independence. Children are judged to be dependent in those spheres of their life in which their own limitations combined with their culture's reservations do not grant independence. *(192)* If the child's natural family cannot provide him or her with the essential nurturing ingredients of dependence, society then engineers a substitute. Here too, the practitioner must deal with a dual involvement; despite the fact that both the helping and the living situation are merged, the effects of the child's previous primary surroundings will continue to linger in his or her thinking, wishes, associations, and behavior and will provide him or her with contacts, residual experiences, values, interests, and hopes for the future.

The helping of individuals on either an associate or a primary level requires working with each individual's ongoing experience. This is true even in the most intimately cloistered interview room and the most detached residential child-care setting. In working at an associate level, clients may act toward their helper as if their "significant others" (their ongoing primary relationships) were right there watching them over their shoulder. Consequently, clients are apt to weigh the implications of change in terms of their relationship to both their helper and those personally significant to them outside of the interview situation who are forever present.

The helper, therefore, must deal with the client's omnipresent circle of others as if they were literally with the client. Working with a client on a primary level involves a similar dual focus. One part of the helper's approach entails the involvement of clients in such a way that the helping process serves as a new primary nurturing relationship for children in the absence of their own; the other part requires a recognition of past, ongoing, and future relationships which are paramount factors in the child's life. *(186; 187; 191)*

Primary Group Systems

When helping occurs within the context of a group, the helping process can either be aimed at changing the behavior of the group as a whole, or it can be designed to affect each individual member through the medium of the group. In the event of affecting the group as a whole, the group members are dealt with as parts of a larger whole, the emphasis being upon the group's adaptation to a larger social system. Although individual differences and needs are not negated, the group members understand that individuality is deemphasized in favor of group cohesion and group integration. It is assumed that individual adaptation occurs according to the group's change of goals, values, orientation, and behavioral norms.

Individual change does occur, but the change is a spontaneous consequence of overall norm changes. Individual adaptation occurs because each individual has the capability and opportunity to do so. This approach is most pertinent in work with children and youth with an adequate range of "normal" development; expectations set for their group experience elicit individual challenges for socialization. The same approach may occur in summer camp, for instance, when a cabin group fails to fit into the overall program and organization of the camp. Then, efforts to effect change are apt to be directed at the group as a whole in order to secure for the group members and the overall camp a camp experience that enhances development. In such an approach, the verbal short-hand designation of "working with the group" is most appropriate.

A second approach, commonly described as social group work, group counseling, group therapy, peer counseling, or group guidance counseling, is to work with the focus revolving around members' development. The primary objective is to assist individuals with their developmental difficulties, rather than with their group's integration within a larger overall context. Changing the behavior and value system of the group as a whole is considered to be relevant only to the extent that group members are specifically and individually helped.

As with the individual-interview system, individuals in

groups can be helped on an associate or a primary level. At the associate level, the group may be comprised of various unrelated members (e.g., a group of teenagers with similar personal problems) or it may be made up of the individual members of a single family, which is dealt with as a unit.[1] In these situations, the helping process is geared toward effecting change for each individual within the context of the group. Interactions within the group serve as a testing and learning resource for dealing with personal difficulties in everyday lives. The group becomes an arena for practicing new behavior, thinking, and feelings. Regardless of the composition of the group, whether family or nonfamily members, the helping process relies upon the system of the group.

Assisting individuals in a group with their specific developmental requirements always has potential relevance for other group members. Frequently, the concerns of one group member have relevance for the others. Group members can come in as trainers, cohelpers, or for general support. Noteworthy also is the continuous interrelationship between individual developmental factors and group developmental factors or social forces (realities), as we saw in the foregoing developmental formulations. In the words of C. H. Cooley, as quoted by R. R. White, "Society and individuals are inseparable phases of a common whole, so that whenever we find an individual fact we may look for a social fact to go with it." (387, 107) These interplays between individual and group developmental phenomena are hinted at in the schematic chart of Table 5.1.

The treatment effort, we note, is directed toward changing interactions, self-concepts, behavioral capacities, ranges of knowledge, and feelings of group members in order that each client can deal more competently with his or her daily life expectations. To assure the group's success, helpers must associate themselves with the group and perceive themselves as a part of the group. The helper must serve as the instrumental group member who introduces actions to further the purpose for which the members are joined together. (378)

At a primary level, the group provides the arena for everyday life experiences. The helping agent introduces and pursues caring (parent-like) activities; the group members' relationships are sibling-like. The same framework applies as outlined in the discussion of the primary dyadic group system.[2]

---

[1] The reader's attention is called to a wide range of publications in regard to family therapy, e.g., 29; 202; 321; 365.

[2] The author has dealt with this approach in separate publications. (186; 187; 191)

TABLE 5.1 INTERRELATED DEVELOPMENTAL
OBJECTIVES IN INDIVIDUAL AND GROUP INTERVENTION

Individual Developmental Objectives	Group Developmental Objectives
1. Self-realization	⟷ 1. Clarity in group norms and values
2. Personal competence	⟷ 2. Tolerance of individual differentiation
3. Competence in relating to and identifying with others	⟷ 3. Group cohesion
4. Competence in problem-solving	⟷ 4. Division of labor and clarification of group roles
5. Evolving cultural role expectations	⟷ 5. Group decision-making and maintenance

Auxiliary Systems

In the action systems outlined thus far, the child has been the pivotal figure in the helping activities. The practitioner worked directly with the child or a group of children. In the case of the auxiliary system, the professional works with key adults who are instrumental in the child's life. This alternate approach is actually not too farfetched because child development is also, in a sense, societal development.

It is worth noting at this point that even when the practitioner deals only with one parent, the other parent is still in existence, however marginal his or her role might be in the child's actual everyday life situation. In cases in which there is one parent in the child's life, this single parent assumes full parental functions. Whether helpers are working with a single parent or both, they attempt to assist these key persons with their parenting efforts in their behavioral, attitudinal, and ideational interactions with the child.

Work with parents requires full knowledge of the parent's situation, the parent's interaction patterns with the child, and the position the parents choose in relation to other parents and the community in general. This action system involves parents with the helper, while the service to be rendered is directed at altering the child's developmental process. If the focus were to be placed upon the parents themselves a different action system would be called for. The parents, in such instances, would become clients in their own right and the intervening efforts would be geared toward their own personal requirements.

When the helping professional is working with parents, a distinct but interdependent (auxiliary) system is formed in which the parents stand as the instrumental partners in the child's development and the helping agent is the facilitator of this vital partnership. Work with other key persons in the child's life, such as teacher, counselor, community worker, employer, pastor, etc., introduces a similar auxiliary system with the focus upon helping the respective instrumental person to affect and enrich his special interactive experience with the child.

The major intervention process in these situations would be that of consultation. All consultation, whether it occurs between two professionals or between a professional and lay person, is different from the other forms of intervention. In consultation, consultant and consultee become temporarily interdependent, but they join as quasi equals. Each engages the other, and has a desire to create a common frame of reference. However, they do not join in action to apply this knowledge. It is important to avoid the fallacy of viewing and treating the teacher as if he were the object of the helping process rather than a cohelper.

Systems for Program, Structure, and Policy Alteration

Like the auxiliary system, the system of program, structure, and policy alteration does not introduce an interaction process between child and helper. Rather, it introduces a shift in the form and content of intervention. Those aspects of a program, structure, or policy which have a direct bearing upon the child's development within his ongoing life situation become the focus. To illustrate by our previous example, the boy's learning difficulties could be viewed and dealt with as a curriculum problem (program), a question of organizational class placement (structure for learning), or a matter related to the school's educational orientation (policy). Change, then, would have to be directed toward a condition more conducive to learning, with the assumption that an alteration would create conditions favorable to the child's learning. This illustration is knowingly within a middle-class bias in which continuation in and adaptation to school is conceived as a central objective of helping.

In the system of program structure or policy alteration, the child's development is kept as the basic consideration. Content, policy, or structural alterations are viewed for their specific (clinical) impact, not for their general social relevance and desirability. Equally, interpersonal issues within the system remain outside this action system's field of concerns. Helping within the context of a program-alteration system involves the processes of specific planning and policy review. Helping proceeds within .a framework of consultation. In this action system, help is structured so that helper and other persons in the system devote themselves jointly to the task of altering content, structure, or decisions. In each event, interpersonal relationships are only relevant insofar as they facilitate the pursuit of a particular task.

The action system for the purpose of program, structure, or policy alteration is sometimes inaccurately viewed as "working with a community" and as analogous to working with individuals or groups. Although a helper can work with a total community, in our rather complex society the helping process deals more likely with distinct aspects of community life. A neighborhood might solicit the aid of an expert in community organization work to assist with the development of curfew rules for its teenage population. Such a situation requires that the helping agent deal with issues of curfew policies rather than that he or she intervene within a system of clients.

THE HELPING RELATIONSHIP

The helping process has been portrayed thus far as a continuous process of interaction between helper and client. Every such interaction sequence finds its beginning at the moment a first contact is made, whether in person, by phone, or by letter. People in search of change in their situation begin to establish their part in the interaction continuum, simultaneously evaluating their prospective helper's share in this venture. At the same time, helpers evaluate the applicant's potential involvement with them and their service. When they have both agreed to explore the possibility of a commitment to the service situation, the person seeking help submits himself or herself to client status, even if merely tentatively and temporarily. From this point on, both parties need each other in a fashion illustrated by the following comment of a helping professional who has discovered a minimal readiness on the part of the client: "I once worked with a schizophrenic boy who was very lonely. I discovered that I was very lonely too, because he gave me little opportunity to relate to him."

Agreement for Help Giving/Receiving

Helper and client reach a tacit or mutually contracted understanding of their mutual but different dependency needs and the necessary boundaries of such dependence. The term dependence is applied here to mean the aspect of a dynamic relationship in which part of the client's individuality is entrusted to the care and direction of the helper, who, in turn, needs the trust of the client in order to initiate and effect helpful intervention. Most important is the inherent mandate for each party to provide as well as demand some sense of personal dependence. Aspects of this kind of dependence foster interactive processes for helping combined with change and for change combined with learning. Oscillating states of dependence and independence (192) allow for periods of imitating, caring, identifying, and, throughout, for *experiencing* free communication of feelings, mutual understanding, and the development of competence.

The relationship serves as the vehicle for assessing the client's situation and impacting it in such a way that the relationship can eventually be terminated and the client can reestablish independence from it. Such a relationship produces, for the people involved, a differentiated, one action system "in which the seer and the seen, the observer and the observed, become one, although at the same time they remain two." (23b, 151) In essence, the intervention process is the *experience of a relationship* in which helper and client work together to find solutions applicable to their own immediate life situations. Clients are after change in their perplexing or troublesome personal situation, and helpers are after opportunities to prove themselves competent in the particular intervention repertoire they have chosen. In the words of one sensitive counselor: "As I create or give as well as take I become therapist, artist, creator, as well as a consumer creature."[3]

THE PROCESSES OF ASSESSMENT AND INTERVENTION

The helping process has thus far been conceived of as an action sequence enriched (or thwarted) by relationship factors. This section presents a systematic review of the major segments and subcomponents of the process. An outline of a dynamic model of *assessment* (diagnosis) and intervention (treatment) is shown in Table 5.2.

Assessment and Treatment—A Continuous Process

Traditionally, assessment has been thought of as a prelude and prerequisite to intervention. We shall view it differently. Assessment is defined as a process of recognizing the characteristics and operations of a situation with the objective of coming to some form

---

[3] I express my appreciation for this statement although the source has been lost.

TABLE 5.2 SCHEMATIC MODEL OF
THE ASSESSMENT AND INTERVENTION PROCESS

Steps in the Helping Process
1. Observing the situation
2. Ordering and assessing the observation
3. Predicting the course of development *without* intervention
4. Predicting the course of development *with* intervention
5. Formulating a tentative hypothesis and an alternate
6. Purposeful intervention and acknowledged *non*intervention
7. Observing anew after intervention
8. Reassessment based on new observations and formulation of a new hypothesis

Subsegments of the Helping Processes"

Assessment Processes		Intervention Processes
Study	Appraisal	Focused Intervention
Observation (1)	Prediction *without* intervention (3)	Purposeful intervention (6)
Ordering and assessing the observations (2)	Prediction *with* intervention (4)	
Observing anew after intervention (7)	Formulation of a hypothesis (5)	
	Reassessment based on new observations and formulation of a new hypothesis (8)	

" Numbers in parentheses refer to the steps in the list above.

---

of conclusion. The accent is on cognition of the situation and not on depicting malfunctioning or deviation. In order to avoid the latter, the assessment is to be based upon thinking in terms of a system *(6)* rather than in terms of a medical model. For the latter reason, the designations *assessment* and *intervention* are used in favor of the more commonly applied and medically oriented terms *diagnosis* and *treatment*.

The assessment process is equivalent to the research processes of fact finding and hypothesis testing. Assessment includes (1) an effort to establish and define the ongoing levels of behavior in each appropriate dimension of functioning; (2) a prediction of the implications of such behavior for future functioning; (3) determination of the degree of divergence of this predicted functioning from normal functioning; and (4) an estimation of possible avenues available to correct predicted divergence. In contrast to research, however, assessment activities are inherently committed to utilizing what has been discovered[4] and to helping amend what has proved to be troublesome in the client's functioning.

Assessment and intervention are interrelated but separate phases of a single continuum. While the doctrine of the specific etiology of disease, or the matching a single unit of cause and effect, has been a most constructive force in medical research, as René Dubos alerts us in *Mirage of Health*, (54) all such studies and the application of the model of causality in the treatment of disease have failed to combat the great medical problems of our time. Dubos challenges the health sciences to search for a more dynamic approach, to give fuller attention to the concepts of multiple causality, and to recognize that purposeful change creates both a removal of the undesirable condition and a new condition. The latter is apt to be vested, like all novel situations, with new dilemmas.

Multiple causality allows for the artistic component of assessment and denies the earlier assumption that assessment is primarily limited to the helping person's establishment of an initial (clinical) evaluation to guide him or her in his intervention effort. Diagnosis that is concerned with etiology is inherently in conflict with the notion of multiple causation. The former seeks to narrow down the number of relevant factors, while the notion of multiple causation directs our attention to seeking out and linking together an ever-increasing field of possibilities. In changing times, a concern with cause and antecedents becomes less relevant than attention to that which needs to be done and the impact of that which has been done. With our concern for action, the effect of any steps in intervention becomes of greater interest than questions pertaining to the particular historical or causative circumstances.

Assessment and intervention, as they are perceived in this chapter, involve a range of continuously interwoven processes. Assessment activities are intimately intertwined with all transactions of helping, including a sense of urgency to initiate activities which may lead to change. Assessment means that there is the possibility and hopeful promise for change. Consequently, assessment means initiating intervention, and intervention means a shift, however temporary, from assessment to treatment. Discovery and the utilization of one's findings occur simultaneously! To illustrate, in the searching inquiry asked of a client by a counselor or social worker, "What would you like to have different?" or "In which way do you picture I might be of help to you?" the

---

[4] Research ventures also have the concomitant ethical obligation to report and to share what has been discovered. But the obligation of the helper to share with the client that which has been discerned does differ from research procedures and practice.

inquiry by the counselor or social worker is not focused on the difficulties or problems but rather on the client's hopes. What changes are anticipated? In short, what *can be* replaces what ought not to be.

Assessment and intervention can be conceived of as interdependent activities which simultaneously permeate all spheres of the helping situation. Each process depends upon a continuous system of mutual feedback. Each minute or overall effort to effect change depends upon a previous appraisal, a set of predictions, and the selection of a momentary hypothesis. First a hypothesis is made. Action will follow with the understanding that the hypothesis is conceived of as momentary and subject to immediate revision when a new hypothesis is formulated to introduce still further action. This process is infinite because a new situation is created by every activity.

The assessment process highlights what can be learned, while the treatment process focuses on what needs to be done based on what has been learned. To illustrate, in an initial interview, helpers might appropriately convey a sense of empathy to the client in order to foster a trust in dependence and encourage the client to confide in them. Empathy and support are prerequisite to obtaining essential observations.[5]

At the same time, empathy and support can themselves produce change since a client's troubles are frequently related to complications in primary contacts and relationships. Thus, the helper is simultaneously assessing and intervening. The development of a relationship based on treatment, that is, a commitment to an action system, furthers significant sharing and discovery on the part of the client of very personal information. This is useful for assessment and directs the helper in his or her efforts to effect change. Assessment, therefore, is both a precursor to and a partner in intervention, while only the experience of intervention can confirm or refute that which has been assessed.

Study Processes

Observing and ordering what is observed are on one end of the assessment (diagnostic) continuum, while renewed observations and reordering of previous as well as new observations are on the other. Observing is the empirical activity of the assessment process, but here inductive thinking comes to an end. Distilling the recognizable facts from a host of life factors requires a process of classification and a shift to a deductive thought process. Deductive

[5] C. B. Truax and associates established in their research that accurate empathy, along with nonpossessive warmth and genuineness, is one of the key variables in regard to effective work and outcome in therapeutic helping. (*16*, 302–344)

reasoning is employed in all diagnostic thinking in the assessment of that which is observable and classifiable. One must select pertinent information from among many items in order to assess; and one cannot know what is pertinent or relevant without a deductive appraisal.[6]

Study activities proceed simultaneously within three separate spheres. They can be pictured as a configuration of spatial, temporal, and qualitative considerations. First, one must determine what territory is in question. There is the dual focus upon the problematic situation per se and upon the circumstances associated with it. Second, one must determine what point in time is in question. There are two time dimensions. The horizontal dimension is the ongoing contemporary life situation, while the ever-present vertical antecedents constitute the "living past," which includes previous relevant factors in a person's experience, history, and social heritage. Ongoing observations gain added significance in the light of looming past events. Third, one must determine what quality of data are in question. Observations may entail overt as well as covert behavior, observable as well as inferential or hidden data.

The helping person, in using the three spheres, has to order the observations he or she makes. Observing requires the cognitive process of ordering and classifying what is observed. The latter does involve a process of labeling. Whether a person wants to or not, one does label. The actual mental process of sorting out, of ordering one's observations (findings), incorporates a miniature assessment process. The most minute observational data are studied, appraised, and screened in relation to a set frame of reference. In many ways, this study process is akin to a shift from using a kaleidoscope to looking through a microscope using alternately higher and lower power.[7]

Since the process of observing occurs within the context of the observer's frame of reference, it is the observer's role to note an event for its behavioral content, its psychological relevance, its cultural implications, and its social significance. Gathering observed or inferred information requires learning what a person does, thinks, and feels—not what a person doesn't do. The latter would merely emphasize what the observer expects. It would define the observer rather than the observed.

[6] Although the gathering of data involves inductive reasoning, a valid case could be made that all observing requires basically deductive reasoning. The mind always projects and directs observations into the scope of deductible general knowledge.

[7] This helpful analogy has been adapted from an illustration introduced by Gordon McLeod, a former student at the School of Social Work, University of British Columbia, Vancouver, B.C.

The observer would order the selected data within the context of the theoretical framework which he or she considers applicable. In short, observers denote, with the assistance of their client, what they consider to be pertinent data. The findings then actually represent the helping person's estimate of the material he or she has labeled and, thereby, rendered significant. In the search for clarity, the questions posed should be at the center of all study, appraisal, and intervention. Therefore, in order to gain understanding, one needs to know what one has to know—what questions to pose. Unless one questions clearly one cannot receive an answer, either from others or from oneself. Thus, the question rather than the answer becomes the most important factor *in the study process.*

In one respect, social distance and noninvolvement enhance objective judgment. However, intimate material, such as private feelings and personal beliefs, can only be shared and reviewed when client and helper perceive and feel that they are very much involved in the same working situation. Only when the helper perceives that he or she is close and is part of the client's world can the client communicate deep feelings and the more perplexing but vital details of his or her life situation. This occurs because "we care what happens to people only in proportion as we know what people are."[8]

The statement "Leo walked somewhat aloof about three steps behind the other boys crowding around me [the counselor]" connotes Leo's physical and emotional distance from the other boys. Part of this could be accounted for in a study of the spatial relationships of the people in the situation. But, at the same time, there is a sensed (inferred) observation in the words *somewhat aloof.* Leo is described as walking *emotionally* apart from the others. Such an observation requires projection into the situation. The observer must see and feel himself or herself as a participant. *(375; 398)*[9] Needed information may be found such sensed observations. They

[8] A quote attributed to Henry James by a former student, Severra Austin, School of Social Work, University of Washington, 1970/72.

[9] B. Wright, in a study of the relationship between emotional involvement and professional development, calls special attention to participant observation. An emphasis upon, and preoccupation with objective observation denies opportunities for sensing subtle communications of affect because observers maintain too much emotional distance to allow themselves to be receptive to subtle observable material. In addition, as observers they may tend to exclude themselves, in spite of their presence, from the observational field. Actually, any observation brings about a participation. The dilemma revolves around the degree of participation. If the emphasis shifts from intrusive observation to intrusive participation, the attention shifts from observing the interactions to a preoccupation with the participant's own actions and the client's reactions to him or her. Participant observation, in contrast to mere observation or intrusive participation, allows the observer sufficient freedom to observe and to participate, to utilize what he or she has observed, and to evaluate the ongoing impact of his or her role as a participant observer *(398)*

involve intuitive reactions, and they add telling information, without which more testable (objective) findings would remain impoverished and incomplete.

Appraisal Processes

Appraisal processes involve the conversion of ordered observed material into a series of applicable propositions. Conceptually, the helper engages in "if . . . then" propositions. From these propositions, a selection is made of the most promising operational predictions. Appraisal constitutes, on the one hand, an assessment and disposition of findings; on the other, a preparation for action. Basically, the mode of reasoning is oriented toward future actions. Previous observations are viewed as data for planning rather than as an account of findings. In fact, previous ordering and assessing of relevant material has probably already been undertaken with the aim of formulating a pertinent course of action.

It is this emphasis upon prediction, at this point of the helping process, which assists helper and client alike to focus upon activities to come. Both are concerned with the promise of the future, as they "read" it from their accounting of the client's ongoing and hoped for life situation. For example, a client might be described as anxious. Such a discovery is important for the appraisal of the helper's activities and the client's potential behavior in the immediate future, rather than for establishing a mere descriptive account of the client.

Appraisal processes occur at two different loci on the assessment continuum. First, appraisal processes emerge into the foreground when observations are fitted together and plans for action are derived from them. Secondly, appraisal processes become of particular concern again when past actions are appraised to predict subsequent actions. In any event, three interrelated predictions must be formulated in order that a proper appraisal can be made:

1. Observed material is applied to predict subsequent development or events under prevailing circumstances. The client's immediate development is forecasted as if he or she were to receive no further help. In other words, his subsequent life situation and development is predicted without purposeful intervention.
2. Observed material, including the prediction of subsequent development without purposeful intervention, is utilized for an alternate prediction of subsequent development in light of introducing projected intervening (treatment) activities.
3. The two alternate predictions of the subsequent outcome of develvelopment is forecasted as if he or she were to receive no further help. In other words, his subsequent life situation and development is predicted without purposeful intervention.

Although appraisal is the responsibility of the helping person, the actual process of appraisal has to be viewed and handled as a joint enterprise of client and helper. For example, in the previously cited case example, Leo's counselor might conclude from the appraisal of Leo's behavior that he has difficulty relating to his peers. Correspondingly, Leo himself may want to convey to the counselor his own findings that he feels apart from his peers and wishes that others would sense his state of detachment.

Making Diagnostic Predictions

Diagnostic client's situation, the first of the three essential diagnostic predictions may be ventured. *If*, on the basis of preceding observations, no intervening activities are initiated, *then* the situation is expected to continue to go on as appraised. The proposition is that no purposeful intervention is necessary if the natural course of development is considered within the range of desirable behavior or if it is known that no potentially available intervention would be of significance for the present. In Leo's situation, it would run as follows: *If* the counselor let things proceed as they are, *then* Leo will continue in his solitary fashion, but at least he will remain in the presence of peers and possibly either find or accidentally drift into some closer peer contacts.

The second prediction involves the alternate proposition: *If* on the basis of preceding observations the situation is to be changed by means of purposeful intervening activities, *then* the client will be able to learn new (added) relationship skills with peers. In this instance, the helper's understanding of the ongoing situation is combined with his knowledge of the impact of purposeful intervention and his assessment of his client's potential capacity for change. For Leo and the worker it would mean, *if* the worker does something, *then* Leo's group experience could take on a new variation.

The third alternate prediction then is derived from the second. *If*, on the basis of preceding alternate predictions, the following intervening activities were to be introduced . . . *then* the situation would be changed to the one predicted as a more desirable course of development within the visible circumstances. This third prediction includes a plan for action which will detrmine which observed information and subsequent predicted propositions will emerge as the material to give the direction for further work. The actual plan of action has yet to be fully worked out.

Earlier, it was surmised that Leo would be unable to bring himself into effective association with peers unless some intervening life experiences were to foster such capabilities. Such an appraisal has the inherent value judgment that closer association is desirable and potentially possible. Each decision to foster support or acquiesce to change or absence of change (status quo) involves a value commitment. Helpers do take stances whether they want to or not. They can do no other. They do ultimately decide upon the nature of the desired change. The helper might decide that Leo either needs to be brought into closer association with age-mates or with the counselor. Each alternative is based upon a different appraisal of observed material. In turn, each set of findings and assessment suggests a different form of intervention.

Appraisal is also influenced by the avilability of additional needed skills and resources and by the helper's awareness of their existence. The breadth and depth of every assessment is markedly determined by the helper's competence, the accessibility of resources, the auspices of the helper's professional efforts, and the value system of his or her professional reference groups. Prediction for change, therefore, is directly related to the helper's (and client's) notion of how much change can be accomplished using the time and resources that are available and worthwhile. In the helping process, assessment only has meaning as long as it leads to a design for action; but such material also provides boundaries to the helper's efforts.

The ability to make hunches is a vital quality. A hunch can be thought of as a momentary assessment or a spontaneous reaction which allows for probing for more comprehensive understanding. (309, 88) Once such an appraisal has pronounced, it still must be verified by subsequent events. A renewed assessment is in order in the light of intervention or nonintervention. Such a reassessment in the process of appraisal can verify or cancel previous judgments. This process is like Norbert Wiener's aphorism: "I don't know what I have said until I have heard the response to it."

Intervention Processes

In intervention, as in assessment, all activities are ultimately related to the particular value systems, knowledge base, and selected techniques of each professional discipline. Each discipline has its chosen theoretical reference system which defines sound and proper procedures and techniques and a valid method of intervention.

In intervention there is a reliable theoretical frame of reference, a mobilization of interpersonal relationships, and a selection and execution of techniques. Techniques enhance the interpersonal relationships while the quality of interpersonal interactions make the techniques accessible to the client. It is the content and context of the interpersonal experience which determines the intervention.

The techniques applied must be considered for their impact on the interpersonal experience. To illustrate, attentive listening can foster the helper's experience of sharing the client's thoughts and feelings and lead to a better comprehension of the client's situation. We must be mindful, however, that neither the experience of listening nor the techniques employed (e.g., paraphrasing) make up the intervention effort (treatment). Rather, the purposeful creation and utilization of the experience serve as the means, context, and vehicle for the introduction of activities which are geared toward the desired changes.

Selecting Interventive Techniques

In spite of the danger of being too mechanistic, we suggest that intervention be perceived as an activity which incorporates the following proposition: If action x is introduced, then the predicted outcome o will occur (if x then o). In each step of intervention, i.e., each minute step or the total step of programmed intervention, this proposition is in order.

Let us return to a previously cited illustration. If Leo is to become more personally involved with his peers and feel less aloof, then he has to experience a sense of closeness with at least one other group member. Let us assume that none of the group members seem ready for this. The helping agent, then, may be the first link to provide such an experience of closeness for Leo. *If a sense of closeness is desirable in this instance, then* the worker must provide an opportunity for it. We may assume that the worker might turn to Leo and engage him in conversation. His prediction and expectation would be to find a common experience through conversation. In terms of the above formula, if conversation with Leo is undertaken (action x), *then* more involvement with worker may ensue (outcome o).[10]

In brief, all intervention activities are an aggregation of many minute steps based upon previously established or intuitively sensed predictions. Each step is a development toward the desired outcome. Each intervention activity is introduced as the most efficient means of bringing about the desired change. It follows, then, that each treatment step must be evaluated for its outcome, to determine if the predicted outcome (o_1) coincides with the actual outcome (o_2).

For instance, assuming that Leo's hobby is a subject of personal interest to him, a conversation with Leo about his model cars might result in introducing ideas which Leo would have in com-

---

[10] This intervention formulation, in turn, builds upon the conceptual knowledge that personal mutual involvement breeds closeness, and mutual engagement in a conversation is an initial step towards mutual involvement.

mon with some of the other boys. In the event that Leo did not respond, the worker would be faced with a new assessment situation: reference to Leo's hobby (x = planned action) did not produce the desired and predicted outcome (0_1 = conversation). Rather it produced no usable response (o_2 = no conversation). This single episode in the intervention process illustrates that the helper *selects* appropriate actions, based on his or her *assessment* of the existing circumstances and a prediction of which ones out of a potential range of intervention activities most likely will bring about the desired objectives.

Concern with the quality of the performance in applying one's understanding of the client and the available intervention techniques shifts the emphasis from the helper's scientific selection of techniques (the science of helping) to the qualitative, personal skills and the artful application of skills and knowledge (the art of helping). *(23b)*

Structure and Dynamics

Intervention activities have to be clearly defined for their structural and dynamic components. Structural factors such as a specified appointment period, reliance upon the worker's role as helper, contractual commitments, etc., serve merely to facilitate dynamic functional processes. Dynamics must be relevant to the structural circumstances (the reality) of the helping situation. For example, to set a definite appointment introduces a combination of structure and dynamics. "This is your time with me" is structural. "I want to be with you" and "you can count on me" are dynamic. *If* the client knows that a definite appointment time is his time, *then* he is more likely to know that he will be welcome. Therefore, making a definite appointment time becomes essential if such an activity will facilitate the desired outcome. On the other hand, it may be unnecessary if a structural arrangement which rests upon a mutual tacit understanding helps the client relate more effectively.

The importance of differentiating between structural and dynamic components in intervention might be further elaborated by the following situation. Client and helper may be engaged in discussing a particular topic. The topic label constitutes a structural phenomenon. The dynamic consideration is how client and helper use the topic and how their relationship is manifested by the topic. Focus upon a particular topic can serve as a structural aid to be utilized therapeutically with the client, or it can be an obstacle for the client in searching out and elaborating on his or her concerns.

Depth or Strength of Intervention

The concern about going deep, getting close, being intensive, going beyond surface material, engaging in long or short term treatment are concerns that might be viewed as issues for the assessment process rather than methodological considerations. We suggest that the concern should not be with the quality of the interaction but with the objectives to be obtained. *How* to engage onself in the helping process depends upon *what* is to be achieved. Intervention may deal with insight, when insight into the client's own functioning assures him more reliable accessibility to his immediate ongoing experience. Intervention may deal specifically with support, when the ordinary client-helper interaction is not supportive enough to encourage ongoing developmental change in itself. Intervention may deal with environmental manipulation, when different environmental experiences are more likely to assure the client a clearer effective use of his ongoing life experiences.

The material in this chapter stresses the utility of a rather mechanistic frame of reference to make the helping process orderly. Such a systematic understanding is the prerequisite for creative work, because clarity about what one is all about frees a person to be creative as the process itself goes on.

DIMENSIONS OF PSYCHOSOCIAL INTERVENTION

The three dimensions of development discussed in earlier chapters provided us with a framework of knowledge about human development. Intervention builds upon such knowledge in order to select appropriate activities for introducing conditions that may help the child develop salutory patterns. Most importantly, intervention can only predict, initiate, and pursue within known patterns of development. We have introduced throughout this book three major dimensions of psychosocial functioning: understanding (cognition), feeling (affect), and doing (behavior). Each dimension relies upon a different constellation of factors in the developmental process. We submit, therefore, that dynamic intervention requires a pervasive understanding of these dimensions and their developmental processes. *(190)* Let us examine each of these.

Cognition

Intervening in cognitive processes and changes in cognition require efforts directed primarily toward effecting a client's understanding of a situation. Client and helper attempt to clarify the client's understanding of relevant aspects of his or her life. Efforts may also be directed toward introducing new perspectives, hitherto unknown. When circumstances are perceived and understood in a new perspective, a client is apt to feel and act differently. For example, if Leo knew the other boys' bantering behavior and exaggerated talk were more for their own entertainment, and less of an actual attack on him and were common actions by kids of his age, he might feel freer to become part of the group and to join in their activities more fully. An extension of comprehension may explain past events, or it may be related to ongoing experiences. Knowing differently may mean feeling and acting differently.

Affect

Changes in affect effect a person's emotional involvement in ongoing experiences and past or future ones. The helping effort is directed towards impacting clients' feelings about themselves and others who are significant to them, as well as the social, ideational, and physical world around them. In Leo's case, the focus would then be upon his feeling so aloof from others. Having him express his feelings about others and his fears, hopes, and uncertainties about himself, might achieve the objectives of a freer sharing of affect, a relief from the burden of his feelings, and sense of personal emotional closeness to worker. Altogether, helping would involve the understanding that if Leo could feel differently about himself, he would then perceive and behave differently.

Behavior

Change in behavior, as the primary target of intervention, shifts the emphasis to the action component of the helping situation. Clients are assisted with knowing how and what to do in order to widen their repertoire of behavior for more effective mastery of everyday life requirements such as interpersonal contacts, problem situations, and the acquisition of new knowledge and skills. For Leo, it may mean that as he learns more effective ways to interact with his worker and other group members, he will add behavioral skills for effective participation with others in his everyday life contacts. Acquisition of more effective behavioral skills lead also to a better comprehension of situations and, therefore, to feeling more adequate in dealing with them. (190)

A DYNAMIC MODEL OF
ASSESSMENT AND INTERVENTION

Thus far we have reviewed the components of the processes of assessment and purposeful intervention. It is important that we look at this process as a unit, that is, as a dynamic model of helping.

Assessment and intervention occur through the interaction of a helper and client as they create change within one action system. Helper and client project their past and ongoing experiences into their temporarily joint endeavor—the helping situation, or action system. Helpers contribute their professional knowledge, skills, and value commitments. Their accumulated professional experience is projected into the particular helping situation where that experience can be verified, altered, and expanded. Clients bring their ongoing concerns and their living past, which become part of the client-helper situation. It is important to sort out what part of the client's dilemma is due to his previous experience and what has been activated by the social context of the new experience of the helping situation.

A meeting, an interactive encounter of client and worker, becomes the working situation, a temporary social arena for ongoing experiences in social change and development, whether such learning concerns knowledge, behavior, or attitudes (affect). No one interactive system can be studied or dealt with separately since helping activities in one system are inmeshed with experiences in others. Interactions in the helping situation allow one to sense and discern the course of events in other systems. Concurrently, the course of events (the change effort within the helping situation) reaches into other life spheres of the parties involved. Change occurs beyond the context of the action system, be it an interview, therapy session for an individual client, family, special group, or consultative conference.

Pronouncements on assessments or intervention activities reflect the helper's attempts to understand rather than to classify or label people and their situations. Within the helping system, the helper uses descriptive or definitive diagnostic labeling as mental shorthand which abbreviates complex narrative accounts. As observations are ordered and totaled under one descriptive label or another, they become clarified in the helper's thinking process and he or she is able to communicate them to others. While doing so, the helper has an opportunity to check out once more the validity of his or her assertions.

To state and sum up one's findings is a check on one's own thinking: Does one say what one means? Does one mean what one says? Assessment pronouncements serve to purify thought and admittedly to label beyond the facts. Above all, diagnostic clarifiers, labels, have to be viewed as transitory. Each hypothesis is always tentative until tested and then must be immediately appraised in light of a subsequent change. Like the god Janus, the helper must look backward and forward at the same time to understand the actions just completed and the new situation emerging for the client's changing life situation.

The theme of this chapter has been to bring assessment and intervention considerations into one field of interrelated, intertwined processes. We have seen how fact-finding always involves intervening change. Intervention, in turn, instantly creates a new condition of which the helper and the client are a part, and from which they cannot divorce themselves. Assessment and intervention are concurrent processes. Although the conception of assessment and intervention as inseparable processes muddy a research effort, they constitute the lifeline for the helping activities.

The helping process is furthered by a lack of clear demarcation between assessment and intervention activities (except in a schematization). As client and helper join together to effect change, it is, in fact, their joint investment rather than the blueprint of helping which determines the ultimate nature and outcome of the helping process. Above all, it is the client's situation which defines the nature of the helping process and the helping system to be utilized; while the helping relationship frees both client and helper to study what needs to be assessed and to act upon what must be changed.

The helping process, in summary, brings helper and helpee by tacit or contractual understanding into one action system. Helpers enter such a helping situation with the clear expectation that their involvement will make the difference which makes a difference. In striving to accomplish such a difference, the helper does not change people (nor could anyone else do such a trick). Rather, the helper creates conditions predictively that enable the individual client(s) involved to develop their capacity for changing selected aspects of their particular life situations.

CHAPTER 6
The three dimensions of child development applied

Our attention in this chapter turns from theory to practice; from studying child development and the helping process conceptually to the application and the broad implications of such knowledge for people who work with children. Rather than providing a handbook or a how-to-do-it kit, this chapter demonstrates our conviction that any kind of professional helping requires a conceptual frame of reference for human development. As a heuristic frame of reference, this chapter should serve student or parent, care giver or professional helper.

DEVELOPMENTAL PHASES

In an earlier chapter, it was suggested that every individual is in a constant state of developmental change. Individuals vary from each other in so many aspects, yet the progression of development is the same for all. Efforts to bring about changes in a child's behavior and personality, therefore, can be directed to the developmental process itself instead of to an individual's behavior per se.

Each of the theories heretofore presented makes use of developmental phases rather than age norms. Chronological ages may suffice as general guides, but they are insufficient aides for judging a child's developmental progress. Complications may reflect either a developmental problem or inappropriate expectations regarding what is thought to be the "right" behavior for a child of a given age.

To illustrate, if an eleven-year-old who is usually capable of adjusting to temporary separations from his or her parents without behavioral repercussions needs to resolve some uneasiness by a socially acceptable device, the child may make phone calls to the parents to compensate for their absence. If children of this age are unable to cope with a separation of only a few weeks, it should not be concluded immediately that they are emotionally unstable, retarded, or in any serious way "abnormal." As was implied in each theorist's findings, children's behavior may be quite in keeping with their particular developmental rate.

Finding the factors which might be at work in situations of this sort constitutes a major challenge to the helping professional, whose task is to treat children according to their own developmental schedules. Helpers may find that eleven-year-old clients have difficulty parting or separating from them. Children may be too old to cling to their helper's hand, but they can be allowed, for example, to hold on to a note from the helper showing the time and place of their next session with the counselor. We submit that an understanding of the loosely defined phases proposed by these theorists provides a valuable aid in assessing each client's immediate developmental needs.

Making investigations in the light of general developmental phases permits the practitioner to review more realistically the present manifestations, past developmental patterns, and future ramifications of a child's behavior. In addition, to really be of help to children their past, present, and future experiences must be dealt with as they are viewed by the children themselves. Any individual recalls feelings about past events somewhat differently from the way they actually occurred, and his or her rememberance of the past tends to color present experiences. Similarly, one's future—to the extent that one can sense it—is comprehended in terms of the past and present. Thus, while constructive intervention takes place within the individual's current life, it must also deal with changes in his or her feelings and conceptions about the past and future.

The three theories also suggest that whatever individuals do, think, or feel regarding any area of their life at any given time in the continuum of development is intrinsically linked to their self-image, their family (and immediate peers), and their key reference groups. All individuals are dealing with their inner experiences and their primary and secondary environments, and the way a person integrates these three spheres affects the way he or she relates to them. Consequently, clients cannot be helped toward desirable adaptive behavior unless their perceptions, feelings, and behavioral expectations regarding these three spheres are altered accordingly.

A Five-Phase Spectrum of Development

Suggestions for the practical application of the conceptual knowledge of the three theories will be presented within a five-phase spectrum of development later on in this chapter. The five phases into which the spectrum is divided are (1) establishing dependence upon dependence, (2) establishing dependence upon self-care, (3) establishing dependence upon primary relationships, (4) establishing dependence upon personal competence and secondary relationships, and (5) establishing dependence upon primary relationships in a secondary world.

These phases are based upon different observable levels of dependence. As was more fully described in Chapter 4, the securing of dependence in any one area also allows independence in that very area. In addition, every acquisition of independence frees an individual to establish a more advanced dependence in a new area; and, in turn, each new base of dependence assures the individual a greater autonomy in previously acquired spheres of independence. We hold that secure dependence points to freedom to act independently, because energies can be invested competently as long as dependence is assured. Basic shifts in the nature of dependence have been pinpointed (by the author), because of their appropriateness in assessment and intervention in developmental dilemmas or problems.

Implications of Development for Assessment

The three dimensions of child development—affect, behavior, and cognition—have certain implications for assessment within the context of the dyadic group, primary group, auxiliary, and organizational helping systems (outlined in the previous chapter). Initial observations are only invitations to further study and appraisal. The helper must explicitly assess what he or she wants to know regarding affect, behavior, or cognition, and then each of these aspects of human functioning must be evaluated in terms of the others.

Let us now proceed as if we were in an actual situation and wished to apply our learning. It is important to recall Piaget's observation that an individual first experiences a situation *affectively* before he or she can comprehend it and explain and utilize that understanding of it. This suggests that separate assessments should be made which differentiate between clients' first feelings about a situation, later understandings, and realistic plans for coping with it. We recall that when infants first sense a situation, they respond emotionally to it; only much later (usually more than a year) do they discover that situation behaviorally. Even more time is needed before they can comprehend, describe, and explain their behavior appropriately. A similar progression of learning occurs with each new chain of experiences at any point in one's life.

Developmental Assessment

Assessing an individual's developmental status and readiness, then, requires an evaluation of (1) his or her capacity to perceive through the five senses (see, hear, feel, etc.); (2) his or her awareness of these sensory experiences; and (3) his or her comprehension of these experiences. The child must at least be aware of sensory experiences in order to incorporate their content knowingly into his or her behavior. Most importantly, *knowing* and *understanding the knowing* are two different steps—days, weeks, months, or even years apart. Appraisals or assessment must differentiate between clients' understanding of the situation, their acceptance of new models of dealing with it, and their capacity for incorporating this understanding into their behavior.

The way children deal with their ongoing experiences provides rich cues for assessment. Initial or early experiences are first processed empirically (inductively) and behaviorally: an item of food is judged by one's first bite. Later, developmentally or experientially, the new experience is reviewed logically: does it make sense? Later on, the whole matter is reevaluated deductively: *(264)* does it fit into the scheme of things? In our work with people, experiences are assessed for such a fit into the scheme of things as well as for the behavioral, affective or cognitive aspects.

The steps in the learning process have significant relevance to the assessment of the child's ability to communicate. Even when the words children use express just what they intend to say, they may also carry a message which children are not able to articulate. The helper wants to know what children *mean,* not what they say, Piaget suggests that, in assessment, attention should focus upon the child's comments rather than on the particular questions put to the child. Very often children will try to provide the right answer to the adult's question, rather than responding to it as they truly think and feel. Piaget's techniques for inquiring into children's understanding of their own communications can serve as a guiding model for sorting out with children what they really conceive, that is, how they think as they see things.

"What?" Not "Why?" Is the Question

The foregoing points call to our attention that little genuine information is obtained in work with young children by questions such as, "Why do you think it happened?" Questions that ask why can be a senseless probe because they imply that there must be a specific explanation where most likely there is none. The child is probably unable to establish the relevant causative factors. Furthermore, the concept of multiple causation dictates that any one event has more than one explanation.

From Piaget we also learned that in questions that ask why, one meaning is related to cause and the other to goal. An individual on the developmental level of early childhood may conceive of a question that asks why merely in terms of goal orientation, that is, in terms of what happened. Causal considerations, as has been pointed out, are possible only with more advanced comprehension.

We learned from Erikson that "history taking influences history," (92) a concept that supports the currently diminished use of history taking as an essential facet of the study and assessment of individuals.

What Else to Be Assessed?

Study of early childhood development, in many ways, is an inquiry into the parent-child relationship. The modality of caring or mothering, that is, the readiness of parents to include their child in their thoughts, in their bodily posture and movements while holding the child, and in their social life and daily routine, furnishes helpful hints on the child's potential developmental progress within this first phase. The infant's own modality, as well, holds relevant clues to his or her developmental achievements or retardation.

Erikson's material on the child's modality in association with each developmental phase suggests that children's play behavior and general approach to their body, to space, and to time may reveal to an observer the children's own developmental preoccupation. A child's shift from a totally incorporative mode to one of incorporative holding, for example, can serve as such a developmental index. (To illustrate, in infancy or later in life we differentiates between "clutching" (incorporating) and "holding" (incorporative holding).) Moreover, Piaget suggests that in early infancy development, just watching to see whether an infant looks, looks for, looks at, reaches for, or grasps will provide telling data about a child's developmental progression. (194b) Assessment can include much about a child's qualitative thinking. While intelligence quotients are an ego-dependent quantitative measure, a developmental assessment can reveal more about the quality of thinking and possible thinking deficiencies. (139, 70)

The extent to which early deprivation has been compensated for is an essential consideration which can be assessed by a study of the symptoms of primary dependence. Guides to the level of the child's dependence are the interactive behavior between the primary nurturing person and child, the latitude of this person's permissive acceptance of the child's dependence, and this person's efforts to avoid excessively frustrating experiences for the child. Other clues to a child's degree of dependence are the responses of the parent and child in separation situations.

The extent of generalized behavior as opposed to specific responses is another clue to the child's developmental level. Gross emotional, intellectual and behavioral responses to specific situations can indicate that children have not successfully completed the first (infancy) phase, for as they formulate a sense of trust in their primary experiences, they begin to expand their spheres of attention in terms of a more specific interest in the separate aspects of their environment. Assessment inquiries can center on the delineation and variety of boundaries children have learned to recognize and incorporate into their behavior.

A valuable medium for assessing acquired abilities is the play situation, where children reveal not only the aspects of development which preoccupy them at the moment, but also the things that puzzle and possibly worry them. In playing, children play life over; they are whatever they play at in fantasy and in life. The professional observer can gain much, moreover, from what children leave out of their play. For example, if the child's play or drawings quite clearly leave out certain family members, it would appear that, as far as the child is concerned, the "denied" family member is very expendable. Another source for assessment is the way a child holds onto and releases objects and people. Early in life, holding on is a major modality and release is accidental. The ability to do both, and to hoard and retain as well, however, indicates a relatively developed self-control.

Sibling and competitive rivalry are part of usual development, although rivalrous possessiveness may imply that a child is still struggling with important and perhaps cumulative aspects of the first two phases. Children who display excessive interest in their own sex or curiosity about the other sex may well be grappling with typically third-phase developmental issues. The practitioner can detect possibly inadequate sexual acceptance by assessing children's relationships, particularly with people of the opposite sex, and evaluating their behavior in terms of what is appropriate for their sex.

Assessment of School-Age Children

In the fourth phase, children are primarily concerned with improving the *quality* of their social interactions and relationships and understanding the specifics and complexities of their social objectives and social environments. In this phase, children are in the "age of reason," energetically delving, searching out, and reinventing things through reason to find out "what makes them tick."

In assessment, a practitioner will be interested in exploring the *quality* of a child's efforts to master life at home and away from home. Competence in relating to persons over a range of circumstances is one index of a child's developmental lacks and accomplishments. Another index is children's readiness to see themselves as part of a larger group that is, in turn, related to society in general. Children's explanations about their activities, especially descriptive accounts of their work and their plans regarding projects and experiments provide an accessible view of their mode of thinking. Attention could also be directed toward assessing the ability of the child to gather facts and to employ objective measuring devices, such as a measuring stick, instead of making mere subjective guesses.

Children in this developmental span are preoccupied with rules. The way they search out, devise, and relate to rules and their ability to grant that these rules are essential components of their interactions can provide the observer with indicators of their developmental progress. On the social plane, children's sense of relativity is demonstrated by their capacity to respond differently to people in different roles and their readiness to assume tasks with varied role demands. For example, children's capacity to baby-sit for another child depend on whether they are able to put aside some of their own preoccupations and interests as they play with their charge.

Since learning does not occur on a straight line, but from area to area, to assist the child, the question has to be repeatedly asked: In which *area* of learning or development has the breakdown occurred? (This question becomes particularly pertinent for work with autistic children.)

The child can be studied for progress in discerning relationships and in applying what has been learned from one situation to another. Play and leisure pursuits are rich resources for observing and learning more about children; in such activities they will toy with tasks and ideas with which they are wrestling in real life.

In this connection, persons working with children may want to remain cognizant of the fact that when a child experiences new materials or events, he or she progresses through two steps of discovery. Whether the experience is with new things, ideas, values, sounds, or sound makers, a child encounters the nature and order of such a novelty first and then tends to leave the experience alone for a while (often to the adult's dismay) returning to it later. In such a return, the child then tends to have a clear purpose in mind. The novelty, no longer novel, now fits in his schema of things, events, and possible actions.

Assessment of Adolescent Development

A client whose adolescent development we wish to assess can be appraised for readiness and capacity to relate to the world of peers and elders. The practitioner may want to evaluate to what extent adolescents' activities are tied in with their attempts to discern their own standards of living and to what degree their activities reflect a resistance to standards per se. Furthermore, the helper may want to reflect upon the youth's progress in finding his or her identity in the several spheres of adolescent development since adolescents face simultaneously many challenges associated with movement toward youth status and young adulthood.

A closer look would reveal, qualitatively, the adolescent's (1) sense of certainty as a person in his or her own right; (2) sense of appropriate timing; (3) sense of sexual adequacy; (4) sense of social competence; (5) sense of workmanship; (6) sense of authority integration; and (7) sense of forming an ideology. Any of these social challenges and promises of adulthood can be a source of acute concern in an individual's total development.

In earlier phases, we are concerned with the child's capacity to differentiate between various social roles and with his or her general adaptation of them. In this fifth (adolescent) phase, the focus would have to be on teenagers' versatility in playing the many roles they pursue readily and, hopefully, happily. It is a time to hate in order to be hateful and a time to be in love with love. We suggest that a review of the range and variation of the social roles or stances assumed within any one day is more informative than an intensive inquiry into one role preoccupation. In adolescence, individuals can mentally reverse a sequence of events so that it becomes clear why something happened. They are then at a point where they can make their own choices.

In earlier phases, sibling rivalry is related to children's wish to be close to and fully possessed by the person for whom they and their contemporaries are competing. In adolescence, sibling rivalry may reveal similar dynamics, or it may indicate the more advanced phenomenon of status—a striving to be the person closest to the one in the authority position. Consequently, in work with adolescents or adults the helper may want to determine the nature of the rivalry. Is the rivalrous person striving for secure dependency, that is, to be *with* the person—which would be a vestige of an earlier developmental struggle? Or is the person competing for a position of status and greater independence, that is, *to take the place of the person*—which would be a factor more intimately tied in with movements toward adult development?

Many of the youth's temporary and experimental activities are valuable indices of his or her integration of age-bound social demands and of emotional readiness. The youth's play activities and tomfoolery may reveal preoccupation with acting "small" while trying to deal with previous and still vitally important concerns; while acting "big," on the other hand, would hint at his or her ambitious thrust toward greater maturity. In the cognitive area, helpers may want to ask themselves to what extent youths are searching for explanations in order to comprehend their social and physical surroundings, their ideational world, and their own lot within them. These may be questions which have plagued the youth for many years.

A good number of the preceding points can also be applied in working with adults, so long as they are adapted to the adult's unique social situation. In particular, a worker may want to be mindful of the fact that an adult experiences developmental phases *as an adult*. Thus, the practitioner may find it useful to assess a client's problems in terms of the developmental phase or phases which are particularly significant to the client. The practitioner may want to intervene within one developmental phase or within the progression from one phase to the next. Yet, in all the searching inquiries, a dual question is inherent: Does the individual operate on the demonstrated level because of his or her developmental accomplishment or because it is a novel situation? (*172,* 20; *192*)

THE DYADIC GROUP SYSTEM

We shall now review the implications of the three dimensions of human development for professional intervention, within the framework of the combined sequential developmental phases.[1] Further, we shall apply these developmental phases to each of the four helping systems outlined in Chapter 5.

Phase I: Establishing Dependence upon Dependence

In their earliest years, children have no social perspective. They depend indiscriminately upon the adult who happens to be with them, while the adult senses concurrently an immediate and full responsibility for a totally dependent child. Thus, it is essential to human survival that nurturing include more than food, clothing, and shelter.

Moreover, the importance of touch as a basic body and life experience has direct implications regarding racism and other forms of skin-deep value judgments. Open acknowledgement and

[1] See the integrated developmental phases, Chapter 4, and Table 4-1, column 4.

communal support for values such as "black is beautiful" (or similar skin-oriented value judgments) have direct bearing upon child-caring when a person's skin color is directly associated with distinct personal and communal values. (34, 1)

Nurturing care encourages activities leading toward dependence, and discourages activities which would frustrate the child. Of course, momentary frustrations are natural and inevitable. But children's attempts to relieve their frustrations through aggression, as we learned from Sears, often require careful handling. Such aggression may reflect last-resort measures in which children try to bail themselves out of difficult situations; such aggression may also be directly related to the child's personal reaction to the caring person, as in cases where a child attempts to blackmail a caring adult into removing the frustrating conditions.

A helper who is fostering dependence must keep in mind the vulnerability of that dependence when it is in the making. A child who starts to depend on an adult reacts very sensitively to any variation in the dependence interactions, so any such alteration should be undertaken cautiously in order that it may foster rather than hinder such interactions. In this connection, sibling rivalry should be recognized as evidence that dependence seems worthwhile enough to the participants to compete or contend for it. The caring adult should welcome it as such.

Phase II: Establishing Dependence upon Self-care

Developmental problems that appear when children are beginning to help themselves and to desert their earlier total dependence are frequently related to the availability or withdrawal of the helping person's care. During this time, helping continues exclusively on a primary level with an emphasis on encouraging children to carry out more and more activities on their own. Helping in this way involves finding safe alternatives for actions as well as for prohibiting actions. Permissiveness now entails both letting children try on their own and providing a safe harbor in which they may find refuge before and after making such attempts. Frustration is now permitted to exist in a controlled way for purposes of challenge. A parent or helping agent needs to make a distinction between dealing with the assimilative activities of a child, which proceed best with the least external reinforcement, and the accommodative efforts, which are best supported with reinforcement.

Language as a tool of communication and an advanced form of dealing with dependence deserves attention here. A single phrase, such as "you do"-"you do get me dressed right now," can convey a whole series of activities in which children perceive that they are the central actors. The language children use is that of their elders; their communication, the helper may note, still reflects only their own impressionistic understanding. As we learned from Piaget, the depth of children's comprehension of their own language varies according to their level of development. The significance of words such as *good* or *bad* is linked to the child's dependence upon the adult who says these words, rather than to the actual meaning.

Helping at this point in children's lives also means working within the confines of their comprehension; they will understand their experiences through reasoning by proximity, judging by external appearances, and locating action by visually perceiving motion. Children are taught to label each experience, action, and feeling, and their efforts to separate them can be encouraged. Children can be shown that they can be angry without necessarily expressing their anger merely by kicking, screaming, or other body language. This understanding holds direct implications for helping with aggression. It is not the adult's explanation of the child's aggression which is apt to be communicated, but rather the adult's own mode of aggressiveness, even in verbal explanations, which serves to act upon the child's aggression. In this way children themselves experience control regarding *how much* and *when* aggression will be tolerated, rather than merely hearing about the essence of their aggression.

Play in the child's life and play in the helping situation can be a reflection of the child's everyday experiences at this time in development. Play yields pertinent information which neither the child nor the adult could verbalize or fully act out in the office interview, at home, or within the lifespace of a residential treatment program.

Phase III: Establishing Meaningful
Secondary Dependence upon Primary Relationships

As children become old enough to venture beyond the physical and interpersonal confines of their homes, they begin searching for new kinds of relationships. In a helping situation, likewise, they are now capable of proceeding either on an associate or a primary level. On either level, in contrast to the helper's fostering satisfaction in dependence in an earlier phase, a new emphasis should be placed upon promoting modification in the child's sense of dependence. Efforts are now directed toward helping children feel important among others and toward preparing them to live in a way that others can count on, so that they can become individuals who are secure among and dependent upon others.

As children gain more experience, they become particularly attuned to the supporting and controlling functions of the adults around them. For the helping professional, it becomes important to communicate clearly and firmly to the child what constitutes acceptable attitudes and forms of behavior. To illustrate, in a treatment situation, clients can learn to differentiate between expressing themselves freely during the interview and maintaining greater controls in the waiting room or hallway when meeting their worker. Similarly, boundaries are explored and established when client and helper discuss the problems of the client's everyday life.

Both speech and actions serve as tools of reasoning. What children do or say while relating to their helping person may represent as much a process of reasoning out ideas in the presence of another as a communication of ideas. Children deal with one problem at a time; analogies are out of the question. Judgments are made by end results as the child experiences them at the moment. Experiences, things, and persons are either *good* or *bad*. A friend is a friend or no friend at all. Shadings or degrees have yet to emerge.

Parent and helper need constantly to remain aware of the fact that children must have cognitive readiness. It is neither lack of motivation nor lack of practice which hampers learning; but rather the absence of cognitive structure for adequate comprehension. For individuals to understand, they must be able to reconstruct what is to be understood.

Even when children can master a certain task it does not necessarily imply that they can perform similar tasks. A child might be able to fold and place paper napkins on a dining table, but be unable to place the silverware. Each learning, at this point of development, is a separate feat of learning. Moreover, learning, now as well as at other points in life, "requires comprehension. . . . Knowledge must be assimilated, incorporated into a system that can accommodate it—for it [learning] to be meaningful." (324, 22)

Counselors should remember that with children of this age or at this point in development, much of their energy is devoted to becoming their own parents, that is, to their affective sense of selfhood. This requires doing things the way the parent, most likely of the same sex, presumably would do it. Children's preoccupation is with themselves, their everyday world. They are attempting to master every problem set before them.

We learned, by combining the three dimensions of human development, that by becoming one's own parent, boys and girls prepare for their respective societal roles. They want to do well, and even if they fail or think they fail, commendation may be given to their courage for trying, because the desire to move ahead and to succeed is as deserving as eventual mastery. Ample time and opportunities for play and the indulging of fantasies of accomplishment now become of utmost importance in care on a primary level. Play has to afford the child opportunities to become what everyday life does not yet allow him or her to become.

In regard to cognitive development spoken communication highlights various points in a child's development. Language as a major tool of the helping process in working with individuals is particularly relevant. As we found, early in a child's development, speech stands for action. "You said so" means "you did so." In the child's mind, an event described may easily become an event which occurred. Children may use language appropriately without realizing the meaning of the words. A child may speak of walking on the left side of the street without having much of a notion of what constitutes left or right. The helper's attention should be devoted, therefore, to a child's actual range of language comprehension, rather than the words or statements per se.

Phase IV: Establishing Dependence upon
Personal Competence and Secondary Relationships
In working with individuals during this phase, helping efforts are directed toward using previously acquired "safety zones" of dependence. New experiences beyond those of primary dependence can be sorted out with the cooperation of the primary caring person. Helping is then directed toward mobilizing children's trust in their own initiative and toward encouraging them to be self-starting and self-perpetuating. Desires to perform in this way are frequently classified as autonomous strivings.[2] Helping means enabling clients to see how their individual creative activities and involvement can gain for them an important position in their world. To succeed means for an individual in this phase to do better than he or she did before. Competitive feelings and activities should be recognized by the helper as reflecting a desire to come out all right by oneself.

Play remains important for communication and common explorations, but in this phase, it is losing some of its socially equalizing quality. This should be recognized in child care and play therapy. Roles and role expectations become relevant now. Concerns for rules and for working out mutual regulations help the child sort out and understand interpersonal interactions, which are employed to advantage at this time to clarify relationships and new centers of authority. It is clear that the interview can aid in disclosing and measuring concerns far beyond those of the immediate helping situation.

At no time in the child's life is his or her insistence upon equality as important; fairness and justice exist when equality is as-

---

[2] In assessment, a distinction can be made between autonomous *doing*, which is a strong desire to *do* for oneself that is most in tune with very early developmental experience, and autonomous *striving*, which is a strong desire to *achieve* for oneself, more in line with the developmental concerns of phase IV, here under consideration.

sured. To this end, helpers play various roles—caring adult, guiding elder, social educator, representative of the adult world, and an older person who identifies and plays with the child. The child knows these roles, and helpers can, therefore, draw upon whichever role expectation they consider relevant.

Phase V: Establishing Dependence upon
Primary Relationships within a Secondary World

A dyadic relationship between client and helping adult presents a perplexing situation for teenagers who are developing and solidifying their own balance between dependence and independence. In a primary situation, the focus is upon resolving the personal need for dependence and/or independence in everyday living. The adolescent's conception of the caring person gradually shifts from that of a parent surrogate to that of a supportive trustee. In an interview situation on the associate level, the aim is to help clients become independently contributing members of their own and the larger society. If helpers see themselves both as counseling specialists, who partake in interpersonal relationships, and as representatives of the larger society to which both client and helper belong, then clients will deal simultaneously with personal and societal relationships.

It is important, in this connection, for the practitioner to realize that adolescents are shifting their value system from a childhood one to an adult one, and comparing their own values to those evidenced by adults. Therefore, any difference between what helpers "preach" and what they practice is likely to be challenged, overtly or covertly, by the client. If valid situational differences are causing different value systems, such factors need to be considered and possibly explored by all parties concerned. Frequently, an understanding of individual differences and capacities will help the adolescent accept different standards.

In a dyadic helping situation, speech is usually the major vehicle for solving problems. Language is employed to test, to think through, to dare oneself and others, to boast, to confess, to examine, or to discard varying life experiences—until finally talking about one or another form of living becomes a commitment to it. Language, therefore, facilitates role experimentation. Thinking aloud together forms a major interrelationship matrix in which the client plays with thoughts and words in place of behavioral experimentation. With more and more facility, the adolescent starts to comprehend through abstractions. Although reasoning, which involves abstract thinking, does not spring into being automatically as an extension of concrete learning, and although it has to be engendered anew on this level, all concrete learning contributes to its generation.

PRIMARY GROUP SYSTEMS

Each time a client is considered for service within a group system, two questions have to be answered: (1) What does group membership mean to the client developmentally? (2) In what way does the client use his or her helping agent as the central person in the group situation? The individual's investments in four major facets of group membership must be determined:

1. Dependence upon individual group members and upon the helping agent as the central person
2. Utilization of the group situation as a social arena for working out old or new relationships, skills, ideas, values, and behavioral patterns
3. Use of the group situation for becoming part of the immediate social unit and a larger social context
4. Dependence upon the group as a social reference system which influences thoughts, feelings, beliefs, and behavior in other associations beyond this particular group (*189*, 29–30)

Phases I and II: Establishing Dependence upon Dependence and Dependence upon Self-care

Working with a group that is functioning within developmental phases I or II most likely requires that the helper establish close one-to-one interpersonal relationships with individual members. It is questionable, therefore, whether most children in these elementary developmental phases can be effectively served by the group system, because development at this time depends fundamentally upon a continuous, concentrated interaction with a central adult.

However, certain children at this level might find help, for example, autistic children or children whose primary requirement is to develop and acknowledge their sense of need for a caring person. For these children, it is desirable to stimulate their sense of rivalry and their expression of it. Expressing rivalrous feelings affords children a situation in which the caring person can finally relate to their desire for care. Their struggle with others for such care is not a dynamic conflict, but a means for getting added and more personally differentiated adult care, nurturing, and involvement.

Phase III: Establishing Dependence upon Primary Relationships

A successful group experience requires a group which is small enough to guarantee ample personal contacts between children and adults within a sibling or peer situation. When two or more individuals demand personal adult attention, rivalry becomes apparent in (1) the striving for a favored position near the central adult and (2) the maintaining of a safe distance between one's own position and those of others who might threaten such security. In this phase, the cause of primary competition among peers is the desire to win and maintain the support of the central person: competition among peers for other reasons remains a by-product. On this basis, helping persons should take into account that their interactions with each client need to be considered first, even when events force them to deal with interpersonal strife between two or more clients. In this phase, there is neither awareness nor understanding of competitive hierarchical relationships; so the helping person can be a special friend to many, as long as one client at a time is number "one" and feels "I am really recognized."

In work with individuals in a group system during this phase, toys, pets, equipment, and group members (including the central adult) serve as important accessories for living out personal struggles through play. The language of play, physical motion, and verbal utterances should all be seen as efforts to communicate with others, and the message rather than the content of speech, play, and actions should be attended to.

Within this phase, much of a group's play is nominally the same as that of developmentally more advanced children (playing cowboys, house, etc.); however, there is a notable difference in the content of the play behavior. In the younger phase, a single reference point might encompass a whole play episode; for instance, sudsing doll clothing might stand for playing house. Play develops into an increasingly more meaningful group experience as the child grows older. "Let's build a hide-out" means "let's do something together."

The helping agent has to keep in mind that the child in this phase still sees group norms and rules in the momentary present, which means that group discussions and activities should relate to the individual group member's current needs and to the planning of effective activities for the immediate future.[3]

Phase IV: Establishing Dependence upon Personal Competence and Secondary Relationships

In work with groups, it is presumed, developmentally, that children in this fourth phase are able to perceive and assume different roles. In group membership, they shift from a preoccupation with social contacts and activities needing close personal relationships and a sense of belonging together. The need for a sense of dependence upon a few key persons gives way to a desire for

---

[3] Teachers of kindergarten and first and second grade will find it helpful to apply Jean Piaget's finding regarding teaching and curriculum development (especially 4, 131–141).

security within the group. Children can now conceive of themselves as being members of their family, school class, and group simultaneously.

The capacity to comprehend reversibility (a Piagetian idea) reaches also into communication exercises and group dynamics. Not until a person can think in terms of reversibility can such a person successfully handle and learn from feedback and paraphrasing. These techniques require a cognitive readiness for reversibility and an affective maturity by which the individual can answer the question: "What kind of feelings were in that thought?" (126, 104)

Primary group care, which from this point on may substitute as an alternative to family living, provides a basic nurturing environment supported by the activities of group living. A client's change to dependence upon peers and the group as a whole permits helping persons to use such new forms of dependence for therapeutic purposes. They may now deal with relationships other than those between each client and themselves because they no longer have to act solely as the central figure.

Whereas previously the group has been visualized and labeled by the child as the helper's group, from this point on, the individual members' activities, encouraged by the helper, will strongly influence the group's character. Play, talk, and work gain increasing importance as social catalysts, and interpersonal experiences continue to be valuable for the immediate social satisfactions they can yield. Individual members want to see themselves succeed and measure up to the others' expectations. Much of one's association with peers is carried on to measure, improve, and maintain self-esteem. Continuous and stimulating interpersonal experiences are the essential motivating factors for relationships.

In group deliberations during this phase, much attention is devoted to questions of group-shared rules and regulations. Fit retributions for violations are part of the concern. There is a consciousness that the seat of authority tends to be more and more found in the child's own friendship groups rather than in the world of his or her elders. Such awareness has particular relevance in helping group members with their group deliberations. Fairness for a group at this point emerges from planning and sticking to standards which they have developed.

To sum up, working with the group system on the associate and primary levels means enabling each client to feel that he or she genuinely counts in the eyes of the other group members, and through such experiences to feel that this is his or her group. A group experience during this phase has to assure ample opportunities for talk and play, for much ado about what to do, which may appear to the adult as much ado about nothing. Work and play become intermingled as if each were the other. The group, in essence, becomes a second testing ground of dependence. Group games and competitive or individual activities are employed for the development of plans, rules, and regulations. Cognitive learning now focuses upon universality, and the group acts as a handy laboratory for thinking through experiences and ideas which might bear on the creation of social rules and standards. Helping by means of the group system entails encouraging group experiences for the mutual benefits to be derived from them, rather than putting emphasis upon the productions of the group as a whole.

Phase V: Establishing Dependence upon
Primary Relationships within a Secondary World

The group plays a vital role in the way of life of contemporary teenagers. Adult participation, from the adolescent's perspective, is an intrusion. A central adult may have to learn a group's norms and culture before he or she can effectively communicate with the group members; as the intruder, it is up to the adult to adjust. The group, if skillfully worked with, can be a useful tool with which to influence developmental lags or to avert developmental complications.

On a primary level, group living such as that provided by a unit within an institutional program may offer a starting point and a retreat to which a child may return when life in the outside world becomes too stormy. The group provides a social and psychological base for belonging. The helping person is a part of that base and is to be available when the teenager needs the sort of adult guidance and support which cannot be furnished by the group alone.

On the associate level, it is essential to determine which aspects of existing or predicted developmental lags or complications the group experience is intended to help. Within this phase, the group takes over more and more adult prerogatives, but at the same time (regardless of the adolescent's and his friends' outward behavior) adult authority continues to stand without question in certain well-defined areas. It is not surprising, therefore, that problems involving a division of authority are frequently encountered. At this stage, both authorities—the old and the new—must begin to blend.

An important consideration is the size of the group. For young people who are primarily preoccupied with self-integration and its myriad aspects, a small, intimate, and closed circle of members is desirable. On the other hand, adolescents who are moving ahead to societal integration and who need to experiment with their newly integrated selves in terms of the society at large can be helped significantly within a larger group of diverse but similarly focused individuals. For these adolescents, productive involvement in organizational functioning, social structure, and a wide range of role experimentation becomes an essential facet of their group experience and provides a useful means for gaining experience in becoming full members of their society.

The abundance of talk and random activities of teenagers in this developmental phase shows that they are endlessly thinking about and experimenting with the many alternatives before them. The helper hopefully refrains from labeling these explorations as actual commitments too quickly. Such trials reflect the adolescent's efforts to apply newly acquired abilities and to test conflicting feelings about his or her developmental capacities.

In working with a group of adolescents, the study of adolescents' versatility and diffusiveness of behavior is often more productive than the study of such behavior's actual content. Sometimes the behavior of several teenagers within the group gives cause for anticipating a state of anarchy. This may alarm many adults who are concerned about this autonomous trend of many youth-group members. In order to be helpful, the adult then needs to delineate the group's structure with firmness and clarity, because an adolescent can only attain a proper degree of independence and a sense of identity within a context that is well defined.

Many intragroup dealings at this time have to do with the adolescent's own role expectations and with developing ones that he or she can meet. In working with a family as a group, this issue is often crucial. The family members need to be studied for both diffusion and possible incompatible duplication of roles. Discerning what are compatible and attainable role expectations for the client is a major function of the helping person, and the aim is to gradually equalize the adolescent's and his or her society's expectations of the role of the young person.

Teenagers are frequently preoccupied with procedures and rules and their applications as if they were the judiciary. This is their way of dealing with some of the problems which face them, and since such activities are often beneficial, they are to be fostered. Mental consideration of all possibilities and probabilities, ceaseless discussion of what constitutes fairness and justice, loud squabbles over contradictions, and trying out ifs—all of these are measures which reflect an adolescent's struggles to find his or her place and to mold a sense of equity. Such activities deserve attention and time in a group session. Much of their verbalizations may be role experimentation or relationship testing within a familiar and protected social unit. Individual clashes and social conflicts can be most welcome for their value in casting private confusions and resentments into the open arena of the group, where they may be dealt with as problems common to all of the group members within this developmental phase.

Rap sessions are not only a desirable medium; they also easily become the adolescent's way of life. For example, a heated argument over the right of one group member to miss a group session without valid reasons may reflect the personal conflict of all group members concerning dependence versus independence. A group discussion for the ostensible purpose of resolving this question might simultaneously benefit each individual's own strivings to balance dependence and independence by further identifying an acceptable set of role expectations for the group members.

We referred to a change in the adolescent's conception of authority and a consequent change in the helping agent's role. In addition to the intermediary role as the relevant society's representative and the enunciator of its expectations, the helping person necessarily has to modify his or her position within the group to accommodate the client's personal conflict with authority. Within a group, such a struggle is twofold. It consists of (1) the primary struggle of the individual against the majority, as represented by the single member's reaction to the authority of the rest of the group, and (2) the struggle of an individual to win a position of authority within a group of other separate individuals.

Opposition to the central adult, or competition for his or her attention, may be undertaken to secure a better position within the group and not to improve the youth's relationship with the central adult. Rivalry in this phase, therefore, has a new meaning; it is no longer engaged in for the purpose of depending upon or receiving care from the adult, but to win the right to *exercise* such care by first mobilizing it via the adult in authority. The shift is from the desire for care to the desire to become the authority for the provision of care, or at least a desire to be second in command.

Basically, the group with its helper provides an atmosphere for experimentation, for dealing with that which perplexes the young person. The fact that group experiences vary so much from client to client within this developmental phase may be explained by the variety and velocity of expressions of personality among adolescents rather than by any appreciable differences in their developmental processes.

AUXILIARY SYSTEMS

In an auxiliary system, the understanding is that the child or adolescent will remain in the center of this type of helping situation, while the parent, teacher, counselor, or other significant concerned person who has sought help receives consultation in order to improve his or her participation in the child's developmental progress.

In working with a child's close associates or life partners, helpers must share their specialized knowledge and skills to broaden the adult's perspective and, thereby, affect the child-adult relationships. Much of the helping effort could be usefully concerned with assessing children's current situations and interpreting their behavior in terms of their developmental readiness rather than by chronological age, as is generally the practice. Parents are frequently relieved and encouraged to find that a complication is due to a difference in the time at which their child's developmental readiness occurred. ,

In working with parents, two not always compatible ideas may need joint consideration: (1) the notion that a good parent is one who is active and *does* something to a child and (2) the realization that a child's ordinary development may sometimes be in a state of subtle balance where it is best to wait. Therefore, the counselor can make it clear that attentive parenthood includes selective periods of inactive parenthood.

We learned that punishment does not tend to foster an alternative way of behaving; instead, it conveys personal disapproval and, thereby, impairs the closeness of the relationship. On the other hand, noninterference, or so-called permissiveness, leaves children directionless and, at times, at the mercy of their own guilt, which may make them feel as rejected and isolated as punishment would. Both approaches to child care, strict control and permissiveness, ought to be reviewed by parent and counselor for their bearing on the life of the child under study. Counseling of this kind means moving from an examination of the techniques themselves, to weighing the implications of such techniques.

Phase I: Establishing Dependence upon Dependence

In working with parents of children in this first phase, it becomes the helping professional's responsibility to use his or her understanding of the pervasive nature of the early years and the quality of the child-parent relationship during those years. What the baby does to the mother, the baby's family, and the family's place in the community require as much attention as what mother, family, and community do to baby. With such understanding labels like "the rejecting mother," "the unwanted child," "the abused child," "the deprived child," etc., may become obsolete.

Piaget, Erikson, and Sears all agree that development depends upon the patterns of experiences. In evaluating child-parent relationships, then, the parents patterns of regularity play a vital part in the baby's responding to recurring experiences—for example,

the extent to which a mother assures her child a sense of predictability by her outward behavior. Investigating child-caring patterns
may help in discerning the effects of child-caring efforts. Feeding,
weaning, toilet training, and the other cycles of caring and separation should be considered in terms of their connection with previously established patterns of dependence; the child's main dilemma in each cycle may be to replace an old dependence pattern
with a new one.

Child training is also parent training. In order to avoid a parental preoccupation with doing "the right thing," it may be helpful
to remember the hypothesis that can be derived from all three
theories: child and parent learn best from each other. Above all,
concurrent learning depends upon discovery through trial and error
and through *mutual* adaptation.

The vulnerability and innocence of infants create a powerful
urge in mother, family, and society to give all that is wanted and
more. Parents can be assured that it is safe, desirable, and beneficial to be a giving parent, and that to instill a sense of trusting
dependence is the first major parental task of child rearing.

Phase II: Establishing Dependence upon Self-care

In this phase, the gradual release of close parental control over
the child demands that decisions be made about what, how,
when, and where the child's self-care and independence can be
encouraged and at what points the parent's direct care ought to be
continued. Again, attention is to be given to the specific considerations with which parents are dealing. Using the toilet, returning
books to the bookcase, and staying in bed when told, are activities
which might demonstrate a child's struggle in a world of many
demands. The helping person, as an authority on human growth
and development, may assure the parent that the ups and downs
in child training are inherent developmental crises which in no
way deny the quality of the person's caring. It should be stressed
that evidence of a child's acceptance of parental care takes many
forms. For example, the exasperation of mothers at their children's
sudden insistence upon feeding themselves may be mediated
when the mother learns that such crude attempts at self-feeding
are positive signs of the client's dependence upon her and the
desire to emulate her, rather than a rejection of her and her skills in
feeding.

When the child starts on his or her own do-it-yourself developmental course, parents need to know that their withdrawal of
care in any area without demonstrated readiness on the part of the
child constitutes a general threat to his or her sense of dependence.
Such withdrawals can serve as powerful and dangerous weapons
of control. To be specific, a remark such as "If you do not come

right away I'll have to leave you" should be considered in light of the message conveyed and its future effects, and not only for its immediate handiness.

The professional helper should share theoretical information with the parent whenever it might promote better caring practices. For instance, parents may discover with real bewilderment that their children no longer respond to them as they used to. Knowing that external pressures of a situational change, such as a move or the birth of another child, can decrease internal control while increasing the need for dependence may permit the parent to regard the condition as a new learning situation rather than as a child's or a parent's failure.

Labeling can be applied as a useful device for linking a preceding experience to a later related event. However, in these childhood phases, labeling serves primarily to establish a connection between related experiences rather than to explain their logical interrelationships. For example, a child having burned his or her tongue because the cocoa was too hot may hear the experience labeled: "tongue hurts, hot cocoa." The child becomes aware that there is some connection between hurting his tongue and hot cocoa, but the logic of hot drinks burning tongues will remain a mystery for some time.

The theoretical contention that play embodies a child's attempts to master developmental tasks holds the following message for parents: All of life may become play, but not all play may become life. Young children may get themselves fully dressed in play; that does not necessarily mean, however, that henceforth they can dress themselves. Piaget's and Erikson's recognition of play as one of the most essential developmental and autotherapeutic processes holds as much significance for the parent as it does for the professional helper. In fact, we may assume that if children are provided with ample opportunities for unhampered play, particularly in the early phases of development, they may deal more precisely with their problems than the parent and helper could. Therefore, suggestions to a parent for providing play opportunities should concern the helping professional just as much as alerting a parent to the importance of a balanced diet, sufficient sleep, and other benefits for the child.

Phase III: Establishing
Dependence upon Primary Relationships
In this phase, the nature of the immediate child-care relationship—whether between mother and child or father and child in a two-parent family or parent and child in a single-parent family—requires particular attention for the variations in the family constellations and differential relationship patterns.

Previously made judgments about what it is safe to do for the child now must be augmented by decisions about interpreting the child's feelings and actions. Parents may take comfort, perhaps, in the knowledge that a child's true feelings need not always be expressed in actions which will require direct response from the parents. Subconscious communication is a normal part of life. A parent's comments, such as, "I know she has really done nothing that should get me so upset that I feel like screaming at her," reflect a common reaction to the intermingling of the child's affective, cognitive, and behavioral processes with the parent's own life experiences.

In interpreting children's needs, the helping professional will likely have to stress for the parent the continuing importance of play with objects, pets, and peers, which now may take place as much outside the range of the parents' supervision as within. Parents may want to consider that in playing with their children they are introducing and instilling their own values, standards, and ideas, and that these will affect a child's future. Whether the emphasis is on exploring, winning, having fun, or just being together, playing together will breed later developmental consequences. Parents may have to decide, therefore, which attitudes and aptitudes to encourage; for example, whether competition, pleasure seeking, sociability, or creativity will contribute most to their child's developing personality.

With a child's intuitive actions approaching more and more rational forms of behavior in this phase, it is hard for any adult to realize that despite some gains, a child's actual social competence is still just beginning. Parents may have to differentiate between teaching behavioral practices and expecting a child's adherence to standards which those practices exemplify. Expectations of courtesy, order, responsibility, and good hygiene, for example, will probably not be fulfilled yet. Although children's behavior falls within the sphere of adults' mores, parent and helper should note that the comprehension of the meaning of such mores does not. Children see their behavior as theirs alone, and, therefore, it may be easily misinterpreted by onlookers.

To sum up, this phase is characterized by the child's independent explorations in thinking, feeling, and acting, and parents need to be shown visibly that their boy or girl still fundamentally relies on them and wants nurturing care both within the home and outside.

Phase IV: Establishing Dependence upon
Personal Competence and Secondary Relationships

In this phase, it may be necessary to deal with the child's parents, teacher, or any other significant adult in the child's life. Such individuals will be depended upon for the kind of nurturing benefits they can provide when the child needs it and will also be societal representatives when the child requires that type of contact. The helping professional, being aware of the child's increased comprehension of the world around him, should lead the parent to investigate, for example, children's questioning of parental authority and their comparing of their own family's ways of doing things with those of others; in this way parents can determine whether the child has a personal psychological conflict or a cognitive crisis caused by discovering two unlike but nevertheless acceptable kinds of behavior. The child's questioning may appear to be a personal challenging of the rights of parenthood, when actually it is only a pondering of the numerous alternatives for behaving "correctly."

It is noteworthy that in this phase we often pay more attention to children's comments than to his actions. In working with parents during this phase, a reliance upon spoken communication as a major gauge of the child-parent relationship develops; and the preoccupation with parents' activities is replaced by a new interest in verbal communication between child and parent. Thoughts and feelings are now often communicated through an expanding group of symbols, both verbal and nonverbal. The child is able to grasp the fuller meaning of words such as *don't* and gestures such as when a mother shakes her finger in disapproval. Much of the effectiveness of this kind of helping may depend on the joint attempt of parent and helping agent to acquire an accurate picture of the child's activities away from home. Practitioners can often help parents find revealing indications of their child's relationship to them in the child's out-of-home behavior; for in spite of children's apparent lack of interest in their family's activities and economic concerns while at home, they cannot help but display their parents' care, behavior, and values when they are away from home.

Phase V: Establishing Dependence upon
Primary Relationships within a Secondary World

This phase holds a special challenge to the concerned helper and parent who are working jointly to solve an adolescent's difficulties. Parents and helpers are in the position of having to prove themselves as dependable people to the adolescent, at a time when he or she is outgrowing dependence. An adolescent's natural strivings are toward independence.

Adolescence represents a distinct period of development between childhood and adulthood, but a period in which the adolescent is a *dependent without childhood status*. Parents often need to be reminded that adolescent behavior is not an isolated behavioral phenomenon and that it cannot be considered separately from the social context within which it is experienced. It is important for a helper to remember that adolescent behavior often includes experimentation with extremes and that adolescent behavior and thoughts are transitory.

In work with parents or other key persons, the helper should try to anticipate realistically the youth's immediate future. What tomorrow holds for and requires of the adolescent are at least as important as what has happened yesterday.

Erikson's material interprets adolescence in a highly civilized world as a prolonged conflict between the need for identity and temporary role diffusions. This prolonged conflict will entail a simultaneously prolonged dependence upon responsible caring elders. Such caring adults continue to serve as sounding boards for the youth's feelings, thinking, and actions while the adults' authority remains undiminished.

An adolescent's development is continually affected by opportunities offered not only by the family but by other social institutions beyond the parents' immediate personal control. To help parents see themselves as *sharing* contributors to an adolescent's development rather than as solely responsible for it may encourage them to deal with and try to impact the institutions that affect adolescents as well as the adolescents themselves.

SYSTEMS FOR PROGRAM, STRUCTURE, OR POLICY ALTERATION

In the previous chapter, we mentioned that helpful intervention may mean altering certain conditions which impinge upon an individual's life situation in order to prevent, control, or alter developmental complications.

All three theories, particularly those of Erikson and Sears, point out that nurturing persons can instill in the child a basic sense of security only as deep as their own. Therefore, it becomes important that parents themselves are assured emotional, social, ethnic, and economic security. This premise becomes a *social* issue, because individuals, parents, and families can expand their potentialities only so far as the community supports and grants such expansion, and only so far as individuals are prepared to invest in the community's development.

The importance of being a participating member of one's community carries over in the work of persons who assume parental functions. Nurses, child-care workers, homemakers, foster-home parents, and teachers need to feel and act as members of their respective communities in order to be able to pass on a sense of continuity to those entrusted to them. Arrangements of working hours, pay scale, social prestige for one's work, and the location of one's place of work become important considertions in assuring helpers a place in their community.

The fact that personality development is anchored in the family's sense of well-being stresses the importance of the helping services. Aid to dependent families, family counseling, day care, national health insurance, family income insurance, housing developments, and numerous other forces tend to promote the economic, psychosocial, and physical security of families. Questions of peace or war, the threat of contamination of vegetation due to nuclear fallout, fear of unemployment, the staggering cost of living, ageisms and sexisms, second-class citizenship due to racial, religious, or ethnic discriminations, and other phenomena of "advanced" civilization become as much child-development questions as the ones related to reading readiness, personal security, and proper social motivations.

In short, helping persons need to concern themselves as much with the social, psychological, ethnic, ideational, and physical context in which the child is to develop as with the child's own psychosocial functioning. To be specific, a boy or girl can only drink a glass of milk as body-building food and as a symbolic expression of mother's goodwill so long as his or her mother's *personal* faith is anchored in her own deep conviction that the milk is *good*, that it is uncontaminated, and that she can afford it again the next day.

Sears' finding that differences in child-rearing practices are less related to the socioeconomic status of the parents per se than to the parents' access to more recent knowledge, stresses the importance of making new understanding as accessible as possible to all groups and strata. Moreover, his findings that age differences and the age span of all the children in a family are correlated to the quality of mothering argue for the importance of homemaker services, family planning, the evaluation of adoptive or foster-home placements, and graded supplementary support in such programs as aid to dependent families.

Although this book deals with child development, Erikson's reminder that development continues throughout adulthood hints at the need for reform in social programs, services, and policies intended to affect adults. (Such reforms might hold particular import for the situations in which the older members of our society frequently find themselves.) Children need to grow up in an environment which fulfills the need of the adults around them; because, when parents cannot find satisfaction in life, they tend to take their frustrations out in all of their life experiences, including their relationships to their children. What society does to its elders it also does to its new generation. The latter also senses what the future has in store for them.

Finally, the three theories under study here make us conscious of both the continuum of development and the intermittent critical periods in its progress. They have made us aware that there are particularly untimely periods for separating children from familiar surroundings. Such periods may be noted (1) during the second half of the first year of life when children become cognizant of regularity in their own personal existence and recognize the dependability of those who care for them; (2) around the time when they begin to leave their own family nest and establish new contacts, thereby endangering their sense of security in their basic family relationships; and (3) when they reach adolescence and feel the need (and are urged) to relinquish more of their dependence upon their family in order to establish new social relationships. The potential separation crises of these periods should be heeded in arranging a foster home or institutional placement and in changing a child's daily existence from institutional to family living.

Phase I: Establishing Dependence upon Dependence

All three dimensions of development build upon the significance of maternal care in producing whatever society wants the infant eventually to be. In our society, food, clothing, and sheler seem to be virtually assured to everyone, regardless of his or her status. But food, clothing and shelter serve as powerful symbols in the act of giving and in the giver's relationship to the receiver. Therefore, in infancy and early childhood, as we learned, giving should be deliberately structured so as to engender dependence as a healthy first step in the long progression of child development.

Continuous care within the same home has a vital influence on a child who may eventually have to be institutionalized. If the child is to achieve a trusting sense of dependency, his or her early experiences should provide a reliable security. Dependable consistency in care at this age may assure a better adaptability if the child's later life should have to be varied. For this reason, the idea of an interdependence between mother and child reemphasizes the value of early adoption and of such arrangements as those provided by rooming-in hospitals, where parents stay with a child during the child's hospitalization.

To recapitulate, maximally beneficial conditions are those which assure mothers or other central caring persons time and resources to exercise their full capabilities in child care.

Phase II: Establishing Dependence upon Self-care

This second phase encompasses a young child's continuing need for individual nurturing care. Unavoidable separation such as that caused by hospitalization of a child or parent necessitates substitute nurturing for the child; in the case of a child's hospitalization, a nurse or other hospital staff member is the person entrusted with the care of the child and the logical person to provide it. Most children who are separated from their parents within this phase are not ready for day care unless it can assure sustained individual attention throughout the period they are away from home. Separations, then, have to be considered in light of the capabilities for self-care which the individual child can master, as well as the amount of nurturing care he or she still requires when in a hospital, at a day-care or detention center, with a baby-sitter, and the like.

Much space in this book is devoted to the importance of play in child development, especially of spontaneous play. Budgeting and programming of children's services would do well to take this into account. A community must ask itself if the budgets of its hospitals, foster homes, and aid to dependent families guarantee sufficient funds and opportunities for children to grow and benefit through play. Play constitutes a child's most reliable device for self-help.

Phase III: Establishing
Dependence upon Primary Relationships

In this phase young children tend to relate to the caring adult of their own grouping. In regard to foster care, then, these questions arise: Do contemporary child-care services realize the importance of differentiating relationships between a child and a caring adult according to the ethnic heritage of the child, and do they provide the youngsters in their care with ample opportunities for adequate social relationships with persons of different backgrounds? Do such services offer the social status and the educational and financial resources to make possible the employment of men and women who can act as wholesome carriers of traditions to the children they are helping?

Modern emphasis upon the nurturing aspects of care, which assure the institutionalized child opportunities to associate with a readily available caring person, indicates that many services are trying to answer these questions positively. Two contemporary trends are underscored: (1) acceptance of the family mode of living as the most desirable form of living for all children regardless of their social or developmental complications; (2) recognizing that nurturing child care is as essential to solving a child's problems as the rehabilitative effort to solve the original complications which brought the child to the institution in the first place.

Economic, social, functional (blindness or deafness), and mere psychological maladjustments are no longer accepted as valid reasons for separation from family living or as justifications for institutional placement. However, if medical or psychopathological conditions cause family living to be interrupted for either medical or psychosocial treatment, the agency involved must provide a quality of child care since the need for nurturing is as basic as the needs for food, clothing, and shelter. Understanding the importance of such care may call for a reevaluation of the policies, services, and programs of our children's hospitals, convalescent homes, detention centers, and other institutions for children of preschool age who still need either family care or a workable substitute.

A small group should form the basic living unit for proper care. A young child's sense of belonging is clearly related to his group living with caring adults, immediate peers, and even any pets that are a part of the living unit, whether it is the family or an alternative arrangement.

Phase IV: Establishing Dependence upon Personal Competence and Secondary Relationships

When we review our programs, services, and policies for children in this phase, we discover reassuringly that our practices seem much better in tune with developmental demands than they are in other phases. We seem to find real evidence for Erikson's observations that society accepts children best when the children consider themselves children and wholeheartedly devote their energies to being children.

Significant adults and respected institutions serve as bearers of values to a child within this phase. Our own political, economic, and social attitudes and behavior continually affect the values being instilled in our children. It is important, therefore, that educational, recreational, religious, and social-welfare programs be geared to serve all three major dimensions of the development of the child within their trust. As Piaget so well substantiated, a child perceives and operates as a child, and much differently from an adult. This may reveal a periodic need for reevaluating such programs as Little League ventures, and other events which are primarily patterned after adult prototypes.

Currently, one frequently hears the concern expressed that the next generation, the children of today, should demonstrate more evidence of their pride in our American heritage. Our contemporary knowledge suggests that a child's capacity to identify with his elders and their joint heritage is directly related to the quality of his or her personal relationship with them. The more realistic one generation's social and national identification is, the more it will be assured and reflected in the next.

Phase V: Establishing Dependence upon
Primary Relationships within a Secondary World

Although there is only a limited lag between knowledge and practice in child development, a different and theoretically predictable situation exists in adolescent development. The adolescent's pattern of psychosocial dependence need not parallel that of his or her maturational development. Also, the span of adolescence carries a distinct and separate developmental status which fits neither the mores of childhood nor those of young adulthood and for which proper structural provisions have never been made in the institutions that deal with it. Adolescence chiefly remains a period of developmental no-man's-land. The adolescent is viewed neither as child nor adult, and, therefore, he or she is intermittently treated as either, neither, or both. *(184)*

We would like to propose that adolescence be regarded as a separate state with special needs. Perhaps it could be considered first and foremost as a time for exploration. Each adolescent needs to explore with his or her teachers their related ideas, and with his or her parents their joint needs for belonging to one another. The youth may require an indeterminate amount of time for vocational planning, for choosing companionship, or for accepting one out of many philosophies of life; and it may be necessary for guiding adults to grant it to him or her as well as to encourage his or her participation in a special program particularly suited to his or her individual needs. The Peace Corps or Vista, for instance, with its combination of adult sponsorship and well-defined spheres of action and opportunities for creative investment for the youth might serve as such a means for certain adolescents' continued development.

A custom accepted by some communities in which curfew regulations are worked out by adolescents for themselves is another example of a policy or program which can have a desirable influence upon individuals in this phase. It seems that there is a need to encourage social institutions which will permit adolescents, in this exploratory time, to work out ideas and to investigate interpersonal relationships, while furthering their own preparation for adulthood and having an ongoing investment in their society. Above all, the adolescent, youth, or young adult, wants to know when the process of being an adolescent or nonadult stops, at least as far as the society is concerned. *(126, 109)*

There is no justification discernible in Erikson's, Sears', or Piaget's work for the current tendency to regard parents as culprits who are seen as the cause of their children's failures or delinquent exploits. As far as the three dimensions are concerned, delinquency, like all other social phenomena, cannot be explained away by or analyzed in terms of any *one* factor. Delinquency must be understood in all its ramifications—psychological and social, individual, and institutional.

In working with adolescents, each youth has to be dealt with as an individual rather than as a representative of an age, sex, ethnic, or cultural group, or as a person typed by any one aspect of his or her behavior. Whether a child, adolescent, or youth, each is *an individual person within a social situation*.

SUMMARY

The foregoing material stresses that, in spite of vast gaps in our contemporary knowledge of human development and behavior, we know far more than we apply. A systematic understanding of child development could free all of us who live and work with children to further our knowledge and creativity.

In examining the implications for practice of the three dimensions of child development for each of the four helping systems, we have reviewed the developmental phases within their approximate age spans. Although we have repeatedly stressed that a child's chronological age should not serve as an exacting criterion for evaluating his or her behavior, we have, nonetheless, for convenience kept our discussion within the limits of an ordinary chronology. It is important for the helper—whoever he or she may be, whatever his or her particular role, and whatever the specific field—to remember that individual development is never fully completed, never regular, normal, or on schedule at any one point in an individual's life. Few children will develop cognitively in *all* aspects of knowing; few children will successfully resolve *all* affective conflicts at the respective modal phases; and few will achieve full satisfaction or tension reduction from *every* goal-directed response in behavioral learning. As indicated earlier, helpers may find themselves dealing with a schoolage child whose major difficulty stems from earlier developmental issues or whose behavioral patterns resemble more closely one typical of an earlier phase.

Thus, a helping person must not only recognize the developmental goals and tasks typical of the phase the child should be undergoing, but he or she must also recognize the dominant developmental patterns—emotional, cognitive, and behavioral. It is possible that the themes of several developmental phases are manifested in the child at a given point as we examine different aspects of his or her functioning. Therapeutic intervention, then, must take into account the typical phase for the child's age range, on the one hand, and the other, the aspects of other developmental phases that are actually operating in the evolvement of the particular child's personality.

A clearer understanding of a child's actual level of functioning and the meaning of his or her life experiences can guide the helping person in assuring the client, so that the client will gain more salutary experiences and a belief in his or her own competence while the common but disquieting fear of not being adequate is dispelled. Furthermore, in all of child development, and in all facets of the professional helping efforts, it is the *nature* of the interpersonal relationship which is paramount. Every interpersonal relationship holds the beginning of a personal promise of mutual significance. But again, each such personal promise depends upon an overall social atmosphere in which there can be potential trust and hope. The burning questions of our day, the problematic issues of international and intergroup relationships, seem to be directly correlated to the degree of personal satisfaction and meaningfulness individuals can find for themselves. This quality of integrated satisfaction would not only promise but assure a change towards the better.

Since all child development and child-rearing practices are anchored in a trust in human beings, we need to aim at achieving in the human community at large the very trust we try to foster in the interpersonal relationships of our children.

Above all, our knowledge, skills and convictions must assure our children and youth that they are a part of their own future and that their future is a part of their society's developmental past and also, particularly, of its present. Child development, we learned, is human development, child, and caring adult all in one. "For," to quote Erik H. Erikson one more time, "only people with equal dignity can love each other." (126, 79).

Bibliography
of text
references

1. Adams, P., L. Berg, N. Berger, et al., *Children's rights*, New York, Praeger, 1972.
2. Aebli, H., *The development of intelligence in the child*, University of Minnesota Press, 1950.
3. Allman, P. D., A validation study of a Piagetian type diagnosis of community college students' cognitive functioning abilities, *Dissertation Abstracts International*, April 1973, *33:* 5463.
4. Almy, M., Reviews of three Piaget publications, *American Journal of Orthopsychiatry*, January 1976, *46* (1): 174–177.
5. Almy, M., E. Chittenden, and P. Miller, *Young children's thinking*, New York, Teachers College Press, 1967.
6. Anderson, R. E., and I. E. Carter, *Human behavior in the social environment*, Chicago, Aldine, 1974.
7. Anthony, E. J., The significance of Jean Piaget for child psychiatry, *British Journal of Medical Psychology*, 1956, *29:* 20–34.
8. Ayers, J. D., and M. Haugen, Measurement or training: an examination of method in conservation studies, *Canadian Journal of Behavioral Science*, January 1973, *5* (1): 67–76.
9. Bakker, C., and M. K. Bakker-Rabdau, *No trespassing*, San Francisco, Chandler and Sharp, 1973.
10. Bandura, A., *Principles of behavior modification*, New York, Holt, Rinehart and Winston, 1969.
11. Bandura, A., and R. H. Walters, *Social learning and personality development*, New York, Holt, Rinehart and Winston, 1963.
12. Bee, H., *Social issues in developmental psychology*, New York, Harper & Row, 1974.
13. Beilin, H., The development of physical concepts, in T. Mischel, (ed.), *Cognitive development and epistemology*, New York, Academic Press, 1971, pp. 86–119.
14. Beilin, H., Developmental stages and developmental processes, in D. R. Green, M. P. Ford, and C. B. Flamer (eds.), *Measurement and Piaget*, New York, McGraw-Hill, 1971, pp. 172–197.

15. Berelson, B., and G. A. Steiner, *Human behavior—an inventory of scientific findings*, New York, Harcourt Brace Jovanovich, 1964.

16. Bergin, A. E., and S. L. Garfield (eds.), *Handbook of psychotherapy and behavior control*, New York, Wiley, 1971.

17. Berne, E., *Principles of group treatment*, New York, Oxford University Press, 1966.

18. Bettelheim, B., *The informed heart: autonomy in a mass age*, New York, Macmillan, 1960.

19. Bettelheim, B., The problem of generation, *Daedalus*, 1962, *91* (1): 68–96.

20. Bijou, S., and D. M. Baer, *Child development: a systematic and empirical theory*, Vol. I, Englewood Cliffs, N.J., Prentice-Hall (Appleton), 1961.

21. Bijou, S., and D. M. Baer, *Child development: universal stages of infancy*, Vol. 2, New York, Wiley, 1965.

22. Bloom, S., *The paradox of helping*, New York, Wiley, 1975.

23a. Boehm, W. W., *The social casework method in social work education*, Vol X, New York, Council on Social Work Education, 1959.

23b. Boehm, W. W., Social work: science and art, *Social Service Review*, 1961, *35* (2): 144–153.

24. Bramer, L. M., *The helping relationship*, Englewood Cliffs, N.J., Prentice-Hall, 1973.

25. Brearly, M., and E. Hitchfield, *A guide to reading Piaget*, New York, Schocken Books, 1967.

26. Breger, L. (ed.), *Clinical-cognitive psychology: models and integrations*, Englewood Cliffs, N.J., Prentice-Hall, 1969.

27. Breger, L., *From instinct to identity: the development of personality*, Englewood Cliffs, N.J., Prentice-Hall, 1974.

28. Bregman, L., Growing older together: temporality, mutuality, and performance in the thought of Alfred Schutz and Erik Erikson, *Journal of Religion*, April 1973, *53*: 195–215.

29. Briar, S., The family as an organization: an approach to family diagnosis and treatment, *Social Service Review*, 1964, *38* (3): 247–255.

30. Bronfenbrenner, U., Freudian theories of identification and their derivatives, *Child Development*, 1960, *31* (1): 15–40.

31. Brown, R., *A first language: the early stages*, Cambridge, Mass., Harvard University Press, 1974.

32. Bruner, J. S., *Beyond the information given*, New York, Norton, 1973.

33. Bryant, P., *Perception and understanding in young children: an experimental approach*, New York, Basic Books, 1974.

34. Burden, D., F. Jones, B. Rees, et al., *Applicability of Erikson's theory of growth and development to Black Americans*, unpublished manuscript, University of Washington, 1975.

35. Bush, D. G., The moral judgement of children at two Piagetian cognitive stages: preoperational thought and concrete operational thought, *Dissertation Abstract International*, March 1973, *33* (9-B): 4483.

36. Carbonara, N., *Techniques for observing normal child behavior*, Western Psychiatric Institute and Clinic, University of Pittsburgh, 1961.

37. Carey, S., and N. Block, Should philosophy and psychology remarry? *Contemporary Psychology*, 1973, *18* (12): 597–600.

38. Case, R., Learning and development: a neo-Piagetian interpretation, *Human Development*, 1972, *15* (6): 339–358.

39. Case, R., Piaget's theory of child development and its implications, *Phi Delta Kappa*, September 1973, *55*: 20–25.

40. Cassel, R. N., Critical contributions of Piaget to developmental psychology, *Psychology*, February 1973, *10* (1): 42–45.
41. Chambers, J., Maternal deprivation and the concept of time in children, *American Journal of Orthopsychiatry*, 1961, *31* (2): 406–419.
42. Chinn, P. C. (ed.), *Mental retardation: a life cycle approach*, St. Louis, Mosby, 1975.
43. Coelho, G. V., D. A. Hamburg, and J. E. Adams (eds.), *Coping and adaptation*, New York, Basic Books, 1974.
44. Coles, R., Cautious hope—dimension of a new identity (essay review of the book by E. H. Erikson), *New Republic*, June 8, 1974, pp. 22–23.
45. Coles, R., *E. H. Erikson: the growth of his work*, Boston, Little, Brown, 1970.
46. Coles, R., The measure of man I and II, *New Yorker*, November 7, 1970, pp. 51–131, November 14, 1970, pp. 59–140.
47. Corman, H., and S. K. Escalona, Stages of sensorimotor development: a replication study, *Merrill-Palmer Quarterly*, October 1969, *15* (4): 351–361.
48. Crews, F., American prophet, *New York Review of Books*, October 16, 1975, pp. 9–15.
49. CTB/McGraw-Hill Conference, *Measurement and Piaget*, New York, McGraw-Hill, 1971.
50. Décarie, T. G., *Intelligence and affectivity in early childhood: an experimental study of Jean Piaget's object concept and object relations*, New York, International Universities Press, 1965.
51. Dempsey, A. D., Time conservation across cultures, *International Journal of Psychology*, 1971, *6* (2): 115–120.
52. Dollard, J., et al., *Frustration and aggression*, New Haven, Yale University Press, 1941.
53. Droz, R., and M. Rahmy, *Understanding Piaget*, New York, International Universities Press, 1976.
54. Dubos, R. J., *The mirage of health*, Garden City, N.Y., Doubleday (Anchor Books), 1961.
55. Duckworth, E., The having of wonderful ideas, *Harvard Educational Review*, 1972, *42* (2): 217–231.
56. Elkind, D., *Children and adolescents (interpretive essays on Jean Piaget)*, New York, Oxford University Press, 1970.
57. Elkind, D., Children's discovery of the conservation of mass, weight and volume: Piaget republication study II, in I. F. Sigel and F. H. Hooper (eds.), *Logical thinking in children*, New York, Holt, Rinehart and Winston, 1968, pp. 11–19.
58. Elkind, D., Erik Erikson's eight ages of man, *New York Times Magazine*, April 5, 1970, pp. 25–27, 84–92, 110–118.
59. Elkind, D., Jean Piaget: measuring young minds, in R. I. Evans, *Jean Piaget: the man and his ideas*, New York, Dutton, 1973, pp. xxi–xli.
60. Elkind, D., Two approaches to intelligence: Piagetian and psychometric, in D. R. Green, M. P. Ford, and C. B. Flamer (eds.), *Measurement and Piaget*, New York, McGraw-Hill, 1971, pp. 12–33.
61. Elkind, D., and J. H. Flavell (eds.), *Studies in cognitive development: essays in honor of Jean Piaget*, New York, Oxford University Press, 1971.
62. Emling, J. F., In the beginning was the response, *Religious Education*, January 1974, *69*: 53–71.
63. Erikson, E. H., Autobiographic notes on identity crisis, *Daedalus*, Fall 1970, *99* (4): 730–759.

64. Erikson, E. H., The California loyalty oath: an editorial, *Psychiatry*, 1951, *14* (3): 244–245.
65. Erikson, E. H., *Childhood and society*, 2nd rev. ed., New York, Norton, 1963.
66. Erikson, E. H., Childhood and tradition in two American Indian tribes, in O. Fenichel et al. (eds.), *The psychoanalytic study of the child*, Vol. *I*, New York, International Universities Press, 1945, pp. 319–350.

67. Erikson, E. H., Clinical observations of play disruption in young children, in M. R. Haworth (ed.), *Child psychotherapy*, New York, Basic Books, 1964, pp. 264–276.
68. Erikson, E. H., Clinical studies in childhood play, in R. C. Barker et al., *Child behavior and development*, New York, McGraw-Hill, 1943, pp. 411–428.
69. Erikson, E. H., *Comments on permissiveness*, paper read at a staff training session, Department of Child Psychiatry and Child Development, University of Pittsburgh, 1955.
70. Erikson, E. H., The concept of identity in race relations: notes and queries, *Daedalus*, 1966, *95* (1): 145–171.
71. Erikson, E. H., Concluding remarks, in J. A. Mattfeld and C. G. Van Aken (eds.), *Women and the scientific professions*, Cambridge, Mass., MIT Press, 1965, pp. 232–245.
72. Erikson, E. H., Configurations in play: clinical notes, *Psychoanalytic Quarterly*, 1937, *6*: 139–214.
73. Erikson, E. H., *Dimensions of a new identity*, New York, Norton, 1974.
74. Erikson, E. H., in J. M. Tanner and B. Inhelder (eds.), *Discussions on child development*, Vol. *III*, New York, International Universities Press, 1958, pp. 16–18, 38–52, 70–90, 91–168, 189–215.
75. Erikson, E. H. in J. M. Tanner and B. Inhelder (eds.), *Discussions on child development*, Vol. *IV*, New York, International Universities Press, 1960, pp. 136–154, 165–175.
76. Erikson, E. H., The dream specimen of psychoanalysis, *Journal of the American Psychoanalitic Association*, 1954, 2 (1): 5–56.
77. Erikson, E. H., Ego development and historical change, in P. Greenacre et al. (eds.), *The psychoanalytic study of the child*, Vol. *II*, New York, International Universities Press, 1946, pp. 359–396.
78. Erikson, E. H., Ego identity and psychosocial moratorium, in H. Witmer and R. Kotinsky, *New perspective for research*, Washington, D.C., U.S. Department of Health, Education, and Welfare, 1956, pp. 1–23.
79. Erikson, E. H., Eight ages of man, in S. I. Harrison and F. McDermott, *Childhood psychopathology*, New York, International Universities Press, 1972, (chap. 8), pp. 109–132.
80a. Erikson, E. H., Erikson speaks out, *Newsweek*, December 21, 1971, 85–89.
80b. Erikson, E. H., The first psychoanalyst, *Yale Review*, Autumn 1956, 40–62.
81. Erikson, E. H., Ghandi's autobiography: The leader as a child, *American Scholar*, 1966, *35* (4): 632–646.
82. Erikson, E. H., *Ghandi's truth: on the origin of militant nonviolence*, New York, Norton, 1969.
83a. Erikson, E. H., in B. Schaffner (ed.), *Group processes: transactions of the first conference*, New York, Josiah Macy, Jr., Foundation, 1954, pp. 60–63.

83b. Erikson, E. H., in B. Schaffner (ed.), *Group processes: transactions of the second conference*, New York, Josiah Macy, Jr., Foundation, 1956.

84. Erikson, E. H., in B. Schaffner (ed.), *Group processes: transactions of the fourth conference*, New York, Josiah Macy, Jr., Foundation, 1959, pp. 100–101, 159–160.

85. Erikson, E. H., Identity and the life cycle: selected papers, *Psychological Issues* (monograph), Vol. 1, No. 1, New York, International Universities Press, 1959.

86. Erikson, E. H., Identity, psychosocial and the human life cycle, *International encyclopedia of the social sciences*, New York, Crowell, 1968, Vol. 7, pp. 61–65, and Vol. 9, pp. 286–292.

87. Erikson, E. H., *Identity: youth and crisis*, New York, Norton, 1968.

88. Erikson, E. H., The initial situation and its alternatives, in M. R. Haworth (ed.), *Child psychotherapy*, New York, Basic Books, 1964, pp. 106–110.

89a. Erikson, E. H., Inner and outer space: Reflections on womanhood, *Daedalus*, Vol. 93 (2), Spring 1964, 582–606. Also in R. J. Lifton, (ed.), *The woman in America*, Boston, Houghton Mifflin, 1965, pp. 1–26.

89b. Erikson, E. H., *Insight and responsibility*, New York, W. W. Norton, 1964.

90. Erikson, E. H., Introduction, in: G. B. Blaine and C. McArthur (eds.), *Emotional problems of the student*, New York, Appleton-Century-Crofts, 1961, pp. xii–xxv.

91. Erikson, E. H., *Juvenile delinquency*, (paper read at a staff training session), Department of Child Psychiatry and Child Development, University of Pittsburgh, 1954.

92. Erikson, E. H., *Life history and historical moment*, New York, W. W. Norton, 1975.

93. Erikson, E. H., Memorandum for the conference on the draft, in: Tax, Sol (ed.), *The draft: A handbook of facts and alternatives*, Chicago, The University of Chicago Press, 1967, pp. 280–283.

94. Erikson, E. H., Memorandum on identity and Negro youth, *Journal of Social Issues*, 1964, 20 (4): 29–42.

95. Erikson, E. H., Memorandum on youth, *Daedalus*, 1967, 96 (3): 860–870.

96. Erikson, E. H., Observations on Sioux education, *Journal of Psychology*, 1939, 7: 101–156.

97. Erikson, E. H., Observations on the Yurok: Childhood and world image, *American Archaeological Ethnology*, 1943, 35 (10): 257–301.

98. Erikson, E. H., On the nature of psycho-historical evidence: In search of Ghandi, *Daedalus*, 1968, 97 (3): 695–730.

99. Erikson, E. H., On the sense of inner identity, in: *Conference on health and human relations*, New York, McGraw-Hill, 1953, pp. 124–146.

100. Erikson, E. H., Once more the inner space, in: Strouse, J. (ed.), *Women and analysis*, New York, Grossman Publishers, 1974, pp. 320–340.

101. Erikson, E. H., Ontogeny of ritualization, in: R. M. Lowenstein et al. (eds.), *Psychoanalysis—a general psychology (essays in honor of Heinz Hartman)*, New York, International Universities Press, 1966, pp. 601–622.

102. Erikson, E. H., The origin of psychoanalysis, *International Journal of Psychoanalysis*, 1955, 36 (1): 1–15.

103. Erikson, E. H., Play and actuality, in: M. W. Piers (ed.), *Play and development*, New York, W. W. Norton, 1972, pp. 127–167.

104. Erikson, E. H., The problem of ego identity, *Journal of American Psychoanalytic Association*, 1956, 4 (1): 56–121.
105. Erikson, E. H., Problems of infancy and early childhood, in: P. G. Davis (ed.), *The Encyclopedia of Medicine*, Philadelphia, F. A. Davis, 1940, pp. 714–730.
106. Erikson, E. H., Psychoanalysis and the future of education, *Psychoanalytic Quarterly*, 1936, 4: 50–66.
107. Erikson, E. H., Psychoanalysis and ongoing history: problems of identity, hatred, and non-violence, *American Journal Psychiatry*, 1965, 122: 241–250.
108. Erikson, E. H., Reflections on the dissent of contemporary youth, *International Journal of Psychoanalysis*, 1970, 51 (1): 11–22. Also in: *Daedalus*, Winter 1970, 99 (1): 154–176.
109a. Erikson, E. H., Reflections on Dr. Borg's life cycle, *Daedalus*, Spring 1976, 105 (2): 1–28.
109b. Erikson, E. H., Remarks, in: *Healthy personality development in children as related programs of the government*, New York, Josiah Macy Jr. Foundation, 1952, pp. 80–95.
110. Erikson, E. H., Review: psychoanalysis for teachers and parents, *Psychoanalytic Quarterly*, 1936, 5: 291–293.
111. Erikson, E. H., The roots of virtue, in: J. Huxley (ed.), *The humanist frame*, New York, Harper & Row, 1961, pp. 145–166.
112. Erikson, E. H., Sex differences in the play configurations of pre-adolescents, *American Journal Orthopsychiatry*, 1951, 21 (4): 667–692. Also in R. E. Herron and Brian Sutton-Smith, *Child's play*, New York, John Wiley, 1971, pp. 126–144. Also in S. J. Beck and H. B. Molish, *Reflexes to intelligence*, Glencoe, Ill., Free Press, 1959, pp. 290–299.
113. Erikson, E. H., Studies in the interpretation of play . . . part 1: clinical observations of play disruption in young children, *Genetic Psychological Monograph*, 1940, 22: 557–671.
114. Erikson, E. H., in: M. J. E. Senn (ed.), *Symposium on the healthy personality*, New York, Josiah Macy, Jr. Foundation, 1950.
115a. Erikson, E. H., *Toys and reasons*, New York, Norton, 1977.
115b. Erikson, E. H., Toys and reasons, in: Clara Thompson, *An outline of psychoanalysis*, New York, Random House, 1955, pp. 227–247. Also in: Mary R. Haworth (ed.), *Child psychotherapy*, New York, Basic Books, 1964, pp. 3-10.
116. Erikson, E. H., Traumatische Konfigurationen im Spiel, *Imago*, 1937, 23: 447–516.
117. Erikson, E. H., Wholeness and totality: A psychiatric contribution, in: C. J. Friedrich (ed.), *Totalitarianism*, Cambridge, Mass., Harvard University Press, 1954, pp. 156–171.
118. Erikson, E. H., The wider identity, in: Erikson, K. (ed.), *In search of common ground: conversations with Erik H. Erikson and Huey P. Newton*, New York, Norton, 1973, pp. 44–70.
119. Erikson, E. H., Womanhood and the inner space, in: Strouse, J. (ed.), *Women and analysis*, New York, Grossman Publishers, 1974, pp. 291–319 and 320–334.
120. Erikson, E. H., *Young man Luther: a study in psychoanalysis and history*, New York, Norton, 1958.
121. Erikson, E. H., Youth and the life cycle: an interview, *Children*, 1960, 7 (2), 43–49.
122. Erikson, E. H., Youth: Fidelity and diversity, *Daedalus*, 1962, 91 (1): 5–27.

123. Erikson, E. H., and J. Erikson, The power of the newborn, *Mademoiselle,* June, 1953, *62:* 100–102.
124. Erikson, E. H., and K. T. Erikson, The confirmation of the delinquent, *Best articles and stories,* 1958, 2 (7): 43–46.
125. Erikson, F. H., *Play interviews of four-year-old hospitalized children,* Purdue, Ind., Monograph Society for Research in Child Development, 1958.
126. Erikson, K. T., *In search of common ground: conversations with Erik H. Erikson and Huey P. Newton,* New York, Norton, 1973.
127. Esman, A., A man for all reasons, (an essay book review), *Psychiatry and Social Science Review,* March 1971, 5 (3): 25–26.
128. Evans, R. I., *Dialogue with Erikson,* New York, Harper & Row, 1967.
129. Evans, R. I., Dialogue with Erik Erikson, (a book summary), *Psychiatry and Social Science Review,* April 1967, 1 (4): 9–13.
130. Evans, R. I., *Jean Piaget: the man and his ideas,* New York, Dutton, 1973.
131. Feigl, H., Principles and problems of theory construction in psychology, in W. Dennis (ed.), *Current trends of psychological theory,* University of Pittsburgh Press, 1951, pp. 179–213.
132. Feldman, C. F., et al., *The development of adaptive intelligence,* San Francisco, Jossey-Bass, 1974.
133. Flanagan, J., The critical incident technique, *Psychological Bulletin,* 1954, *51* (4): 327–358.
134. Flavell, J. H., Comments on Beilin's "The development of physical concepts," in T. Mischel (ed.), *Cognitive Development and Epistemology,* New York, Academic Press, 1971, pp. 121–128.
135. Flavell, J. H., *The developmental psychology of Jean Piaget,* New York, Van Nostrand, 1963.
136. Freud, S., *The ego and the id.,* London, Hogarth, 1950.
137. Freud, S., *The problem of anxiety,* New York, Norton, 1936.
138. Furth, H. G., *Piaget and knowledge,* Englewood Cliffs, N.J., Prentice-Hall, 1969.
139. Furth, H. G., Piaget, IQ, and the nature-nurture controversy, *Human Development,* 1973, *16* (1): 61–73.
140. Gaudia, G., Race, social class, and age achievement of conservation on Piaget's task in H. Bee (ed.), *Social issues in developmental psychology,* New York, Harper & Row, 1974, pp. 272–283.
141. Ginsburg, H., *The myth of the deprived child,* Englewood Cliffs, N.J., Prentice-Hall, 1972.
142. Ginsburg, H., and S. Opper, *Piaget's theory of intellectual development,* Englewood Cliffs, N.J., Prentice-Hall, 1969.
143. Gitelson, M., and E. H. Erikson, Play therapy, *American Journal of Orthopsychiatry,* 1937, 8 (3): 499–524.
144. Goldstein, J., A. Freud, and A. J. Solnit, *Beyond the best interest of the child,* New York, Free Press, 1973.
145. Gorman, J. F., Some characteristics of consultation, in L. Rapoport (ed.), *Consultation in social work practice,* New York, National Association of Social Workers, 1963, pp. 21–32.
146. Gorman, R. M., *Discovering Piaget: a guide for teachers,* Columbus, Ohio, Merrill, 1972.
147. Haley, J., *Strategies of psychotherapy,* New York, Grune & Stratton, 1963.
148. Hall, C., and G. Lindzey, *Theories of personality,* 2nd ed., New York, Wiley, 1970.

149. Hall, E., A conversation with Jean Piaget, *Psychology Today*, 1970, *3* (12): 25–32, 54–56.

150. Halleck, S. L., The impact of professional dishonesty on behavior of disturbed adolescents, *Social Work*, 1965, *8* (2): 48–56.

151. Hamlyn, D. W., Epistemology and conceptual development, in T. Mischel (ed.), *Cognitive development and epistemology*, New York, Academic Press, 1971, pp. 3–24.

152. Harris, D. B. (ed.), *The concept of development*, University of Minnesota Press, 1957.

153. Hartmann, H., *Ego psychology and the problem of adaptation*, New York, International Universities Press, 1958.

154. Havighurst, R. J., *Human development and education*, New York, Longmans, 1953.

155. Hebb, D. O., *The organization of behavior*, New York, Wiley, 1949.

156. Henry, J., Book review of E. H. Erikson, Childhood and society, 2nd ed., *American Journal of Orthopsychiatry*, 1965, *35* (3): 616–620.

157. Hess, J. L., Piaget sees science dooming psychoanalysis, *New York Times*, October 19, 1972, pp. 45–46.

158. Honzik, M. P., Sex differences in the occurrence of material in the play constructions of pre-adolescents, *Child Development*, March 1951, *22* (1): 15–35.

159. Howe, I., A great man's greatness, book review of E. H. Erikson, Gandhi's truth, *Harper's* April 1970, *240* (1439): 100–105.

160. Inhelder, B., Development theory and diagnostic procedures, in D. R. Green, M. P. Ford, and C. B. Flamer (eds.), *Measurement and Piaget*, New York, McGraw-Hill, 1971, pp. 148–171.

161. Inhelder, B., Memory and intelligence in the child, in D. Elkind and J. H. Flavell (eds.), *Studies in cognitive development*, New York, Oxford University Press, 1969.

162. Inhelder, B., and J. Piaget, Closing remarks, in CTB/McGraw-Hill Conference, *Measurement and Piaget*, New York, McGraw-Hill, 1969, pp. 210–213.

163. Inhelder, B., H. Sinclair, and M. Bovet; *Learning and the development of cognition*, Cambridge, Mass., Harvard University Press, 1974.

164. Kaplan, D. M., Since Freud, *Harper's Magazine*, August 1968, *237*: 55–60.

165. Keniston, K., *Do Americans really like children?* unpublished paper presented at 1975 Annual Meeting of Orthopsychiatry, New York, Carnegie Council on Children, 1975.

166. Kessen, W., Early cognitive development: hot or cold, in T. Mischel (ed.), *Cognitive development and epistemology*, New York, Academic Press, 1971, pp. 288–304.

167. Kessen, W., Intellectual development in children: a conference on Piaget's contributions in relation to other theories of children's thinking, *Items*, Social Science Research Council, 1960, *14* (3): 25–30.

168. Kluckhohn, C., and H. A. Murray, *Personality in nature, society and culture*, New York, Knopf, 1956.

169. Kohlberg, L., From is to ought, in T. Mischel (ed.), *Cognitive development and epistemology*, New York, Academic Press, 1971, pp. 151–235.

170. Kohlberg, L., Stage and sequence: the cognitive development approach to socialization, in D. A. Goslin (ed.), *Handbook of socialization theory and research*, Skokie, Ill. Rand McNally, 1969, pp. 347–380.

171. Kuhn, T. S., *The structure of scientific revolutions*, University of Chicago Press, 1970.

172. Lawson, A. E., and J. W. Renner, *A quantitative analysis of responses to Piagetian tasks and its implications for curriculum*, unpublished paper, University of Oklahoma, 1974.

173. Levin, H., and R. R. Sears, Identification with parents as a determinant of doll play aggression, *Child Development*, 1956, 27 (2): 135–153.

174. Lickona, L., Piaget misunderstood: a critique of the criticisms of his theory of moral development, *Merrill-Palmer Quarterly of Behavioral Development*, 1969, 15 (4): 337–350.

175. Lippitt, R., et al., *The dynamics of planned change*, New York, Harcourt Brace Jovanovich, 1958.

176. Lohr, E., *Current biography*, New York, H. W. Wilson, 1952, pp. 522–523.

177. Lovell, K., The philosophy of Jean Piaget, *New Society*, August 11, 1966, 222–226.

178. Lubin, G. I., J. F. Magary, and M. K. Poulsen (eds.), *Piagetian theory and the helping professions*, University of Southern California Press, 1975.

179. Lynd, H. M., *On shame and the search for identity*, New York, Harcourt Brace Jovanovich, 1958.

180. Maas, H. S., The place of research in child welfare programs in Child Welfare League of America, *Six papers on child welfare problems*, New York, Child Welfare League, 1953, pp. 11–18.

181. Maccoby, E. E., Role-taking in childhood and its consequences for social learning, *Child Development*, 1959, 30 (2): 239–252.

182. Maccoby, E. E., The taking of adult roles in middle childhood, *Journal of Abnormal Social Psychology*, 1961, 61 (3): 493–503.

183a. Magary, J. R. et al. (eds.), *Proceedings: second annual university affiliated program conference: Piagetian theory and the helping professions*, Los Angeles, University Publishers, 1972.

183b. Magary, J. R. et al. (eds.), *Proceedings: seventh annual university affiliated program conference: Piagetian theory and the helping professions*, Los Angeles, University Publishers, 1978.

184. Maier, H. W., Adolescenthood, *Social Casework*, 1965, 46 (1): 3–9.

185. Maier, H. W., Application of psychological and sociological theory to teaching social work with groups, *Journal of Education for Social Work*, 1967, 3 (1): 22–31.

186. Maier, H. W., Child (and youth) care as a method of social work, in Child Welfare League of America, *Training of child-care staff*, New York, Child Welfare League, 1963, 62–81.

187. Maier, H. W., The child care worker, in John B. Turner (ed.), *Encyclopedia of Social Work—1977*, New York, National Association of Social Work, 1977, pp. 130–134.

188. Maier, H. W., A child's cognitive conquest of space and time, *Indian Journal Social Research*, 1961, 2 (2): 31–38. Also in: Piagetian conference planning and educational committee, *Proceedings: second annual UAP conference: Piagetian theory and the helping professions*, Los Angeles, University Publishers, 1972, 20–33.

189. Maier, H. W. (ed.), *Group work as part of residential treatment*, New York, National Association of Social Workers, 1965.

190. Maier, H. W., Human functioning as an interpersonal whole: the dimensions of affect, behavior and cognition, in *Teaching of competence*

in the delivery of direct services, New York, Council on Social Work Education, 1976, pp. 60–71.

191. Maier, H. W., Learning to learn and living to live in residential treatment, *Child Welfare*, 1975, *54* (6): 406–420.

192. Maier, H. W., A new perspective on the role of dependence and independence in human development, University of Washington, 1977 (Manuscript in Preparation for Publication).

193. Maier, H. W., A sidewards look and what comes into view, in *Social work in transition: issues, dilemmas, and choices*, School of Social Work, University of Washington, 1974, pp. 138–147.

194a. Maier, H. W., A sidewards look at change, *Social Service Review*, June 1971, *45* (2): 126–136.

194b. Maier, H. W., Sensori-motor phase knowledge applied to beginnings in professional helping, in: J. R. Magary, et al., (eds.), Precedings: *seventh annual university affiliated program conference: Piagetian theory and helping professions*, Los Angeles, University Publishers, 1978.

195. Mayer, M. F., The parental figures in residential treatment, *Social Service Review*, 1960, *34* (3): 273–285.

196. Mays, W., Jean Piaget: the man and his work, *Hibbert Journal*, 1957, *56:* 134–139.

197. Medinus, G. R., *An investigation of Piaget's concept of development of moral judgment in six to twelve-year-old children from the lower socio-economic group*, unpublished doctoral dissertation, University of Minnesota, 1957.

198. Millar, S., Piaget and play, *The psychology of play*, London, Penguin Books, 1968, pp. 164–168.

199. Miller, N. E., and J. Dollard, *Social learning and imitation*, New Haven, Yale University Press, 1941.

200. Miller, N. E., et al., Reformulation of the frustration and aggression theory, *Psychological Review*, 1941, *48:* 337–342.

201. Millett, N. E., Inner space, *Sexual politics*, New York, Doubleday, 1970, pp. 210–220.

202. Minuchin, S., *Families and family therapy*, Cambridge, Mass., Harvard University Press, 1975.

203. Mischel, T., Piaget: cognitive conflict and the motivation of thought, in T. Mischel (ed.), *Cognitive development and epistemology*, New York, Seadin's Press, 1971, pp. 311–355.

204. Modgil, S., *Piagetian research: a handbook of recent studies*, New York, Humanities Press, 1974.

205. Monane, J. H. *A sociology of human systems*, Englewood Cliffs, N.J., Prentice-Hall (Appleton), 1967.

206. Munn, N. L., *The evolution and growth of human behavior*, Boston, Houghton Mifflin, 1955.

207. Munroe, R. L., *Schools of psychoanalytic thought*, New York, Holt, Rinehart and Winston, 1955.

208. Murchison, D. (ed.), *The psychological register*, Vol. *III*, Worcester, Mass., Clark University Press, 1932.

209. Mussen, P., J. Conger, and J. Kagan, *Child development and personality*, 4th ed., New York, Harper & Row, 1974.

210. Nass, M., The superego and moral development in the theories of Freud and Piaget, in R. S. Eissler and associates (eds.), *The psychoanalytic study of the child*, Vol. *XXI*, New York, International Universities Press, 1966, pp. 51–68.

211. Newcomb, T., and C. Tavris, What does college do for a person?—Frankly very little (a conversation with Theodore Newcomb) *Psychology Today*, *8* (4), September 1974, 76–81.

212. *Newsweek* Special report, Erik Erikson: The quest for identity, *Newsweek*, December 21, 1970, 84–89.

213. Odier, C., *Anxiety and magic thinking*, New York, International Universities Press, 1956.

214. Overton, A., Establishing the relationship, *Crime and delinquency*, 1965, *11* (3): 224–238.

215. Parsloe, P., H. Goldstein et al., *A unitary approach to social work practice*, Scotland, University of Dundee Press, 1975.

216. Peller, L., *The psychoanalytic study of the child*, Vol. IX, New York, International Universities Press, 1954, pp. 178–198.

217. Phillips, R., Doll play as a function of the realism of the materials and length of the experimental session, *Child Development*, 1945, *16:* 123–145.

218. Piaget, J., An autobiography, in R. Evans (ed.), *Jean Piaget: the man and his ideas* (and Addendum), New York, Dutton, 1973, pp. 103–143.

219. Piaget, J., Autobiography of Jean Piaget, in E. G. Boring et al. (eds.), *A history of psychology*, Vol. *IV*, Worcester, Mass., Clark University Press, 1952, pp. 237–256.

220. Piaget, J., The biological problem of intelligence, in D. Rapoport (ed.), *Organization and pathology of thought*, New York, Columbia University Press, 1951, chap. 7, pp. 176–192.

221. Piaget, J., *Biology and knowledge: an essay on the relations between organic regulations and cognitive processes*, University of Chicago Press, 1971.

222. Piaget, J., The child and modern physics, *Scientific American*, 1957, *196* (3): 46–51.

223. Piaget, J., *The child and reality: problems of genetic psychology*, New York, Grossman, 1973.

224. Piaget, J., *The child's conception of movement and speed*, New York, Basic Books, 1970.

225. Piaget, J., *The child's conception of physical causality*, London, Routledge & Kegan Paul, 1930.

226. Piaget, J., *The child's conception of time*, New York, Basic Books, 1970.

227. Piaget, J., *The child's conception of the world*, London, Routledge & Kegan Paul, 1951.

228. Piaget, J., Children's philosophies, in C. Murchison, *A handbook of child psychology*, Worcester, Mass., Clark University Press, 1934, pp. 534–547.

229. Piaget, J., Closing remarks, in D. R. Green, M. P. Ford, and C. B. Flamer (eds.), *Measurement and Piaget*, New York, McGraw-Hill, 1971, pp. 210–213.

230. Piaget, J., Cognitive development in children: the Piaget papers, in R. E. Ripple and V. N. Rockcastle (eds.), *Piaget rediscovered: a report of the conference on cognitive studies and curriculum development*, Ithaca, New York, School of Education, Cornell University Press, 1964, pp. 6–48.

231. Piaget, J., *Comments on Vygotsky's critical remarks*, Cambridge, Mass., MIT Press, 1962, Appendix.

232. Piaget, J., *The construction of reality and the child*, New York, Basic Books, 1954.

233. Piaget, J., The development in children of the idea of the homeland

and of relations to other countries, *International Social Science Journal,* 1951, 3 (3): 561–578. Also in Ihsan Al-Issa and W. Dennis (eds.), *Cross cultural studies of behavior,* New York, Holt, Rinehart and Winston, 1970, pp. 286–307.

234. Piaget, J., Development and learning, *Journal of Research Teaching,* 1964, 2 (3): 176–186.

235. Piaget, J., in J. Tanner and B. Inhelder (eds.), *Discussions on child development,* Vol. *I* (1953), London, Tavistock, 1956, pp. 31–33, 69–72, 89–94, 104–105.

236. Piaget, J., in J. Tanner and B. Inhelder (eds.), *Discussions on child development,* Vol. *II,* London, Tavistock, 1956, pp. 58–62, 256–263.

237. Piaget, J., in J. Tanner and B. Inhelder (eds.), *Discussions on child development,* Vol. *III,* New York, International Universities Press, 1958, pp. 114, 154–162.

238. Piaget, J., *Essay on operative logic,* Paris, Dunod, 1972.

239. Piaget, J., *Études d'épistémologie génétique,* Paris Presses Universitaires de France, 1968.

240. Piaget, J., Explanation in psychology and psycho-physiological parallelism, in P. Fraisse and J. Piaget (eds.), *Experimental psychology: its scope and method,* Vol. *1,* New York, Basic Books, 1968, pp. 53–191.

241. Piaget, J., Foreword, in Thérèse G. Decarie, *Intelligence and affectivity in early childhood,* New York, International Universities Press, 1965, pp. xi–xv.

242. Piaget, J., Foreword, in Millie Almy, *Young children's thinking,* New York, Teachers College Press, 1967, pp. iii–vii.

243. Piaget, J., Foreword, in M. Schwebel and J. Ralph, *Piaget in the classroom,* New York, Basic Books, 1973, pp. ix–x.

244. Piaget, J., Foreword, in B. Inhelder, H. Sinclair, and M. Bovet, *Learning and the development of cognition,* Cambridge, Mass., Harvard University Press, 1974, pp. ix–xiv.

245. Piaget, J., Foreword, in E. J. Anthony, *Explorations in child psychiatry,* New York, Plenum, 1975, pp. vii–ix.

246. Piaget, J., The general problems of the psychobiological development of the child, in J. Tanner and B. Inhelder (eds.), *Discussions on child development,* Vol. *IV,* (1956), New York, International Universities Press, 1960, pp. 3–34, 35–83, 87–135, 171–175.

247. Piaget, J., The genetic approach to psychology of thought, *Journal of Educational Psychology,* 1961, 52 (6): 275–281.

248a. and b. Piaget, J., Genetic epistemology, (a) *The Columbia Forum,* Fall 1969, 12 (3): 1–71. Also in (b) R. I. Evans, *Jean Piaget: the man and his ideas,* New York, Dutton, 1973, pp. xlii–lxi.

249. Piaget, J., *Genetic epistemology,* New York, Columbia University Press, 1970.

250. Piaget, J., *The grasp of consciousness,* Cambridge, Mass., Harvard University Press, 1976.

251. Piaget, J., How children form mathematical concepts, *Scientific American,* 1953, 189 (5): 74–79.

252. Piaget, J., *Insights and illusions of philosophy,* New York, World Publishing Co., 1971.

253. Piaget, J., The intellectual development of the adolescent, in G. Caplan and S. Lebovici (eds.), *Adolescence: psychosocial perspectives,* New York, Basic Books, 1969, pp. 22–26.

254. Piaget, J., Intellectual evolution from adolescence to adulthood, *Human Development,* 1972, 15: 1–12.

255. Piaget, J., Introduction, in M. Laurendeau and A. Pinard, *The development of the concept of space in the child*, New York, Basic Books, 1969.

256. Piaget, J., *The judgment and reason in the child*, New York, Harcourt Brace Jovanovich, 1928.

257. Piaget, J., *The language and thought of the child*, New York, Harcourt Brace Jovanovich, 1926.

258. Piaget, J., *Logic and psychology*, New York, Basic Books, 1957.

259. Piaget, J., *Main trends in interdisciplinary research*, New York, Harper & Row, 1973.

260. Piaget, J., *The mechanisms of perception*, New York, Basic Books, 1969.

261. Piaget, J., *The moral judgment of the child*, New York, Macmillan, 1955.

262. Piaget, J., On correspondences and morphisms, in *Newsletter of the Jean Piaget Society*, April 1976, 5 (3): 6–8.

263. Piaget, J., *On the development of memory and identity*, Worcester, Mass., Clark University Press, 1968.

264. Piaget, J., Operational structures of the intelligence and organic controls, in A. Kraczmar and J. C. Eccles (eds.), *Brain and human behavior*, New York, Springer-Verlag, 1972, pp. 393–398.

265. Piaget, J., *The origin of the intelligence in children*, New York, International Universities Press, 1952.

266. Piaget, J., Piaget's theory, in P. Mussen (ed.), *Carmichael's manual of child psychology*, New York, Wiley, 1970, pp. 703–732.

267. Piaget, J., *Play, dreams and imitation of childhood*, London, Heinemann, 1951.

268. Piaget, J., Le point de vue de Piaget, *International Journal of Psychology*, 1968, 3 (4): 281–299.

269. Piaget, J., Preface, in M. Laurendeau and A. Pinard, *Casual thinking in the child*, New York, International Universities Press, 1962, pp. xi–xv.

270. Piaget, J., Principal factors determining intellectual evolution from childhood to adult life, in Harvard Tercentenary Conference, *Factors determining human behavior*, Cambridge, Mass., Harvard University Press, 1937, pp. 32–48. Also in D. Rapoport (ed.), *Organization and pathology of thought*, New York, Columbia University Press, 1951, pp. 154–175.

271. Piaget, J., *The principles of genetic epistemology*, New York Basic Books, 1972.

272. Piaget, J., Problem of consciousness and symbolic process, in H. E. Abramson (ed.), *Problems of consciousness: transactions of the fourth conference*, New York, Josiah Macy, Jr., Foundation, 1954, pp. 136–177.

273. Piaget, J., in P. S. Osterrieth et al., *Le probleme des stades en psychologie de l'enfant*, Symposium de l'association de langue Française, Paris, Presses Universitaires, 1956, pp. 33–105.

274. Piaget, J., Psychologie der Frühen Kindheit, in D. Katz, *Handbuch der Psychologie*, 2nd ed., Basel, Switzerland, Benno Schwabe, 1959, pp. 275–315.

275. Piaget, J., *Psychology and epistemology*, New York, Viking Press, 1972.

276. Piaget, J., *The psychology of intelligence*, London, Routledge & Kegan Paul, 1950.

277. Piaget, J., Quantification, conservation, and nativism, *Science*, November 1968, 162: 976–979.

278. Piaget, J., The relations of affectivity to intelligence in the mental

development of the child, *Bulletin of the Menninger Foundation,* 1962, *26:* 112–137. Also in S. I. Harrison and J. F. McDermalt (eds.), *Childhood psychopathology,* New York, International Universities Press, 1972, chap. 11, pp. 167–175.

279. Piaget, J., Response to Brian Sutton-Smith, *Psychological Review,* 1966, 173 (1): 110–112. Also in R. E. Herron and B. Sutton-Smith, *Child's play,* New York, Wiley, 1971, pp. 337–340.

280. Piaget, J., Response to Harry Beilin's paper on developmental stages and developmental process, in D. R. Green, M. P. Ford, and C. B. Flamer (eds.), *Measurement and Piaget,* New York, McGraw-Hill, 1971, pp. 192–194.

281. Piaget, J., The right to education in the modern world, in UNESCO, *Freedom and Culture,* New York, Columbia University Press, 1951, pp. 69–116.

282. Piaget, J., The role of action in the development of thinking, in H. Furth, W. Overton, and J. Gallagher, *Yearbook of developmental epistemology,* New York, Plenum, 1970.

283. Piaget, J., *Science of education and the psychology of the child,* New York, Orion Press, 1970.

284. Piaget, J., *Six psychological studies,* New York, Random House, 1967.

285. Piaget, J., The stages of intellectual development of the child, *Bulletin of the Menninger Clinic,* 1962, 26 (3): 120–128. Also in S. Harrison and J. F. McDermalt (eds.), *Childhood psychopathology,* New York, International Universities Press, 1972, chap. 10, pp. 156–166.

286. Piaget, J., *Structuralism,* New York, Basic Books, 1970.

287. Piaget, J., The theory of stages in cognitive development, in D. R. Green, M. P. Ford, and G. B. Flamer (eds.), *Measurement and Piaget,* New York, McGraw-Hill, 1971, pp. 1–11.

288. Piaget, J., The theory of stages in cognitive development, in *Proceedings of the CTB/McGraw-Hill conference on ordinal scales of cognitive development,* New York, McGraw-Hill, 1971.

289. Piaget, J., Time perception in children, in J. T. Fraser, *The voices of time,* New York, Basic Books, 1965, pp. 202–216.

290. Piaget, J., *To understand is to invent: the future of education,* New York, Grossman, 1973.

291. Piaget, J., *Understanding causality,* New York, Norton, 1974.

292. Piaget, J., and B. Inhelder, Diagnosis of mental operations and theory of the intelligence, *American Journal of Mental Deficiency,* 1947, 51 (3): 401–406.

293. Piaget, J., and B. Inhelder, *The growth of logical thinking from childhood to adolescence,* New York, Basic Books, 1958.

294. Piaget, J., and B. Inhelder, *Memory and intelligence,* New York, Basic Books, 1973.

295. Piaget, J., and B. Inhelder, *Mental imagery in the child,* New York, Basic Books, 1971.

296. Piaget, J., and B. Inhelder, Mental images, in P. Fraisse and J. Piaget (eds.), *Experimental psychology: its scope and method,* New York, Basic Books, 1969, pp. 153–190.

297. Piaget, J., and B. Inhelder, *The origin of the idea of chance in children,* New York, Norton, 1975.

298. Piaget, J., and B. Inhelder, *The psychology of the child,* New York, Basic Books, 1969.

299. Piaget, J., and B. Inhelder, Social and affective interactions, in

Z. Cantwell and P. A. Suajian, *Adolescence: studies in development*, Itasca, Ill., Peacock, 1974, pp. 201–210.

300. Piaget, J., B. Inhelder, and H. Sinclair, *Memoire et intelligence*, Paris Presses Universitaires de France, 1968.

301. Piaget, J., B. Inhelder, and A. Szeminska, *The child's conception of geometry*, New York, Basic Books, 1960.

302. Piaget, J., and D. McNeill, Cognitions and conservations (a book review), *Contemporary psychology*, 1967, *12* (11): 530–533.

303. Piaget, J., Vinh-Bang and B. Matalon, Note on the law of the temporal maxim of some optico-geometric illusions, *American Journal of Psychology*, 1958, *71*: 277–282.

304. Piers, M. W. (ed.), *Play and development*, New York, Norton, 1972.

305a. Pincus, A., and A. Minahan, *Social work practice: model and method*, Itasca, Ill., Peacock, 1974.

305b. Poulsen, M. K. et al. (eds.), *Piagetian Theory and the Helping Professions;* Los Angeles, University Publishers, 1976.

306. Pribram, K. H., Neurological notes on the art of educating, in E. R. Hilgard (ed.), *Theories of learning and instruction: sixty-third yearbook of education*, Vol. 63, University of Chicago Press, 1964, pp. 78–111.

307. Pufall, P., R. E. Shaw, and A. Syrdal-Lasky, *Development of number conservation, Child Development*, March 1973, *44* (1): 21–27.

308a. Rapaport, D., A historical survey of psychoanalytic ego psychology, in E. H. Erikson, Identity and the life cycle, *Psychological Issues* (monograph), 1959, *1* (1): 5–17.

308b. Rapaport, D., *Organization and pathology of thought*, New York, Columbia University Press, 1941, pp. 154–192.

309. Redl, F., The art of group composition, in S. Schulze, *Creative group living in a children's institution*, New York, Association Press, 1951, pp. 79–96.

310. Redl, F., *When we deal with children*, New York, Free Press, 1966.

311. Redl, F., and D. Wineman, *The aggressive child*, New York, Basic Books, 1957.

312. Reeves, N., *Womankind: beyond the stereotypes*, Chicago, Aldine, 1971.

313. Renner, J. W., *Content and concrete thought*, unpublished mimeographed paper, University of Oklahoma, 1974.

314. Renner, J. W., Learning, motivation and Piaget, *Engineering Education*, March 1974, 416–419.

315. Renner, J. W., J. Brock, et al., Piaget is practical, *Science and Children*, 1971, *9* (2): 23–26.

316a. Renner, J. W., and A. E. Lawson, Piagetian theory and instruction in physics, *The Physic Teacher*, 1973, *11*(3): 165–169.

316b. Riegel, K., Dialectic Operations: the final period of cognitive development, *Human Development*, 1973, *16*(5): 346–370.

317. Ripple, R. E., and V. N. Rockcastle (eds.), *Piaget rediscovered: a report of the conference on cognitive studies and curriculum development*, Ithaca, N.Y., School of Education, Cornell University Press, 1964.

318. Rogers, C. R., *Characteristics of a helping relationship*, Supplement No. 27, Ottawa, Department of National Health and Welfare, March 1962.

319. Rothenberg, B. B., and R. G. Courtney, A developmental study of unconservative choices in young children, *Merrill-Palmer Quarterly*, October 1969, *15* (4): 363–373.

320. Ryan, J. R., Early language development: towards a communica-

tional analysis, in M. P. Richards (ed.), *The integration of a child into a social world*, England, Cambridge University Press, 1974, pp. 185–213.

321. Satir, V., *Conjoint family therapy*, Palo Alto, Calif., Science and Behavior Books, 1968.

322. Schasre, R. W., and J. Wallach (eds.), *Readings in changing interpretations of behavior*, Los Angeles, University of Southern California Press, 1965.

323. Schiamberg, L. B., Piaget's theories and early childhood education, *Children*, May–June 1970, *17* (3): 114–116.

324. Schwebel, M., and J. Raple, *Piaget in the classroom*, New York, Basic Books, 1973.

325. Sears, R. R., Attachment, dependency and frustration, in J. L. Gewirtz (ed.), *Attachment and dependency*, Washington, D.C., V. H. Winston & Sons, 1972, pp. 11–27.

326. Sears, R. R., Child psychology, in W. Dennis et al., *Current trends in psychology*, University of Pittsburgh Press, 1947, pp. 50–74.

327. Sears, R. R., Comparison of interview with questionnaire for measuring mothers' attitudes toward sex and aggression, *Journal of Personality and Social Psychology*, 1965, 2 (1): 37–44.

328. Sears, R. R., *Dependency*, unpublished manuscript, Palo Alto, Calif., Stanford University, 1961.

329. Sears, R. R., Development of gender role, in F. A. Beach (ed.), *Sex and behavior*, New York, Wiley, 1965, pp. 133–163.

330. Sears, R. R., Dependency motivation, in M. R. Jones (ed.), *Nebraska Symposium on Motivation*, University of Nebraska Press, 1963, pp. 25–64.

331. Sears, R. R., Effects of frustration and anxiety on fantasy aggression, *American Journal of Orthopsychiatry*, 1951, *21*, (3): 498–505.

332. Sears, R. R., Experimental analysis of psychoanalytic phenomena, in J. M. Hunt (ed.), *Personality and the behavior disorders*, Vol. *1*, New York, Ronald Press, 1944, pp. 306–332.

333. Sears, R. R., Frustration and aggression, in P. L. Harriman, *Encyclopedia of psychology*, New York, Philosophical Library, 1971, pp. 215–218.

334. Sears, R. R., Identification as a form of behavior development, in D. B. Harris, *The concept of development*, University of Minnesota Press, 1957, pp. 149–161.

335. Sears, R. R., *Identification, sex typing and guilt*, unpublished manuscript, Palo Alto Calif., Stanford University, 1957.

336. Sears, R. R., Influence of methodological factors on doll play performance, *Child Development*, 1947, *18* (4), pp. 190–197.

337. Sears, R. R., *Mark Twain's dependency and despair*, unpublished paper read at the Conference of the American Psychological Association, New York, September 1961.

338. Sears, R. R., The multiple department concept, *American Psychologist*, 1970, *25* (5): 428–433.

339. Sears, R. R., Personality, *Annual Review of Psychology*, 1950, 1: 105–118.

340. Sears, R. R., Personality development in contemporary culture, *Proceedings of the American Philosophical Society*, 1948, 92 (5): 363–370.

341. Sears, R. R., Personality development in the family, in J. M. Seidman (ed.), *The child: a book of readings*, New York, Holt, Rinehart and Winston, 1958, pp. 117–137.

342. Sears, R. R., Relation of early socialization experiences to aggression in middle childhood, *Journal of Abnormal Social Psychology*, 1961, *63* (3): 466–492.

343. Sears, R. R., Relation of early socialization experiences to self-concepts and gender role in middle childhood, *Child development*, June 1970, *41* (2): 267–289.

344. Sears, R. R., Relationship of fantasy aggression to interpersonal aggression, *Child development*, 1950, 21 (1): 5–6.

345. Sears, R. R., Reporting research to parents, *Journal of Nursery Education*, 1960, *16*: 25–32.

346. Sears, R. R., Social behavior and personality development, in T. Parsons and E. A. Shils, *Toward a general theory of action*, Cambridge, Mass., Harvard University Press, 1951, pp. 465–478.

347. Sears, R. R., *Survey of objective studies of psychoanalytic concepts*, New York, Social Science Research Council, 1951.

348. Sears, R. R., A theoretical framework for personality and social behavior, *American Psychologist*, 1951, 6 (9): 476–483.

349. Sears, R. R., et al., *Patterns of child rearing*, New York, Harper & Row, 1957.

350. Sears, R. R., et al., Effect of father separation on preschool children's doll play aggression, *Child development*, 1946, 17 (4): 219–243.

351. Sears, R. R., and S. S. Feldman (eds.), *The seven ages of man*, New York, Kaufman, 1973.

352. Sears, R. R., E. E. Maccoby, and H. Levin, Patterns of child rearing, in George G. Thompson (ed.), *Social development and personality*, New York, Wiley, 1971, pp. 4–12.

353. Sears, R. R., L. Rau, and R. Alpert, *Identification and child rearing*, Stanford, Calif., Stanford University Press, 1965.

354. Sears, R. R., and J. W. Whiting, Some child-rearing antecedents of aggression and dependency in young children, *Genetic Psychology Monograph*, 1953, *47*: 135–236.

355. Secord, P., and C. Backman, *Social psychology*, New York, McGraw-Hill, 1964.

356. Sharp, E., *Thinking is child's play*, New York, Dutton, 1969.

357. Sheehy, G., Catch-30 and other predictable crises of growing up adult, *New York Magazine*, February 18, 1974, 7 (7): 30–44.

358. Shulman, E. D., *Intervention in human services*, St. Louis, Mosby, 1974.

359. Sigel, I. E., and F. H. Hooper, *Logical thinking in children—research based on Piaget's theory*, New York, Holt, Rinehart and Winston, 1968.

360. Singer, J. L., *The child's world of make-believe*, New York, Academic Press, 1973.

361a. Skinner, B. F., *Beyond freedom and dignity*, New York, Bantam Books, 1971.

361b. Smith, F. N., An adult model of human consciousness, in Magary, J. R. et al. (eds.), *Proceedings: Seventh Annual university affiliated program conference: Piagetian theory and helping professions*, Los Angeles, University Publishers, 1978.

362. Smith, J. M., Erik H. Erikson's sex role theories: a rhetoric of hierarchical mystification, *Today's speech*, Spring 1973, *21*: 27–31.

363. Solnit, A. J., An essay review: the life and works of Erik H. Erikson, *Children*, September–October 1971, *18* (5): 192–193.

364. Solomon, Barbara B., Conceptualization of identity in social work practice, *Social Service Review*, 1967, *41* (1): 1–9.

365. Somer, M. L., Group process within the family unit, in *The family is the patient: the group approach to treatment of family health problems,* New York, National Association of Social Workers, 1965, pp. 22–31.

366. Stein, I., *Systems theory: science and social work,* Metuchen, N.J., Scarecrow Press, 1974.

367. Strouse, Jean (ed.), *Women in analysis,* New York, Grossman, 1974.

368. Sutton-Smith, B., Piaget on play: a critique, *Psychological Review,* 1966, *173* (1): 104–110.

369. Sutton-Smith, B., *A rejoinder to Piaget's response,* mimeographed paper, Bowling Green, Ohio, Bowling Green State University, 1966.

370. Sutton-Smith, B., What play tells you about children, *Education,* 1964, *13* (4): 31–36.

371. Svoboda, C. P., Sources and characteristics of Piaget's stage concept of development: a historical perspective, *Journal of Education,* April 1973, *155:* 28–39.

372. Taber, M., Social work as interference in problem-definitions, *Applied Social Studies,* May 1970, 2 (2): 59–68.

373. Tessler, R. C., and N. A. Polansky, Perceived similarity: a paradox in interviewing, *Social Work,* September 1975, *20* (5): 359–363.

374. Theakston, R. T., and N. Isaacs, *Some aspects of Piaget's work,* London, National Froebel Foundation, 1964.

375. Tillich, P., *The spiritual and theological foundation of pastoral care,* paper read at the Conjoint Meeting of the Council for Clinical Training and the Institute of Pastoral Care, Atlantic City, 1956.

376. Universities' National Anti-War Fund AD, Congress and the war, *The Daily,* University of Washington Press, June 2, 1970, p. 4.

377. Vikan, A., On developmental heterogeneity: the case for Piaget, *Psychological Reports,* December 1972, *31* (3): 735–740.

378. Vinter, R. D., The essential components of social group work practice, in P. Glasser et al. (eds.), *Individual change through the small group,* New York, Free Press, 1974, pp. 9–33.

379. Vygotsky, L. S., *Thought and language,* Cambridge, Mass., MIT Press, 1962, pp. 9–24.

380. Wambach, R. L., *Sex differences in play configurations of pre-adolescent children: a comparative study,* unpublished doctoral dissertation, University of Washington, 1974.

381. Watzlawick, P., J. H. Beavin, and D. D. Jackson, *Pragmatics of human communication,* New York, Norton, 1967.

382. Watzlawick, P., J. Weakland, and R. Fisch, *Change,* New York, Norton, 1974.

383. Westman, J. (ed.), *Individual differences in children,* New York, Wiley, 1973.

384. White, R. W., Competence of the psychosexual stages of development, in M. Jones (ed.), *Nebraska Symposium on Motivation,* University of Nebraska Press, 1960, pp. 97–140.

385. White, R. W., The concept of healthy personality: what do we really mean? *The counseling psychologist,* 1973, *4* (2): 3–12.

386. White, R. W., *The enterprise of living: growth and organization of personality,* New York, Holt, Rinehart and Winston, 1972.

387. White, R. W., *Lives in progress,* 2nd ed., New York, Holt, Rinehart and Winston, 1966.

388. White, R. W., Motivation reconsidered: the concept of competence, *Psychological Review,* 1959, *66:* 297–333.

389. Whitman, L. E., *Adult developmental tasks as suggested by the writings*

of Erik H. Erikson, unpublished master's thesis, School of Social Work, University of Washington, 1968.

390. Whittaker, J. K., *Social treatment,* Chicago, Aldine, 1974.

391. Winklebleck, Layne, *A model for assessment,* unpublished paper, American Lake, Veterans' Administration Hospital, Washington, 1974.

392. Witmer, H. L., Delinquency and the adolescent crisis, *Facts and Facets,* Washington, D.C., U.S. Department of Health, Education and Welfare, 1960.

393. Witmer, H. L., and R. Kotinsky, *Personality in the making,* New York, Harper & Row, 1952.

394. Wolff, P. H., The developmental psychologies of Jean Piaget and psychoanalysis, *Psychological Issues* (monograph), 2, 1960.

395. Wolff, P. H., Piaget's tension-motion theory of intelligence and general development psychology, in L. Breger (ed.), *Clinical-cognitive psychology,* Englewood Cliffs, N.J., Prentice-Hall, 1969, pp. 228–245.

396. Wolff, P. H., What Piaget did not intend, in G. I. Lubin, J. F. Macary, and M. K. Poulsen, *Piagetian theory and the helping professions,* University of Southern California Press, 1975, pp. 3–14.

397. Woodward, M., Concepts of space in the mentally subnormal studied by Piaget's method, *British Journal of Social Clinical Psychology,* 1962, *1* (1): 25–37.

398. Wright, B., *Attitude toward emotional involvement and professional development in residential child care,* unpublished doctoral dissertation, University of Chicago, 1957.

399. Zehrer, F. A., Review of patterns of child rearing, *American Journal of Orthopsychiatry,* 1958, *28* (2): 430–431.

Complete bibliography
of original and
collaborative works of
the three theorists*

ERIK H. ERIKSON

Original Writings

1930. Die Zukunft der Aufklärung und die Psychoanalyse, *Zeitschrift der Psychoanalytik Paedagogie*, 1930, 4: 201–216.

1931a. Psychoanalysis and the future of education, *Psychoanalytic Quarterly*, 1935, 4: 50–68.

1931b. Bilderbücher, *Zeitschrift der Psychoanalytik Paedagogie*, 1931, 5: 13–19.

1936a. Psychoanalysis and the future of education, *Psychoanalytic Quarterly*, 1936, 4: 50–66.

1936b. Review: psychoanalysis for teachers and parents, *Psychoanalytic Quart.*, 1936, 5: 291–293.

1937a. Configurations in play: clinical notes, *Psychoanalytic Quarterly*, 1973, 6: 139–214.

1937b. Traumatische Konfigurationen im Spiel, *Imago*, 1937, 23: 447–516.

1939. Observations on Sioux education, *Journal of Psychol.*, 1939, 7: 101–156.

1940a. Studies in the interpretation of play, *Genetic Psychological Monograph*, 1940, 22: 557–671.

1940b. Problems of infancy and early childhood, in P. G. Davis (ed.), *The cyclopedia of medicine*, Vol. 12, Philadelphia, Davis, 1940, pp. 714–730.

1941. Further explanations in play construction, *Psychological Bulletin*, 1941, 38: 748.

1942. Hitler's imagery and German youth, *Psychiatry*, 1942, 5: 475–493.

1943a. Observations on the Yurok: childhood and world image, *American Archaeological Ethnology*, 1943, 35 (10): 257–301.

1943b. Clinical studies in childhood play, in R. C. Barker et al., *Child behavior and development*, New York, McGraw-Hill, 1943, pp. 411–428.

1945a. Childhood and tradition in two American Indian tribes, in O.

* Listings are arranged by year of original publication.

Fenichel et al. (eds.), *The psychoanalytic study of the child*, Vol. 1, New York, International Universities Press, 1945, pp. 319–350.

1945b. Plans for the veteran with symptoms of instability, in L. Wirth, *Community planning for peacetime living*, Palo Alto, Calif., Stanford University Press, 1945.

1946. Ego development and historical change, in Phillis Greenacre et al. (eds.), *The psychoanalytic study of the child*, Vol. II, New York, International Universities Press, 1946, pp. 359–396.

1949. R. Benedict, in A. L. Kroeber (ed.), *Ruth Fulton Benedict: a memorial*, New York, Viking Fund, 1949.

1950a. *Childhood and society*, New York, Norton, 1950.

1950b. In M. J. E. Senn (ed.), *Symposium on the healthy personality*, New York, Josiah Macy, Jr., Foundation, 1950, pp. 91–146.

1951a. Sex differences in the play configuration of pre-adolescents, *American Journal of Orthopsychiatry*, 1951, 21 (4): 667–692. Also in R. E. Herron and B. Sutton-Smith *Child's play*, New York, Wiley, 1971, pp. 126–144. Also in S. J. Beck and H. B. Molish, *Reflexes to intelligence*, New York, Free Press, 1959, pp. 290–299.

1951b. Statement to the Committee on Privilege and Tenure of the University of California in the California Loyalty Oath: an editorial, *Psychiatry*, 1951, 14 (3): 244–245.

1952. Remarks, *Healthy personality development in children as related programs of the federal government*, New York, Josiah Macy, Jr., Foundation, 1952, pp. 80–95.

1953. On the sense of inner identity, *Conference on health and human relations*, New York, McGraw-Hill, 1953, pp. 124–146.

1954a. *Juvenile delinquency*, paper read at a teaching seminar, Department of Child Psychiatry and Child Development, University of Pittsburgh, 1954.

1954b. Wholeness and totality: a psychiatric contribution, in C. J. Friedrich (ed.), *Totalitarianism*, Cambridge, Mass., Harvard University Press, 1954, pp. 156–171.

1954c. The dream specimen of psychoanalysis, *Journal of American Psychoanalytic Association*, 1954, 2 (1): 5–56.

1954d. Identity and totality: psychoanalytic observations on the problems of youth, *Human Development Bulletin*, Chicago, The Human Development Student Organization, 1954, 50–82.

1954e. On the sense of inner identity, in R. P. Knight and C. R. Friedman (eds.), *Psychoanalytic psychiatry and psychology, clinical and theoretical papers, Austen Riggs Center*, Vol. I. New York, International Universities Press, 1954, pp. 131–170.

1954f. Problems of infancy and early childhood, in G. Murphy and A. J. Bachrach, *Outline of abnormal psychology*, New York, Random House, 1954, pp. 3–36.

1954g. In B. Schaffner (ed.), *Group processes, transactions of the first conference*, 1954, New York, Josiah Macy, Jr., Foundation, 1956, pp. 60–63, 205–206, 303–304.

1955a. In B. Schaffner (ed.), *Group processes, transactions of the second conference*, 1955, New York, Josiah Macy, Jr., Foundation, 1956.

1955b. Toys and reasons, in C. Thompson, *An outline of psychoanalysis*, New York, Random House, 1955, pp. 227–247.

1955c. Sex differences in the play configurations of American adolescents, in M. Mead and M. Wolfenstein (eds.), *Childhood in contemporary cultures*, University of Chicago Press, 1955, pp. 324–341.

1955d. The origin of psychoanalysis, *International Journal of Psychoanalysis*, 1955, *36* (1): 1–15.

1955e. Comments on permissiveness, paper read at Staff Training Session Department of Child Psychiatry and Child Development, University of Pittsburgh, 1955.

1956a. Comments at a roundtable discussion about a consideration of the biological, psychological, and cultural approaches to the understanding of human development and behavior, in J. M. Tanner, *Discussions on child development*, Vol. IV, New York, International Universities Press, 1960, pp. 133–154, 165–175.

1956b. The problem of ego identity, *Journal of American Psychoanalytic Association*, 1956, *4* (1): 56–121.

1956c. Ego identity and the psychosocial moratorium, in H. Witmer and R. Kotansky, *New perspective for research*, Washington, D.C., U.S. Department of Health, Education and Welfare: 1956, pp. 1–23.

1956d. The first psychoanalyst, *Yale Review*, Autumn 1956, 40–62.

1957. Sigmund Freud's Psychoanalytik Krise und Trieb und Umwelt in der Kindheit, in Frankfurter Beiträge zur Sozialogie, *Freud in der Gegenwart*, Frankfurt, Germany, Europäische Verlaganstalt, 1957, pp. 10–30, 43–64.

1958a. *Young man Luther: a study in psychoanalysis and history*, New York, Norton, 1958.

1958b. In J. Tanner and B. Inhelder (eds.), *Discussions on child development*, Vol. III (comments on a roundtable discussion), New York, International Universities Press, 1958, pp. 16–18, 38–52, 70–90, 91–215.

1958c. The nature of clinical evidence, *Daedalus*, 1958, *87* (4): 65–87.

1959a. Identity and the life cycle: selected papers, *Psychological Issues* (monograph), *1* (1), New York, International Universities Press, 1959.

1959b. Late adolescence, in D. H. Funkenstein (ed.), *The student and mental health*, New York, World Federation for Mental Health and The international Association of Universities, 1959, pp. 66–106.

1960. Youth and the life cycle: an interview, *Children*, 1960, *7* (2): 43–49.

1961a. The roots of virtue, in J. Huxley (ed.), *The humanist frame*, New York, Harper & Row, 1961, pp. 145–166.

1961b. Introduction, in G. B. Blaine and C. C. McArthur (eds.), *Emotional problems of the students*, New York, Englewood Cliffs, N.J. (Appleton), 1961, pp. xiii–xxv.

1962a. Youth: fidelity and diversity, *Daedalus*, 1962, *91* (1): 5–27.

1962b. Reality and actuality, *Journal of American Psychoanalytic Association*, 1962, *10* (3): 451–473.

1963a. (Ed.), *Youth: change and challenge*, New York, Basic Books, 1963.

1963b. The golden rule and the cycle of life, in R. W. White (ed.), *The study of lives*, Englewood Cliffs, N.J., Prentice-Hall, 1963, pp. 412–428.

1963c. *Childhood and society*, 2nd rev. ed., New York, Norton, 1963.

1963d. Eight ages of man, in S. I. Harrison and J. F. McDermott (eds.), *Childhood psychopathology*, New York, International Universities Press, 1972, pp. 109–132.

1964a. Inner and outer space: reflections on womanhood, *Daedalus*, 1964, *93* (2): 582–606. Also in R. J. Lifton (ed.), *The woman in America*, Boston, Houghton Mifflin, 1965, pp. 1–26.

1964b. *Insight and responsibility*, New York, Norton, 1964.

1964c. Memorandum on identity and Negro youth, *Journal of Social Issues*, 1964, *20* (4): 29–42.

1964d. Toys and reasons, in M. R. Haworth (ed.), *Child psychotherapy,* New York, Basic Books, 1964, pp. 3–10.

1964e. The initial situation and its alternatives, in M. R. Haworth (ed.), *Child psychotherapy,* New York, Basic Books, 1964, pp. 106–110.

1964f. Clinical observation of play disruption of young children, in M. R. Haworth (ed.), *Child psychotherapy,* New York, Basic Books, 1964, pp. 264–276.

1965a. Psychoanalysis and ongoing history: problems of identity, hatred and non-violence, *American Journal of Psychiatry,* 1965, *122:* 241–250.

1965b. Concluding remarks, in J. A. Mattfeld and C. G. Van Aken (eds.), *Women and the scientific professions,* Cambridge, Mass., MIT Press, 1965, pp. 232–245.

1966a. The ontogeny of ritualization in man, *Philosophical Transactions of the Royal Society of London,* 1966, Series B, 251: 337–349.

1966b. The ontogeny of ritualization, in R. M. Lowenstein et al. (eds.), *Psychoanalysis—a general psychology* (essays in honor of Heinz Hartman), New York, International Universities Press, 1966, pp. 601–622.

1966c. Gandhi's autobiography: the leader as a child, *American Scholar,* 1966, *35* (4): 632–646.

1966d. The concept of identity in race relations: notes and queries, *Daedalus,* 1966, *95* (1): 145–171.

1967a. Memorandum on youth, *Daedalus,* 1967, *96* (3): 860–870.

1967b. Memorandum for the conference on the draft, in S. Tax (ed.), *The draft: a handbook of facts and alternatives,* University of Chicago Press, 1967, pp. 280–283.

1967c. Book review of Sigmund Freud and William C. Bulitt, Thomas Woodrow Wilson: twenty-eighth president of the United States, *International Journal of Psychoanalysis,* 1967, *48* (3): 462–468.

1968a. *Identity: youth and crisis,* New York, Norton, 1968.

1968b. Identity, psychosocial and the human life cycle, *International encyclopedia of the social sciences,* New York, Crowell, 1968, Vol. 7, pp. 61–65, and Vol. 9, pp. 286–292.

1968c. On the nature of psycho-historical evidence: in search of Gandhi, *Daedalus,* 1968, *97* (3): 695–730; Also in R. J. Lifton and R. Olson, *Explorations in psychohistory,* New York, Simon & Schuster, 1974, pp. 42–77.

1969. *Gandhi's truth: on the origins of militant nonviolence,* New York, Norton, 1969.

1970a. Reflections on the dissent of contemporary youth, *International Journal of Psychoanalysis,* 1970, *51* (1): 11–22. Also in *Daedalus,* 1970, *99* (1): 154–176.

1970b. Autobiographic notes on identity crisis, *Daedalus,* 1970, *99* (4): 730–759.

1970c. Erik Erikson: the quest for identity, (special report), *Newsweek,* December 21, 1970, 84–89.

1972a. Play and actuality, in M. W. Piers (ed.), *Play and development,* New York, Norton, 1972, pp. 127–167; Also in R. J. Lifton and E. Olson, *Explorations in psychohistory,* New York, Simon & Schuster, 1974, pp. 109–135.

1972b. Inner and outer space, in N. Reeves (ed.), *Womankind—beyond the stereotypes,* Chicago, Aldine, 1972, pp. 164–168.

1972c. On protest and affirmation, *Harvard Medical Alumni Bulletin,* 1972, *46:* 30–32.

1973. The wider identity, in K. T. Erikson, *In search of common ground: conversation with Erik H. Erikson and Huey P. Newton*, New York, Norton, 1973, pp. 44–70.

1974a. Womanhood and the inner space and once more the inner space, in J. Strouse (ed.), *Women and analysis*, New York, Grossman, 1974, pp. 291–319, 320–340.

1974b. *Dimensions of a new identity*, New York, Norton, 1974.

1974c. Genetic identification and identity; pathographic: The clinical picture of severe identity confusion, in Z. Cantwell and P. A. Svajian (eds.), *Adolescence: studies in development*, Itasca, Ill., Peacock, 1974, pp. 128–135.

1975. *Life history and the historical moment*, New York, Norton, 1975.

1976a. *Toys and reason*, New York, Norton, 1977.

1976b. Reflections on Dr. Borg's life cycle, *Daedalus*, Spring 1976, *105* (2): 1–28.

Collaborative Writings

1937. With M. Gitelson, Play therapy, *American Journal of Orthopsychiatry*, 1937, *8* (3): 499–524.

1953. With Joan Erikson, The power of the newborn, *Mademoiselle*, June 1953, pp. 62, 100–102.

1958. With Kai T. Erikson, The confirmation of the delinquent, *Best articles and stories*, 1958, *2* (7): 43–46.

JEAN PIAGET

Original Writings*

1923. *The language and the thought of the child*, New York, Harcourt Brace Jovanovich, 1926.

1924. *The judgment and reason in the child*, New York, Harcourt Brace Jovanovich, 1928.

1926. *The child's conception of the world*, London, Routledge & Kegan Paul, 1951.

1927a. *The child's conception of physical causality*, London, Routledge & Kegan Paul, 1930.

1927b. *The child's conception of time*, New York, Ballantine Books, 1971.

1928. Psychology, in E. L. Schaub (ed.), *Philosophy today*, 1928, 263–288.

1931. Children's philosophies, in C. Murchison, *Handbook of child psychology*, Worcester, Mass., Clark University Press, 1931, pp. 377–391.

1932. *The moral judgment of the child*, New York, Macmillan, 1955.

1936a. *The origin of intelligence in children*, New York, International Universities Press, 1952.

1936b. The biological problem of intelligence, in D. Rapoport (ed.), *Organization and pathology of thought*, New York, Columbia University Press, 1951, pp. 176–192.

1937a. *The construction of reality in the child*, New York, Basic Books, 1954.

1937b. Principal factors determining intellectual evolution from childhood to adult life, in Harvard Tercentenary Conference, *Factors determining human behavior*, Cambridge, Mass., Harvard University Press,

* This is a complete bibliography of all the works of Piaget that have been published in English.

1937, pp. 32–48. Also in D. Rapoport (ed.), *Organization and pathology of thought*, New York, Columbia University Press, 1951, pp. 154–175.

1941. *The child's conception of numbers*, New York, Humanities Press, 1952.

1946a. *Play, dreams and imitation in childhood*, London, Heinemann, 1951.

1946b. *The child's conception of movement and speed*, New York, Basic Books, 1970.

1947. *The psychology of intelligence*, London, Routledge & Kegan Paul, 1950.

1948. *To understand is to invent: the future of education*, New York, Grossman, 1973.

1951a. Psychologie der Frühen Kindheit, in D. Katz, *Handbuch der Psychologie*, 2nd ed., Basel, Switzerland, Benno Schwabe, 1959, pp. 275–315.

1951b. The development in children of the idea of the homeland and of relations to other countries, *International Social Science Journal*, 1951, 3 (3): 561–578. Also in I. Al-Issa and W. Dennis (eds.), *Cross-cultural studies of behavior*, New York, Holt, Rinehart and Winston, 1970, pp. 286–307.

1951c. The right to education in the modern world, UNESCO, *Freedom and culture*, New York, Columbia University Press, 1951, pp. 67–116.

1952. Autobiography of Jean Piaget, in E. G. Boring et al. (eds.), *A history of psychology*, Vol. IV, Worcester, Mass., Clark University Press, 1952, pp. 237–256.

1953a. Genetic psychology and epistemology, *Diogenes*, 1953 (1): 49–63.

1953b. *Logic and psychology*, New York, Basic Books, 1957.

1953c. How children form mathematical concepts (with biographic sketch), *Scientific American*, 1953, *189* (5): 74–79.

1953d. Roundtable discussion, in J. M. Tanner and B. Inhelder (eds.), *Discussion on child development*, Vol. I, London, Tavistock, 1956, pp. 31–33, 69–72, 89–94, 104–105.

1953e. Problem of consciousness and symbolic processes, in H. E. Abramson, *Problems of consciousness: transactions of the fourth conference*, March 24–31, 1953, Princeton, N.J., New York, Josiah Macy, Jr., Foundation, 1954, pp. 136–177.

1954b. Roundtable discussion, in J. M. Tanner and B. Inhelder (eds.), *Discussion on child development*, Vol. II, London, Tavistock, 1954, pp. 58–62, 256–263.

1954c. Les relations entre l'intelligence et l'affectivité dans le développement de l'enfant, *Bulletin de Psychologie*, March, April 1954, pp. 522–535, 699–701.

1955a. Roundtable discussions, in J. M. Tanner and B. Inhelder (eds.), *Discussion on child development*, Vol. III, New York, International Universities Press, 1955, pp. 114, 154–162.

1955b. The development of time concepts in the child, in P. H. Hoch and J. Fubin, *Psychopathology of childhood*, New York, Grune and Stratton, 1955, pp. 34–44.

1955c. Perceptual and cognitive structures in the development of the concept of space in the child, *Proceedings of the Fourteenth International Congress of Psychology*, Amsterdam, Northland, 1955, pp. 41–46.

1956a. Impressions of a visit to Soviet psychologist, *Acta Logica*, 1956, *12*: 216–219.

1956b. The definition of stages of development, in J. M. Tanner and B. Inhelder (eds.), *Discussions on child development*, Vol. IV, New York,

International Universities Press, 1960, pp. 3–34, 35–83, 89–97, 98–135, 171–175.

1956c. Equilibration and the developmental structures, ibid., pp. 98–115.

1956d. The general problems of the psychobiological development of the child, ibid., pp. 3–28.

1956e. Reply to comments concerning the part played in the psychobilogical development of the child and introductory discussion, ibid., pp. 77–83, 87–97.

1956f. Les stades du développement intellectuel de l'enfant et de adolescent, In P. S. Osterrieth, et al., *Le problème des stades en psychologie de l'enfant, Symposium de l'Association de psychologie scientifique de Langue Française,* Paris, Presses Universitaires, 1956, pp. 33–105.

1957a. The child and modern physics, *Scientific American,* 1957, *196* (3): 46–57.

1957b. *Études d'épistémologie génétique,* Paris, Presses Universitaires de France, 1957.

1958a. Assimilation and sensori-motor knowledge, in H. Furth, *Piaget and knowledge,* Englewood-Cliffs, N.J., Prentice-Hall, 1969, pp. 52–54.

1958b. Assimilation and perception, ibid., pp. 144–147.

1959a. Peering into the mind of a child, *UNESCO Courier,* 1959, *12:* 4–7.

1959b. Learning and knowledge, in H. G. Furth, *Piaget and knowledge,* Englewood-Cliffs, N.J., Prentice-Hall, 1969, pp. 235–239.

1960. Individual and collective problems in the study of thinking, *Annals of the New York Academy of Sciences,* 1960, *91:* 22–37.

1961a. *The mechanisms of perception,* New York, Basic Books, 1969.

1961b. The genetic approach to psychology of thought, *Journal of Educational Psychology,* 1961, *52* (6): 275–281.

1962a. *Comments on Vygotsky's critical remarks,* Cambridge, Mass., MIT Press, 1962, Appendix.

1962b. Preface, in Monique Laurendeau and A. Pinard, *Causal thinking in the child,* New York, International Universities Press, 1962, pp. xi–xvi.

1962c. The relation of affectivity to intelligence in the mental development child, in I. Harrison and F. McDermott, *Childhood Psychopathology,* New York, International Universities Press, 1972, pp. 167–175. Also, in *Bulletin of the Menninger Clinic, 26* (3): 1962, 129–137.

1962d. The stages of intellectual development of the child, in I. Harrison and F. McDermott, *Childhood psychopathology,* New York, International University Press, 1972, pp. 157–166. Also in *Bulletin of the Menninger Clinic, 26* (3): 1962, 120–128.

1962e. Foreword, in Thérèse Gouin-Décarie, *Intelligence and affectivity in early childhood,* New York, International Universities Press, 1965, pp. xi–xv.

1962f. Will and action, *Bulletin of the Menninger Clinic, 26* (3): 1962, 138–145.

1963a. Perception, in P. Fraisse and J. Piaget (eds.), *Experimental psychology: its scope and method,* Vol. 6, New York, Basic Books, 1968, pp. 1–62.

1963b. Explanation in psychology and psychophysiological parallelism, ibid., Vol. 1, New York, Basic Books, 1968, pp. 153–191.

1963c. Language and intellectual operations, in Furth, H. *Piaget and knowledge,* Englewood-Cliffs, N.J., Prentice-Hall, 1969, pp. 121–130.

1964a. Cognitive development in children: the Piaget papers, in R. Ripple and V. Rockcastle (eds.), *Piaget rediscovered: a report of the Conference* on *Cognitive Studies and Curriculum Development,* Ithaca, N.Y., School of Education, Cornell University, 1964, pp. 6–48.

1964b. Development and learning, *Journal of Research in Science Teaching,* 1964, 2 (3): 176–186.

1964c. Psychology and philosophy, in Wohlman, B. and E. Nagel (eds.), *Scientific psychological principles and approach,* New York, Basic Books, 1964, pp. 28–43.

1965a. Time perception in children, in J. Fraser, *The voices of time,* New York, Basic Books, 1965, pp. 202–216.

1965b. *Insights and illusions of philosophy,* New York, World Publishing, 1971.

1966a. Response to Brian Sutton-Smith, *Psychological Review,* 1966, *173* (1): 111–112. Also, in R. Herron and B. Sutton-Smith, *Child's play,* New York, Wiley, 1971, pp. 337–340.

1966b. Henri Pieron, 1881–1964, *American Journal of Psychology,* 1966, *79:* 147–150.

1967a. Foreword, in M. Almy, *Young children's thinking,* New York, Teachers College Press, 1967, pp. iii–vii.

1967b. *Six psychological studies,* New York, Random House, 1967.

1967c. Adolescence: thought and its operation; the affectivity of the personality in the world of adults, in A. Cantwell and P. Svajian, *Adolescence: studies in development,* Itasca, Ill., Peacock, 1974, p. 44.

1967d. Cognitions and conservations, *Contemporary Psychology,* 1967, *12:* 523–533.

1967e. *Biology and knowledge: an essay on the relations between organic regulations and cognitive processes,* University of Chicago Press, 1971.

1968a. *On the development of memory and identity,* Worcester, Mass., Clark University Press, 1968.

1968b. Quantification, conservation, and nativism, *Science,* 1968, *162:* 976–979.

1968c. *Structuralism,* New York, Basic Books, 1970.

1968d. *Genetic epistemology,* New York, Columbia University Press, 1970.

1968e. Le point de vue de Piaget, *International Journal of Psychology, 3* (4): 1968, 281–299.

1969a. Genetic epistemology, *The Columbia forum,* 1969, *12* (3): pp. 1–11. Also in I. Evans, *Jean Piaget: the man and his ideas,* New York, Dutton, 1973, pp. xlii–lxi.

1969b. The intellectual development of the adolescent, in G. Caplan and S. Lebovici (eds.), *Adolescence: psychosocial perspectives,* New York, Basic Books, 1969, pp. 22–26.

1969c. Introduction, in M. Laurendeau and A. Pinard, *The development of the concept of space in the child,* New York, Basic Books, 1969.

1969d. *Science of education and the psychology of the child,* New York, Orion Press, 1970.

1969e. Response to Beilin's paper, in D. Green, M. Ford, and C. Flamer (eds.), in CTB/McGraw-Hill Conference, *Measurement and Piaget,* New York, McGraw-Hill, 1971, pp. 192–194.

1969f. The theory of stages in cognitive development, ibid., pp. 1–11.

1969g. Closing remarks, ibid., pp. 210–213.

1969h. Foreword and Autobiography, in H. Furth, *Piaget and knowledge: theoretical foundation,* Englewood-Cliffs, N.J., Prentice-Hall, 1969, pp. v–vii, 253–556.

1970a. Piaget's theory, in P. Mussen (ed.), *Carmichael's manual of child psychology,* 3rd ed., Vol. 1, New York, Wiley, 1970, pp. 703–732.

1970b. *The principles of genetic epistemology*, New York, Basic Books, 1972.

1970c. *Psychology and epistemology*, New York, Grossman, 1971.

1970d. Mainstreams in interdisciplinary research, in Mouton, *Main trends in human sciences*, Geneva, UNESCO, 1970, pp. 467–528, Also, *Main trends in interdisciplinary research*, New York, Harper & Row, 1973.

1971. *Understanding causality*, New York, Norton, 1974.

1972a. A structural foundation for tomorrow's educational prospects, *UNESCO*, 1972, 2 (1): 12–27.

1972b. Piaget now, *Times Educational Supplement*, February 18 and 25, 1972, pp. 19–21.

1972c. *The child and reality: Problems of genetic psychology*, New York, Grossman, 1973.

1972d. *Essay on operative logic*, Paris, Dunon, 1972.

1972e. Intellectual evolution from adolescence to adulthood, *Human Development*, 1972, 15: 1–12; Also, in C. Guardo, *The adolescent as individual: issues and insights*. New York, Harper & Row, 1975, pp. 108–117.

1972f. Operational structures of the intelligence and organic controls, in A. Kraczmar and J. Eccles (eds.), *Brain and human behavior*, New York, Springer-Verlag, 1972, pp. 393–398.

1973a. An autobiography, in R. Evans, *Jean Piaget: the man and his ideas*, New York, Dutton, 1973, pp. 103–143.

1973b. Foreword, in M. Schwebel and J. Ralph, *Piaget in the classroom*, New York, Basic Books, 1973, pp. ix–x.

1974a. Foreword, in B. Inhelder, H. Sinclair, and M. Bovet, *Learning and the development of cognition*, Cambridge, Mass., Harvard University Press, 1974, pp. ix–xiv.

1974b. *The Grasp of Consciousness*, Cambridge, Mass., Harvard University Press, 1976.

1975a. The role of action in the development of thinking, in H. Furth, W. Overton, and J. Gallagher, *Yearbook of developmental epistemology*, New York, Plenum, 1975.

1975b. Foreword, in E. Anthony, *Explorations in child psychiatry*, New York, Plenum, 1975, pp. vii–ix.

1976a. On correspondences and morphism, *Newsletter of the Jean Piaget Society*, April 1976, 5 (3): 6–8.

1976b. The possible, the impossible and the necessary, *The Genetic Epistemologist*; Vol. VI, #1, October 1976, pp. 1–12.

Collaborative Writings

1947. With B. Inhelder, Diagnosis of mental operations and theory of the intelligence, *American Journal of Mental Deficiency*, 1951, 51 (3): 401–406.

1948a. With B. Inhelder, *The child's conception of space*, New York, Humanities Press, 1956.

1948b. With B. Inhelder and A. Szeminska, *The child's conception of geometry*, New York, Basic Books, 1960.

1951. With B. Inhelder, *The origin of the idea of chance in children*, New York, Norton, 1975.

1955. With B. Inhelder, *The growth of logical thinking from childhood to adolescence*, New York, Basic Books, 1958.

1958. With Vinh-Bang and B. Matalon, Note on the law of the temporal maximum of some optico-geometric illusions, *American Journal of Psychology*, 1958, 71: 277–282.

1959. With B. Inhelder, *The early growth of logic in the child*, New York, Harper & Row, 1964.

1961. With W. Beth, *Mathematical epistemology and psychology*, Dordrecht, Holland, Reidel, 1961.

1963a. With P. Fraisse (eds.), *Experimental psychology: its scope and method*, New York, Basic Books, 1969.

1963b. With B. Inhelder, Mental images, in P. Fraisse and J. Piaget (eds.), *Experimental psychology: its scope and method*, Vol. 7, New York, Basic Books, 1969, pp. 85–143.

1963c. With B. Inhelder, Intellectual operations and their development, ibid., pp. 144–205.

1966a. With B. Inhelder, *The psychology of the child*, New York, Basic Books, 1969.

1966b. With B. Inhelder, *Mental imagery in the child*, New York, Basic Books, 1971.

1966c. Biology and cognition, *Diogene, 54:* 3–26.

1967a. With D. McNeill, Cognitions and conservations: two views (review of *Studies in cognitive growth*, by J. Bruner, R. Olver, and P. Greenfield), *Contemporary psychology*, 1967, *12* (11): 530–533.

1967b. With P. Fraisse and M. Reuchlin, *History and method*, Vol. I, New York, Basic Books, 1967.

1968. With B. Inhelder, *Memory and intelligence*, New York, Basic Books, 1973.

1969a. With B. Inhelder, Mental images, in P. Fraisse and J. Piaget (eds.), *Experimental psychology: its scope and method*, New York, Basic Books, 1969, pp. 153–190.

1970. With B. Inhelder, A talk with Piaget and Inhelder on how children learn, in E. Hall (ed.), *Psychology today*, May 1970, 25–32, 54–55.

1974. With B. Inhelder, Social and affective interactions, in Z. Cantwell and P. Svajian, *Adolescence: studies in development*, Itasca, Ill., Peacock, 1974, pp. 201–210.

ROBERT R. SEARS

Original Writings

1936a. Experimental studies of projection: I. attribution of traits, *Journal of Social Psychology*, 1936, *7:* 151–163.

1936b. Functional abnormalities of memory with special reference to amnesia, *Psychological Bulletin, 33:* 224–274.

1936c. Review of Lewin's, A dynamic theory of personality, *Psychological Bulletin*, 1936, *33* (7): 548–552.

1937a. Experimental studies of projection: I. ideas of reference, *Journal of Social Psychology, 8:* 389–400.

1937b. Initiation of the repression sequence by experienced failure, *Journal Experimental Psychology, 20*, 570–580.

1941a. Frustration and aggression, in P. Harriman, *Encyclopedia of psychology*, New York, Philosophical Library, 1941, pp. 215–218.

1941b. Non-aggressive reactions to frustration, *Psychological Bulletin*, 1941, *48* (4): 343–349.

1942. Success and failure: a study of motility, in Q. McNemar and M. Merill (eds.), *Studies in personality*, New York, McGraw-Hill, 1942, pp. 235–258.

1943. *Survey of objective studies of psychoanalytic concepts*, New York, Social Science Research Council, 1951.

1944a. Experimental analysis of psychoanalytic phenomena, in J. Hunt (ed.), *Personality and the behavior disorders*, Vol. I, New York, Ronald Press, 1944, pp. 306–332.

1944b. Personality and motivation, *Review Educational Research*, 1944, *14* (5): 368–380.

1947a. Child psychology, in W. Dennis et al., *Current trends in psychology*, University of Pittsburgh Press, 1947, pp. 50–74.

1947b. Influence of methodological factors on doll play performance, *Child Development*, 1947, *18* (4): 190–197.

1948. Personality development in contemporary culture, *Proceedings of American Philosophical Society*, 1948, *92* (5): 363–370.

1950a. Relation of fantasy aggression to interpersonal aggression, *Child Development*, 1950, *21* (1): 5–6.

1950b. Ordinal position in the family as a psychological variable, *American Sociological Review*, 1950, *15* (3): 397–401.

1950c. Personality, *Annual Review of Psychology*, 1950, *1:* 105–118.

1951a. Social behavior and personality development, in T. Parsons and E. Shills, *Toward a general theory of action*, Cambridge, Mass., Harvard University Press, 1951, pp. 465–478.

1951b. Effects of frustration and anxiety on fantasy aggression, *American Journal of Orthopsychiatry*, 1951, *21* (3): 498–505. Also, in I. Sarason (ed.), *Contemporary research in personality*, New York, Van Nostrand, 1962, pp. 134–139.

1951c. A theoretical framework for personality and social behavior, *American Psychologist*. 1951, *6* (9): 476–483.

1957. Identification as a form of behavior development, in D. Harris, *The concept of development*, University of Minnesota Press, 1957, pp. 149–161.

1958. Personality development in the family, in J. Seidman (ed.), *The child: a book of readings*, New York, Holt, Rinehart and Winston, 1958, pp. 117–137.

1960a. Transcultural variables and conceptual equivalence, in B. Kaplan (ed.), *Studying personality cross-culturally*, New York, Harper & Row, 1960, pp. 445–455. Also, in I. Al-Issa and H. Dennis (eds.), *Cross-cultural studies of behavior*, New York, Holt, Rinehart and Winston, 1970, pp. 164–174.

1960b. Reporting research to parents, *Journal of Nursery Education*, 1960, *16:* 25–32.

1961a. *Mark Twain's dependency and despair*, paper read at the American Psychological Association, New York, September 1, 1961.

1961b. Relation of early socialization experiences to aggression in middle childhood, *Journal of Abnormal Social Psychology*, 1961, *63* (3): 466–492.

1961c. *Dependency* (manuscript), Palo Alto, Calif., Stanford University, Mass., 1961.

1963. Dependency motivation, in M. Jones (ed.), *Nebraska Symposium on Motivation*, University of Nebraska Press, 1963, pp. 25–64.

1965a. Development of gender role, in F. Beach (ed.), *Sex and behavior*, New York, Wiley, 1965, pp. 133–163.

1965b. Comparison of interviews with questionnaire for measuring mothers' attitudes toward sex and aggression, *Journal of Personality and Social Psychology*, 1965, *2* (1): 37–44.

1970a. The multiple department concept, *American Psychologist*, 1970, *25* (5): 428–433.

1970b. Relation of early socialization experiences to self-concepts and gender role in middle childhood, *Child Development*, 1970, *41* (2): 267–289.

1972. Attachment, dependency and frustration, in J. Gewirtz (ed.), *Attachment and dependency*, Washington, D.C., V. H. Winston, 1972, pp. 1–27.

Collaborative Writings

1940. With C. Hovland and N. Miller, Minor studies of aggression: Measurement of aggressive behavior, *Journal of Psychology*, 1940, *9* (2): 277–281.

1941a. With C. Hovland, Experiments on motor conflict, *Journal of Experimental Psychology*, 1941, *28:* 280–286.

1941b. With N. Miller et al., Reformulation of frustration and aggression theory, *Psychological Review*, 1941, *48:* 337–342.

1941c. With J. Dollard et al., *Frustration and aggression*, New Haven, Yale University Press, 1941.

1946. With M. Pinter and P. Sears, Effect of father separation on preschool children's doll play aggression, *Child Development*, 1946, *17* (4): 219–243.

1950. With G. Wise, Relationship of cup-feeding in infancy to thumbsucking and the oral drive, *American Journal of Orthopsychiatry*, 1950, *20:* 123–138.

1953. With J. Whiting, Some child-rearing antecedents of aggression and dependency in young children, *Genetic Psychological Monograph*, 1953, *47:* 135–236.

1956. With H. Levin, Identification with parents as a determinant of doll play aggression, *Child Development*, 1956, *27* (2): 135–153.

1957. With E. Maccoby and H. Levin, *Patterns of child rearing*, New York, Harper & Row, 1957.

1965. With L. Rau and R. Alpert, *Identification and child rearing*, Palo Alto, Calif., Stanford University Press, 1965.

1971. With E. Maccoby and H. Levin, Patterns of child rearing, in G. Thompson (ed.), *Social development and personality*, New York, Wiley, 1971, pp. 4–12.

1973. With S. Feldman (eds.), *The seven ages of man*, New York, Kaufmann, 1973.

Index

A

Abnormal, *see* Deviant
Accommodation, 20, 22–23, 33, 34, 38, 39, 40, 42–43, 45, 46, 48, 56, 232. *See also* Adaptation; Predictability
defined, 22–23
Activation, 83
Adaptation, 2, 22, 31, 32 ,36, 185, 250. *See also* Accommodation; Assimilation
Adler, A., 8
Adolescence, 64–65, 108, 109–120, 175, 189, 230–231, 236, 238–240, 240–242, 247–248, 253–254. *See also* Operation, formal; Indentity, phase of
affect development, 108, 109, 120, 125–126
cognitive development, 64–68
Adult authority, *see* Authority, adult
Adulthood, 20, 27, 43, 53, 68n, 70, 120, 120–122, 126, 175, 190, 231. *See also* Maturity
Adultmorphic, 173
Aebli, H., 257
Affect development, 5, 5n, 10–11, 25, 26, 35, 71–132, 156n, 220, 224–225. *See also* Erikson, E. H.
Affect theory, compared, 165–188
Aggressiveness, 106, 137, 138–139, 139n, 147, 154–155, 157, 159, 162–163, 164, 232–233. *See also* Frustration–aggression theory and Frustration
Almy, M., 12, 16, 238n, 257
American scene, *see* Contemporary issues
Anderson, R. E., 87, 257
Animism, 49–50
Anthony, E. J., 16, 257
Appraisal process, 209, 214–216. *See also* Assessment process
Assessment process, 208–211, 221–222, 225–231. *See also* Helping process; Professional intervention
Assimilation, 20, 22–23, 31, 33, 42, 43, 51, 56, 232. *See also* Accommodation; Adaptation; Rhythmicity; Play
defined, 22–23
Associate frame of reference, *see* Frame of reference
Attachment, 36, 41, 101, 102–103, 112, 145–147, 149–150, 160, 227, 232, 243, 250–251. *See also* Mutual regulation; Separation
Attention seeking, negative, 158
defined, 158, 159
positive, 159
Austin, S., 213n
Authority, adult, 43, 53, 116, 117, 125–127, 186, 240, 247
Authority diffusion, *see* Authority, adult
Autism, *see* Autistic processes
Autistic processes, 32, 42, 143, 144, 237
Autonomy, phase of, 94–99. *See also* Affect development; Early childhood, affect development

Auxiliary helping system, 200, 205–206, 221, 242–248

B

Baer, D. M., 8, 258
Bandura, A., 7, 8, 257
Basic trust, phase of, 89–94. *See also* Infancy, affect development
Bee, H., 257
Behavior modification, 17. *See also* Behavioral development; Operant Behavior; Sears; Skinner
Behavioral development, 3, 7, 10–11, 17, 35, 133–164, 220, 224–225, 232 compared, 165–188. *See also* Learning theory; Sears
Behavioral learning, *see* Behavioral development; Sears
Beilin, H., 257
Bergson, H., 13
Bijou, S., 8, 258
Binet, A., 13
Birth, *see* Newborn
Bisexuality, 82, 86, 115, 151n, 169n. *See also* Female; Male, Sex differentiation; Sexism
Black power, 85n, 114, 130. *See also* Newton, H. P.
Blake, W., 84, 184, 258
Bloss, P., 71–72
Body experience, 31, 90, 91–92. *See also* Reflexive processes; Sensorimotor processes
Boehm, W., 199, 208, 218, 258
Bramer, L. M., 258
Briar, S., 258
Brown, R., 30n, 258
Bryant, P., 59n, 258
Burden, D., 232, 258
Burlingham, D., 72

C

Carbonara, N., 258
Career, 115, 119, 120–121, 127
Carter, I., 87, 257
Casework, *see* Dyadic group system, associate level
Causal relations, *see* Causality
Causality, 5, 29, 33–34, 35, 38, 40, 42, 43, 44
Cause and effect, 37, 43, 135, 139. *See also* Causality; Empirical approach; S–R formulation; Sears; Sensorimotor process
Change, x, 2, 5, 62, 118–120, 160, 171, 174, 206–207, 221
Child care work, 17, 248. *See also* Dyadic group, primary level
Childhood development, 45–54, 100–105, 176–177, 232–235, 237–238, 245–246, 251–252. *See also* Operation, concrete; Industry, phase of
Child-rearing, 17, 85, 86, 99, 123, 125, 141, 148
definition (Sears') 141
Classifying, cognitive process of, 49, 55, 57, 58

Clemens, Samuel, *see* Mark Twain
Clinical counseling, *see*Professional helping
Coelho, G.V., 112, 259
Cognitive development, 7, 10–11, 12–70, 219–220,
     224–225. *See also* Piaget, J.
   compared, 165–191
Coles, R., 77, 259
Collecting, process of, 97
Communication, 35, 84, 101, 116, 186, 190, 200, 208,
     221, 226, 232–233, 234, 235, 239, 240, 247
Community organization, 206–207
Competence, *see* Industry, phase of; White, R. W.
Concrete operation, *see* Operation, concrete, phase of
Conflict, 196, 241
Conscience, 44–45, 53, 63, 96, 98–99, 101, 154, 160,
     162, 186
Conservation, 47, 49, 55, 56, 57, 58n, 60, 60n. *See
     also* Reversibility
Consistency, *see* Prediction
Consultation, *see* Auxiliary system
Contemporary issues, xi, 74, 75, 81, 98, 114, 118,
     122–130
Continuity, *see* Unity–in–continuity
Contracting, 207–208. *See also* Mutual regulation
   secondary schemata, stage of, 36–37
Cooley, C. H., 204
Cosmic order, *see* Universal order
Counseling, *see* Dyadic group system
Counter-culture, 74, 75, 81, 114, 118, 124, 126
Crisis, developmental, 75, 76–77, 81, 82, 85, 87, 101,
     110, 112, 118, 121, 141, 174–175, 188. *See also*
     Polarity
Cross-cultural issues, *see* Cultural
Cultural change, 118–120, 124
Culture, 27, 58, 60n, 64, 70, 79, 85, 94, 101, 104, 109,
     127, 130, 141, 148, 160, 167

D
Darwin, C., 82n
Daycare, 249
Daydreaming, 105
Death, 122, 132
Déecarie, T., 170n, 259
Deductive, *see* Thinking, inductive/deductive
Defense mechanism, 82
Dependence, 95, 96, 105, 109, 125, 142, 143, 144–147,
     148, 149–150, 151–153, 157, 158, 159–160,
     161–163, 164, 188, 202, 207–208, 237. *See also*
     Dependence/Independence development
   defined (Sears'), 144–145
Dependence/Independence development, 31,
     176–177, 179, 207–208, 225, 227. *See also*
     Dependence
Dependence upon dependence, phase of, 91–92, 94,
     176, 231–232, 237, 243–244, 250–251. *See also*
     Infancy
Dependence upon personal competence, phase of,
     176, 235–236, 238–240, 246–247, 252–253. *See
     also* School–age development
Dependence upon primary relationship, phase of,
     176, 233–235, 237–238, 245–246, 251–252.
     See also Childhood development
Dependence upon primary relationship within
     a secondary world, phase of, 177, 236, 240–
     242, 247–248, 253–254. *See also* Adolescence
Dependence upon self-care, phase of, 176, 231–232,
     237, 243–244, 251. *See also* Early childhood
     development
Deprivation, 227
Developmental continuum compared, 173–178,
     178–180
Developmental delay, 225–226
Developmental phase, 79, 142, 174, 223–225
Developmental readiness, 226
Deviation, 196, 197, 209, 224
Dewey, J., 21
Diagnosis, *see* Assessment
Dialectic thinking, *see* Thinking, dialectic
Dollard, J., 134, 136, 138, 259

Dreams, 48, 62, 66
Dubos, R., 210, 259
Dyadic group, defined, 199
Dyadic group, associate level, 199–203, 231–236, 240
   defined, 202
   primary level, 202, 232, 240
Dyadic unit, 136–137, 139–140, 145, 163
Dynamic model of helping, 220–222

E
Early childhood, 41–45, 94–99, 149–161, 173, 174,
     180–183, 231–232, 237, 244–245, 251. *See also*
     Autonomy, phase of; Preconceptual phase;
     Secondary motivational system,
     family-centered
   affect development, 94–99
   behavioral development, 149–161
   cognitive development, 41–45
Ego, 82, 88
Egocentric, 40–41, 42, 46, 48, 50, 59, 61, 67n, 93, 181n
Ego development, *see* Affect development *and*
     Erikson, E. H.
Ego ideal, 103, 113
Ego synthesis, 77, 85
Einstein, A., 14, 16, 60n
Elkind, D., 16, 30, 74, 259
Emotion, *see* Affect development
Empirical approach (*also* Thinking), 7, 9, 18–19, 50,
     133, 134, 137, 167–168, 190, 226
Energy, psychic, 23, 91, 95, 106, 110. *See also*
     Reflexive development; Sensorimotor
     development
   defined, 23
Ends and means, *see* Reasoning
Epigenetic, 81
Equilibration, 22, 23, 26, 28, 29, 46, 56, 64, 68, 87,
     175. *See also* Mutual regulation; Homeostasis;
     Heterostasis
Equilibrium, *see* Equilibration
Equity, *see* Judgment, equity
Erikson, E. H., ix, x, xi, 4, 6–11, 71–132, 135, 140,
     165–191, 227, 243, 245, 248, 249, 253, 254,
     255, 259–263, 276–280
   basic assumptions, 83–86
   biography, 71–75
   concept of development, 86–89
   developmental chart, 131, 176–177
   research and writings, 72–75, 259–263, 276–280
   theory formation, 78–80
Erikson, F. H., 263
Eirkson, K. T., 263
Ethnic factors, 75, 76, 78, 248. *See also* Culture
Etiology, 21–22, 80, 139, 210
Evolutionary change, 19, 21, 23, 29, 79, 86
Exercises of reflexes, stage of, 31–32
Existential thinking, *see* Thinking, existential

F
Fantasy, 51, 52, 100, 140, 155, 188
Father, 127, 148, 154, 157, 159
Faulkner, W., 119
Feedback, 23, 239
Feeding, 91, 143, 145, 146, 147, 152–153, 226, 244
Female, 81, 86, 103, 104, 107, 108, 121, 127, 129, 151,
     153–154, 157–158, 159, 181. *See also* Bisexual;
     Sexual differentiation
Fidelity, *see* Identity formation, phase of
Flavell, J. H., 18, 24, 26, 263
Foster parents, 248. *See also* Dyadic group, primary
     care
Foster parent work, *see* Dyadic group, primary level
Formal operation, *see* Operation, formal, phase of
Frame of reference, x, 9–10, 165, 212, 216, 223
Freud, A., 8, 72, 73, 75
Freud, S., 7, 8, 12, 72, 73, 75, 76, 77, 78, 80–81, 81n,
     82n, 83, 86, 87, 102, 110, 128, 129, 132, 172n,
     263
Frustration, 92, 94, 95, 100, 138, 139n, 147, 154–155,
     225, 232. *See also* Aggression

Frustration-aggression theory, 138–139. *See also* Aggression; Frustration
Furth, H., 227, 263

G

Gandhi, M., 74, 121n, 122, 127, 260, 261
Generational issues, 75, 76, 80, 88, 94, 121–122, 123, 126–127, 134, 143, 250. *See also* Mutual regulation
Generativity, phase of, 121–122
Geometrical concept formation, 64–65
Gorky, 127
Gorman, J. F., 263
Grasping, 32, 33, 34, 35, 92
Group, 52, 55, 200–203, 203–205, 237–242. *See also* Dyadic group system; Primary group system
Group care, 239–240
Group counseling, *see* Primary group system work, associate and primary levels
Group therapy, *see* Primary group system, associate level
Group work, *see* Primary group system, associate level
Guilt, sense of, 53, 102, 105. *See also* Conscience; Autonomy, phase of

H

Habits, 31, 38, 94, 183
Haley, J., 263
Harris, D. B., 264
Helping, defined, 196
Helping process, 195–222
    defined, 195
Helping, professional, 6, 10, 17, 39, 165, 197–198, 223–255. *See also* Professional intervention
Helping techniques, 195–222, 217–219
Heterostasis, 19, 26, 87, 165, 171–172
Hierarchical thinking, *see* Thinking, hierarchical
Historic perspective, 74–76, 77, 81, 227, 261
Hitler, A., 127
Homburger, E., *see* Erikson, E. H.
Homburger, T., 71
Homeostasis, 19, 23, 26, 86–87, 95, 165, 171–172
Honzik, H., 104, 264
Hope, *see* Basic trust, phase of
Hull, C. L., 7, 134, 135, 137
Human development, ix, 2, 30–41, 196–197
Hypothesis testing, 209, 211, 221
Hypothetical thinking, *see* Thinking, hypothetical

I

Id, 82
Identification, affect, 93–94
    behavioral, 131, 139, 151–153, 156–157, 157–158, 160, 163, 164, 184–185
    cognitive, 25, 41, 44–45, 60
    defensive, 157
    negative, 113–114
Identity, phase of, 61, 62, 101–102, 108–109, 109–120, 123, 125, 188, 230, 244, 248. *See also* Adolescenthood, Operation, formal, phase of
Illegitimate generalization, 48
Imitation, 25, 34, 40, 42–43, 51–52, 62–63, 139, 183, 184
Inductive thinking, *see* Thinking, inductive/deductive
Individual interview system, *see* Dyadic group
Industry, phase of, 106–109
Infancy, phase of, 2, 3, 6, 30–41, 79, 83, 85, 89–94, 142, 143–149, 170, 180–183, 228, 231–232, 237, 243–244, 250–251
    affect, development, 89–94
    behavioral development, 143–149
    cognitive development, 30–41
Infant, *see* Infancy, phase of
Inhelder, B., 27, 49, 59, 264
Initiative, phase of, 100–105
Instinct, 27

Integrity, phase of, 122
Intervention, *see* Professional intervention
Interviewing, *see* Dyadic group system
Intimacy, phase of, 120–121
Intuitive thought, phase of, 45–54
Invention of new means through combination, stage of, 39–41

J

Jefferson, T., 74, 121n, 127
Jones, F., 232, 258
Judgment, equity, 67–68
    expiratory, 63
    distributive, 63, 68
    moral, 52, 201
Juxtaposition, 44, 47

K

Keniston, K., 264
Klein, M., 8
Kohlberg, L., 7n, 264
Kuhn, T. S., 265

L

Labeling, 42, 50–51, 160, 212, 213, 221, 233, 245
Language, 30n, 41, 42, 43, 44, 46, 50–51, 52, 60, 62, 66, 83, 101, 116, 185–186, 232–233, 234, 236
Latency, *see* School-age child development, phase of
Lattices, 57, 58
    defined, 57
Lawson, A. E., 64n, 172, 265
Learning theory, *see* Behavioral development; Sears; Skinner, S—R formulation
Leisure, *see* Play
Levin, H., 161, 265
Lewin, K., 7
Libidinal theory, *see* Freud, S.
Libido, defined, 80–81. *See also* Energy
Life cycle, 88, 101, 119, 121, 122, 124, 126–127, 132. *See also* Generational issues; Mutual regulations
Life style, 118
Limit setting, 97–98
Linear thinking, *see* Thinking, linear
Logical thinking, *see* Thinking, logical
Loyalty oath, 74, 260
Luther, M., 74, 121n, 127, 262

M

Maas, H., 265
McLeod, G., 212n
Male, 81, 103, 104, 107, 108, 121, 127–129, 151, 153–154, 157–158, 181. *See also* Bisexuality; Sexual differentiation
Mark Twain, 137, 162, 272
Masturbation, 153
Maturation, 4, 17, 20, 22, 24, 31, 32, 38n, 58n, 81, 85, 90, 91n, 92, 95, 107, 112, 139, 174, 178, 178n, 181–183
Maturity, *see* Adulthood
Mayer, M. F., 266
Memory, 25, 59n, 184
Men, *see* Male; Bisexuality; Sexual differentiation
Millett, N. E., 75, 127, 129, 169n, 266
Mishel, S., 266
Modalities, 104, 129, 227
Modality, incorporative, 31–32, 91, 92
Monane, J. H., 266
Moral judgment, *see* Judgment, moral
Moratorium, 114–116
Motor behavior, *see* Reflexive behavior; Sensorimotor behavior
Mowrer, O., 8, 134
Mutation, 13, 19
Mutual regulation, 83, 88, 92, 94, 98, 99, 110, 120–127, 144, 145–146, 196, 217n, 235, 244. *See also* Adaptation; Generational issues
    defined, 83

N

National health insurance, 249
Nationalism, 98. *See also* Contemporary issues
Negative identification, *see* Identification, negative
Nesting, 57, 58, 62
Newborn, 26, 79–84, 85, 89–90, 91, 140–141, 170
Newcomb, T., 9, 267
Newton, H. P., 74, 80, 85n, 86, 127, 263. *See also* Black power
"Normal" development, 3, 196, 197
Norms, 118, 123, 124
Numbers, concept of, 49, 59
Nursing, *see* Sucking

O

Obedience, 45, 52
Object, concept of, property of, recognition, and relationship, 33, 34, 35, 36, 37, 38, 40, 43, 44, 47, 48–49, 49–50, 52, 55, 60, 64, 66, 142, 156n, 238
Occupation, *see* Career
Odier, C., 8, 186
Oedipus issues, 76, 102–103, 108, 112–113, 123, 127, 154n, 157, 186–187
Ontogeny, 79
Operant behavior, 17, 137, 144. *See also* Learning theory; Skinner
Operations, 23, 24, 25, 29, 41, 54–63, 64–68
  defined, 24
Operation, concrete, defined, 24
  phase of, 24, 25, 29, 41, 54–63
Operation, formal, 29, 64–68
Opposing pulls, *see* Polarity
Orality, 91
Ordering, 55, 56, 57
Ordinal position, 147–149
Organizational system, 200, 206–207, 248–255
Oscillation, 4, 119, 171, 208. *See also* Dialectic thinking; Dependence/independence development

P

Parent support, *see* Auxiliary system
Part and whole, *see* Whole-and-part
Participant observation, 213, 283
  defined, 213n
Peers, 52, 88, 102, 107, 108–109, 117, 118, 125, 151, 202, 203, 204, 239
Perception, 25–26, 31, 36, 37, 60
Permanency, 36, 49, 58, 156n. *See also* Reversibility; Rhythmicity
Permissiveness, 99, 100–101, 146, 147, 154, 155, 159, 162–163, 232, 243
Phasal development, 4, 27–29, 29–30, 32n, 86–89, 149, 165
Phase, *see* Phasal development
Phase of, *see* respective name of phase
Phenomenological, 77n
Physical care and comfort, 90, 91. *See also* Infancy
Physiology, 5n, 79
Piaget, J., ix, xi, 4, 6, 11, 12–70, 113, 135n, 140n, 165–191, 233, 238n, 239, 243, 245, 252, 254, 267–271, 280–285
  basic assumptions, 17–27
  biography, 12–16
  concept of development, 27–29
  definition of terms, 22–24
  developmental chart, 69, 176–177
  research and writing, 14–16, 267–271, 280–285
  theory formation, 18–19
Plato, 89n
Play, 5, 25, 35, 39, 39n, 40, 42, 45, 51, 52, 62–63, 72, 73, 83–84, 93, 97, 104–105, 108–109, 114, 117, 140n, 155, 158–159, 183, 228, 229, 233, 234, 235, 236, 238, 239, 245, 251. *See also* Play disruption
  defined, 83
Play disruption, 84, 105
Playfulness, *see* Play

Polarity, 81n, 82, 87, 95, 96, 106–107, 119, 123–234, 169, 171, 175. *See also* Oscillation; Thinking, dialectic
Power struggle, 94–99, 112–113, 114, 118–120
Preconceptual, phase of, 41–45. *See also* Early childhood development
Predictability, 36–39, 40, 43, 50, 87, 90, 92, 93, 143, 160, 243. *See also* Accommodation; Rhythmicity
Preschool-age child, *see* Childhood development
Prevention, *see* Helping, professional; Professional intervention
Pribram, K. H., 38, 271
Primary circular reactions, stage of, 32–34
Primary drive, 135–136, 139, 143–144
Primary group system, 203–205
  associate level, 203–205
    defined, 203
  primary level, 204–205
    defined, 204
Primary process, cognitive, 24–26
Professional intervention, 195–197, 207–208, 208–211, 216–219, 224
Psychoanalytic theory, 7, 8–9, 16, 75–77, 78, 82, 102, 131, 132, 134, 137, 169, 172. *See also* Erikson, E. H., Freud, A.; Freud, S.
Psychosexual development, 73, 75, 76, 77, 80–81, 86. *See also* Psychoanalytic theory
Psychosocial development, 86–89
Punishment, 53, 63, 149, 153, 155, 160, 162–163, 243

R

Racism, 231–232, 249. *See also* Newton, H. P.
Rank, O., 8
Rapaport, D., 43, 76n, 271
Reasoning, 2, 3, 19, 25, 26, 28, 36, 37, 43, 46, 48, 50, 56, 58, 59, 65, 67, 74, 77, 78, 81, 82, 87, 88, 119, 123, 124, 134, 137, 160, 165, 167, 211–212, 238. *See also* Thinking
Recall, 25, 38, 40
Reciprocity, 62, 63
Redl, F., 216, 271
Rees, B., 232, 258
Reeves, N., 127, 129, 271
Reflexive action, 3, 30–32, 91, 169. *See also,* Rhythmicity
Regression, 88, 174
Regularity, *see* Predictability
Reinforcement, *see* Behavioral development; Learning theory
Relationship formation, 93, 97–98, 105–107, 117
Religion, 80, 85, 90, 116, 119
Renner, J. W., 64n, 271
Reversibility, 24, 29, 54–55, 62, 239. *See also* Permanency
Rhythmicity, 31, 32, 33, 43, 59, 89, 181. *See also* Sensorimotor, phase of
Rivalry, *see* Sibling rivalry
Rogers, C., 7
Role diffusion, 113–114. *See also* Identity, phase of
Role selection, 113–114, 115, 117. *See also* Identity, phase of
Rudimentary behavior, 41n. *See also* Infancy
  defined, 142
Rudimentary thinking, *see* Thinking, rudimentary
Rules, 52, 63, 67–68, 238, 240, 241

S

S-R formulation, 17, 33, 136–137, 169. *See also* Learning theory; Sears; Skinner
  defined (Sears'), 136
Schema, 24, 28, 32, 34, 35, 44, 46, 48, 174, 184, 230
  defined, 24
  secondary, 36
Schemata, *see* Schema
Scheme, *see* Schema
School-age child development, phase of, 54–63, 106–109, 161–163, 188–190, 228–229, 232–235, 237–238, 245–246, 251–252

affect development, 106–109
  behavioral development, 161–163
  cognitive development, 54–63
Schwebel, M., 6, 272
Sears, P. S., 134, 287
Sears, R. R., ix, x, xi, 4, 6, 11, 78, 133–164, 165–188,
    232, 243, 248, 249, 254, 272–273, 285–287
  basic assumptions, 138–141
  biography, 133–135
  concept of development, 141–143
  developmental chart, 176–177
  research and writing, 134, 272–273, 285–287
  theory formation, 135–138
Secondary circular reaction, stage of, 34–36. See also
    Sensorimotor, phase of
Secondary motivational system, based upon beyond
    family-centeredness, 142, 161–163
  defined, 142
Self, 35, 40, 43, 95, 97, 182. See also Self control
Self-control, 95, 96
Sensorimotor development, phase of, 29–41, 166. See
    also, Infancy, phase of; Newborn; Rhythmicity
Separation, 94, 232, 250, 251. See also, Attachment;
    Mutual regulation
Seriation, 57–58
Serson, J. W. (Ms. Joan Erikson), 72n. 263
SES, see Socioeconomic factors
Sex, see Bisexual; Female; Male; Sexism; Sex
    typing; Sexual differentiation; Sexuality
Sex typing, 102, 115, 127, 147–149, 151, 157
Sexism, xi, 2n, 73, 81, 86, 104, 121, 127–129, 151, 249
Sexual differentiation, 18, 73, 82, 84, 102, 104n,
    127–129, 139, 181, 188, 191
Sexuality, 115, 127–129, 140, 153–154, 157
Shakespeare, 73n
Shaw, B., 127
Shifflette, M., 114n
Sibling rivalry, 99, 105, 228, 230, 237, 242
Sinclair, H., 27, 47, 59
Skinner, B. F., 7, 135, 137, 164, 273
Smith, E. A., 4, 19n, 178n
Smith, F. N., xi, 16n, 27n, 273
Smith, J. M., 127, 129, 273
Social activists, 74–75, 81, 124, 126
Social group work, see Primary group systems
Socioeconomic factors, 141, 147–149, 160, 249, 251,
    252
Somatic order, 81, 87
Space, 21, 29, 33, 38, 43, 44, 59, 60, 84, 104, 105,
Speed, concept of, 47, 59, 60
Spock, B., 87
Stage, 28, 32n. See also Phases
Strouse, J., 128, 129, 274
Structure of thought, defined, 54
Study process, see Assessment
Sucking, 31, 32, 33, 91, 137, 146–147
Superego, see Conscience; Unconscious
Sutton-Smith, B., 39n, 274
Svoboda, C. P., 68n, 274
System theory, 199, 200, 201

T
Teething, 92
Temporal space, see Time tertiary circular reactions,
    stage of, 37–39
Tension reduction, 136
Terman, L. M., 133
Tertiary circular reactions, stage of, 37–39
Theory formation, 7, 9, 18–19, 78–80, 165, 166–168
Therapy, see Helping, professional
Thinking, dialectic, 74, 81, 82, 87, 119, 123, 124, 172,
    174–175
  ends and means, 56
  existential, 74–77
  hypothetical, 65, 67
  inductive/deductive, 59, 78, 134, 137, 167, 211–212,
    212n
  linear, 50, 57, 58, 88, 238
  logical, 19, 28, 43, 48
  rudimentary, 2, 3, 32
Tillich, P., 213, 274
Time, 21, 29, 30, 35, 44, 47, 60, 60n, 84, 115
Toddlerhood, see Early childhood, phase of
Toilet training, 95, 96, 142, 148, 153, 154, 244. See also
    Sensorimotor development
Transformation, 47, 54, 64, 68, 88
Trial and error learning, 36, 156, 184, 244
Traux, C., 13, 211
Two-way pull, see Polarity

U
Unconscious, 76, 82, 182, 188
Unity-in-continuity, 4, 5, 6, 19, 22, 28–29, 76, 140,
    141–142, 167, 168

V
Ventis, L., 77n
Vinter, R. D., 204, 274

W
Wambach, R., 104n, 129, 274
"Warmth," 140, 143, 148, 152 defined, 140
Weaning, 142, 152, 153, 244
West, P., 130n
White, R. W., 8, 204, 274
Whitman, L., 121n, 274
Whittaker, J. K., 275
Whole-and-part, 47, 54, 63, 66
Wiener, N., 216
Winklebeck, L., 275
Women, see Female
Wolff, P., 9, 275
Work, 51, 109, 115, 120–121, 239
Wright, B., 213n, 275

Y
Youth, 74–75, 81, 124, 126